Dugald Stewart, William Hamilton

Lectures on political Economy

Vol. I

Dugald Stewart, William Hamilton

Lectures on political Economy
Vol. I

ISBN/EAN: 9783337077747

Printed in Europe, USA, Canada, Australia, Japan

Cover: Foto ©ninafisch / pixelio.de

More available books at **www.hansebooks.com**

THE COLLECTED WORKS

OF

DUGALD STEWART.

VOL. VIII. *a*

LECTURES

ON

POLITICAL ECONOMY.

NOW FIRST PUBLISHED.

VOL. I.

TO WHICH IS PREFIXED,

PART THIRD

OF THE

OUTLINES OF MORAL PHILOSOPHY.

BY

DUGALD STEWART, ESQ.

EDITED BY

SIR WILLIAM HAMILTON, BART.

EDINBURGH:
T. & T. CLARK, 38 GEORGE STREET.
1877.

ADVERTISEMENT BY THE EDITOR.

THIS, and the ensuing Volume of Mr. Stewart's *Collected Works*, come before the public under very different circumstances from his other writings. The other writings were once and again elaborated by the Author, and by himself carefully conducted through the press; whereas the following *Lectures* were not destined for publication,—at least, in the state in which they now appear. That Mr. Stewart, however, intended ultimately to publish his Course of Political Economy, seems certain; and, with this view, during the latter years of his life, he had revised, corrected, amplified, and re-arranged its constituent parts. But whether he had finally completed this preparation is doubtful; for the Lectures thus remodelled by him in his retirement, have, for the most part, unhappily perished. As now printed from those Original Manuscripts which have escaped the fate of the others revised for publication, the course consists principally of what was written so far back as the beginning of the century, with such additions and corrections as were occasionally interpolated up to the Session of 1809-10, the last year of Mr. Stewart's academical labours. Fortunately, he did not in his course of *Political Economy*, as in that of *Moral Philosophy*, either trust to the extemporaneous resources of his memory and eloquence for the exposition of his *own* opinions, or read from their original context the passages which he had occasion to quote from *other* authors; but that, in *both* respects, all, or nearly all, was fully written out. I say *fortunately*—for while the Lectures on *Psychology and Morals* have been not inadequately supplied by his correlative publications, those on *Political Economy* are replaced by no printed substitute. Still, under the circumstances, it became a question with Mr. Stewart's Trustees, whether, in the discharge of the duty which they owed to the reputation of the deceased, they should, or should not, publish what remained of the Course of Political Economy. In this difficulty, they, with great propriety, sought advice from the most competent of Mr. Stewart's older friends and pupils; and in particular, from the Marquis of Lansdowne and Viscount Palmerston. But, as perhaps was to be expected, these noblemen, however favourable to the alternative of publication, found themselves unable, without an examination of the Manuscripts, to express a definite opinion; and the result was, that the decision devolved exclusively upon the Editor. An examination convinced me of the importance of the documents which still remain; in reference to which, it may be observed, that while Mr. Stewart was habitually accurate in all his statements, whatever he committed to writing was more especially sure of being thoroughly meditated and carefully expressed. "Ignorabat inepta." Although, therefore, we must always regret the loss of many important writings, old and new, still I feel confident, that the manuscripts remaining, however their value might be enhanced did they exhibit the Course in its original integrity, with the addition of subsequent improvements, will, even in their present state, be found eminently worthy of publication. For although they may not fulfil all the intentions of the Author, still, even without his last emendments, they afford a systematic view of Political Science in its most important doctrines, written too with the eloquence, wisdom, and enlightened liberality which distinguish all the works of Mr. Stewart. Many changes and considerable progress in the doctrines of Political Economy, have, undoubtedly, been made since these Lectures were delivered; but these Lectures themselves have exerted a powerful influence in determining this advancement. For while Mr. Stewart's instruction inculcated, more or less articulately, these improved opinions, no master, perhaps, ever exerted a stronger and more beneficial influence on his disciples. "His disciples," to quote the words of Sir James Mackintosh, "he lived to see among the lights and ornaments of the Council and the Senate; and without derogation from his writings it may be said, that his disciples were among his best works." As an introduction to Political Economy and Politics, these Lectures, as they stand, will be found, I am persuaded, among the best extant; and though they may not exhaust all the problems of the science, they omit none of primary importance. In particular, they will prove a valuable preparative and accompaniment to a study of the *Wealth of Nations;* affording, as they do, a criticism and supplement to the immortal work of Smith. The doctrines of Smith are not, however, considered to the exclusion of those of minor authors; and we have here commemorated and canvassed, with an enlightened impartiality, the speculations of many able but now forgotten thinkers.

In regard to the unfortunate loss of the manuscripts, the most articulate information which I am able to afford is that supplied by Mr. Stewart's son, Colonel Stewart, in the following letter addressed to Mr. Henry Foss, (of the well-known publishing house of *Payne & Foss,*) and by that gentleman subsequently communicated to the public in *Notes and Queries*, Vol. XI., No. 284, April 7, 1855.

"CATRINE, *March* 30, 1837.

"SIR,—You were so obliging, some time since, as to say that you would mention the literary property that I wished to publish in your intercourse with the other members of your profession, in whose line such business lay. You need not, however, farther trouble yourself on this head ; because, finding myself getting on in life, and despairing of finding a sale for it at its real value, I have destroyed the whole of it. To this step I was much induced by finding my locks repeatedly picked during my absence from home, some of my papers carried off, and some of the others evidently read, if not copied from, by persons of whom I could procure no trace, and in the pursuit or conviction of whom, I never could obtain any efficient assistance from the judicial functionaries.

" As this may form, at some future period, a curious item in the history of literature in the present century, (as a proof of the encouragement and protection afforded to literary labour during the present reign, by a people reckoning themselves amongst the most enlightened and civilized communities of the earth,) I subjoin a list of the works destroyed as unsaleable, written by my father, Dugald Stewart, author of the *Philosophy of the Human Mind*, &c. :—

" 1*st*, *The Philosophy of Man as a Member of a Political Association.* (Incomplete.)

" 2*d*, His *Lectures on Political Economy*, delivered in the University of Edinburgh ; reduced by him into books and chapters, containing a very complete body of that science, with many important rectifications of Adam Smith's speculations.

" 3*d*, One hundred and seventy pages of the continuation of the *Dissertation prefixed to the Encyclopædia Britannica.*

" Written by me :—

. . . .

"2d, An Account of the Life and Writings of Dugald Stewart, together with all his Correspondence. Among others, with Madame de Staël, La Fayette, Jefferson, and many other literary and well-known characters, French and English; with Anecdotes from his Journals kept during his residence in Paris, before and at the commencement of the Revolution, and during his visits to that city with Lord Lauderdale, during the Fox Administration. *All of which I burnt.*"

The other nine works (some of them very voluminous) written by Colonel Stewart, and by him destroyed, it is unnecessary articulately to specify. Mr. Foss, in a note, observes,— " I believe there was no foundation for Colonel Stewart's suspicions respecting his locks having been picked." This conjecture, I have no doubt, is correct; and should it seem strange that a man of Colonel Stewart's ability and filial veneration should, on so groundless a suspicion, have been actuated to so rash a proceeding; we may perhaps find an explanation in the circumstance, that when on professional service in India, he had suffered from an attack of coup-de-soleil; a malady which, I believe, often manifests its influence in the most capricious manner, and long after an apparent disappearance of the affection.

It is therefore to be understood, that the *Lectures on Political Economy* do not appear as the Course was, by the Author, prepared for publication. Parts, indeed, as finally completed, seem by accident to have escaped the fate of the other emended Lectures and revised additions,—such as the *Introduction to the Course*, and the *Notes upon the Bullion Report*, (Vol. I.) But these shew only as exceptions, although it is not improbable that other portions, as the Lectures upon the *Theory and Forms of Government* (Vol. II.) are now nearly in the state in which they were left for publication by the Author. On this, however, not being able to speak with certainty, I prefer silence to conjecture, and leave the reader to his own surmises in regard to the extent and importance of the loss.

And here, the subjoined abstract by Miss Stewart, of the Contents of seven volumes, in quarto, of her father's manuscripts,—volumes in which the corrected and amplified Lectures were fairly transcribed,—may enable the reader to form an opinion of how much has perished, compared with what has been preserved and printed from the older copies. It is, perhaps, hardly necessary to warn him, that in this Table the distinction of *volume* is altogether an arbitrary division, being determined by the extent of room which the paper of each happened to supply. In general, also, the list is printed as it was found written, though some changes might seem occasionally to be obvious.—(In reference to the prefixes within square brackets, see p. xvi.)

(VOL. I.)

	PAGE
[*?] Allegiance to Government,† Part I.,	5
Part II.,	33
(Intended for *Part III. of Dissertation.*)	
Theory of Government‡—Introduction,	47
Simple Forms of Government,	48
Of Democracy and Democratic States,	51
Of Aristocracy,	76
Of Monarchy,	88
Of Mixed Governments,	106
Of the English Constitution,	132
[*?] Introduction to a Course of Elementary Lectures on Political Economy,§ Part I.,	165
Part II.,	185
(In continuation,) Part III.,	206

† [See Note †, *infra*, Vol. I. p. 9.]   ‡ [See Note *, *infra*, Vol. I. pp. 21, 29.]
§ [See Note *, *infra*, Vol. I. p. 9.]

ADVERTISEMENT BY THE EDITOR. xiii

	PAGE
Of Population,	224
Of Population as it is affected by the State of Manners, &c.,	233
Of Population as it is affected by Plenty or Scarcity, &c.,	238
Of Agriculture, Manufactures, and Population, considered in Relation to each other,	
I. State of the Actual Cultivators of the Soil,	258

(VOL. II.)

(Continuation of the *Lectures on Population*.)

Comparative Advantages of Small and of Great Farms,	1
Policy of Enclosures,	8
II. Of Agriculture and Population, as they are affected by the Distribution of Landed Property,	22
III. Of Agriculture and Population, in Connexion with the influence of Manufactures,	42
Appendix to Article III.,	79
What are the Effects with respect to Population of the Substitution in Manufactures of Machinery in place of Human Labour?—(For continuation of this Lecture, see p. 172,)	105
(Former part of this Lecture, see p. 104.)	
National Wealth,	220

(VOL. III.)

I.	1
II. Division of Labour,	36
III. Of Money,	67
IV. Of the relative Value of Money and of Commodities,	103
Continuation,	116
V. Of the Real and Nominal Prices of Commodities,	149
VI. Of Interest,	185
(New Chapter, see p.),	213
Appendix—Containing an Abridgment of some Chapters of fundamental importance in *The Wealth of Nations*, with a few occasional Remarks.—(A Fragment?)	228
Of the Component Parts of the Price of Commodities,	245
Of the Natural and Market Price of Commodities,	248
Of the Rent of Land,	258

Part ii.—Of the Produce of Land, which sometimes does, and sometimes does not, affect Rent,	267
(Heads of an additional Lecture to be inserted after those on the Economical System,)	275

(Vol. IV.)

(The First Lecture has no title; but it seems to be on the Practical Doctrines of the Mercantile or Commercial System of Political Economy,)	1
Of Drawbacks,	50
Of Bounties,	52
Of Treaties of Commerce,	53
Colonies,	56
Miscellaneous Observations on the Freedom of Trade,	58
Of the Expediency of Anti-usurious Laws,	81
Appendix,	151
Of the Corn Trade,	155
i.—Of the Inland Corn Trade,	166
Appendix,	266
Extract of a Letter to Mr. Stewart from Francis Horner, Esq., dated 6th April 1805,	270
ii.—Of the Trade carried on by the Merchant Importer of Grain for Home Consumption,	273

(Vol. V.)

iii.—Of the Trade carried on by the Merchant Exporter of Grain for Foreign Consumption,	1
iv.—	28
Miscellaneous Observations on the Corn Trade,	29
Appendix to the Lectures on the Corn Trade; quotation from the *Edinburgh Review*, July 1807,	64
Quotation from the *Monthly Review*, 1822,	67
Of the Commerce of Land, (Primogeniture,)	70
Appendix,	111
Note from M. Garnier's *Translation of the Wealth of Nations*,	115
Laws relating to the Poor,	125
History of the Poor-Laws in England,	128

ADVERTISEMENT BY THE EDITOR. xv

	PAGE
Of the Poor-Laws in Scotland,	205
Of Poor and Charity Workhouses,	237
Of Benefit Clubs and Friendly Societies,	255
Conclusion of Lectures on the Laws relating to the Poor,	279

(Vol. VI.)

Of the Education of the People, ... 1
Appendix, ... 46

[*] Essay on the Probable Effects of the Progress of Science, and of the Diffusion of Knowledge on the future Fortunes of the Human Race, (intended to form the concluding Chapter of my *Dissertation* prefixed to the *Encyclopædia;* [and accordingly in this edition so arranged.])—

Section i., ... 56
ii., ... 87
iii., ... 114
[*] Note, ... 130
[*] Appendix, ... 134

Notes on the *Bullion Report*,† (sent by Mr. Stewart to Lord Lauderdale, in February, March, and April 1811.)—

Note I., ... 138
II., ... 164
III., ... 182
IV., ... 190
V., ... 222
VI., ... 225
Of the Present Depreciation of the Paper Currency, I., . 257
II., . 265

(([Vol. VII.] Folio MS., marked M.)

[*] Lectures on the Varieties of the Race.

[*] Introduction, ... 1
[*] Comparative influence of Physical and Moral Causes on National Character, ... 59
[*] Notes, ... 86

† [Extant, see *infra*, Vol. I., p. 431, *seq.*]

	PAGE
President de Goguet, ...	96
Origin and History of Property, ...	99
Of the Institution of Marriage, ...	154
Origin of Ranks, ...	180

The ensuing sentences, in Miss Stewart's handwriting, but apparently of a later date, immediately follow the preceding list of the seven manuscript volumes :—

"The above is the Index [or rather the Table of Contents] of Seven Volumes of MSS. transcribed, under my father's own inspection, from his older MSS., with considerable alterations and additions, during the last four years of his life. These MSS. were delivered to my brother, after my father's death, according to his will. . . .

"I took a copy of the Index before delivering the MSS. to my brother."

Though principally occupied with topics of *Political Economy*, it will farther be observed, that the destroyed manuscripts comprised also copies of Lectures, of Essays, and of fragments on *other matters of Philosophy*, as is seen from the contents of the Volumes labelled VI. and VII., in the articles there distinguished by an *asterisk*, [*]. In Volume I., the articles marked by an *asterisk and interrogative*, [* ?], appear to have been intended, as equally adapted, to stand either among the *Lectures on Political Economy*, or among the chapters of the *Preliminary Dissertation*, Part III. Accordingly, in the only case where an option was possible, the former alternative has been preferred in the present edition of the *Collected Works*.

I here also subjoin a summary of the separate Course of *Political Economy* in its *earlier* form, as I find it in Mr. Stewart's handwriting. This, as observed in the footnote at p. 21, Vol. I., excludes the Lectures on *Politics proper*, a subject comprised in the general Course of *Moral Philosophy*. These

Lectures are now incorporated with those on *Political Economy;* and, as printed, appear in Vol. II.

PLAN OF LECTURES ON POLITICAL ECONOMY,
For Winter 1800-1801.

i.—Introductory Lecture on the Object and Utility of Political Economy.
ii.—Lectures on the Rise and Progress of this Branch of Science. —Its connexion with Natural Jurisprudence.—View of the systems of Grotius and his Successors; and of the train of thought by which these seem to have led to the modern study of Political Economy.
iii.—Preliminary Review of some fundamental Laws which seem to be essential to all the various forms of Civilized Society; particularly of the Institution of Marriage, and of the Laws which protect the Right of Property.

POLITICAL ECONOMY.

I.

OF POPULATION.

i.—Of Population, as it is affected by the State of Manners relative to the connexion of the Sexes.
ii.—Of Population, as it is affected by the means of Subsistence enjoyed by the People.
 1.—Of National Habits with respect to Food.
 2.—Of Agriculture, Manufactures, and Population, considered in relation to each other.—State of the Actual Cultivators of the Soil; —Great and Small Farms;—Enclosures;—Distribution of Landed Property;—Agrarian policy of the Romans and of other ancient Nations;—Effects with respect to Population;—Essential Distinction between their Condition and ours, in consequence of the Abolition of Domestic Slavery, and other causes; and absurdity of reasoning from their institutions, as applicable to the present State of Society.—Law of Entails.

Influence of Manufactures in encouraging Agriculture among Nations which exclude the institution of Domestic Slavery.—Subordination of Manufactures to Agriculture.—Errors of some modern Statesmen on this subject.—Discouragements which still exist to the Progress of Agriculture.

Digression concerning the effects of some particular forms of Manufacturing Industry, lately introduced into this Country.—Cotton Mills, &c.—General question concerning the tendency of Mechanical contrivances for abridging labour, to increase or to diminish the Population of a Country.

How far the Number of a people, compared with the extent of their Territory, may be regarded as a test of National Prosperity.—Mischievous consequences of encouraging Population without a corresponding increase in the funds necessary to support it. Question resumed concerning the Subordination of Manufactures to Agriculture.—Application of these reasonings to the present state of Great Britain.—Objection, which has been stated to these liberal views of Political Economy, from their supposed tendency to produce or to accelerate the mischiefs of an Excessive Population.—Critical Examination of a late *Essay on the Principle of Population, as it affects the Future Improvement of Society.*—[London, 1798, by Malthus.]

APPENDIX.

Of the Means which have been employed to ascertain the State of Population in particular instances.—Number of Houses;—Quantity of Consumption in the article of Food;—Register of Births, Deaths, and Marriages.

Miscellaneous observations and inquiries, chiefly relating to the question concerning the progressive or declining Population of Great Britain;—Population of France.

Population of China.—Application of this extreme case, to illustrate the principles formerly stated concerning the evils of an excessive Population, and the danger of proposing Population as an ultimate object of policy, instead of advancing it through the medium of National Wealth.

II.

OF NATIONAL WEALTH.

i.—Of Productive and Unproductive Labour.
ii.—Of the Principles on which the *Effective* Powers of Labour depend.
iii.—Of Money. Examination of the opinions of Locke, Law, and Berkeley.
iv.—Of the Real and Nominal Price of Commodities. Examination of Mr. Smith's reasonings on this subject.
v.—Of the Principles by which the relative Values of Money and of Commodities are adjusted in Commercial transactions.
vi.—Of the Accumulation of Stock; of Money lent upon Interest.
vii.—Of the Freedom of Trade.
    1.—Of Restraints on Domestic Commerce and Industry.
    2.—Of Restraints on the Commercial intercourse of Different Nations.
viii.—Of the Corn Trade.
ix.—Of the Commerce of Money.
x.—Of the Commerce of Land.
xi.—Of Taxes.

III.

OF THE POOR.

i.—History of the Poor-Laws in England.
ii.—State of the Poor in Scotland.
iii.—Of Charity Workhouses.
iv.—Of Friendly Societies.
v.—General Principles, and Miscellaneous Observations on the Subject.—Rumford.

IV.

OF CORRECTIVE POLICE.

i.—Of Penitentiary Houses and Solitary Confinement;—Panopticon of Mr. Bentham, &c. &c.
ii.—Of the General Principles which ought to regulate the Punishment of Crimes.

V.

Of Preventive Police.

i.—Of the Effects which might be expected from a well organized and vigilant Police, in restraining the Commission of Crimes.

ii.—Of the Effects which might be expected on the Morals of the Lower Orders from a Systematical Attention to their Instruction, and to their early Habits.

VI.

Of Education.*

i.—Of Education, considered in its relation to the objects of Political Economy.—Attention due to it by the Legislator. —Change produced in the circumstances of Mankind by the invention of Printing.—National Education.

ii.—Importance of the Education of the Female Sex.—Pernicious tendency of some late systems to obliterate the characteristical qualities bestowed on them by Nature, and to counteract her obvious intentions with respect to their peculiar sphere in Civilized Society.

iii.—Of Education, considered in its relation to Intellectual Improvement, and to the advancement of Human Knowledge.—State of Academical Education in Modern Europe.

The present publication, then, of the Lectures on Political Economy, as has been stated above, is taken from Mr. Stewart's *older* manuscripts, most of which are still extant. As the work, however, passed through the press, various deficiencies were discovered, which had not been detected on a cursory perusal of the documents,—deficiencies which, indeed, only became apparent by a careful comparison of the different Plans or Tables of Contents of the Lectures, with two sets of Notes taken in 1809, the last year in which the Course was delivered, and

---

* [Much in relation to this subject will be found in the *Dissertation*, Part III.,—probably transferred from these Lectures.]

which had been kindly sent to me, in the hope of their proving useful in the arrangement of the Lectures. Of these copies of Notes, the one was the joint work of Mr. James Bridges, W.S., and of the late Mr. John Dow, W.S.; the other was by the late Mr. James Bonar, Solicitor of Excise, Edinburgh, and obligingly communicated to me by his son, through Mr. Constable. The former Notes, as Mr. Bridges informs me, were taken in short-hand, and afterwards written out; and, from a comparison of them with Mr. Stewart's manuscripts, they have been found remarkably copious and accurate, frequently corresponding word for word with the original. The latter appear to have been written without the aid of short-hand, as they are not so comprehensive and articulate as the former; while sundry quotations, particularly in the earlier portions of the Course, have been copied *verbatim* from the works of their respective authors.

As the deficiencies, in consequence of the destruction of the original manuscripts, became fully manifest, it was necessary to choose between the alternatives;—either to print only what remained of Mr. Stewart's autograph, or to supply the blanks from this or that copy of the Notes. The latter alternative was deemed preferable; inasmuch as thus is fulfilled the Author's plan as followed in his *final* Course, while there is every reason to believe, that where the Lectures are deficient, the Notes, especially those of Mr. Bridges, may be safely relied on, as fully and faithfully recording the Author's opinions in the language of his prelections.* Of these Notes, therefore, I have

---

* Mr. Bridges, in the letter to me which accompanied the five volumes of his Notes, says:—" Mr. Stewart was jealous at the time of our labours, and stated to Mr. Dow and myself, that he would take it for granted we would not publish our notes. But presuming that you have the sanction of his family for your work, I not only do not feel myself to be acting contrary to this pledge, but rather deem myself to be discharging a duty to his memory and to the public, in thus communicating these volumes to you."

availed myself largely, particularly in the Chapters on *Labour*, on *Money*, and on *Trade;* while the whole of what is advanced on the Maintenance of the *Poor*, and on *Education*, is supplied from the same source. Although, however, the Notes of Mr. Bridges are very complete, in so far as Mr. Stewart's own remarks and speculations are concerned, the numerous citations adduced by him are, for the most part, left to be inserted. In this respect, I have found the Notes of Mr. Bonar of great utility, in pointing out a quotation, and in marking its length, so that they have materially assisted in supplying the chief deficiency in those of Mr. Bridges. And here it is to be observed, that the commencement and termination of the passages supplied from the Note-books of Mr. Stewart's pupils, are articulately marked as *interpolations;* and, when not otherwise stated, they are from the transcript of Mr. Bridges. The quotations have, however, in general, been filled up from the original works.

To Mr. Bridges and to Mr. Bonar, I have, therefore, to offer my best thanks for the use of these valuable Note-books. But I have, likewise, to express my acknowledgments to Mr. James Gibson Craig, for his kindness in communicating to me a copy of Notes in his possession, taken of Mr. Stewart's Course of *Political Economy*, by the late Lord Jeffrey in 1802. I should have gladly availed myself of these, had not the writing been found so extremely difficult to decipher, and the Notes themselves been of so early a date.

Nor can I conclude this Advertisement without gratefully thanking my friend and colleague, Professor More, for the valuable, and often laborious, assistance he has been always kindly ready to afford me, from the treasures of his library; while his extensive acquaintance with books and the literature of Political Economy, has enabled him to discover for me many of the scarce pamphlets adduced, lying perdue in the public collections.

It should finally be observed, that, here as elsewhere, the footnotes of the Author are referred to by *numerals*, those of the Editor, by *asterisk, obelus*, &c. To the latter, likewise, in this work, belongs *all* that is inclosed within *square brackets*, whether in text or annotation; and, in general, the distribution of the Lectures into *Book, Chapter, Section*, &c., to say nothing of the *Running Titles*. In the *Table of Contents*, however, the distinction of square brackets has been omitted, as in the present volumes the Editor is for that Table *exclusively* responsible.

W. H.

EDINBURGH, *December* 1855.

CONTENTS.

I.—OUTLINES OF MORAL PHILOSOPHY.
PART THIRD—(APPENDIX.)
OF MAN CONSIDERED AS THE MEMBER OF A POLITICAL BODY.

CHAPTER I.

OF THE HISTORY OF POLITICAL SOCIETY, .   PAGE 3

CHAPTER II.
OF THE GENERAL PRINCIPLES OF LEGISLATION AND GOVERNMENT.

SECT. 1. *Of Political Economy*, ... 4
SECT. 2. *Of the Different Functions of Government, and of the various Forms in which they are Combined in the Constitutions of Different States*, ... 5

II.—LECTURES ON POLITICAL ECONOMY.
INTRODUCTION.
OF THE OBJECTS AND PROVINCE OF POLITICAL ECONOMY.

CHAPTER I.
OF THE TITLE AND COMPREHENSION OF THE SCIENCE, . . 9

CHAPTER II.
OF THE CONTENTS AND DISTRIBUTION OF POLITICAL ECONOMY PROPER, OR OF PART FIRST, ... 30
  i. *Population*, ... 31
  ii. *National Wealth*, ... 33
  iii. *The Poor,—their Maintenance*, ... 47
  iv. *Education;—Prevention, Reformation, Correction of Crime*, . 49

CHAPTER III.

PRELIMINARY DISTINCTION OF POSITIVE LAWS INTO TWO CLASSES, AND THE RELATION OF THESE TO POLITICAL ECONOMY PROPER,—OR TO PART FIRST, ... 57

PART FIRST.—OF POLITICAL ECONOMY PROPER.

BOOK FIRST.

OF POPULATION.

CHAPTER I.

OF POPULATION CONSIDERED AS AN ARTICLE OF THE NATURAL HISTORY OF MAN, . . . 60

CHAPTER II.

OF POPULATION CONSIDERED AS AN ARTICLE OF POLITICAL ECONOMY, . 67

SECT. i.—*Of Population as affected by the Political Institutions which regulate the Connexion between the Sexes,* . . 67
    SUBSECT. 1. Marriage compared with Concubinage, . . 67
    SUBSECT. 2. Monogamy compared with Polygamy, . . 82
SECT. ii.—*Of Population as affected by the State of Manners relative to the Connexion between the Sexes,* 92
SECT. iii.—*Dependence of Population on the Means of Subsistence enjoyed by the People,* 98
    SUBSECT. 1.—Dependence of Marriage and Population on the notion held in regard to the competent support of a Family, ... 98
    SUBSECT. 2.—Of Agriculture and Manufactures considered in relation to Population, . . . 113
        First.—Of Population in connexion with Agriculture, 113
            1.)—Kinds of Farm Tenure, . . . 113
            2.)—Farm Burdens, ... 118
            3.)—Size of Farms, ... 124
            4.)—Enclosures, ... 132
            5.)—Size of Properties, ... 138

	PAGE
Second.—Of Population (and Agriculture) as affected by Manufactures,	152
1.)—On the Employment of Children in Factory Work: its Advantages and Disadvantages,	183
2.)—Of Machinery as a Substitute for Labour: its Advantages and Disadvantages,	188
SUBSECT. 3.—Is the Density of Population in Proportion to the Extent of Country, a certain Index of National Prosperity,	198
APPENDIX.—*Of the Means which have been employed to ascertain the Population in particular instances,*	211

BOOK SECOND.

OF NATIONAL WEALTH.

CHAPTER I.

OF PRODUCTIVE AND UNPRODUCTIVE LABOUR,	253
SECT. i.—*Specially, on the System of the Economists,*	269
SECT. ii.—*On the Circumstances which render Labour more Effective,*	309
SUBSECT. 1.—On the Division of Labour,	310
SUBSECT. 2.—On the use of Machinery as a Substitute for Labour,	316

CHAPTER II.

OF MONEY, THE CIRCULATING MEDIUM,	333
SECT. i.—*Of the Origin and Use of Money,*	333
SECT. ii.—*Of Real and Nominal Prices,*	349
SECT. iii.—*Effects of Plenty or Scarcity of the Precious Metals on Price,*	371
SECT. iv.—*Of Money as the Standard of Value,*	390
SECT. v.—*Of Interest,*	396

APPENDICES TO BOOKS I. AND II.

APP. I., *Extract from Pinto, on Population,*	429
APP. II., *Notes on the Parliamentary Bullion Report,*	431

OUTLINES OF MORAL PHILOSOPHY.

PART THIRD.

[POLITICAL SCIENCE.]

OUTLINES OF MORAL PHILOSOPHY.

PART III.*

OF MAN CONSIDERED AS THE MEMBER OF A POLITICAL BODY.†

CHAPTER I.

OF THE HISTORY OF POLITICAL SOCIETY.

ARTICLE 1. Of the Principles in Human Nature, and of the Circumstances in the Condition of Mankind, which lay the foundation of the Political Union.

ART. 2. Of the Principles in Human Nature, and of the

---

* [Continued from *Works*, Vol. VI. p. 108. This "Part III." is expressly considered only as an "*Appendix*" to the "*Outlines of Moral Philosophy;*" and, in fact, it is merely a Table of Contents, and that too not indicating the order of the Lectures.]

† [" Having, of late, carried into execution (at least in part) the design announced in the foregoing Preface, by a *separate* Course of Lectures on Political Economy, I have omitted in this edition of my *Outlines*, the articles which I formerly enumerated under that general title; substituting in their stead a few others, calculated to illustrate the peculiar and intimate connexion between

this department of Politics and the more appropriate objects of Ethics. The observations which these articles are meant to introduce, may be useful, at the same time, in preparing the minds of students for disquisitions, the details of which can scarcely fail to appear uninviting to those who are not aware of the important conclusions to which they are subservient.—College of Edinburgh, Nov. 2, 1801."—Postscript of Preface to *Outlines of Moral Philosophy*, second and subsequent editions, *Works*, Vol. II. p. 4.

Part III. of the *Outlines* is here reprinted from the second edition, that of 1801, which is identical with those

Circumstances in the Condition of Mankind which lay the Foundation of the Progress of Society.

ART. 3. Of the Institution of Marriage; and its consequences, Political and Moral.

ART. 4. Of the Condition and the Character of the Sexes, as they are modified by different States of Society.

ART. 5. Of the History of Property, considered in relation to Human Improvement and Happiness.

ART. 6. Of the Origin and Progress of the Arts and of the Sciences.

ART. 7. Of the Origin and Progress of Commerce.

ART. 8. Of the Origin and Progress of Government, and of the History of Rank and Subordination.

ART. 9. Of the Origin and Progress of Municipal Systems of Jurisprudence.

ART. 10. Of Diversities in the History of the Species, arising from the influence of Climate and Situation.

subsequent. A few unimportant verbal additions have, however, been interpolated from the first edition, without discrimination; but wherever the change is of any moment, it has been explicitly noticed.]

CHAPTER II.

OF THE GENERAL PRINCIPLES OF LEGISLATION AND GOVERNMENT.

SECT. I.—OF POLITICAL ECONOMY.*

ART. 1. Of the Writings of *Grotius* and his Successors on Natural Jurisprudence, and their influence in suggesting the Modern Speculations concerning Political Economy.

ART. 2. Of the Objects of Political Economy, and the more important general Conclusions to which the study of it has led.

ART. 3. Of the Coincidence of the Principles of Justice and of Expediency, in the Political Conclusions to which they lead. —[Slavery.]—1*st Edit.*

ART. 4. Of the Connexion between just Views of Political Economy, and the Intellectual and Moral Improvement of Mankind.

SECT. II.—OF THE DIFFERENT FUNCTIONS OF GOVERNMENT; AND OF THE VARIOUS FORMS IN WHICH THEY ARE COMBINED IN THE CONSTITUTIONS OF DIFFERENT STATES.

ART. 1. Of the Legislative, Judicial, and Executive Powers.

ART. 2. Of the Simple Forms of Government, according to

---

* [The three following articles appear in the *first* edition only, 1793:]
ART. 1. Of Population.
ART. 2. Of National Wealth.
  1.) Of the Distribution of Wealth among the body of the People,— and of the Regulations respecting the Poor.
  2.) Of the Revenue of the Sovereign.
[After an ART. 3, the same as in the text, there follows:]
ART. 4. Of the instruction of the Lower Orders; and of the Prevention and Punishment of Crimes.

the definitions of Speculative Politicians; and of the Uses to which this theoretical view of the subject is subservient, in the examination of actual Constitutions.

ART. 3. Of Mixed Governments.

ART. 4. Of the English Constitution.

ART. 5. Of the Influence of Forms of Government on National Character and Manners.

ART. 6. Of the Duties arising from the Political Union.

ART. 7. Of the Political Relations of different States to each other; and of the Laws of Morality as applicable to Nations.

LECTURES ON POLITICAL ECONOMY.

LECTURES ON POLITICAL ECONOMY.

INTRODUCTION.

OF THE OBJECTS AND PROVINCE OF POLITICAL ECONOMY.*

[CHAPTER I.]

[OF THE TITLE AND COMPREHENSION OF THE SCIENCE,
IN ITS MOST EXTENSIVE MEANING.]

IT was before intimated,† that when the phrase *Political Economy* occurs in the course of this *Dissertation*, it is to be understood in the most extensive sense of these words. By most of our English writers, as well as by those in the other countries of Europe, this phrase has been hitherto restricted to inquiries concerning *Wealth and Population;* or to what have sometimes been called *the resources of a State*. It is in this limited sense it is used by the disciples of *Quesnai* in France, and also by Sir James Steuart, Mr. Smith, and a long

---

* [This seems to correspond with the "*Introduction to a Course of Elementary Lectures on Political Economy*," as enumerated in the table of contents given by Miss Stewart; (*see* Editor's Advertisement.) It escaped the fate of the other writings in that list, in consequence of an extra copy having been taken. For, its first certainly, and apparently also its second chapter, were latterly intended by Mr. Stewart to be incorporated in the *Third Part* of his *Dissertation;* and various changes were accordingly (about 1819 and down to 1823) made to fit them for this transference; which, however, was never completed. It is perhaps needless to observe, that these alterations are merely superficial, and that the chapters, in all essential respects, correspond with their original accommodation.]

† [*See* above, Vol. I., (*Dissertation,*) p. 22; though probably reference is made to a more proximate passage in the intended previous Lecture or Chapter, entitled, *Allegiance to Government*, now lost.]

list of respectable authors in this Island, both before and after the publication of Quesnai's works. Without, however, presuming to censure in the slightest degree the propriety of their language, I think that the same title may be extended with much advantage to all those speculations which have for their object the happiness and improvement of Political Society, or, in other words, which have for their object the great and ultimate *ends* from which Political regulations derive all their value; and to which *Wealth and Population* themselves are to be regarded as only subordinate and instrumental. Such are the speculations which aim at ascertaining those fundamental Principles of Policy, which Lord Bacon has so significantly and so happily described, as "*Leges Legum, ex quibus informatio peti possit, quid in singulis Legibus bene aut perperam positum aut constitutum sit.*"* In this employment of the phrase *Political Economy*, I may perhaps be accused of a deviation from established practice; but the language does not afford me another expression less exceptionable, for denoting this particular department of Political Science; and the use which Dr. Johnson and other classical authorities have made of the word *Economy*, to denote "disposition and regulation in general," justifies me at least in some measure, for extending its ordinary acceptation when applied to the internal policy of nations.

If we could suppose that this departure from the common language of Political writers were to be sanctioned by general use, its advantages, if I do not deceive myself, would be found of material importance. I shall only mention at present the effect it would necessarily have in keeping constantly before the mind of the speculative Politician, the *Standard* by which the wisdom and expediency of every institution is to be estimated; and in checking those partial views of human affairs which have led so many eminent writers in their zeal for the advancement of *National Riches*, to overlook the more essential objects of the Political Union.

That the idea which I thus propose to annex to this study

* [*De Aug. Scient.* Lib. VIII. cap. iii. *Exemplum Tractatus de Justitia Universali,* Aph. 6.]

is sufficiently precise, must appear evident to all who are conversant with Political inquiries. In the meantime, (as I find it impossible to convey this idea to others by any general definition or description,) a few examples may serve to illustrate the questions which I propose to comprehend under the title of Political Economy, and those subordinate discussions, which, although essentially different in their nature and aim, are apt, from their apparent relation to the same objects, to be confounded together under the same title.

To begin, then, with that science, which, in the judgment of the most enlightened politicians, is the most essential of all to human happiness,—I mean the *Science of Agriculture ;* how various and important are the subjects which belong exclusively to its province ! The general principles of vegetation; the chemical analysis of soils; the theory of manures ; the principles which regulate the rotation of crops, and which modify the rotation, according to the diversities of soil and climate ; the implements of agriculture, both mechanical and animal ;— and a thousand other topics of a similar description. To none of these articles does the *Political Economist* profess to direct his attention; but he speculates on a subject, without a knowledge of which, on the part of the Legislator, that of the other, how generally soever it may be diffused, is of no value. He speculates on the *motives which stimulate human industry ;* and according as he finds these favoured or not in the classes of the people on whose exertions agriculture depends, he predicts the agricultural progress or decline of a nation. He considers with this view the state of landed property, and the laws which regulate its alienation or transmission ; the state of the actual occupiers of the ground; the security they possess for reaping, unmolested, the reward of their labours ; and the encouragement they enjoy in comparison of that held out in the other walks of lucrative enterprise. Nor does he confine his views to the plenty or scarcity of the immediately succeeding seasons, but endeavours to investigate the means of securing permanent abundance and prosperity to his fellow-citizens. In this respect, too, the principles on which he proceeds differ essentially not only from those of the practical agriculturist, but from those which regulate the views of all the other orders of men who think merely of their individual interests. The exertions of the farmer, it may be reasonably presumed, will be proportioned to the recompense he expects; spirited and vigorous after a few years of high prices, and languid when overstocked markets have for a length of time disappointed his just expectations. The manufacturer, on the other hand, and the various orders of annuitants and stipendiary labourers, exult when the farmer repines, and repine when the farmer exults. In the midst of this conflict of contending interests and prejudices, it is the business of the Political Economist to watch over the *concerns of all*, and to point out to the Legislator the danger of listening exclusively to claims founded in local or in partial advantages, to remind him that the pressure of a temporary scarcity brings along with it in time its own remedy, while an undue depression of prices may sacrifice to a passing abundance years of future prosperity;—above all, to recommend to him such a policy, as by securing in ordinary years a regular *surplus*, may restrain the fluctuation of prices within as narrow limits as possible; the only effectual method of consulting at once the real and permanent interests of proprietors, cultivators, and consumers.

What has now been said with respect to agriculture, may be extended to the various other employments of human industry, all of which furnish, in a greater or less degree, interesting subjects of scientific examination. This is exemplified very remarkably in *Manufactures*, in which the chemists and mechanists of the present age have found so ample a field of observation and of study; and to the improvement of which they have so largely contributed by their discoveries and inventions. To the *Philosopher* also, manufactures present a most interesting spectacle, and that whether he takes the trouble or not to enter into the detail of their various processes. What are the circumstances which attract manufacturers to one part of a country in preference to another? in what respects is it in the power of the Legislator to encourage them by roads, canals, harbours, and other public works? what are the effects of that division of labour, which takes place in a manufacturing country, on the intellectual and moral powers of the lower orders? what are the political effects of those mechanical contrivances by which labour is abridged? *these*, and many other questions of a similar nature, depend for their solution, not on that knowledge which is to be acquired in workshops, but on an acquaintance with the nature and condition of man. Such questions, I conceive, belong properly to *that science*, of which I am now endeavouring to describe the objects.

While the Political Economist thus investigates the sources of Agricultural and Manufacturing wealth, he is naturally led to consider these two great divisions of manual industry in their *mutual relations*; to inquire in what manner they act and re-act on each other; and how far it is in the power of the statesman to combine their joint influence for increasing the happiness and improvement of the community. Where the freedom of industry is unjustly restrained by laws borrowed from less enlightened ages, and more especially where that species of industry on which man depends for his subsistence is depressed below its proper level, it is his *duty* to remonstrate against so fatal a perversion of Political Institutions. In doing so, he does not arrogate to himself any superiority of practical knowledge over those whose professional labours are the subject of his discussions; but he thinks himself entitled to be heard, while his conclusions rest, not on the details of any particular art, but on the principles of human nature, and on the physical condition of the human race.

The diversity of pursuits to which individuals betake themselves in the progress of civilized society, in consequence of the various modifications of agricultural and of manufacturing labour, give rise necessarily to a new order of men, whose province it is to facilitate those exchanges which the separation of professions renders indispensable; and who, in thus contributing to the perfection of the social system, open an ample source of emolument to themselves. I allude at present to the order of *Merchants*, a class of citizens entirely dependent on the labours of the farmer and tradesman; but who, in such a complex state of society as that with which we are connected, exert a very powerful influence over both the others. A practical acquaintance with this department of business, more especially when it embraces the great objects of national concern, requires a longer and more systematical education than what is commonly understood to be necessary to qualify the farmer and the tradesman for their respective occupations; and it is, in truth, only to be acquired completely, by that experience which commercial habits communicate. Among the various callings, accordingly, to which the circumstances of modern Europe have given rise, there is none which has discovered a greater jealousy of uninitiated theorists, or a more arrogant contempt for the speculative conclusions of the closet, than the whole tribe of what are commonly called the *monied interest;* that is, *capitalists, great merchants,* and *financiers of every description.* And, unquestionably, in whatever relates to *practical details,* or to a quickness of mercantile combination in estimating the probable profits or losses of a particular adventure, their claims to a superior degree of illumination cannot reasonably be disputed. Still, however, there are many questions relating to trade, to the consideration of which the philosopher, and the philosopher alone, is competent. The *theory of money* (including under this word, *paper credit*) is of itself a sufficient example; a theory which, after all that has been yet written on the subject, and all the prodigies which the thing itself daily accomplishes before our eyes, remains to this hour in much obscurity. It is not, however, to such a subject as that of *money* (which Leibnitz has somewhere justly called a *semi-mathematical* speculation) that I allude chiefly in the foregoing remark. I have an eye more particularly to *Trade* considered in its relation to other objects of Political Science, animating and combining into one system the labours of the farmer and the artificer, in the most remote corners of an extensive territory, encouraging and calling forth the industry of *other* nations, and of other quarters of the globe;—exhibiting, in a word, those stupendous effects, both political and moral, which distinguish the condition of mankind in Modern Europe, from everything else that is known in the history of the species. It is unnecessary for me to say, how important that class of *laws* must be, which affects peculiarly the interests of those whose operations lead to such momentous consequences ; how extensive their utility, where they second the salutary tendencies of commerce ; and how dangerous the mistakes of the Legislator may prove, when they thwart, in concerns of so vast a magnitude, the beneficial arrangements of nature.

For speculations which embrace so complicated a variety of objects, the details of a particular branch of trade are surely not the best preparation ; nor is that quick-sighted regard to personal interest which commercial pursuits communicate, necessarily accompanied with views equally just, concerning questions of public utility. The truth is, that no wise statesman will reckon much on the disinterested benevolence of any one order of individuals; and the only occasions on which their professional knowledge is likely to be turned to national advantage, is when the interest of their order, and the interest of the community, are one and the same. That this is *less* the case with manufacturers and merchants than with farmers and country gentlemen, is frequently remarked by Mr. Smith in the course of his *Inquiry ;** and the same observation has been sanctioned by a still more unexceptionable authority, that of *Sir Josiah Child.*† " Merchants," says this very intelligent and liberal writer, who was himself in an eminent degree conversant with the practical details of trade, " Merchants, while they are in the busy and eager prosecution of their particular objects, although they be very wise and good men, are not always the best judges of commerce, as it relates to the power and profit of a kingdom. The reason may be, because their eyes are so continually fixed on what makes for their peculiar gain or loss, that they have no leisure to expatiate, or to turn their thoughts to what is most advantageous for the kingdom in general."

* [" Manufactures," says Smith, " may flourish amidst the ruin of their country, and begin to decay upon the return of its prosperity." This may serve as a specimen. *Inquiry into the Nature and Causes of the Wealth of Nations*, Book IV. chap. i.]

† [*Discourse on Trade.*]

"The like," he adds, " may be said of all shopkeepers, artificers, and manufacturers, until they have left off their trades, and being rich, *become, by the purchase of lands, of the same common interest with most of their countrymen.*"[1]

The same train of thought might be easily extended to the other subjects which I comprehend under the title of *Political Economy*. But what I have already stated is fully sufficient to illustrate the nature of those general and fundamental principles which I propose to investigate, and to justify the concise and expressive description of them formerly quoted from Lord Bacon, [p. 10,] where he calls them, " *Leges Legum*, ex quibus informatio peti possit, quid in singulis Legibus bene aut perperam positum aut constitutum sit."

According to the idea of Political Economy which I have adopted, this science is not confined to any particular description of Laws, or to any particular department of the general science of Legislation. Among the means, for example, of advancing *national wealth*, what so efficacious as the laws which give security to the right of property, and check an inordinate inequality in its distribution? To secure these ends, is one great aim both of civil and criminal jurisprudence; and therefore, even those regulations which appear, on a superficial view, to be altogether foreign to the subject of *national resources*, may yet involve in the consequences, the most effectual provisions by which national resources are to be secured and augmented.

The science of *Political Economy*, considered in its more extensive signification, as comprehending every regulation which affects the sum of national improvement and enjoyment, must necessarily embrace discussions of a still more miscellaneous nature. Among its various objects, however, one of

---

[1] Even after the trader has become a landed proprietor, he will naturally feel the influence of his former habits of thinking and judging, and will regard with undue partiality the associates of those pursuits to which he is indebted for his fortune. Mr. Ricardo himself, with all his liberality, sometimes betrays in his parliamentary opinions, a stronger fellow-feeling with Fund-holders, than the country gentlemen of England are disposed to sympathize with. (*See* Debate, Feb. 11, 1822.)

the most important is the solution of that problem which Mr. Burke has pronounced to be one of the finest in legislation:— *"to ascertain what the State ought to take upon itself to direct by the public wisdom, and what it ought to leave, with as little interference as possible, to individual discretion."* The mischievous consequences that may result from the tendency of mistaken notions on this point, to produce an undue multiplication of the objects of law, must be evident to every person who has the slightest acquaintance with Mr. Smith's political disquisitions. In point of fact, it is the very problem stated by Mr. Burke, which renders it so difficult to define with precision the object of *Political Economy.* Its general aim is to enlighten those who are destined for the functions of government, and to enlighten public opinion with respect to their conduct; but unless it be previously ascertained how far the legitimate province of the Statesman extends, it is impossible to draw the line distinctly between those subjects which belong properly to the science of Legislation, and those of which the regulation ought to be entrusted to the selfish passions and motives inseparable from human nature.

I have dwelt the longer on this subject, as I was anxious to point out its intimate connexion with the *Philosophy of the Human Mind.* The only infallible rules of political wisdom are founded ultimately on a knowledge of the prevailing springs of human action, and he who loses himself in the details of the social mechanism, while he overlooks those moral powers which give motion to the whole, though he may accumulate a mass of information highly useful in the pursuits of private life, must remain in total ignorance of those primary causes on which depend the prosperity and the safety of nations.

Nor is it in *this* respect alone that the sciences of Morals and of Politics are related to each other; it is justly and profoundly remarked in one of the oldest fragments now extant of Grecian Philosophy, that "among the external circumstances necessary to the happiness of the individual, the *first* place is due to a well constituted State, without which the rational and social animal is imperfect, and unable to fulfil the purpose of its being."* I shall endeavour afterwards to shew, that this observation applies with far less force to that part of the political order which depends immediately on the form of government, than to the system of *Political Economy* which that government encourages. At present I shall content myself with suggesting in general, in confirmation of the Pythagorean maxim just now quoted, that it is in the political union, and in the gradual improvement of which it is susceptible, that the chief provision has been made for a gradual development of our faculties, and for a proportionate enlargement in our capacities of enjoyment, insomuch that it may be confidently affirmed, that by the particular modification of the political order existing in any country, both the intellectual and moral condition of the great body of the people is infallibly determined.

I am perfectly aware of the objections to this doctrine, which will immediately occur to such as have adopted the prejudices which have been so industriously fostered for the last twenty years† by the advocates of civil and religious tyranny, (and by none more zealously than by the existing Government of France,‡) against all those branches of Philosophy which have human affairs for their object. But to these I think it quite superfluous to offer a formal reply; not only because their injustice and absurdity are completely felt and understood by their authors; but because all I could allege on the other side of the question would amount to nothing more than to an apology for the actual state of society in this part of the world, when contrasted with that which existed during the dark ages.

---

* [Mr. Stewart probably refers to the Pseudo-Pythagorean Fragment *On Happiness*, under the name of Thurius; (Gale's *Opuscula*, edition of Amsterdam, p. 663.) But a weightier and surer authority for the same doctrine is that of Aristotle, in his *Politics;* who there shews, that Man, only in Society attains to the perfection of which he is capable, and therefore, that a State is prior in the order of nature, to an Individual or a Family. "The solitary," he says, "is either a god or a beast;" "Man is by nature *political*, in a sense higher than the bee or the ant, or any gregarious animal." As he elsewhere expresses it: "Man is to Man the condition of his highest happiness and improvement,"— 'Ανθρώπῳ ἥδιστον ἄνθρωπος, κ. τ. λ.]

† [In her transcript, Miss Stewart notes—"What date? I think about 1819, but am doubtful."]

‡ [Relative to acts, in and after 1820. See "*Notice sur M. Cousin,*" 1835.]

It was indeed against the authors of the most important blessings transmitted to us by our forefathers, that the outcry was the loudest and most general, not many years ago, in all the absolute monarchies on the Continent; in some of those most remarkably which have since fallen victims to their own blindness and imbecility; and where the people were prepared by unqualified panegyrics on the excellence and tranquillity of despotical Governments, to consider a change of masters as a circumstance of too little importance to their political condition to animate them in struggling against the arms of their invaders. The acknowledged mischiefs and horrors which were produced in France in the earlier stages of her revolution, by what the popular leaders dignified with the title of *Philosophy*, while everything which really merited the name was silenced and proscribed, has furnished to the enemies of human reason too specious a pretence for confounding, under one common appellation, the doctrines of sophistry and the salutary lessons of wisdom. The consequences have been everywhere such as were to be expected. The false theories which were once so generally propagated have been suppressed solely by the terrors of the sword; and that mild Philosophy, which addresses herself to minds unwarped by passion and by the spirit of faction, has been forced to reserve her admonitions for other times. In no country of Europe has this observation been verified in so remarkable a degree as in that where the evil originated; and if it applied to that country exclusively, it would afford much ground of consolation and hope to the human race.

"Di meliora piis, erroremque hostibus illum!"

I blush, however, to confess, that even among ourselves it is only *now* that the more candid and intelligent are *beginning* to acknowledge, that the radical source of the calamities of our age has been the ignorance and prejudices of the people; and that it is only by diffusing the light of knowledge and of liberality in those countries which have survived the general storm, that a provision can be made against those political convulsions which, in our own times, have derived their origin from the artifices of ambitious demagogues, operating on the credulity and profligacy of an uneducated multitude.

This growing change in public opinion, has given rise, of late years, to a much more general attention to speculative politics, than existed at any former period; and from this new direction of the public curiosity the happiest consequences may be anticipated. "Nothing," says Mr. Smith, "tends so much to promote public spirit as the study of politics; of the several systems of Civil Government; their advantages and disadvantages; of the condition of our own country; its situation and interest with regard to foreign nations; its commerce; its defence; the disadvantages it labours under; the dangers to which it may be exposed; how to remove the one, and how to guard against the other. Upon this account, Political Disquisitions, if just and reasonable and practicable, are, of all the works of speculation, the most useful. Even the weakest and the worst of them are not altogether without their utility. They serve at least to animate the public passions of men, and rouse them to seek out the means of promoting the happiness of society."[1]

A very able and candid critic, in some strictures which he did me the honour to make on the First Part of this *Dissertation*,* was pleased to express his regret that I should have announced my intention, in the farther prosecution of my subject, to abstain from all speculations concerning the Theory of Government, and to confine myself exclusively to the modern science of Political Economy. For this omission I might

---

[1] *Theory of Moral Sentiments*, Vol. I. pp. 471, 472, [sixth edition.]

* [Sir James Mackintosh; (see *Edinburgh Review*, Sept. 1816, Vol. XXVII. p. 220.) His words are:—" The mention of Buchanan excites our regret that Mr. Stewart should have excluded from his plan the history of those questions respecting the principles and forms of government, which form one of the principal subjects of political philosophy, properly so called. No writer could have more safely trusted himself in that stormy region. He was much less likely to have been tainted by its turbulence, than to have composed it by the serenity of his philosophical character. Every history of the other parts of moral and political science is incomplete, unless it be combined with that of political opinion; the link which, however unobserved, always unites the most abstruse of ethical discussions with the feelings and affairs of men."]

perhaps find a sufficient apology, in the novelty of Political Economy considered in the light of a science; (no attempt having been made to reduce its principles into a systematical form till the middle of the last century;) but as the reasons which chiefly weighed with me were really of a different nature, and as they are in my own opinion of considerable importance, I shall take this opportunity of submitting them, at some length, to the consideration of my readers.

In most of the Systematical Treatises published by political writers, the attention of the student is directed, in the *first instance*, to an examination and comparison of the different Forms of Government, and is *afterwards* led to some of those subjects which I have comprehended under the title of *Political Economy*. On a superficial view, this arrangement is apt to appear the most natural; for it is to the establishment of Government we are indebted for the existence of the Social Order; and without the executive power of Government, *Law* would be merely a *dead letter*. In this instance, however, I am inclined to think, as in many others, the most obvious arrangement is not the most natural; and that it would be better to *invert* the arrangement commonly followed, by beginning, first with the Principles of *Political Economy*, and afterwards proceeding to the Theory of Government.* My reasons for thinking so are various; but the following are some of the most important.

It is on the particular system of Political Economy which is established in any country, that the happiness of the people *immediately* depends; and it is from the *remote* tendency that

* [The order here indicated has been followed in the present publication: but, it will be observed, that this distribution is different from what may possibly be viewed as Mr. Stewart's ultimate arrangement; (see the preliminary Advertisement.) By that arrangement, the *Theory of Government* and its several *Forms* are, relatively to *Political Economy* proper, considered in the first instance.—It should be mentioned, that Mr. Stewart usually delivered a series of lectures on the Theory and Forms of Government, in addition to, but as a part of his ordinary course of Moral Philosophy. These *Political* lectures were thus altogether distinct from his separate course of *Political Economy*.]

wise forms of Government have to produce wise systems of Political Economy, that the utility of the former in a great measure arises. The one, indeed, leads *naturally* to the other; but it does not lead to it *necessarily;* for it is extremely possible that inexpedient laws may, in consequence of ignorance and prejudice, be sanctioned for ages by a Government excellent in its constitution, and just in its administration; while the evils threatened by a Government fundamentally bad, may, to a great degree, be corrected by an enlightened system of internal policy.

An idea very similar to this is stated by Mr. Hume, (though in a manner somewhat too paradoxical,) in one of his Essays. "We are, therefore, to look upon all the vast apparatus of our Government as having *ultimately* no other object or purpose but the distribution of *justice*, or the *support of the twelve Judges*. Kings and parliaments, fleets and armies, officers of the court and revenue, ambassadors, ministers and privy councillors, are all subordinate in their *end*, to *this* part of administration. Even the clergy, as their duty leads them to inculcate morality, may justly be thought, so far as regards this world, to have no other useful object of their institution."*

In farther illustration of this fundamental principle, it may be remarked, that there are two very different points of view in which *Laws* may be considered;—*first*, with respect to their *origin;* and, *secondly*, with respect to their *tendency*. If they are equitable in *both* respects, that is, if they arise from a just constitution of Government, and if they are favourable to general happiness, they possess every *possible* recommendation; but if they are to want the one recommendation or the other, the former (it ought always to be recollected) is of trifling moment in comparison of the latter. Unfortunately, however, for the world, the contrary idea has very generally prevailed; and has led men to direct their efforts much more to improve the Theory of Government, than to ascertain the just principles of *Political Economy*. What has contributed much to produce this effect is, that every change in an established form of administration,

* [*Essays*, Vol. I., Essay *Of the Origin of Government*.]

presents an immediate field of action to the ambitious and the turbulent; whereas improvements in Political Economy open only those distant prospects of general utility, which, however they may interest the calm benevolence of speculative men, are not likely to engage the passions of the multitude, or to attract the attention of those who aspire to be their leaders.

I before observed, that the mistaken notions concerning *Political Liberty* which have been so widely disseminated in Europe by the writings of Mr. Locke, have contributed greatly to divert the studies of speculative politicians from the proper objects of their attention. On this subject I beg leave to refer to the remarks I offered on Locke and his followers, when treating on the foundation of the duty of *Allegiance ;** and I have only to add at present, that the conclusion to which these and other observations of the same kind lead, is, *not* that the share of political power vested in the people is of trifling moment, but that its importance to their happiness depends on the protection and support it provides for their civil rights. *Happiness* is, in truth, the only object of legislation which is of *intrinsic* value ; and what is called *Political Liberty*, is only one of the means of obtaining this end. With the advantage of good laws, a people, although not possessed of political power, may yet enjoy a great degree of happiness ; and, on the contrary, where laws are unjust and inexpedient, the political power of the people, so far from furnishing any compensation for their misery, is likely to oppose an insurmountable obstacle to improvement, by employing the despotism of numbers in support of principles of which the multitude are incompetent to judge.

On the other hand, it is no less evident, that the only effectual and permanent bulwark against the encroachments of tyranny, is to be found in the political privileges which the Constitution secures to the governed. This, indeed, is demonstrated by the history of all those arbitrary establishments in which the condition of the subjects is decided by the personal character of the Sovereign ; and hence the jealousy with which,

* [Miss Stewart, in her transcript says :—"I fear this chapter on *Allegiance* is lost."]

under better constitutions, every encroachment on these privileges has been watched by the enlightened friends of freedom. The want of them, however, does not, like that of *civil liberty*, necessarily affect the happiness, nor impair the natural rights of individuals; for their value is founded entirely on considerations of political expediency; and, therefore, the *measure* of them, which a wise man would desire for himself and his fellow-citizens, is determined, not by the degree in which every individual consents, directly or indirectly, to the laws by which he is governed; but by the share of power which it is necessary for the people to possess, in order to place their civil rights beyond the danger of violation.—In so far as this object is attained under any establishment, the civil liberty of the people rests on a solid foundation; and their political power accomplishes completely the only purpose from which its value is derived. Nor must it be forgotten, how often it has happened in the history of mankind, that a people, by losing sight of the *end*, in the blind pursuit of the *means*, have forfeited both the one and the other.

These considerations, added to what was formerly stated, appear fully sufficient to justify my general position, that of the two branches of Political Science, (the Theory of Government and Political Economy,) the latter is that which is most immediately connected with human happiness and improvement; and which is therefore entitled, *in the first instance*,* to the attention of the student. But this is not all. Some knowledge of Political Economy is indispensably necessary to enable us to appreciate the different Forms of Government, and to compare them together, in respect of their fitness to accomplish the great ends to which they ought to be subservient: whereas Political Economy may be studied without any reference to constitutional forms; not only because the *tendency* of laws may be investigated abstractedly from all consideration of their *origin*, but because there are *many* principles of Political Economy which may be sanctioned by governments very different in their constitutions; and *some* so essentially con-

* [See note, p. 21.]

nected with the happiness of society that no Government can violate them, without counteracting the very purposes for which Government is established.

In contrasting, as I have now done, the study of Political Economy with that of the Theory of Government, I think it necessary for me once more to repeat, (before concluding this Lecture,*) that I do not mean to deny their very intimate connexion with each other. I have already said that it is only under equitable constitutions that we can have any reasonable prospect of seeing wise systems of policy steadily pursued; and it is no less true, on the other hand, that every improvement which takes place in the internal policy of a State, by meliorating the condition and the morals of the great mass of the people, has a tendency to prepare society for undergoing, without any shock or convulsion, those gradual alterations which time produces on all human institutions.

These observations may *appear* at first view to be contradicted by a passage in the Historical Fragment of Mr. Fox, of which, in consideration of the high authority of that eminent person, I think it necessary for me to take some notice. Speaking of the reign of Charles II., and particularly of the spirit of Government in the year 1675, he observes: " It is to be remarked, that to these times of heat and passion, and to one of those Parliaments which so disgraced themselves and the nation, by the countenance given to *Oates* and *Bedloe*, and by the persecution of so many innocent victims, we are indebted for the Habeas Corpus Act, the most important barrier against tyranny, and best framed protection for the liberty of individuals, that has ever existed in any ancient or modern Commonwealth."

" But the inefficacy of mere laws in favour of the subjects, in case of the administration of them falling into the hands of persons hostile to the spirit in which they had been provided, had been so fatally evinced by the general history of England ever since the grant of the Great Charter, and more especially

---

* [This parenthesis is deleted in the transcript from which Miss Stewart copied, and is omitted by her.]

by the transactions of the preceding reign, that the Parliament justly deemed their work incomplete, unless the Duke of York were excluded from the succession to the Crown."* To the same purpose he has elsewhere said, that "the reign of Charles II. forms one of the most singular as well as one of the most important periods of history. It is the æra of good laws and of bad government. The abolition of the Court of Wards; the repeal of the Act De Heretico Comburendo; the Triennial Parliament Bill; the establishment of the Rights of the House of Commons in regard to Impeachment; the expiration of the License Act; and, above all, the glorious Statute of Habeas Corpus, have therefore induced a modern writer of great eminence [Hume,] to fix the year 1679 as the period at which our constitution had arrived at its greatest theoretical perfection; but he owns, in a short note upon the passage alluded to, that the times immediately following were times of great practical oppression. What a field for meditation does this short observation from such a man furnish! What reflections does it not suggest to a thinking mind, upon the inefficacy of human laws, and the imperfection of human constitutions! We are called from the contemplation of the progress of our constitution, and our attention fixed with the most minute accuracy to a particular point, when it is said to have risen to its utmost perfection. Here we are then, at the best moment of the best constitution that ever human wisdom formed. What follows? A time of oppression and misery, not arising from external or accidental causes, such as war, pestilence, or famine, nor even from any such alteration of the laws as might be supposed to impair this boasted perfection, but from a corrupt and wicked administration, which all the so-much admired checks of the constitution were not able to prevent. How vain, then, how idle, how presumptuous is the opinion that laws can do everything! And how weak and pernicious the maxim founded upon it, that measures, not men, are to be attended to."†

The sentiments of an eminent Scotch Judge with respect to

* [*A History of the Early Part of the Reign of James II.*, Chap. I. p. 38, orig. ed.]
† [Ibid. p. 22, *seq.*]

the Act 1701, (which has been called the Habeas Corpus Act of Scotland,) may be quoted as a supplement to this citation from Mr. Fox. " The Habeas Corpus in England was passed in the reign of Charles II., and you may remember what Mr. Hume says, that that Act for securing the personal liberty of the subject, rendered the constitution of England the best the world had ever seen. The Habeas Corpus Act, however, was rendered altogether nugatory and unavailing in the infamous government which followed, and which produced the Revolution 1688. The Revolution also took place in this country; but there had been no Habeas Corpus Act here, and it was found necessary to pass the Act 1701. In England personal liberty was unavailing without political freedom; and in Scotland, political freedom was discovered to be nugatory without personal liberty. The Act 1701, was meant to consummate the Revolution."[1]

What is the moral to which these reflections lead? *Not*, certainly, that laws are of *little* moment to national felicity; or even that they are of *less* moment than the theoretical plan of the government, but that without the vivifying spirit of an enlightened people, jealous of their rights and determined to preserve them, the wisest political institutions are little better than a dead letter.

Delolme has made some judicious remarks on this subject, when treating of the *Censorial Power* exercised by the people of England over the conduct of government by means of the press. " Whoever considers," he observes, " what it is that constitutes the moving principles of what we call great affairs, and the invincible sensibility of man to the opinion of his fellow-creatures, will not hesitate to affirm, that, if it were possible for the Liberty of the Press to exist in a despotic government, and (what is not less difficult) for it to exist without changing the constitution, this liberty of the press would alone form a counterpoise to the power of the Prince. If, for ex-

[1] Speech of Lord Gillies in the case Duncan *v.* His Majesty's Advocate, as reported in the *Scotsman,* February 8, 1823. [This marks a date, after which the context was written.]

ample, in an empire of the East, a sanctuary could be found which, rendered respectable by the ancient religion of the people, might ensure safety to those who should bring thither their observations of any kind, and that from thence printed papers should issue, which, under a certain seal, might be equally respected, and which in their daily appearance, should examine and freely discuss the conduct of the Cadis, the Bashaws, the Vizier, the Divan, and the Sultan himself,—that would introduce immediately some degree of liberty."*

It is much to be regretted that Mr. Fox had not lent this argument the support of his talents and eloquence, but at the time he wrote, it was too little attended to by our best Whig writers; and, indeed, since the period of his death, the influence of the Press, in consequence of the diffusion of knowledge among the lower orders in every part of the island, and the astonishing multiplication of pamphlets and of periodical prints, has increased to a degree of which, twenty years ago, the most sanguine imagination could not have formed a conception. While this organ of public opinion and of the public will, shall remain unrestrained, the friends of liberty need entertain no serious apprehensions about the fate of our happy constitution. At least, any hazard to which it may be exposed can arise only from some incorrigible defect in the morals and public spirit of the people, which renders them no longer able or worthy to enjoy its blessings.

The following remarks of a profound and eloquent philosopher† will exhaust all that I wish farther to observe on this head. The passage is long, but is so important and so appropriate to my present purpose, that I am unwilling to weaken its effect by attempting to abridge it.

" It is not in mere laws that we are to look for the securities of justice, but in the powers by which these laws have been obtained, and without whose constant support they must fall into

* [*Constitution*, &c., Book II. chap. xii.]

† [Dr. Adam Ferguson, Mr. Stewart's predecessor in the chair of Moral Philosophy, in whose *Essay on the History of Civil Society* the passage is found;— Part III., sect. vi.]

disuse. Statutes serve to record the rights of a people, and speak the *intention* of parties to defend what the letter of the law has expressed; but without the vigour to maintain what is acknowledged as a right, the mere record, or the feeble intention, is of little avail.

" A populace roused by oppression, or an order of men possessed of a temporary advantage, have obtained many charters, concessions, and stipulations in favour of their claims; but where no adequate preparation was made to preserve them, the written articles were often forgotten, together with the occasion on which they were framed.

" The history of England, and of every free country, abounds with the example of statutes enacted when the people or their representatives assembled, but never executed when the crown or the executive was left to itself. The most equitable laws on paper are consistent with the utmost despotism in administration. Even the form of trial by juries in England had its authority in law, while the proceedings of the courts were arbitrary and oppressive.

" We must admire as the key-stone of civil liberty, the statute which forces the secrets of every prison to be revealed, the cause of every commitment to be declared, and the person of the accused to be produced, that he may claim his enlargement or his trial, within a limited time. No wiser form was ever opposed to the abuses of power. But it requires a fabric no less than the whole political constitution of Great Britain, a spirit no less than the refractory and turbulent zeal of this fortunate people, to secure its effects."*

* [From the previous Introduction it thus appears, that we are warranted in dividing the following Lectures on Political Economy into *two Parts*:—to wit, 1°, into a part comprising the matters usually referred to *Political Economy* proper; and 2°, into a part comprising the *Theory of Government and Forms of Administration*, that is, *Politics* proper. In its sequel, the Introduction further enumerates the subordinate constituents of the *First Part;* to wit, 1°, *Population*,—2°, *National Wealth*,—3°, *The Poor*,—4°, *Education:* and these we may consider as so many *Books* into which this Part is distributed.—Of the *Second Part*, this Introduction takes no account.]

CHAPTER II.*

[OF THE CONTENTS AND DISTRIBUTION OF POLITICAL ECONOMY PROPER,—OR OF PART FIRST.]

IN the last chapter I endeavoured to convey a general idea of the nature of those disquisitions which I comprehend under the title of *Political Economy,* and to which I have in this *Dissertation* restricted the meaning of Political Philosophy. In point of fact, the subjects of Population and of National Wealth have of late appropriated the title of Political Economy almost exclusively to themselves; but I flatter myself that the reasons I have assigned for enlarging the province of this science will be found satisfactory.

That the science of Political Economy, in the common acceptation of the phrase, is of modern origin, is universally admitted; and that the same observation is applicable to the other subjects to which I propose to extend the same title, will appear in the course of the following remarks. Indeed, upon all of them many of the conclusions which now very generally unite the suffrages of speculative men, stand in direct opposition to the maxims of ancient policy. It seems, therefore, naturally to occur as an object of preliminary inquiry, what are the peculiarities in the circumstances of Modern Europe which have given birth to this new science, and which have imposed on statesmen the necessity of searching for other lights than what are to be collected from the institutions of Ancient Greece

---

* [Miss Stewart notes upon her transcript,—"All after this is *old.*"—If hereby she means, that the process of accommodating the *Lectures* to the *Dissertation* ceases with the first Chapter, this is manifestly incorrect; as is apparent from the earlier portion, at least, of the following chapter.]

and Rome ? In considering this question, I shall have occasion to point out the natural connexion by which the different branches of Political Economy are united into one department of knowledge, and the easy transitions by which the consideration of any one of them leads to that of all the others. The remarks which I have to offer under this head will serve, at the same time, to explain, why in this part of my *Dissertation* so many of my observations are rather of a prospective, than of a historical or retrospective nature. This view of the subject I found to be unavoidable in treating of a science which, though it has suddenly burst into preternatural maturity, is still in point of years only in a state of infancy.

[POPULATION.]

I.—Among the various objects of Political Economy, one of the most important and interesting has been always understood to be *the augmentation of the numbers of the people ;* and accordingly, I propose to begin the course with an examination of the principal questions to which this subject has given rise.* It is a subject on which much attention has been bestowed both by ancient and by modern legislators, but the relative place which it occupies in the ancient and modern systems of Political Economy, will be found to be essentially different.

Of this difference the most powerful, though not the only cause, is the civil and domestic liberty now enjoyed, in this part of Europe, by the industrious orders of the community, contrasted with that *slavery* which entered into the constitutions of those states which, in the ancient world, were understood to have accomplished, in the most effectual manner, the great ends of government. In consequence of this mighty change produced by the dissolution of the *Feudal system,* the care of the statesman (in as far as population is concerned) is necessarily transferred from the higher classes of the people, to a description of men whose numbers in the *Free States* (as they were called) of Antiquity, were recruited, as they are now

* [This latter clause is deleted in the earlier copy, and omitted by Miss Stewart.]

in the West India Islands,* by importations from abroad. It is this description of men which forms the *basis* of that political fabric, which Sir William Temple has so finely compared to a pyramid; and it is on *their numbers*, combined with their *character* and *habits*, that the stability of the superstructure depends. Their *numbers*, however, it is evident, can in the actual state of things be kept up only by such political arrangements as furnish them with the means of rearing families; and it is into the question concerning the comparative expediency of the various arrangements proposed for that purpose, that the problem of population ultimately resolves. It is well known the efforts of *Augustus* and of the other statesmen of Rome to discourage celibacy, had little or no reference to this class of the community, but were calculated exclusively to keep up the race of citizens, and more especially of the order of nobility.

In consequence of the place which the subject of population necessarily occupies in the systems of modern statesmen, it will be found to be more or less connected with every other article of Political Economy; and accordingly, the most enlightened writers who have of late treated of population, have been led under this general title to discuss a variety of questions, to which it may appear, on a superficial view, to bear a very remote relation; such, for example, is the question with respect to the relative claims of Agriculture and of Manufactures to the attention of the statesman, with a number of other incidental inquiries connected with these different modes of industry. Nothing, however, under this head appears more deserving of notice, than the striking contrast between ancient and modern schemes of policy, considered in their effects on national manners, and on the progressive improvement of mankind; the former checking or altering the natural course of things by means of agrarian laws, and of other restrictive and violent regulations, calculated chiefly to keep up and to multiply the breed of soldiers; the latter (in those countries, at least, where

* [Miss Stewart, in her transcript, notes:—" This must be altered to suit 1823. My father has evidently overlooked it."]

the true principles of Political Economy have made any progress) allowing Agriculture and Commerce to act and re-act on each other, in multiplying the comforts of human life, in developing all the capacities that belong to our nature, and in diffusing as widely as the imperfections of human institutions will permit, the blessings of knowledge and of civilisation among all classes of the community. " The advantages, indeed, which modern policy possesses over the ancient, arises principally from its conformity, in some of the most important articles of Political Economy, to an order of things recommended by nature ;" and where it remains imperfect, its errors may in general be traced to the obstacles which, in a few instances, it still continues to oppose to those beneficent arrangements which would gradually take place of their own accord, if the legislator were only to confine his attention to his proper province.

[NATIONAL WEALTH.]

[II.]*—The various questions concerning *Population*, lead by an easy transition to an examination of the nature and causes of *National Wealth;* a branch of Political Economy which presents a contrast no less striking than that which the former article exhibits, between the maxims of ancient and of modern policy.

As the wealth possessed by some of the most celebrated states of antiquity was acquired not by commerce but by the sword, it had no tendency to encourage a commercial spirit, excepting in so far as it ministered to luxury. Accordingly, we find that commerce was dreaded by the Roman statesmen on account of the luxury which they regarded as its necessary consequence ; and it is a curious circumstance, that after their foreign conquests had brought immense riches into the public treasury, this very dread of the commercial spirit produced the same jealousy about the exportation of the precious metals with which the prejudices of the mercantile system of Political Economy so long inspired the legislators of Modern Europe.

* [This numeral apparently omitted by inadvertence.]

"Exportari aurum," says Cicero, "non oportere, cum sæpe antea senatus, tum, me consule, *gravissime* judicavit."* The same policy continued afterwards (partly indeed from other motives) under the Emperors; and it must be confessed, that in so far as their aim was to keep possession of the riches they had acquired, their views were somewhat more reasonable and consistent than those of our ancestors, for as they had no commodities of their own to give in exchange for the luxuries they imported, they must have paid for every thing in silver and gold. In the degenerate state, however, into which the Roman manners had then fallen, the progress of luxury was not to be checked by legislative restrictions, and the discouragements to commerce served only to prevent the operation of that antidote which nature has so beautifully provided against its pernicious effects, in the general diffusion of wealth among the body of a people, accompanied with that spirit of industry and frugality which commercial pursuits have a tendency to inspire.

The fatal effects which had been found, in the history of so many states, to be produced by a sudden influx of riches from abroad, combined with an ignorance of the salutary tendencies of commerce, led the ancient lawgivers very generally to check, as much as possible, the commercial spirit by the force of positive institutions. Plato prohibits the introduction into his imaginary Commonwealth, of any arts but those which minister to the necessities of human life, and refused to give laws to the Arcadians, because they were rich and loved magnificence;— while Phocion, who saw in the wealth of the Athenians the seeds of their ruin, proposed that artisans should be considered as slaves, and deprived of the rights of citizens. That these ideas correspond perfectly with the prevailing, or rather the unanimous opinion of antiquity, appears from numerous passages in the Greek and Roman authors. At present, I shall only mention Plutarch's *Life of Pericles*, and the 8th, 17th, 20th, and 94th *Epistles of Seneca.*

How different are the ideas which now prevail universally on the same subject! "It is no longer," says Raynal, " a

* [*Pro Flacco*, cap. xxviii.]

people immersed in poverty, that becomes formidable to a rich nation. Power is at present an attendant on riches, because they are no longer the fruit of conquest, but the produce of lives spent in perpetual employment. Gold and silver corrupt only those indolent minds which indulge in the delights of luxury, upon that stage of low intrigue which is called greatness. The same metals put in motion the hands and arms of the people, exciting a spirit of agriculture in the fields, of navigation in the maritime cities, and multiplying over the whole face of the country, the comforts, enjoyments, and ornaments of life."* Montesquieu himself does not seem to have been sufficiently aware of this essential difference between the wealth acquired by commerce and by rapine, in the parallel which he draws between the Carthaginians and the Romans. The former were indeed subdued by the latter, but they must be allowed to have maintained a far more obstinate and glorious struggle for their political existence, than was afterwards exhibited by their conquerors when assailed by the arms of the barbarians.

Agreeably to these remarks, and in direct contradiction to the maxims of *ancient* policy, we find everywhere, when we cast our eyes over the surface of the globe, that the most wealthy states are those where the people are the most industrious, humane, and enlightened, and where the liberty they enjoy, by entering as an elementary principle into the very existence of the political order, rests on the most solid and durable basis. Indeed, it was the general diffusion of wealth among the lower orders of men which first gave birth to the spirit of independence in Modern Europe, and which has produced under some of its governments, and more especially under our own, a more equal diffusion of freedom and of happiness than took place under the most celebrated constitutions of antiquity.

The difference between the condition of ancient and of modern nations, in consequence of the abolition of domestic slavery, has been already remarked, and the effects which it has produced have in no instance been more conspicuous than

* [*Histoire Philosophique des Etablissemens et du Commerce*, &c.]

upon the sources of national opulence. As the ground is now universally cultivated (at least in this part of Europe) by men whose subsistence depends on the fruits of their own industry, the measure of their exertions can be increased only by the multiplication of their wants and necessities; or (as Sir James Steuart expresses it) "by the operation of manufactures and commerce, in rendering men *slaves* to their own passions and desires." Hence the important distinction upon which this ingenious writer has laid so great stress between *labour* and *industry*. "The former," he observes, "may always be procured, even by force, at the expense of furnishing man with his daily sustenance, whereas the latter cannot possibly be established, but by means of an adequate equivalent, proportioned not to what is absolutely necessary, but to what may satisfy the reasonable desire of the industrious, which equivalent becomes, in its turn, the means of diffusing a similar taste for superfluities among all classes of people."[1]

One of the best illustrations I know of this distinction between labour and industry, and of the consequent difference between the ancient and modern system of Political Economy, is to be found in the discourse (commonly, and I think justly, attributed to Xenophon) "*On the Improvement of the Revenue of the State of Athens*."[2] From this work of Xenophon we learn the opinion of the author with regard to the three principal classes of the Athenian people—the *Citizens*, the *Strangers*, and the *Slaves;* and it is particularly remarkable, that even among the lowest order of the citizens, he never once supposes the expediency, or even the possibility, of exciting a spirit of industry by any of the motives which operate so effectually on the minds of the multitude in Modern Europe. On the contrary, his professed object is to secure the same advantages at which Political Economy *now* aims, through the medium of men's natural propensities, by regulations of *police*, altogether

---

[1] Sir James Stenart's *Works*, Vol. II. p. 163, 8vo edition, [*An Inquiry into the Principles of Political Economy*, Book II. chap. xxx.]

[2] A translation of this *Discourse* is introduced into the first volume of the edition of D'Avenant's *Political Works*, published by Sir Charles Whitworth.

unconnected with the habits of the people for whose welfare they were destined.

With this view, he lays down a plan for improving the revenue of the State, (by means of taxes to be imposed on its confederate cities,) in such a manner, as out of it to give every Athenian citizen a pension of three *oboli* a day, or threepence three farthings of our money.

In case the resources he points out for obtaining this revenue should prove deficient, people from all quarters, (he observes,) princes and strangers of note in all countries, would be proud of contributing towards it, to have their names transmitted to posterity in the public monuments of Athens.

Besides providing this daily pension of threepence three farthings for every citizen of Athens, rich and poor, Xenophon proposed to build, at the public expense, a number of trading vessels, a great many inns, and houses of entertainment for all strangers in the sea-ports, to erect shops, warehouses, and exchanges, the rents of which would not only increase the revenue, but add to the beauty and magnificence of the city. In a word, the great aim of this ancient system of Political Economy, (as Sir James Steuart has well observed,) is to accomplish by the labour of slaves, and by the subsidies of strangers, what a free people in our days are constantly performing by their own industrious exertions.[1]

In consequence of this independent industry of our lower orders, and more especially of the action and re-action of manufactures, commerce, and agriculture on each other, there has gradually arisen in the mechanism of modern society, a complexness of parts, and, at the same time, an apparent simplicity of design, essentially different from what fell under the review of ancient politicians.

Among other important consequences resulting from this mechanism, there is one which it may not be improper to mention at present, as it affords a peculiarly striking proof of the essential difference between the state of mankind in ancient and in modern times. The circumstance I allude to is, the

[1] Vol. II. pp. 166-168. [Ibidem.]

effect of internal commerce in circulating *money* through all the different parts of the political body; affording by this very process a sensible illustration of the systematical relations which now connect together all the different orders of men in the same community, and which render every change in the condition of any one order a source either of advantage or loss to all the others. How different the case was in the old world, we may infer from the low price which the necessaries of life bore at a time when the precious metals were in the greatest abundance among the higher classes; and when the pecuniary expenses of some individuals, in articles of luxury and of ornament, were on a scale far exceeding the most extravagant ideas of modern ages.

These, and some other facts of the same kind, demonstrate how much the relation between *prices* and the *quantity* of the *precious metals* depends on that *circulation of money* which is produced by an active internal commerce: But the *only* inference I wish to draw from them at present is, the *disjointed organization* of society in the ancient Commonwealths, when compared with that comprehensive mechanism, which, in such a country as ours, combines so beautifully into one system the different classes and interests of individuals.

Another circumstance which has had a powerful influence on the condition of civilized nations in modern times, is the activity and extent of *maritime* trade, so wonderfully facilitated by the improvements which have taken place in the art of navigation, and so strongly encouraged by the intercourse which *these* have opened with parts of the globe formerly unknown.

' It is observed by Dr. Robertson,* that in the ancient world *land trade* was the principal object, and *maritime trade* only a secondary one. This was not *entirely* owing to the cause to which he ascribes it,—the imperfection of the art of navigation: it was the natural effect of the geographical situation of the three continents to which the operations of commerce were confined. They all either touched, or nearly touched, each

* [*Historical Disquisition concerning the Knowledge which the Antients had of India, and the Progress of Trade, &c.*]

other; and the Mediterranean seas, which they included, served only to facilitate the operations of a commerce, of which the land was the principal element.

Of the extent to which human ingenuity and industry were able, in ancient times, to carry on foreign trade, under the great disadvantages of land-carriage, an idea may be formed from the remains of this species of commerce, still existing in the East; for although since the passage to India by the Cape of Good Hope was opened, the trade from that country to Europe has been carried on by sea, a considerable portion of its valuable productions are, to this day, conveyed by land to other parts of the earth. This mode of communication is, indeed, rendered absolutely necessary, by the unbroken continuity of many of the most extensive provinces of Asia; and in a still greater degree, by the effect of the same circumstances in the Continent of Africa. The religious pilgrimages to Mecca, enjoined by the founder of the Mahometan faith, have contributed to increase, or, at least, to concentrate this commercial intercourse, by drawing annually to the Holy City numerous caravans, both of pilgrims and merchants, from all the countries where the Mahometan worship is established, extending to the shores of the Atlantic on the one hand, and to the remotest regions of the East on the other. During the few days of its continuance, the Fair of Mecca is said to be the greatest on the face of the earth; and of the immense value to which mercantile transactions are there carried on, the most unequivocal proof (as Dr. Robertson remarks) is afforded by the despatch, the silence, the mutual confidence and good faith with which they are conducted.

I have mentioned these facts chiefly as proofs of the extent to which the commercial transactions of ancient nations *may* have been carried, notwithstanding their comparative ignorance of the art of navigation. Accordingly, it has been argued by a late writer, (Mr. Heeren of Göttingen,*) that although *particular states*, in modern times, may have carried their trade to

* [Mr. Stewart, though he did not read German, possessed in manuscript an English translation of Heeren's work on the *Policy and Commerce of the Ancient Nations.*]

a higher degree than single states of the ancient world; yet, on the other hand, commerce was, in the earlier ages, more equally divided among nations than at present, when a few countries in the western parts of Europe are become almost the only seats of the commerce of the globe. It has been observed by the same author, that while, in consequence of our extended navigation and maritime trade, the nations which are in possession of them have made the most important improvements, a multitude of other nations, whose situations now lie out of the road of commerce, have sunk into the lowest state of barbarism. But although there may be some foundation for these remarks, no comparison certainly can be made between the *land trade* carried on of old, and the commerce which has originated in modern Europe, when considered in connexion with human improvement and happiness. Nothing, indeed, can shew this more clearly than the stationary condition in which the race still remains in those parts of the world, where the former species of traffic is carried on upon the greatest scale. The facts which have been collected to illustrate the extent of their traffic serve only to place in the stronger light the peculiar advantages of that maritime intercourse, which unites, by a rapid intercourse, the most remote harbours of the globe; more particularly when combined with that inland trade, which, by means of water conveyance, penetrates in every direction the interior of a continent.

The origin of that maritime commerce which so peculiarly distinguishes modern times, is to be ascribed in a great measure to the discovery of the New World, and of the passage to India by the Cape of Good Hope. The former of these events, more particularly, was necessarily accompanied with the most important consequences; extending, in an incalculable degree, the mutual connexion of nations; and by encouraging the art of man to contend with the dangers of the ocean, throwing a new light on those beneficent arrangements which Providence has made for the improvement of the human race. It is to this event that the subsequent progress of navigation, and of that commercial spirit which now exerts so powerful an influence over the condition of mankind, may be ultimately traced; and, if it had not happened, it may be reasonably questioned whether the circumnavigation of *Africa* would have produced any essential change in the course of trade, or in the relations which had till then connected together the different parts of the globe.

The activity of trade thus excited and maintained by the boldness and skill of modern navigators, has been farther aided, in an immense degree, by the *commerce of money*, so expeditiously and easily carried on in modern times by the simple and beautiful expedient of *bills of exchange*. By means of these, debts and credits may be shifted from one place to another, so as to answer all the purposes of transportation of the precious metals; the same ends being accomplished by this happy invention in foreign commerce, to which coins are subservient in the details of ordinary business.

The invention of bills of exchange has been generally ascribed, since the time of Montesquieu, to the Jews. "It is a known fact," says this eminent writer, "that under Philip Augustus and Philip the Long, the Jews who were chased from France took refuge in Lombardy, and that there they gave to foreign merchants and travellers secret letters drawn upon those to whom they had entrusted their effects in France, which bills were accordingly accepted by their correspondents." "Commerce," he adds, "by this means, became capable of eluding violence, and of maintaining everywhere its ground; the richest merchant having nothing but invisible effects, which he could convey imperceptibly wherever he pleased."*

In these observations, Montesquieu has probably gone a little too far; for although the Jews may have invented the modern *forms* of transactions of this nature, (a fact, however, which is by no means indisputably ascertained,) there are very strong reasons for believing that the practice in question was not altogether unknown among the commercial states of antiquity. The idea, indeed, of thus exchanging one debtor for another, or of a reciprocal transfer of credits, is so extremely obvious, that it could not possibly fail to occur wherever an extensive com-

* [*Esprit des Loix.* Liv. XXI. chap. xvi.]

merce has subsisted between different nations; and, in fact, some traces of such transactions in ancient times, have been discovered by the learned industry of modern writers.

Notwithstanding, however, these circumstances, I believe it may be safely asserted, that it was in modern Europe that this mode of settling accompts, and transacting payments between foreign merchants, was first reduced to a system; a chain of correspondences being established all over the commercial world, among a particular description of traders, whose business it is to negotiate pecuniary transactions; and who, by confining their attention to this branch of commerce, have given a regularity and correctness, formerly unknown, to all other mercantile operations. The improvements which have taken place, during the course of a few centuries, in the general state of political society, all over this part of the world, by giving rise to the establishment of regular posts, and promoting everywhere a disposition to good faith and mutual confidence, are, in truth, (as I shall have occasion afterwards to show,) the foundation of those multiplied mercantile relations, of which the refinements now under our consideration may be regarded as the necessary consequences, and without which they could not possibly have existed.

In a passage already quoted from Montesquieu, [p. 41,] it is observed,—by the invention of bills of exchange, merchants were enabled to elude the grasp of *despotism*. The observation is just, and it touches on a circumstance equally important to civil liberty, and to the prosperity of commerce. Whether these advantages are not in some degree compensated by the selfish independence of capitalists, who by the same causes which increase their influence on public affairs, are released from local connexions, and rendered citizens of the world at large, is a question of more difficult discussion.

Among the various circumstances, however, which distinguish the modern systems of political economy, and add to the intricacy of this branch of study, none is more conspicuous than the *fabric of public credit*, particularly in the great commercial states of Europe; an innovation which not only affects essentially all the branches of trade, in consequence of its intimate connexion with the commerce of money, but in its more remote tendency affects the condition of all the different classes of the community.

One advantage, however, (among many inconveniences,) which may be traced to this innovation, is the attention which sovereigns have been forced to give, for their own sakes, to the advancement of industry and wealth among their subjects; and although their efforts towards this end have not been always enlightened, yet they have almost everywhere contributed materially to ameliorate gradually the condition of the body of the people. The strength of modern empires is now understood to depend on *internal cultivation;* presenting in this respect a striking contrast to those in the Old World, which rose by conquest, and were fed by precarious tribute. The greater the number of such states, which thus found their importance on their internal advantages and resources, and the more liberal the policy by which they are connected, the greater will be the prosperity of each individually; and the more solid will be the foundation which is laid for the future happiness of the human race.

It is remarked by Mr. Hume, in one of his political discourses, that "though all kinds of government be improved in modern times, yet monarchical governments seem to have made the greatest advances towards perfection. It may now," he says, "be affirmed of civilized monarchies, what was formerly said in praise of republics alone, *that they are a government of laws, not of men.* They are found susceptible of order, method, and constancy, to a surprising degree. Property is there secure; industry encouraged; the arts flourish; and the prince lives secure among his subjects like a father among his children. There are, perhaps, and have been for two centuries, near two hundred absolute princes, great and small, in Europe; and allowing twenty years to each reign, we may suppose that there have been in the whole two thousand monarchs, or *tyrants,* (as the Greeks would have called them,) yet of these there has not been *one,* not even Philip II. of Spain, so bad as Tiberius,

Caligula, Nero, or Domitian, who were four in twelve among the Roman emperors."*

Of this very remarkable fact, an explanation may no doubt be found, *in part*, in the diffusion of knowledge among all orders of men by means of the *press*, which has everywhere raised a bulwark against the oppression of rulers in the light and spirit of the people; but much must likewise be ascribed to the influence which juster views of *Political Economy* have had upon the counsels even of absolute princes, by convincing them how inseparably the true interests of governors and the governed are connected together;—a consideration which, while it opens an encouraging prospect with respect to the future history of the world, affords an additional proof of a proposition which I shall afterwards endeavour to illustrate; that the science of *Political Economy*, much more than that part of the theory of government which relates to *forms of administration*, is entitled, in the present circumstances of mankind, to the attention of the speculative politician.

†In treating of the various questions connected with the general title of *National Wealth*, I shall be obliged to confine myself to very partial views on the subject. The field is of immense extent; and one of the most interesting portions of it (that relating to the question about the freedom of trade) has been surveyed already by Mr. Smith, with so great accuracy, that little remains for me but to consider a few incidental questions which have not entered into his plan, and to examine such of his fundamental principles as seem to myself to require limitations or corrections, or which have been disputed on solid grounds by political writers of a later date. An outline of his reasonings on this important article will be necessary for the sake of connexion; but I shall direct my attention more particularly to certain applications of the general doctrine, about which doubts have been suggested either by Mr. Smith

---

* [*Essays*, Vol. I., Essay *Of Civil Liberty*.]

† [All that follows under II., or the head of National Wealth, is deleted in the older transcript.]

himself, or by later writers. Of this kind are the questions,— *First*, with respect to the expediency of restrictions on the *commerce of money*, in the case of pecuniary loans. *Second*, concerning the expediency of restrictions on that branch of commerce which is employed about the *necessaries of life ;* and *Third*, concerning the expediency of restrictions on the *commerce of land.*

But although in my *practical* conclusions on the more important questions, I am disposed to agree with Mr. Smith, I shall have frequent occasion to differ from him widely in stating the first principles of the science, as well as in my opinion of the logical propriety of various technical phrases and technical distinctions which he has sanctioned with his authority. I must take the liberty also to observe, that the *plan of arrangement* of his invaluable work, is far from being unexceptionable; and I am not without hopes, that by the criticisms which I have to offer on its imperfections in this respect, I shall be able to simplify the study of its doctrines to those who may adopt it, (which most persons in this country now do, and, in my opinion, for the most solid reasons,) as the elementary groundwork for their future speculations on that branch of Political Economy to which it relates.

The great variety of subjects which the plan of the *course* embraces, will necessarily confine my attention, *in general*, to those principles of *Political Economy* which are of a universal application. To examine the modifications which may be requisite in particular instances, in consequence of the peculiarities in the physical or moral circumstances of nations, would lead me into details inconsistent with the nature of academic lectures. In discussing, however, the two articles already mentioned, (those of *Population* and of *National Wealth*,) my reasonings will often have a reference to the interests of *our own* country. And if I should be thus occasionally led to deviate a little from systematical method, I flatter myself, that the inconvenience will be more than compensated, not only by the useful information to which I shall be able to *lead your attention*, but by the light which such digressions cannot fail to throw on our general principles. It is, indeed, one of the most fruitful sources of error and paradox in disquisitions of this kind, to reason abstractedly concerning the *resources of states*, without any regard either to existing forms of society, or to varieties in the physical and geographical advantages of different regions. It is a source of error, not only because the soundest general rules ought to be applied with caution in particular cases, but because the greater part of political writers, even when they express themselves in the most general and abstract terms, have been insensibly warped, more or less, in their speculations, by local habits, and local combinations of circumstances to which they have been accustomed. To this source may be distinctly traced many of the apparent diversities in the theories of different politicians; and among others, some of the contradictions between the partisans and the opponents of the agricultural system of *Political Economy*. The very ingenious author himself, of the *Essay on Circulation and Credit*,* has not perhaps always recollected, that, while his antagonists had a view, more especially to a territory like *France, his* mind was occupied about *Holland*. An attentive consideration of this circumstance will, if I do not deceive myself, account, in many instances, for an apparent diversity of opinion among speculative politicians, upon points concerning which there could not possibly have been any disagreement, if both parties had stated fully all the local particulars by which their general principles were *tacitly*, perhaps *unconsciously*, modified in their own habits of thinking.

In studying *Political Economy*, it is more particularly necessary for an inhabitant of these kingdoms, to keep in remembrance the many peculiarities of our situation, combining an immense fund of agricultural riches, with the advantages arising from an insular form, from the number and disposition of our navigable rivers, and from an extent of coast amounting (according to Sir William Petty's computation, a computation which, I apprehend, falls short greatly of the truth) to three

* [Mr. Stewart probably refers to the *Traité de la Circulation et du Crédit*, Amst. 1771, by Isaac Pinto.]

thousand eight hundred miles. Nor ought he to lose sight of the prodigies which the industry and spirit of the people, improving on their natural advantages, have already effected, under the protecting influence of civil liberty; connecting the different parts of our islands by an extended system of inland navigation, which (considering the mountainous surface of the country) may be justly regarded as one of the proudest monuments of human power.

[THE POOR:—THEIR MAINTENANCE.]

III.—The researches of modern politicians concerning the sources of National Wealth, have naturally directed their attention to that unfortunate class of men, who, in consequence either of the imperfections of our social institutions, or of the evils *necessarily* connected with the present condition of humanity, are left dependent on the bounty of their fellow-citizens. The speculation is sufficiently interesting in itself, considered merely in its relation to those orders of the community who are its immediate objects; but it has been found, on examination, to be still more interesting, when considered in its connexion with the general system of *Political Economy.*
. . . . [*Sic.*] To those who have any knowledge of the rise and progress of that part of English policy which relates to this subject, it is unnecessary for me to remark, with what extreme difficulty the speculation is attended, and how frequently the best intended, and apparently the most wisely considered schemes have been found to aggravate the evils they were meant to remedy.

Doubts have accordingly arisen in the minds of many sagacious inquirers, whether it would not have been better if the cause of this class of men had been left entirely to the voluntary charity of their fellow-citizens; and whether the existing system of our poor laws may not be added to the many other instances which human affairs afford, of an officious attempt on the part of statesmen, to accomplish artificially, by the wisdom of man, those beneficent ends, for securing which so beautiful an arrangement has been made by the wisdom of

Providence. That in many individual instances the evils of extreme indigence are thus greatly alleviated, is beyond a doubt: but the question is, how does this interference of law operate with respect to the *general*, and the most important interests of the labouring orders? Is it favourable to their industry, to their economy, and to their domestic virtues? Or is there no reason to apprehend, that while it operates as a palliative to local inconveniences, it aggravates and confirms the radical malady in which they originated?

It must, however, be owned to be a very different question, whether, supposing no legal provision to have been made for the poor, it would have been expedient to introduce the present system of laws; and whether, circumstanced as we actually are, it would be wise to abolish this part of our policy. Among the various opinions concerning the mode of relieving the wants of the lower classes, it seems to be very generally agreed, that a *modification* only of our existing regulations, and not a total *repeal* of them, can be safely attempted; and that the correction of the evils complained of is to be expected less from the *direct* and *immediate* interposition of the Legislature, than from the gradual operation of more remote and powerful causes on the industry, morals, and resources of the people.

It is scarcely necessary for me to add, that these disquisitions with respect to the *poor*, which have for many years past exercised the ingenuity of speculative men all over Europe, furnish another very remarkable illustration of that contrast which the present state of society in this part of the world exhibits, to the condition of mankind under the ancient governments. The disorders which have been now under our consideration, originated in the abolition of a much greater disorder, the institution of Slavery, and they have presented ever since to the politician, one of the most interesting, and, at the same time, one of the most difficult problems, which the science of legislation affords.

[EDUCATION.—PREVENTION, REFORMATION, CORRECTION OF CRIME.]

IV.—The maintenance of the poor is intimately connected with another subject:—The means of encouraging among the body of the people habits of industry, and of a regularity of morals; and of effecting, where it is possible, a reformation in the manners of those who have rendered themselves obnoxious to the laws of their country. The attempts which have been made with this last view by the projects of penitentiary houses and of solitary confinement, do honour to the enlightened benevolence of the present age, and may probably be found susceptible of many improvements for accomplishing, still more effectually, the laudable and important purposes for which they are destined.

With a review of these establishments, the general principles which ought to regulate the *punishment of crimes* have a very close connexion, and accordingly, they have attracted, in the course of the last century, the attention of some very distinguished writers, and more particularly of the Marquis *Beccaria*, whose humane and eloquent *Treatise on Crimes and Punishments* forms one of the most valuable illustrations that has yet appeared, of the connexion between the principles of Ethical Philosophy and the Science of Legislation. In order, however, to apply a radical cure to these evils, it is necessary for government to bestow such a systematical attention on the *Education* of the people, as may afford the means of instruction even to the lowest classes of the community.

It is justly and beautifully observed by Sir Henry Wotton, that " albeit good laws have always been reputed the nerves and ligaments of human society, yet they are no way comparable in their effects to the rules of good nature. For it is in civil as it is in natural plantations, where young tender trees (though subject to the injuries of the air, and in danger even of their own flexibility) would yet little want any under proppings and shoarings, if at first they were well fastened in the root." In the present state of society this may be regarded as one of the most effectual objects of legislation; and the happy effects resulting from the establishments (however imperfect) for that purpose, in Scotland and America, give the strongest encouragement to the farther prosecution of the same plan on more liberal principles.

"In a civilized and commercial country, the education of the common people," as Mr. Smith has well remarked, "requires the attention of the public more than that of people of some rank and fortune. The common people have little time to spare for education. Their parents can scarce afford to maintain them even in infancy. As soon as they are able to work, they must apply to some trade, by which they can earn their subsistence. That trade, too, is generally so simple and uniform, as to give little exercise to the understanding, while, at the same time, their labour is both so constant and so severe, that it leaves them little leisure and less inclination to apply to, or even to think of anything else."*

"An instructed and intelligent people, besides," as is farther observed by the same writer, "are always more decent and orderly than an ignorant and stupid one. They are more disposed to examine, and more capable of seeing through the interested complaints of faction and sedition; and they are, upon that account, less apt to be misled into any wanton or unnecessary opposition to the measures of government. In free nations, where the safety of government depends very much upon the favourable judgment which the people may form of its conduct, it must surely be of the highest importance, that they should not be disposed to judge rashly or capriciously concerning it."†

To the same liberal doctrine a very forcible sanction has been given by a late Bishop of London, (Dr. Porteous,) in the following passage of one of his *Charges to the clergy*, a passage which is well entitled to particular attention, inasmuch as it states, on this very important and long contested question, the opinion of a most intelligent and candid judge, founded on a

---

* [*Wealth of Nations*, Book V. chap. i.] [† Ibid.]

calm review of the causes which have produced the revolutionary evils of our own times.

" Ignorance is the mother of superstition, of bigotry, of fanaticism, of disaffection, of cruelty, and of rebellion. These are its legitimate children. It never yet produced any other, and never will, to the end of the world. And we may lay this down as an incontestable truth, that a well-informed and intelligent people, more particularly a people well acquainted with the sacred writings, will always be more orderly, more decent, more humane, more virtuous, more religious, more obedient to their superiors, than a people totally devoid of all instruction and all education."

I shall only add farther on this subject at present, (and it is an observation which I shall state in the words of Bishop Butler,) that the duty of extending the means of elementary instruction to the lower orders, is now recommended to us by many powerful arguments which did not apply to the state of the world, prior to the invention of printing.

" Till within a century or two, all ranks were, in point of learning, nearly on a level. The art of *printing* appears to have been *providentially* reserved till these latter ages, and then providentially brought into use, as what was to be instrumental, for the future, in carrying on the appointed course of things."

" The alterations which this art has even already made in the face of the world, are not inconsiderable. By means of it, whether immediately or remotely, the methods of carrying on business are, in several respects, improved ; "*knowledge has been increased*," and some sort of literature is become general. And if this be a blessing, we ought to let the poor in their degree share it with us. If we do not, it is certain, how little soever it may be attended to, that they will be upon a greater advantage, on many accounts, especially in populous places, than they were in the dark ages. And, therefore, to bring up the poor in their former ignorance, now that knowledge is so much more common and wanted, would be not to keep them in the same, but to put them into a lower condition of life than what they were in formerly. Nor," concludes this excellent author, in the same spirit which dictated the passage just quoted from Mr. Smith, " nor, let people of rank flatter themselves that ignorance will keep their inferiors more dutiful and in greater subjection to them; for surely there must be danger that it will have a contrary effect, under a free government such as ours, and in a dissolute age."*

To ascertain what are the branches of knowledge best fitted for accomplishing the purposes here described, and to devise the simplest means for their communication, is a more difficult subject of speculation than may at first be imagined. Nor do I apprehend that the field is yet exhausted, notwithstanding the dogmatical assertion of Dr. Johnson, that " education is as well known as it ever *can* be."† Admitting even his observation to be just when applied to the instruction of the *higher orders*, it must be allowed to fail most remarkably in its application to the instruction of the lower, a subject on which very little attention has been hitherto bestowed in modern Europe; and which, in ancient times, was considered as unworthy the notice of a philosopher. The plans of education recommended by some of the most enlightened writers of Greece, had a reference only to those who were called [ἐλεύθεροι,—χαρίεντες (?)]; while the inferior classes were almost entirely overlooked as a part of the social system. In proportion to the progress of society during the last two or three centuries, this order of men have been gradually rising in political importance; but the authors who have hitherto speculated concerning their intellectual improvement, have, in general, (and more especially in our own times,) gone into extremes; some representing it as a duty incumbent on governments to extend gratuitously the means of instruction, (and *that* on the most liberal plan,) to all descriptions of people; and others recommending to statesmen a policy calculated to check completely, among the great mass of their fellow-citizens, the progress of the human mind.

---

* [*Sermon preached at Christchurch.* London, 1745.]

† [The absurdity of this is shown somewhere in the *Dissertation*, by Johnson's own childish superstitions.]

Besides a provision for the general elementary instruction of the lower orders, some politicians have recommended to government a still more watchful and minute interference in the care of the rising generation, and *that*, not only in the case of the labouring classes, but of all ranks and descriptions of men. A celebrated English writer, (Dr. John Brown, author of the *Estimate*,) whose publications at one time attracted a great deal of attention, has laid much stress on this idea, in his *Thoughts on Civil Liberty, Licentiousness, and Faction.* "It is deeply to be regretted," he observes in one passage, "that the British system of policy and religion is not upheld in its native power, like that of Sparta, by correspondent and effectual rules of education; that it is in the power of every private man to educate his child, not only without a reverence for these, but in absolute contempt of them; and that at the Revolution in 1688, the education of youth was still left in an imperfect state; this great Revolution having confined itself to the reform of public institutions, without ascending to the great fountain of political security, the private and effectual formation of the public mind." . . . "The chief and essential remedy of licentiousness and faction, the fundamental means of the lasting and secure establishment of civil liberty, can only be in a general and prescribed improvement of the laws of education, to which all the members of the community should legally submit; and it is for want of a prescribed code of education that the manners and principles, on which alone the State can rest, are ineffectually instilled, are vague, fluctuating, and self-contradictory."

"Nothing," he adds, "is more evident, than that some reform on this great point is necessary for the security of public freedom, and that, though it is an incurable defect of our political state, that it has not a correspondent and adequate code of education, *inwrought* into its first essence: we may yet hope, that in a secondary and inferior degree, something of this kind may yet be *inlaid;* that though it cannot have that perfect efficacy, as if it had originally been of the piece, yet, if well conducted, it may strengthen the weaker parts, and alleviate defects, if not completely remove them."

Some remarks to the same purpose occur in the *Essays on the Spirit of Legislation*, published by the Society of *Berne*, in Switzerland. "A legislator," it is justly observed, "occupied like the father of his country, with the happiness of his people, will watch national education, to the end that children may suck in with the milk, the principles and maxims which may contribute to the public good, and the prosperity of individuals." "Upon this principle," the author adds, "I do not comprehend how we can abandon the public education to masters that depend not on government, or are little concerned with the State."

To this plan, however, of Dr. Brown, (at least in its application to the circumstances of our own country,) many strong and insuperable objections might be stated, and accordingly, several very eminent writers have expressed their doubts, whether some of the important ends which he was so anxious to accomplish, would not be secured more effectually, if governments were to interfere *still less* in regulating the system of education, than they have been commonly disposed to do. Without giving any opinion on this point, I shall content myself with remarking, that these considerations which, in such a country as this, impose on the public as a duty, the task of providing proper instruction for the poor and for the labouring classes, do not apply, with the same force, to the higher orders. It is on the character and habits of these inferior classes, that the stability of every government essentially depends; and it is on *their* account chiefly that regulations of police are necessary, as their condition exposes them peculiarly to the contagious influence of those vices which disturb the general tranquillity.

The education of the *higher orders* is, at the same time, in such a state of society as that in which we live, an object of the last consequence; and if it is one of those to which the superintending care of government cannot be extended with advantage in any considerable degree, it becomes doubly incumbent on those who direct their speculations to subjects of public utility, to contribute their efforts towards an improvement of the principles on which it is conducted. The revolution which has taken place in science and philosophy since the time of Lord Bacon, seems obviously to recommend (in a greater degree than has hitherto been effected in most universities) a correspondent change in the plan of academical instruction. This view of education, indeed, (considered in its connexion with intellectual improvement and the advancement of human knowledge,) properly belongs to the Philosophy of the Human Mind; but there are also many views of the same subject, which will be found to be very intimately connected with the most important objects of Political Economy.

In this respect, as well as in many others, the education of *females* (to whose care the task of early instruction must be, in a great measure, intrusted) will be found not undeserving of attention.

Among the various circumstances, indeed, which discriminate the condition of mankind in modern times, from what it was among ancient nations, nothing is more striking than the rank and consequence of the other sex. I shall not at present inquire into the various causes which have conspired to produce this change. It is of more importance to remark its extensive influence on human character, and on the whole system of European manners. The ancients appear to have attached but little importance to the domestic virtues. They considered *man* almost always in relation to his fellow-citizens; and as their free States were in general composed of a scanty population, and women altogether overlooked, as parts of the social system, the public duties of the individual were understood to be the only ends of his existence; and to enforce the zealous discharge of these duties, was the sole object of those philosophers who devoted themselves to the study of morals. *Plato*, in his *Republic*, proposes as a plan for increasing the happiness of the human race, to destroy conjugal love, and paternal affection, by a community of women and of children; and even those writers who, uninfected by the spirit of paradox or of theory, confined themselves to a faithful delineation of the manners around them, plainly shew, by their silence concerning the other sex, how insignificant the share was which they were then understood to possess in carrying on the business of human life. It is remarked by an ingenious French writer, that the word *woman* does not occur once in the *characters* of *Theophrastus;* and that it may be questioned whether the word *happiness* is, in any passage of the Greek writers, employed in the modern acceptation. As the extent of modern States and the structure of their governments have now detached the greater number of individuals from political concerns, men have been led to concentrate their pursuits within the circle of their domestic relations, and by doing so, have unquestionably opened to the species sources of enjoyment and improvement of which the philosophers of antiquity were unable to form a conception.

Notwithstanding, however, these circumstances, the education of women has, till very lately, been almost entirely overlooked by systematical writers; and among the few who have treated of it, there has been, in general, a strange disposition to run into extremes. One set of theorists, undervaluing the natural endowments of the other sex, and inattentive to their immense importance in the social system, have adhered even in these times to the confined notions of our forefathers; while others, overlooking the obvious and beautiful destinations of nature, have confounded the provinces and the duties of both sexes together, indulging themselves in visionary and licentious projects, equally subversive of the order of political society, and of the purity and refinement of domestic manners.*

---

* [With this *Chapter* terminates Mr. Stewart's last review and occasional alterations of the context, which were continued so recently as 1823. All hereafter is from the olden Manuscripts, chiefly in 1800; and even what is placed as *Chapter Third* of this *Introduction*, stands there only by conjecture.]

[CHAPTER III.]

[PRELIMINARY DISTINCTION OF POSITIVE LAWS INTO TWO CLASSES; AND THE RELATION OF THESE TO POLITICAL ECONOMY PROPER, —OR TO PART FIRST.]

THE President *De Goguet*, in his very learned and valuable work *On the Origin of Laws, Arts, and Sciences*, [1758,] lays much stress, among other fundamental principles, upon a distinction between two different classes or orders of *positive laws*. The *first* comprehends those which *are*, or at least which *ought to be*, common to all the different kinds of political society. The *second*, those which are peculiar to a society which has made some progress in Agriculture, in Commerce, and in the more refined arts of life.

To the *former* of these classes he refers "the laws which sanction the right of property;" "the laws which settle the formalities of marriage;" and "the laws which regulate the punishment of crimes;" to which he adds, "the laws establishing public worship,"—an institution which, in one shape or other, has had a place in all civilized nations. This class of laws (he observes) may be regarded as essential to the very existence of political society, however various may be the forms which the laws may assume in different instances.

Under the *second* class of positive laws, Goguet arranges "the laws which regulate the common transactions of civil life, and the particular interests of the different members of the community." Such are the laws concerning inheritances, successions, sales, and contracts;—"Laws," says Goguet, "which must necessarily vary according to the climate, genius, and particular circumstances of different nations."

In the course of the following disquisitions, I shall have occasion to illustrate some of the causes which produce a diversity in the municipal institutions of different countries; and at the same time to investigate those general principles which ought to be common to them all. It will afterwards appear, that even in the *second* class of positive laws, there are certain principles which are never departed from, without injustice and inexpediency: And, indeed, *one* great object which I have in view in this course, is to ascertain what these principles are. This, I conceive, to be the proper aim of *Political Economy*, in the extensive sense in which I employ that expression.

With respect to the *first* class of positive laws, their nature has been so long understood, and their authority so long recognised among all civilized nations, that they do not appear to form a proper object of philosophical discussion: and a very few years ago I should certainly not have thought of referring to them in this place. In the late rage, however, of political innovation, those fundamental principles which it has been the aim of all wise legislators, both ancient and modern, to consecrate in the opinions of their fellow-citizens, have not escaped the indiscriminate fury of some reformers; and, in various philosophical theories an attempt has been made to expose them to general reprobation and ridicule. I hope, therefore, it will not be considered as altogether superfluous, if I employ one or two lectures (before engaging in any particular discussion) in reviewing some subjects of a more general description. I propose at present to confine myself to *two* of these, the laws relating to the *contract of marriage*, and the laws sanctioning and regulating the *right of property ;*—institutions, which (together with the established solemnities of *public worship*) are justly considered by Goguet as the great pillars of the social system. The last of these articles I shall pass over in *this course*, as being more immediately connected with some of the doctrines of *Ethics.**

* [See *Philosophy of the Active and Moral Powers*, Vol. II. pp. 260-273. *Works*, Vol. VII.]

[PART FIRST.—BOOK FIRST.]

[OF POPULATION.]

In reflecting on the various objects of legislation, our thoughts are naturally attracted, at the commencement of our inquiries, by two speculations, which have already employed the ingenuity of many writers of the first eminence; and to which the title of *Political Economy* has been hitherto, in a great measure, restricted. The aim of the one is to add to the *Population* of a country; that of the other, to increase its *Wealth.* The *common* aim of both is to augment what have been sometimes called the *National Resources.*

Between these two subjects, there is a very intimate connexion, insomuch, that hardly any writer has treated professedly of the one, without introducing many incidental observations on the other. They are both, however, of so very great extent, that it is impossible to do them complete justice, without bestowing on each a separate consideration; and I accordingly intend to examine at some length the principles on which *Population* depends, and various other questions connected with that disquisition, before engaging in any inquiries concerning *the nature and causes of the Wealth of Nations.* On the latter article, indeed, which has been so very fully and ably discussed by Mr. Smith, I shall confine myself within much narrower limits than on some other branches of Political Economy, which are not comprehended in his plan.

The subject of Population may be considered in two points of view,—as an article of *Natural History,* and as an article of *Political Economy.* In the first light, it does not properly fall under our examination here. A few particulars, however, with respect to it deserve our attention, on account of their connexion with some reasonings which will be stated afterwards.

[CHAPTER I.]

OF POPULATION CONSIDERED AS AN ARTICLE OF THE NATURAL HISTORY OF MAN.

THE propagation of animals, and the circumstances on which it depends, are among the most interesting subjects of inquiry in the whole economy of Nature; and when considered in their relation to the physical necessities and the moral habits of different tribes, exhibit the most striking evidences of wise and benevolent design. On this subject, however, I do not mean to enlarge, but shall content myself with referring to *Buffon* and the other writers on Natural History, for an illustration of the beautiful arrangements which are conspicuous in the general laws here presented to our observation.

The propagation of all animals supposes a competency of that kind of food on which the particular tribe is destined to subsist. This provision being equal, the rate at which the multiplication of different races would go, seems to depend on the following particulars:[1]—(1.) The age at which the parent becomes prolific; (2.) The time that elapses in pregnancy; (3.) The frequency of breeding; (4.) The numbers of each brood; and (5.) The period during which the parent continues prolific.

The laws of propagation in our own species appear to vary to a certain extent in different climates; and the general opinion is, that they are most favourable to population in the warmer regions,—a difference, however, which must be partly ascribed to the greater abundance of the means of subsistence. The fact unquestionably is, that nations in those climates *are* populous, even under great defects of government.

M. Moheau, a French author of extensive and accurate information, assures us that the truth of this general observation

[1] Ferguson's *Institutes* [*of Moral Philosophy.*]

with respect to the effects of climate is confirmed by facts, which may be collected within the comparatively narrow limits of France. Other circumstances being the same, the women in the north of France are (according to him) less fruitful than in the south. The same author adds, (upon documents which he thinks entitled to credit,) that whilst in France forty-eight marriages produce at an average two hundred and thirty-two births, the same number of marriages, towards the fifty-second or fifty-third degree of latitude, produce only one hundred and ninety-five births; and beyond the fifty-sixth degree, not more than one hundred and sixty.[1] On so very nice a question, however, the results still require to be verified by farther observations.

Without entering more particularly into this speculation, it is sufficient for our purpose to remark, that in all the habitable parts of the globe, the laws of propagation are sufficient for preserving the race and adding to its numbers, provided other circumstances be not unfavourable. In some situations in which the prolific powers of the two sexes have been less restrained than they generally are by the difficulty of rearing a family, the multiplication of the species has been found to be astonishingly rapid. In *some* parts of America, before the Revolution, the number of inhabitants (according to Franklin) was doubled every fifteen years; in *others*, every twenty-five years. Nor was this owing to the influx of new inhabitants, but to the actual increase of the people. Those who lived to old age frequently saw from fifty-six to one hundred, and sometimes many more, descendants from their own body. The truth is, that marriage, which in this part of the world is a source of so much expense and anxiety to men of middling fortunes, as to deter many from thinking of that connexion, was in America one of the most effectual steps towards prosperity and affluence. The labour of each child before it could leave its father's house,

---

[1] *Recherches sur la Population de la France*, [1778,] p. 139. It is curious that Mr. Hume seems to lean to the contrary idea, and to suppose that women are more prolific in the northern regions. [See his *Essay on the Populousness of Antient Nations*, and the adverse quotation from Columella.]

was (according to Mr. Smith) computed in some parts of the Continent to be £100 clear gain to him; so that a young widow with four or five children was commonly courted as a sort of fortune.

As the rapid progress of population in the English North American Colonies, is probably without parallel in history, it may be proper to state the fact a little more particularly.

The original number of persons who had settled in the four provinces of New England in 1643, was 21,200. Afterwards, it is supposed, that more left them than went to them. In the year 1760, they were increased to half a million. They had, therefore, all along doubled their own number in twenty-five years. In New Jersey, the period of doubling appears to be twenty-two years; and in Rhode Island still less. In the Back Settlements, where the inhabitants applied themselves solely to agriculture, and luxury was not known, they were found to double their number in fifteen years.[1]

The operation of similar causes has produced similar effects, although in a very inferior degree, in all the other European settlements in the New World. The truth is, that an abundance of rich land, to be had for little or nothing, is so powerful an encouragement to population as to overcome all obstacles. No settlements could well have been worse managed than those of Spain in Mexico, Peru, and Quito; yet under all their disadvantages these colonies multiplied very rapidly. The city of Lima, founded since the Conquest, is represented by Ulloa as containing fifty thousand inhabitants near fifty years ago. Quito, which had been but a hamlet of Indians, is represented by the same author as in his time equally populous. Mexico is said to contain a hundred thousand inhabitants, which is a number probably five times greater than what it contained in the time of Montezuma.—Nor is this rapid multiplication of the species peculiar to new colonies. It is experienced in every instance in which the numbers of the people fall greatly short of what their means of subsistence might support. It has been

[1] *Essay on the Principle of Population* [Malthus,—first edition of his *Essay* in 1798,] p. 105.

often exemplified in Flanders, where the effects of those wars, of which that fertile and beautiful province has so long been the occasional seat, have always been obliterated by a few years of peace. It was exemplified in London, after the fatal plague of 1666, the traces of which, in the short period of twenty years, were scarcely perceptible. The same observation has been made with respect to the effects of the famines in China and Hindostan, and of the plagues which so frequently sweep men by thousands from the face of the earth in Egypt and Turkey.

If this rapid increase was to go on unchecked, it is easy to perceive, that the world would, at no very distant period, be overstocked with inhabitants. Dr. Wallace, in his *Dissertation on the Numbers of Mankind*, has shewn that this must have been the case long before the Deluge, even on the very moderate supposition, that the numbers of mankind had doubled every thirty-three and one-third years. His computations on this subject deserve attention, as they lead to important consequences.

Suppose, then, the race to begin with a single pair, that all marry who attain to maturity, and that every marriage produces six children, three males and as many females; two of whom (one male and one female) die before marriage, (according to which hypothesis four will remain to marry and replenish the world,) that in thirty-three and one-third years from the time when the original pair began to propagate, they shall have produced their six children; and that within the second period of thirty-three and one-third years, each of the succeeding couples shall have produced six children, and this to take place continually. On these suppositions, at the beginning of the scheme, the original pair alone are in life; at the end of the first period of thirty-three and one-third years, there are six persons living, viz., the original pair and four others; at the end of sixty-six and two-third years, there will be twelve; at the end of one hundred years, there will be twenty-four living; and at the end of twelve hundred years, (the numbers of mankind continuing to double every thirty-three and one-third years,) the number alive will be 206,158,430,208. According to the computations of the same very learned and ingenious writer, the whole habitable earth does not actually contain, at this moment, more than one thousand millions.

From the facts already stated with respect to our colonies in North America, it appears to be abundantly confirmed by actual experience, that even in circumstances which by no means afforded to the prolific powers of our species their greatest conceivable scope, population has gone on doubling itself every twenty-five years.

Assuming this, therefore, as a general rule, (which is obviously far short of the truth,) that population, when unchecked, goes on doubling itself every twenty-five years, a late anonymous author* argues in the following manner:—

" Suppose the restraints to population, all over the earth, to be completely removed, and consider in what ratio the subsistence it affords can be conceived to increase. If it were to be increased every twenty-five years by a quantity equal to what the whole world at present produces; this would allow the power of production in the earth to be absolutely unlimited, and the rate of its increase much greater than we can imagine any possible exertions of mankind to make it.

" Taking the population of the world at any number, a thousand millions for instance, the human species would increase in the ratio of—1, 2, 4, 8, 16, 32, 64, &c.; [a *Geometrical* ratio.] And subsistence as—1, 2, 3, 4, 5, 6, 7, &c.; [an *Arithmetical* ratio.] In two centuries and a quarter, the population would be to the means of subsistence as 512 to 10; in three centuries, as 4096 to 13; and in two thousand years, the difference would be almost incalculable, though the produce in that time would have increased to an immense extent."

* [Mr. Malthus is here referred to. At the time (c. 1800) when these *Lectures* were originally written, the *Essay on the Principle of Population* had been only anonymously published, in 1798. The second edition, with the author's name, and the reasoning considerably modified, appeared in 1803; and in Mr. Stewart's subsequent courses, (as is seen from the fragment extant of a lecture in 1804, and from the notes taken in 1809, by Mr. Bridges and others,) Mr. Malthus is explicitly quoted.—See *infra, pluries.*]

From this reasoning, which seems to be just in the main, it may be fairly inferred, that although the rapid multiplication of our species be in some states of society incomparably greater than in others, it does not appear to be a part of the order of Providence, that this rapidity should continue or be universal, an insurmountable obstacle being opposed to it by the other physical arrangements of our globe.

These considerations are sufficient, of themselves, to suggest a doubt, How far it is true that a rapidly increasing population is an unequivocal test of a wisely constituted government; and, Whether the mere increase of numbers ought to be a leading object of attention to a legislator. That both of these questions are to be answered in the affirmative, under proper limitations, is beyond dispute; but we may, perhaps, find reason afterwards to conclude, that they have been generally discussed by politicians in too vague and unqualified a form. Within these few years, indeed, the connexion between Population and National Prosperity has been examined with much greater accuracy than before, but not perhaps in such a manner as to unite completely the opinions of speculative politicians in their general conclusions. The very ingenious and intelligent author of *L'Ami des Hommes,* [Mirabeau, the Father,] appears to have wavered a little in his speculations on this point. In the first part of that work he maintains the superiority of National Wealth to Population, and insists that the latter ought to be regarded only as a *secondary* object by the statesman. But in the second part[1] he asserts that Wealth is an inferior object to Population, and that numbers of people are alone the cause of riches.[2]

---

[1] See the letters annexed to *Socrate Rustique,* (by M. Hirzel of Zurich,) translated by Arthur Young in his *Rural Economy.*

[2] Of this contradiction Mirabeau himself takes notice, in a letter addressed to the French translator of a German Treatise entitled *The Rural Socrates.* "I have always," says he, "been scrupulous of making alterations in the Essays I publish, if they go through a second edition; though certainly in one of them there is a very essential correction wanting; for, in second part of *L'Ami des Hommes,* [1755,] I have expressly contradicted what I asserted as a fundamental principle in the first—*That Population was the consequence of Riches;* I was sensible of my error in mistaking the cause for the effect, and have since advanced

Mr. Arthur Young, in his *Political Arithmetic*, (published in 1774,) lays it down as a most important and fundamental principle, that Population should be ever regarded as subordinate to Agriculture. " If a measure," says he, " is beneficial to the latter, give no attention to those who talk of injuring population. If you act primarily from an idea of encouraging populousness, you may injure husbandry; but if your first idea is the encouragement of the latter, you cannot reduce population below that standard which, being adapted to the circumstances of the country, can alone render it a source of national strength and of general happiness."[1]

Before, however, I enter on these discussions, it is necessary for me to consider, on what *political* causes the population of a country depends;—an inquiry of great extent and importance, and which (in the manner I propose to treat it) will lead to an examination of some of the most interesting articles of Political Economy. The slight reference which I have just now made to the speculations of the Marquis de Mirabeau and of Mr. Young, is sufficient to shew how very intimately the different branches of this science are connected together.

that *Riches are the consequence of Population*. The method was simple and easy to have established this latter opinion by some slight additions, explaining the principles on which it is founded; but I was unwilling to lessen the value of the book to the first purchasers, and have invariably persisted in not changing the least sentence in the works once published; or adding anything by way of Appendix, in future editions."—See *Addenda* to *Socrate Rustique*. Translated by A. Young, [in his *Rural Economy*, 1770.]

[1] See *Political Arithmetic*, pp. 264-267. In the last sentence of the above quotation, I have departed a little from Mr. Young's words; but the limitation I have added seems to be absolutely necessary for conveying his idea fully.

[CHAPTER II.]

[OF POPULATION CONSIDERED AS AN ARTICLE OF POLITICAL ECONOMY.]

OF the *political* causes which affect the population of a country. The most important of these may be referred to the three following heads :*—

1. *The Political Institutions which regulate the connexion between the Sexes;*
2. *The State of Manners relative to this Connexion;* and,
3. *The Means of Subsistence enjoyed by the People.*

[SECT. I.—OF POPULATION AS AFFECTED BY THE POLITICAL INSTITUTIONS WHICH REGULATE THE SEXUAL CONNEXION.]

Under the first of these heads an extensive and interesting field of speculation presents itself; first, with respect to the comparative effects of marriage, and of a promiscuous *concubinage;* and, secondly, with respect to the comparative effects of monogamy and of *polygamy.*

[SUBSECT. I.—MARRIAGE COMPARED WITH CONCUBINAGE.]

In the very general observations concerning the *Institution of Marriage* to which I propose to confine myself in this lecture, I shall avoid those views of the subject which have an immediate reference to the more appropriate objects of Political Economy, in *some* of which respects (particularly in its connexion with *Population*) it will necessarily fall again under

* [These will, accordingly, constitute so many *Sections* of this Chapter.]

our review. On the other hand, it would be obviously a trifling with your time, to offer any illustration of those views of expediency which have induced legislators, in every instance, to impose certain limitations on the vague commerce of the sexes; (as with the single exception of Mr. Godwin,) I do not know that any advocates for a promiscuous concubinage are to be found even among the most paradoxical writers of the present age.

In the *Republic* of Plato, indeed, Socrates is introduced as maintaining, that "in a well ordered state, all things ought to be common,—wives, children, and possessions." His arguments for this opinion, which are fanciful and puerile, are examined with much more attention than they deserve, and refuted in a very satisfactory manner, in the second book of Aristotle's *Politics;* to which I beg leave to refer.[1]

I quote the following passages from Mr. Godwin, not with the view of replying to them, (the necessity of which is completely superseded by their unexampled extravagance,) but as a specimen of that order of things which appears to the writer to be imperiously recommended by the principle of *Political Justice.*

"The abolition of marriage would be attended with no evils. In this, as in other cases, the positive laws which are made to restrain our vices, irritate and multiply them. Not to say that the same sentiments of justice and happiness which, in a state of equal property, would destroy the relish for luxury, would decrease our inordinate appetites of every kind, and lead us universally to prefer the pleasures of intellect to the pleasures of sense." [Again:]

"It is true, that in such a state of society, it could not be definitively affirmed who is the father of each individual child. But it may be affirmed, that such knowledge would be of no

---

[1] This part of Aristotle's works, which is certainly one of the most valuable remains of antiquity, may be perused by the *English* reader, in a translation which has been executed, with a considerable degree of spirit and of elegance, by Dr. Gillies. [In Gillies's translation of *Aristotle's Practical Philosophy*, the *Politics* occupy the second volume; and of that volume, see particularly chapters iii. and iv. of Book II.]—Taylor, [*Elements of the Civil Law,*] p. 342.

importance. It is aristocracy, self-love, and family pride, that teach us to set a value upon it at present. I *ought* to prefer no human being to another, because that being is my father, my wife, or my son, but because for reasons which equally appeal to all understandings, that being is *entitled* to preference."*

Of the tendency of such a state of society with respect to *population*, Mr. Godwin has taken no notice, nor indeed was it necessary for his purpose that he should; for it is part of the same system, that if its principles were realized, the species would cease to multiply by propagation, and individuals would become immortal.

Neglecting therefore these paradoxes, (which are much less likely to do mischief than some other passages of the same work, the scope of which is not equally apparent,) I shall assume as a self-evident principle, the political utility of such a contract between the sexes, as is necessary for connecting the offspring with *both* parents, by excluding (as far as *law* can operate) a promiscuous concubinage.

What I propose *chiefly* in introducing the subject here, is to consider (which I shall do very briefly) the institution of marriage as a part of the *moral and physical order of nature;* and to offer a few miscellaneous remarks on the tendency of some modern speculations to weaken the influence of those principles which have so universally consecrated this connexion, among all civilized nations.

The question, whether marriage be an appointment of *nature* or of *municipal law,* has been often and warmly disputed, even among those who acknowledge its *utility* as a political institution. It is a question which (when thus stated at least) savours so much of scholastic refinement, that I should have avoided any reference to it in these lectures, if some late doctrines had not bestowed on it a temporary interest.

The diversity of opinion to which this discussion has given rise, may probably be ascribed, in some degree, to the vague

* [*Inquiry concerning Political Justice,* Book VIII. chap. vi. pp. 850, 852, original edition, 1793.]

manner in which the question has been proposed. Few phrases are more ambiguous than that of *natural law;* and of consequence, the circumstances which are appealed to as tests of it, in one sense, do not at all apply to it when understood in another.

By some writers, the laws of nature with respect to *man* are collected from the customs of savage nations, among whom artificial systems of policy have made little or no progress. By others, every institution is considered as enjoined by nature, or (in other words) as a part of her *law*, which may be inferred by *reason* to be agreeable to her intentions: either from an examination of the principles of our constitution, combined with our physical condition; from the analogy of the other animals whom she has taken immediately under her own guidance; or from the beneficial effects it has a tendency to produce. I need scarcely observe, that what are understood to be *laws of nature*, according to the former definition, will not always be found entitled to that appellation, according to the latter.

That a promiscuous concubinage is the natural result of savage ideas and savage manners, seems to have the universal creed of antiquity. "Nam fuit quoddam tempus," says Cicero, "cum in agris homines passim bestiarum modo vagabantur, et sibi victu fero vitam propagabant; nec ratione animi quidquam, sed pleraque viribus corporis administrabant. Nondum divinæ religiones, non humani officii ratio colebatur: nemo legitimas viderat nuptias; non certos quisquam adspexerat liberos."[1] Of this state of society, Lucretius, in the following verses, has presented a lively picture.

> "Et Venus in sylvis jungebat corpora amantûm.
> Conciliabat enim vel mutua quemque cupido,
> Vel violenta viri vis, atque impensa libido,
> Vel pretium,—glandes, atque arbuta, vel pira lecta."[*]

Agreeably to the same notions, the establishment of marriage is always numbered among the first improvements introduced by those legislators who reclaimed their fellow-citizens from the fierceness and misrule of savage life.

---

[1] *De Inventione*, Lib. I. [cap. ii.]   [*] [*De Rerum Natura*, V. 960.]

"Concubitu prohibere vago, dare jura maritis,
Oppida moliri, leges incidere ligno."[1]

We are told of *Cecrops*, in particular, the founder of the Athenian constitution, that before his time marriage was not known in Greece, and that the burden of children lay upon the mother. To this fact innumerable allusions may be found in the Greek writers; by whom we are also informed, that on account of this circumstance, Cecrops obtained the appellation of Διφυής or *Biformis*. "Cecrops dictus est Biformis, quod legem tulisset, ut fœminæ, quæ virgines adhuc essent, uni viro elocarentur; quas Nymphas vocavit. Ante enim, illius regionis mulieres, more pecudum, promiscue cum viris coibant; nec suo cuique viro uxor erat, sed unaquæque mulier cuivis corporis sui copiam faciebat. Unde etiam nemini constabat, cujusnam filius vel filia esset infans in lucem editus."[2]

I do not intend to enter into a particular discussion of the evidence by which these opinions and traditions are supported, as it is not at all material to the argument I have in view, whether we adopt or reject them. When we reflect, however, on the condition of the human infant, and the impossibility of a mother rearing a numerous offspring solely by her own industry, (at least in the earlier stages of society, and in such a climate as Greece,) it is difficult to avoid a considerable degree of scepticism with respect to facts of so high antiquity in point of date, and of which we have no authentic memorials; more especially as a very strong presumption against them arises from the whole system of the ancient mythology, (a system of which the origin is confessedly lost in the obscurity of the fabulous ages,) and which invariably assigns to each of the deities, not excepting Jupiter himself, but a single wife united with him by a legitimate marriage.[3] The account which Cæsar gives of the manners of the ancient Britons, is indeed entitled to much respect from the known fidelity and accuracy of the writer; but it differs essentially from the state of society in which the Greeks are supposed to have lived before the time

[1] Horace, *Ad Pisones*, 398.   [2] Suidas, v. Προμηθεύς.
[3] Goguet, Book I. chap. i. Art. 1.

of Cecrops, and is by no means liable to the same objections. "It was common," he says, "for a number of brothers, or other near relations, to use their wives promiscuously. The offspring, however, were not common; for each man maintained the children that were produced by his own wife."[1] The information is curious, and of some importance in this disquisition; for while it affords a melancholy proof of the dissolute morals that once prevailed in this island, it illustrates strongly the necessity of a co-operation of both sexes in rearing an infant offspring, and thereby turns our thoughts to one of the most striking circumstances in the condition of man, which suggest the institution of marriage.

Suppose, however, for a moment, that we should adopt the ideas of the ancients on this subject in their full extent. To what other conclusion would they lead, than that the intellectual and moral powers of our species are liable to extreme degradation amidst the ignorance and brutishness of savage manners? To judge of the intentions of nature, requires in many cases (as I already hinted) a comprehensive view of the constitution of man, of the circumstances of his external condition, and of the mutual relations which these two parts of his destiny bear to each other;—and therefore it is not to *History* that we ought to appeal as an infallible standard in such discussions, but to what our own reason pronounces concerning moral fitness and expediency, after availing itself of all the lights it can collect concerning the ends and purposes of our being. Or, if any appeal is made to the actual experience of mankind, it ought certainly to be to the practices of those nations among whom the highest attainments of the race have been exhibited.

Among the many prejudices which have misled the speculations of philosophers concerning the history and destination of *man*, there is perhaps none more absurd and groundless than the idea that the rudest state of our species is that which

---

[1] "Uxores habent deni duodenique inter se communes; et maxime fratres cum fratribus, parentesque cum liberis; sed si qui sunt ex his nati, eorum habentur liberi a quibus primum virgines quæque ductæ sunt."—[*De Bello Gallico*, Lib. V. cap. xiv.]

approaches most nearly to the *state of nature*. The contrary opinion would be in every essential respect more agreeable to the truth; inasmuch as one of the most melancholy and fatal consequences of human ignorance, is a presumptuous confidence in the remote conclusions of reason, in opposition to what is obviously suggested by the state and condition of *man*. We may remark this not only in the moral depravity of rude tribes, but in the universal disposition which they discover to torture and distort the human body;—in one case compressing the eyes at the corners; in a second lengthening the ears; in a third, checking the growth of the feet; in a fourth, by mechanical pressures applied to the head, attacking the seat of thought and intelligence. To allow the *human body* to attain in perfection its fair proportions, is one of the latest improvements of civilized society; and the case is perfectly analogous in those sciences which have for their object to assist nature in the cure of diseases, in the correction of bad morals, or in the regulation of the social order.

In the present instance, without any appeal to *history*, the intentions of nature may be easily collected from *facts* which fall under our daily observation. Of these facts, one of the most striking is the *long period during which the human infant remains in a state of the most complete helplessness and dependence*. The cares of the mother are evidently not sufficient for the task of rearing her offspring till they are able to provide for themselves; and the difficulties of this task, so far from being diminished, must be wonderfully increased by the nature of those occupations on which man depends for his precarious subsistence, in the earlier periods of society. In such a state of things, while the mother is employed in suckling her child, the care of both is obviously devolved by nature on the father; and indeed without his constant and assiduous protection, both the one and the other must inevitably perish.

During the long helplessness of the first infant, (a helplessness which, in our species, Nature seems to protract, in order to bind that union which love had originally formed,) the family multiplies apace. Every new member adds another tie to those which existed before; habit adds her irresistible influence; and thus, without the formalities of a contract or of nuptial rites, those arrangements insensibly arise, which it is the pride of human policy to confirm and to sanctify.

In the rudest period, too, of society, something must be allowed to a sentimental predilection, and to the effect of reciprocal kindnesses and sacrifices. The affection of friendship has never been denied to the savage; and why should we doubt that it may sometimes unite, in its tenderest form, with those passions which prompt to the continuation of the species.

Among the ancient writers, it was often disputed whether the affection of Friendship could possibly exist in its perfection between more than two persons, and I believe that the common decision was that it cannot.[1] For my own part, I confess I can see no good reason in the case of *friendship* for such a limitation; and I am inclined to think that it has been suggested rather by the fables of mythology or the dreams of romance, than by good sense or a practical acquaintance with mankind. What the ancients, however, alleged with respect to friendship, is certainly true of *love* between the sexes. This last affection cannot, at one time, be directed to a variety of objects. It is of an exclusive and suspicious nature; and the jealousy of the one party is roused the moment an apprehension arises that the attachment of the other is in any degree divided. In this circumstance, which is strikingly characteristical of the passion between the sexes, we see not only a provision made for the conjugal union, but (as will appear afterwards more fully) a manifestation of the law of nature on the subject of polygamy.

The delicacy and modesty which seem to be *natural* to the other sex, in a much greater degree than to ours, conspire with the causes already mentioned, in grafting a *moral* union on the

---

[1] Πολλοῖς εἶναι φίλον, κατὰ τὴν τελείαν φιλίαν, οὐκ ἐνδέχεται, ὥσπερ οὐδὲ ἐρᾶν πλειόνων ἅμα. . . . Ἔστι γὰρ φίλος ἄλλος αὐτός. "It is impossible to be a friend (according to the idea of perfect friendship) to more than one, as it is impossible to *love* more than one at the same time. . . . For a friend is a second self."—Aristotle's *Nicomachian Ethics*, [IX. x. and iv. Wilkinson.]— See Wollaston, [*Religion of Nature*, Sect. VIII. § iv.]

instinctive passion. By many writers these are considered as entirely *factitious* principles; but the contrary might be easily proved, if it were worth while at present to enter into the argument. I shall content myself with remarking the conspicuous figure they have been found, in various instances, to make in ruder ages, more particularly among the American tribes and the ancient Germans. The latter are extolled on this very account by Tacitus, who plainly means to insinuate, in the panegyric he bestows on them, an indirect satire on the corrupted manners of his own countrymen. " Publicatæ pudicitiæ nulla venia: non forma, non ætate, non opibus maritum invenerit. Nemo enim illic vitia ridet; nec corrumpere et corrumpi seculum vocatur."[1]

From the shyness and reserve natural to women, and the respect paid to it by the earliest legislators, some writers have very ingeniously traced the ceremonies which have been found occasionally connected with the institution of marriage. Thus among the early Romans, the bride appears to have been carried forcibly from the lap of her mother ; and among the Spartans a marriage assumed the semblance of a rape. " The virgin and her relations," says Dr. [Gilbert] Stuart, " no doubt, understood previously the transaction, and expected this violence. But it was a compliment to her, thus to give an air of constraint to her consent, to relieve her embarrassment and distress, her emotion of fear and hope, anxiety and tenderness."*

The same remark is made, and not ill expressed, by Dr. Taylor.[2] " The seeming violence," he observes, " with which the bride is taken from her mother's lap, the lifting her over the threshold, and many other incidents in the ceremony, would be as proper in the rites of any other nation that did not owe its foundation to an accident of this kind, as they are in the Roman system. There is a propriety, that a sex whose modesty

---

[1] " Nor is any indulgence shewn to a prostitute. Neither beauty, youth, nor riches, can obtain her a husband ; for no one there looks on vice with a smile, or calls mutual seduction the way of the world."—[*Germania*, cap. xix.]

* [*View of Society in Europe*, Note (6), sect. 3, chap. i. Book I.]

[2] *Elements of the Civil Law*, p. 305.

is their charter, who, by a great consent of nations, are to be solicited into this union, and—for a while to refuse it, should in these delicate circumstances be complimented with the appearance of constraint, and with that softer kind of violence which suits so well with their condition, their character, and education. Thus with us, and with the Athenians, as we have seen above, the bride is *given* in marriage, and hardly appears upon the face of the stipulation to be consenting. . . . And though we know what these things mean, ("Scio, voluntate tua coactus es,") yet the moral is sound and warrantable. This compulsion testifies the retirement and abstraction that attended their education, is a pledge of that honour and chastity which they should bring with them to this solemnity, and guarantees the modesty and decorum that is to sweeten and recommend the remainder of this alliance."

These observations are not undeserving of attention, as the show of violence which accompanied the marriage ceremony among the Romans (that in particular of tearing the bride *ex gremio matris*) is commonly considered by the ancient writers as carrying an allusion to a celebrated event in the history of the early ages,—the *Rape of the Sabines.* In this instance we meet with a striking example of that unphilosophical bias, so common both among the Roman and Greek authors, to account for every remarkable phenomenon in the history of man, by referring it to a fabulous origin, instead of endeavouring to resolve it into the general principles of human nature.

After all, the principal support of marriage among rude nations, is undoubtedly the circumstance which was first mentioned,—I mean the long helplessness of the human infant; and, accordingly, in those parts of the world where the means of subsistence are furnished by nature, with little or no exertion on the part of man, the conjugal tie appears to be a much slighter bond of union, than where the parties are drawn more closely together by their common necessities.

In proof of the foregoing conclusions concerning the intentions of nature with respect to the human race, Lord Kames has drawn an additional argument from the economy of the lower animals. "The instinct of pairing," he observes, "is bestowed on every species of animals to which it is necessary for rearing their young, and on no other species. . . . Brute animals which do not pair, have grass and other food in plenty, enabling the female to feed her young, without needing any assistance from the male. But where the young require the nursing care of both parents, pairing is a law of nature."* A variety of other very judicious and pleasing remarks on the economy of nature, relating to the propagation of animals, may be found in the Appendix annexed to his *Sketch on the Progress of the Female Sex.*

Mr. Hume, too, in his Essay *On Polygamy and Divorce,* has referred to the economy of the brutes; but the inference he draws from his premises, is different from that of Kames, and (in my opinion) less philosophical. "Among the inferior creatures," he observes, "nature herself being the supreme legislator, prescribes all the laws which regulate their marriages, and varies those laws according to the different circumstances of the creature. Where she furnishes, with ease, food and defence to the new-born animal, the present embrace terminates the marriage, and the care of the offspring is committed entirely to the female. Where the food is of more difficult purchase, the marriage continues for one season, till the common progeny can provide for itself, and then the union immediately dissolves, and leaves each of the parties free to enter into a new engagement at the ensuing season. But nature having endowed man with reason, has not so exactly regulated every article of his marriage contract, but has left him to adjust them by his own prudence, according to his particular circumstances and situation. Municipal laws are a supply to the wisdom of each individual; and, at the same time, by restraining the natural liberty of men, make private interest submit to the interest of the public. All regulations, therefore, on this head are equally lawful, and equally conformable to the principles of nature, though they are not all equally

* [*Sketches of the History of Man,* Book I. Sk. vi.; Vol. I. pp. 172, 173, original edition, 1774.]

convenient, or equally useful to society."* According to the meaning I annex to the phrases, "principles of nature," and "laws of nature," (and which I have already† endeavoured to shew is the proper meaning of the expression,) this last conclusion of Mr. Hume's involves a contradiction in terms.

I have hitherto touched only upon those advantages of marriage which are obvious to the most careless inquirer, and which could not fail to force themselves on the notice of men in the most rude and ignorant ages. If I were to enter more deeply into the subject, and to consider it in connexion with the happiness of human life, with the preservation of morals, and with the progressive improvement of the species, volumes might be written without exhausting the subject. Much might also be said on the connexion of this institution with the subject of *population*, not only as an arrangement absolutely necessary for preserving undiminished the prolific powers of the other sex, but as no less indispensable (even in the present state of society) for rearing children with success, amidst the diseases and dangers of infancy. Of this a judgment may be formed from the barrenness of those connexions where the circumstances of the parents do not allow them to bestow that care on their offspring to which affection and duty prompt in more favourable situations. "The tender plant," to borrow the words of Mr. Smith, "is produced, but in so cold a soil and so severe a climate, soon withers and dies."‡

What then would the consequences be, in the present state of things—I shall not say of the abolition of marriage—but of any considerable relaxation in the ideas of men concerning the sacredness of this connexion, and the duties which it imposes?

These different considerations, which I must content myself with barely hinting at, illustrate sufficiently the wisdom of that advice which Plato (notwithstanding his own paradoxes on the subject) gives to his *Legislator*, when he directs him to take his stand from the institution of marriage, and for the better

---

* [*Essays*, Vol. I.]
† [See above, Vol. I. p. 186, *seq.*; Vol. II. p. 5, *seq.*; Vol. III. p. 158, *seq.*]
‡ [*Wealth of Nations*, Book I. chap. viii. Vol. I. p. 120, 10th edit.]

ordering of his commonwealth, to begin where that also begins, the arrangement of the conjugal union.* Agreeably to the same idea, this union is beautifully called by Cicero, " the Seminary of the republic." " Cum sit hoc natura commune animantium, ut habeant lubidinem procreandi : prima societas in ipso conjugio est; proxima in liberis; deinde una domus, communia omnia. Id autem est principium urbis, et quasi Seminarium reipublicæ."†

The stress which these two eminent philosophers and the other political writers of antiquity have so justly laid on the institution of marriage, has been appealed to in support of an absurd opinion already mentioned, that it is altogether an invention of human policy. But marriage (as I hope sufficiently appears from the foregoing observations) is the result (in the first instance) of that order of things which nature herself has established ; and the proper business of the legislator is here, as in other cases, limited to the task of seconding and enforcing her recommendations, by checking the deviations from her plan which are occasioned by the vices and follies of individuals. The fact is precisely similar with respect to *Property.* The idea of property is not created by municipal laws. On the contrary, one of the principal circumstances which suggested the necessity of laws and magistrates, was to guard against those violations to which the property of the weak was found to be exposed amidst the turbulence of barbarous times. It is with great propriety, therefore, that Horace classes these two *objects* of law together, the preservation of property and the protection of the marriage bed ;—objects, however, which so far from being the *creatures* of municipal institutions, may be justly considered as the chief *sources* from which municipal institutions have taken rise.

" Oppida cœperunt munire, et ponere leges,
Ne quis fur esset, neu latro, neu quis adulter."‡

They are indeed the two great pillars of the political fabric, and whatever tends to weaken them, threatens, we may be assured, the existence of every establishment essential to human

* [See *De Legibus*, Libb. IV. and VI.] † [*Officia*, I. xvii.]
Taylor, [*Elements*, &c.] p. 264. ‡ [*Sermones*, I. iii. 105.]

happiness. If in some of the preceding remarks, therefore, I may be thought to have expressed myself with an unnecessary diffuseness, the importance of the subject, contrasted with the tendency of some late speculations concerning it, will, I trust, be a sufficient apology for the space which I have allotted to an article which has been so often exhausted by the ingenuity both of ancient and of modern writers.

One particular question connected with the institution of marriage affords, (it must be owned,) when we abstract altogether from the precepts of revelation with respect to it, a fair field for argument,—Whether marriage ought to be considered by the legislator, merely as a civil contract, liable, like other civil contracts, to be dissolved by the mutual consent of the parties? My own opinion on this point may be anticipated from what I have already said, but it would encroach too much on our time, to explain particularly the principles on which it is founded. I must content myself, therefore, with referring to a short Essay *On Polygamy and Divorce*, by Mr. Hume, in which the argument is stated with equal conciseness and force. The manner, too, in which the subject is treated by this eminent writer, is peculiarly adapted to those politicians who have argued for a *liberty of divorce*, as he disclaims all regard to what he is pleased to call the common superstitious notions concerning the nature of marriage, and founds his reasonings entirely on considerations of *political expediency*.

On a superficial view of the question, Mr. Hume confesses, that a liberty of divorce may appear favourable to population, by removing, what is with many a powerful obstacle to marriage, the indissoluble nature of the connexion. It is, however, extremely remarkable, that " at the time when divorces were most frequent among the Romans, marriages were the most rare; and Augustus was obliged, by penal laws, to force men of fashion into the married state; a circumstance which is scarcely to be found in any other age or nation. The more ancient laws of Rome, which prohibited divorces, are extremely praised by *Dionysius of Halycarnassus*. 'Wonderful was the harmony,' says the historian, 'which this inseparable union of interests produced between married persons, while each of them considered the inevitable necessity by which they were linked together, and abandoned all prospect of any other choice or establishment.'"* It conveys, indeed, a most delightful idea of the domestic manners of the Romans, when we consider a fact about which all their writers are agreed, that Carvilius Ruga, who lived A. U. C. 520, was the first person who divorced his wife. The ground of his separation was her barrenness; a pretext which, when considered merely in a political view, is much less ridiculous than many which at a later period were considered by this people as perfectly valid; and yet we are informed [among others] by *Valerius Maximus*, that although the divorce stood unimpeached in law, the morality of his conduct was *then* regarded as very questionable. " Repudium inter uxorem et virum, a condita urbe usque ad vicesimum et quingentesimum annum, nullum intercessit. Primus autem Sp. Carvilius uxorem, sterilitatis causa, dimisit. Qui quanquam tolerabili ratione motus videbatur, reprehensione tamen non caruit: quia nec cupiditatem quidem liberorum, conjugali fidei proponi debuisse arbitrabantur."[1]

At a later period of the Roman history, when a new jurisprudence taught that marriage, like other partnerships, might be dissolved by the abdication of one of the associates, the consequences were fatal to the virtues and to the comforts of domestic life. "Passion, interest, or caprice," to borrow the words of Mr. Gibbon,† " suggested daily motives for the dissolution of marriage; a word, a sign, a message, a letter, the mandate of a freedman declared the separation; the most tender of human connexions was degraded to a transient society of profit or pleasure. According to the various conditions of life, both sexes alternately felt the disgrace and the injury; an inconstant spouse transferred her wealth to a new family, abandoning a numerous, and a perhaps spurious progeny to the authority and care of her late husband; a beautiful virgin might be dismissed to the world, old, indigent, and friendless." " A specious theory," the same author adds, " is confuted by this

* [*Essays*, Vol. I. *On Polygamy*, &c.]   † [*Decline and Fall*, &c., chap. xliv.]
[1] *Dicta Factaque*, &c. II. i. 4.

free and perfect experiment, which demonstrates that the liberty of divorce does not contribute to happiness and virtue. The facility of separation would destroy all mutual confidence, and inflame every trifling dispute: the minute difference between a husband and a stranger, which might so easily be removed, might still more easily be forgotten; and the matron, who, in five years, can submit to the embraces of eight husbands, must cease to reverence the chastity of her own person."

Of the profligacy of manners produced at Rome by the facility of divorce, a very striking picture is given by Seneca—" Vices," he observes, "cease to be disgraceful so soon as they become general. What woman *now* blushes to be divorced, since those of the first rank number their years, not by the names of the consuls, but by those of their husbands? Divorce," he adds, " is the object of marriage, and marriage that of divorce."[1]

[SUBSECT. II.—MONOGAMY COMPARED WITH POLYGAMY.]

The remarks which have been already made, appear to be sufficient for illustrating the conformity of the institution of marriage to the *law of nature*, in so far as this can be inferred either from an examination of the principles of our constitution, from the analogy of the lower animals, or from the beneficial effects with which it is attended.

These arguments, indeed, conclude, *in general*, much more strongly against vague love on the part of the *female* than of the *male;* although, if attentively examined, they will be found to suggest powerful motives, both of a moral and political nature, for a reciprocal obligation. The question, however, whether a plurality of wives might not be allowed to the same individual, is so different, in many respects, from that which has been hitherto treated, that although some of the foregoing considerations may be of use, yet the aid of some additional reasonings is necessary, in order to establish the general conclusion.

Polygamy may be conceived to be of two kinds, according as it consists in a *plurality of wives*, or in a *plurality of husbands*. Of the latter, (Πολυανδρία,) modern travellers have furnished

[1] *De Beneficiis*, Lib. III. cap. xvi.—[See Martial, VI. vii.]

us with some very curious instances; but the circumstances in which it can possibly take place are so extremely rare, that it does not merit a particular discussion. It is accordingly mentioned as a subject upon which there can be no diversity of sentiment, even by those writers who consider the other species of Polygamy as a matter which the law of nature leaves to the legislator to regulate at discretion. The partiality of our sex to their own prerogative has been complained of loudly, and perhaps not entirely without justice in the present age. But it is not altogether a modern evil. It is amusing to observe its influence, even on the speculations of Grotius and of St. Augustine—" Suscipiendæ prolis causa erat," says St. Augustine, in defending the polygamy of the patriarchs, " uxorum plurium simul uni viro habendarum inculpabilis consuetudo; et ideo, unam feminam maritos habere plurimos honestum non erat. Non enim mulier eo est fœcundior; sed meretricia potius turpitudo est vel quæstum vel liberos vulgo quærere."*

To the same purpose the author of the treatise *De Jure Belli et Pacis*, who, although in general by no means a loose moralist, seems disposed to vindicate the sensual indulgences of his own sex, in countries which did not enjoy the light of revelation; and even goes so far as to exclude from his *definition* of the marriage connexion, any obligation to fidelity on the part of the husband. " Conjugium naturaliter esse existimamus talem cohabitationem maris cum fœmina quæ fœminam constituat quasi sub oculis et custodia maris; nam tale consortium, et in mutis animantibus quibusdam videre est. In Homine vero, qua animans est utens ratione, ad hoc accessit fides, qua se fœmina mari obstringit."

" Nec aliud ut conjugium subsistat natura videtur requirere. Sed nec divina lex amplius videtur exegisse, ante evangelii propagationem. Nam et viri sancti ante legem plures una uxores habuerunt; et in lege præcepta quædam dantur his, qui plures una habuerunt; et regi præscribitur, ut nec uxorum nec equorum nimiam sibi adsciscat copiam, ubi Hebræi

* [*De Doctrina Christiana*, Lib. III. c. xxii.; also *De Civitate Dei*, Lib. c. vii. See also, ibidem, c. xviii., and XVI. c. xxxviii.]

interpretes notant, octodecim sive uxores sive concubinas regi fuisse concessas, et Davidi Deus imputat quod uxores ei complures, et quidem illustres, dedisset."[1]

Passing over, therefore, that sort of Polygamy which consists in a plurality of *husbands*, as an almost singular anomaly in the history of human affairs, I shall confine myself in what follows to the case of a plurality of *wives;* and it is in this restricted sense that I should wish the word Polygamy to be always understood, when I may have occasion to employ it afterwards in the prosecution of this disquisition.

That the practice of Polygamy has been very general among mankind in some of the earlier stages of society, more particularly in climates which exalt the imagination and inflame the passions, is a fact about which there can be no dispute. It does not, however, seem to have been universal among rude nations. It was unknown among the ancient Germans, excepting in the case of a few individuals, who affected a distinction of this sort as an appendage of their superior rank. "Severa illic matrimonia, nec ullam morum partem magis laudaveris. Nam *prope soli barbarorum* singulis uxoribus contenti sunt, exceptis admodum paucis, qui non libidine, sed ob nobilitatem, plurimis nuptiis ambiuntur."[*]

"This," says Montesquieu, "explains the reason why the kings of the first race had so great a number of wives. These marriages were less a proof of incontinence than a consequence of dignity; and it would have wounded them in a tender point, to have deprived them of such a prerogative. This explains likewise," the same author adds, "the reason why the example of our kings was not followed by their subjects."[2]

---

[1] *De Jure Belli*, &c., Lib. II. cap. v. [§§ 8, 9.]

The argument in favour of Polygamy is still more avowedly and explicitly stated by Euripides, in a fragment which remains of his Tragedy of *Ino*, and which I shall quote in the Latin version.

"Haud scripta recte jura sunt connubiis. Decuit beatum pluribus se uxoribus

Sociare, quantas alere sufficeret domus; Ut inaudientem pelleret penatibus, Bonam volenti corde servaret sibi. Nunc una sola accipitur, immenso nimis Vitæ periclo; nam priusquam intrat domum Nova nupta, nulla moris exploratio est."

[*] [Taciti *Germania*, cap. xviii.]
[2] *Esprit des Loix*, Livre XVIII. chap. xxv. See also Stuart, [*View*, &c., Note (14,) sect. 3, chap. i., Book I.]

It is to be remarked, however, that in the foregoing passage, Tacitus mentions the manners of the Germans as, in this particular, an exception, and almost a singular one, to the customs of rude nations. "Nam prope soli barbarorum singulis uxoribus contenti sunt." Dr. [Gilbert] Stuart, whose peculiar ideas concerning the importance of women in the earlier times, were strongly contradicted by the supposed prevalence of Polygamy, has accordingly, in quoting this passage, suppressed entirely the clause which was unfavourable to his conclusion.*

Having mentioned this author, I cannot help adding, in farther illustration of the same subject, that in controverting the common opinions concerning the condition of the female sex among barbarous nations, he has stated one assertion much more strongly than facts authorize him. "It is a proof," says he, "of the antiquity of *Monogamy*, that when a plurality of wives is uniformly indulged, which happens not till the ages of property, there is always one of them who seems more peculiarly the wife, the rest appearing only as so many concubines."†

It cannot be denied that this observation is countenanced by *some* facts mentioned by travellers; and, wherever such a preference of *one* female is found to be invariably and exclusively attached to her *condition*, and not to result from a temporary caprice of passion, we may reasonably conclude Polygamy to be a deviation from the purer manners of former ages. From the following passage of Captain Cook, with respect to the inhabitants of the *Friendly Islands*, which may seem, on a superficial view, to favour Dr. Stuart's remark, I should rather be disposed to conclude, that Polygamy is contrary to the established maxims, and is affected only by the *chiefs* (as Tacitus tell us it was among the ancient Germans) as a mark of superior rank and consequence. "Whether their marriages," he [Cook] observes, "be made lasting by any kind of solemn

---

* [But see his *View of Society*, &c., pp. 23, and 201, 202, where the passage in question is adduced, translated, and fully canvassed. I quote from the original edition.]

† [*View*, &c., Note (14,) § 3, c. i. B. I.]

contract, we could not determine with precision; but it is certain that the bulk of the people satisfied themselves with one wife. The chiefs, however, have commonly several women, though some of us were of opinion that there was only one that was looked upon as mistress of the family."[1] Cantova says expressly of his Caroline Islanders, (whose manners, in many striking particulars, resemble those of the tribes visited by Cook,) that a plurality of wives was among them an appendage of greatness.[2]

The observations made by a late very intelligent and authentic traveller,* into the interior parts of Africa, directly contradict the assertion in question. After stating that "the negroes, whether Mahometan or Pagan, allow a plurality of wives," he adds, "the Mahometans alone are by their religion confined to *four;* and as the husband commonly pays a great price for each, he requires from all of them the utmost deference and submission, and treats them more like hired servants than companions. They have, however, the management of household affairs, and each in rotation is mistress of the household, and has the care of dressing the victuals, and of overlooking the female slaves."[3]

I have laid the less stress on the manners of savages and barbarians in the article of marriage, because it appears to me, as I already hinted, altogether absurd to appeal to *them* as the standard by which we are to judge of the *laws* of nature; meaning by *these* the *moral* laws which she recommends to man by her own established order. In the present instance, her intentions cannot possibly be mistaken, by those who attend to that wonderful circumstance in her providential economy, the balance which she everywhere maintains in the comparative numbers of the two sexes.[4]

---

[1] Cook's *Voyages*, Vol. I., p. 400. Irish edition.

[2] "La pluralité des femmes est une marque d'honneur et de distinction."— *Lettres Edifiantes et Curieuses.* Tome XV. p. 310.

* [This refers to *Mungo Park*, who was well known to Mr. Stewart after returning from his first travels in Africa, of which expedition the account was published in 1799.]

[3] [*Travels*, &c.] p. 268.

[4] For Dr. Arbuthnot's speculations on this subject, (founded on the doctrine

This balance, indeed, does not seem to be anywhere mathematically exact, but it universally varies within so narrow limits, as to shew manifestly, that the inequalities which exist, whatever their final cause may be, have no relation whatever to the question of *Polygamy*.

The proportions are probably not precisely the same in different countries, and, even in the same country, they are variously stated by different writers. But there is a general coincidence in the statements which relate to *this* part of the world, more than sufficient for all the purposes of the present argument.

Major Graunt, (who assisted Sir William Petty in his inquiries relative to Political Arithmetic,) from an examination both of the London and Country Bills, states fourteen males to thirteen females; from whence he infers that " the Christian religion prohibiting polygamy, is more agreeable to the *Law of Nature*, than Mahometanism and others that allow it."

" This proportion of fourteen to thirteen," says Dr. Derham, " I imagine is nearly just. In the hundred years of my own parish register, although the burials of males and females were nearly equal, being 636 males and 623 females in all that time; yet there were baptized 709 males, and but 675 females, which numbers are in the proportion of 13.7 to 13." " This surplusage of males," Dr. Derham adds, " is very useful for the supplies of war, the seas, and other such expenses of the men above the women."[1]

According to the author of *Métrologie*, [M. Paucton,] whose conclusions are chiefly founded on observations made in Germany, 104 boys are born for 100 girls.[2] He adds, however, that a greater number of the former die in infancy, so that towards the age of puberty, the two sexes are nearly equal.

The same author states " the number of men who die in a country to be to that of women as 27 to 25. In general," he says, " it has been remarked that when women have passed a

of Chances,) see *Philosophical Transactions*, No. 338.—[For a disquisition and some more recent authorities on the Proportion of the Sexes, see above,

Works, Vol. VII. p. 112, *seq.*, and Note C. p. 380, *seq.*]
[1] *Physico-Theology*, pp. 175, 176.
[2] *Métrologie*, p. 485.

certain age, their longevity may be more presumed on than that of men, more especially in the case of women who are married."[1]

Moheau, who is commonly considered as very accurate in his details, declines any particular statement of the proportions of the two sexes *born* in France; and contents himself with observing, that the actual population of women exceeds that of men in the proportion of seventeen to sixteen.[2]

Of late years this subject has been examined with far greater accuracy than had been attempted before: by Mr. Suessmilch in Germany; by Mr. Wargentin in Sweden; and by Dr. Price in England. From their combined observations, it seems to be established beyond a doubt, *First*, that the number of *males and females born*, invariably *approach* to equality. *Secondly*, that the excess is in favour of the males. *Thirdly*, that this excess is partly counterbalanced by their greater mortality. It is extremely remarkable too, that this greater mortality does not appear to be owing merely to the *accidents* to which men are liable in consequence of their own excesses, and the professional hazards to which they are exposed, but to some peculiar delicacy or fragility in the male constitution. It is observed sensibly even in infancy and childhood: nay, the number of still-born males exceeds proportionally that of still-born females.

The numbers *born* at Berlin during the four years beginning with 1752, were, *males*, 9219; *females*, 8743; or 21 to 20.

The numbers that died under two years of age, were, *males*, 3118; *females*, 2623; or 7 to 6.

The numbers that died upwards of eighty years of age, were, *males*, 135; *females*, 215; or 5 to 8.

The numbers that died between ninety-one and one hundred and five, were, *males*, 21, *females*, 55.[3]

From the account given by *Mr. Muret* of his observations made at *Vevey* in the *Pays de Vaud*, it appears, that for twenty years ending in 1764, there died in that town, during

[1] Ibid. p. 485.
[2] *Recherches*, &c., p. 71.
[3] Price [*On Annuities*, &c.] Vol. II. p. 263.

the first month after birth, of males 135, to 89 females; and in the first year, 225 to 162.

In Berlin, according to Suessmilch, 203 males die in the first month, and but 168 females; and in the first year, 489 to 395. The tables of these two writers shew, that, both at Vevey and Berlin, the *still-born males* are to the *still-born females* as 30 to 21.

From a variety of different accounts, both in England and on the Continent, mentioned by Dr. Price,[1] it appears, that in a long list of towns, although the proportion of males and females born is no higher than 19 to 18, yet the proportion of boys and girls (under ten years of age) that die is 8 to 7; and, in particular, the still-born males are to the still-born females as 3 to 2; a proportion which agrees remarkably with that of 30 to 21, as deduced from the observations at Berlin and Vevey.

I shall only add farther on this very interesting article, that Dr. Price has suggested a doubt whether this difference in point of mortality between the two sexes *be natural*. The following facts prove that his suspicions are not altogether unsupported by evidence.

" It appears, from several registers in Suessmilch's works, that this difference is much less in the country parishes and villages of Brandenburg, than in the towns. And agreeably to this, it appears likewise, from the accounts of the same writer, that the number of males in the country comes much nearer to the number of females.

" In 1056 small villages in Brandenburg, the males and females in 1748 were 106,234, and 107,540; that is, were to one another as 100 to 101¼. In 20 small towns, they were 9544, and 10,333; or as 100 to 108¼. In Berlin, they were (exclusive of the garrison) 39,116 and 45,938; or as 100 to 117½.

" In the years 1738 and 1745, the number of inhabitants in New Jersey was taken by order of the Government, and they were distinguished particularly into *males* and *females* under and above sixteen.

[1] [Ibid.] Vol. I. p. 360, *et seq.*

" In 1738 the number of—
Males under sixteen was, 10,639; Females, 9,700.
Males above sixteen was, 11,631; Females, 10,725.

" In 1745, the numbers were,—
Males under sixteen, 14,523; Females, 13,754.
Males above sixteen, 15,087; Females, 13,704.

"The inference from these facts," says Price, "is very obvious. They seem to shew sufficiently, that human life in males is more brittle than in females, only in consequence of adventitious causes, or of some particular debility that takes place in polished and luxurious societies, and especially in great towns."* We may add, that in so far as their accuracy is to be relied on, they shew, that in proportion as simple and natural manners prevail, the balance between the *births* of the two sexes is the more accurately preserved.

The facts which have been already stated relate almost entirely to this quarter of the globe, and lead to a conclusion in favour of Monogamy which is undisputed among political writers. I may be thought perhaps to have entered more into details than was absolutely necessary; but (independently of their connexion with our present argument) I could not avoid the opportunity which the subject afforded me of turning your attention to one of the most striking provisions which the economy of nature has made, for those moral and political arrangements which are subservient to the happiness of the individual, and the multiplication of the race.

With respect to other parts of the globe, our information is much less correct; and here accordingly speculative men have found themselves more at liberty to indulge their ingenuity and fancy. "In Japan," says Montesquieu, upon the authority of Kaempfer, "there are born rather more girls than boys; and at Bantam, the former exceed the latter in the proportion of *ten to one.*"† Hence, he seems disposed to infer, that the law which permits polygamy is physically conformable to the inhabitants of such countries; a conclusion which some other

* [Ibid.] † [*Esprit*, &c., XVI. iv.]

authors have apprehended to be farther confirmed by the prematurity and rapid decay of female beauty in some regions of the East. But there is good reason to suspect the accuracy of the documents on which Montesquieu proceeds. The Japan account, which makes the proportion of females to males to be as 22 to 18, is inconclusive, as the numbering the inhabitants of a great city can furnish no inference applicable to the present question. And the account of the births at Bantam is not only *so contrary* to the analogy of all the other facts with which we are acquainted, as to surpass belief, but (as we are assured by Mr. Marsden) is positively *false*. " I can take upon me to assert," says he, " that the proportion of the sexes throughout Sumatra, does not differ sensibly from that ascertained in Europe ; nor could I ever learn, from the inhabitants of the many eastern islands whom I have conversed with, that they were conscious of any disproportion in this respect."*

From the remarks which have been now made, it may be safely concluded, that it is the duty of the legislator to prohibit *polygamy*, and to employ all the authority he possesses in enforcing a law so strongly recommended, both by the physical and moral condition of our *species*. It might besides be easily shewn, that while he thus employs the most essential of all expedients for the *multiplication* of the race, he takes the most effectual measures for securing the *happiness* and *morals* of a people ; but this last consideration is foreign to our present subject ; and it has been so well illustrated by Mr. Hume, that nothing of importance remains to be added to his observations. I have alluded to it chiefly, in order to recommend his Essay [*On Polygamy and Divorce*] to your attention, at a period when those moral principles which the most sceptical writers of former times treated with respect, have been rejected with contempt by some theorists, whose paradoxes, from the particular circumstances of the times, have had, in various parts of Europe but too extensive an influence on the opinions of the multitude. Among the numberless wild ideas which have been started within these few years by political projectors, there are few

* [*History of Sumatra.*]

more alarming than one which appears from the *Moniteur* of the 16th April 1798, to have been proposed in the Senate of the Cisalpine Republic by *Campagnoni*.[1]

[SECT. II.—OF POPULATION AS AFFECTED BY THE STATE OF MANNERS RELATIVE TO THE CONNEXION BETWEEN THE SEXES.]

When the legislator, however, has prohibited polygamy, he has only removed one of the *obstacles* to population, by preventing particular individuals from engrossing a number of females. The rate at which it proceeds will depend on the number of marriages which are actually contracted; and this seems to be a circumstance which depends more on *the state of manners* in a society, than on the regulations of the politician.

The ancient lawgivers, indeed, considered it as one grand object of legislation to promote population by direct rewards to marriage, and by punishing celibacy. This was the case among the Hebrews, the Persians, and the Greeks; and still more remarkably among the *Romans*,—to whose institutions I shall confine my attention at present.

In the history of this celebrated people we meet with regulations in favour of marriage, from the time of Romulus downwards. When the censorship was established, one great object of it was to discourage celibacy, which the censors endeavoured to do, by condemning those who were unmarried, to pay a certain fine called *Mulcta uxoria*. It even appears from a fragment of a speech of P. Scipio Africanus, when censor, (preserved by Aulus Gellius,) that it was the practice for the censor not only to punish the unmarried, but to reward those who had families.[2] These laws, however, in favour of matrimony, which were certainly superfluous at a period when the

---

[1] The speech to which I refer, and which was plainly calculated to insinuate an apology for Polygamy in particular cases, is quoted by *D'Ivernois* in his *Tableau Historique et Politique*, p. 25.

[2] Animadvertimus, in oratione P. Scipionis, quam censor habuit ad populum de moribus, inter ea quæ reprehendebat, quod contra majorum instituta fierent, id etiam eum culpasse, quod filius adoptivus Patri adoptatori inter Præmia Patrum prodesset.—*Noctes Atticæ*, Lib. V. cap. xix.

advantages enjoyed by a Roman citizen as father of a family, were of themselves a sufficient encouragement, became afterwards little more than a dead letter, when, in the progress of national corruption, the aversion to marriage increased to such a degree, as neither to yield to the prospect of reward nor the fear of punishment. Julius Cæsar and Augustus, both attempted to remedy the evil, by reviving and improving the ancient institutions. The latter, more especially, seems to have considered the extension and application of these as a principal object of his reign; and it is very remarkable, that by the measures he pursued for that purpose, he incurred a more general odium than by any other part of his policy.

Among the other curious facts mentioned on this subject, by Suetonius and Dion Cassius, the following particulars deserve to be selected, as strongly expressive of the general state of manners in the Augustan age. "The Emperor," we are told, "sometimes brought forward the children of his own family into the place of public assembly, and exhorted his audience to profit by his example; but his zeal in this matter was far from being acceptable to the people." It is added, that "he was frequently accosted in the theatres and places of public resort, with general cries of dislike; and that, in consequence of the complaints which were brought to him of the impossibility of supporting the extravagance of women of rank, he was obliged to correct many of the edicts he had published, or to abate much of their rigour;—that, in order to obviate the objections which were made to women of high condition, he permitted the nobles to marry emancipated slaves;—that the law, nevertheless, was still eluded;—that pretended marriages were contracted with children, or females under age, and the completion of course indefinitely deferred;—that to prevent such evasions or frauds, it was enacted that no marriage could be legally contracted with any female under ten years of age, nor the completion of any marriage be delayed above two after the date of the supposed contract."[1]

[1] Ferguson, [*History of Roman Republic*, &c., Book VI. chap. iii.; who cites Dion Cassius, Book LIV. chap. xvi., and Suetonius in Octavius, chap. xxxiv.]

The reflections of Dr. Ferguson on the spirit of these laws are just and philosophical, and are expressed with his usual eloquence. "Under this wretched *succedaneum* for good policy, it seemed to be forgotten that where mankind are happy, and children are born to bless and to be blessed, Nature has provided sufficient inducements to marriage; but that where the people are debased, marriage itself, and the pains which are employed to enforce it, are an additional evil; and that a sovereign, whose arrival at power has made a state, into which mankind are powerfully led, by the most irresistible calls of affection, passion, and desire, a kind of workhouse into which they must be driven by the goad and the whip; or a prison, in which they must be detained under bars and fetters of iron, is justly an object of execration to his people. And the Romans, accordingly, seemed to feel themselves, on the present occasion, treated as the property of a master, who required them to multiply merely to increase the number of his slaves; and they resisted this part of the Emperor's administration more than any other circumstance of the state of degradation into which they had fallen."*

During the reigns of the succeeding emperors, the evils which Augustus was so anxious to correct, continued, and even increased, as we learn (among other authorities) from Pliny[1] and from Tacitus.[2] This last author expressly contrasts the manners of the Romans in this particular with those of the Germans, and remarks, that whereas the latter people, without either rewards or punishments, considered marriage as the first duty of a citizen, and a family as the chief blessing resulting from marriage; the former, with all their laws, abhorred the one relation, and dreaded to be placed in the other.

In modern Europe, the evil as yet has not arrived at such an extreme. It is, however, evidently on the increase, as sufficiently appears from the growing disrelish for marriage among all classes of people. This arises from various causes: above

---

* [Ibidem.]
[1] *Epistolæ*, Lib. IV. xv.
[2] *Annales*, Lib. XV. [L. III. c. xxv. *Germania*, c. xix.]

all, perhaps, from men forming to themselves, in consequence of the progress of luxury, a false idea of competency, which prevents them, even when their situation is easy and comfortable, from choosing to embarrass themselves with the cares of a family. It arises, too, in part from that prevailing taste for unlawful pleasure, in our sex, which is both a cause and an effect of celibacy ; and which, while it multiplies the objects of temptation to one half of the species, deprives, in the same proportion, a number of the other of any prospect of ever establishing themselves in an honourable connexion. In some countries of Europe, the evil does not rest here, but by extending its influence to the morals of married women, discourages those men from the conjugal union, who, in other circumstances, would have placed their chief happiness in domestic enjoyments.

These evils are common, in some degree, to all the great European monarchies, and arise from the general state of modern manners. But, in some countries, they are greatly aggravated by the celibacy of the clergy, and in many more by the numerous standing armies which are chiefly composed of men, who, by their profession, are led to prefer a single life. To these ecclesiastical and military celibataries, we may add the domestic servants of both sexes, very few of whom are disposed or have it in their power to marry ; and the younger sons of noble families, in those countries where the Law of Primogeniture is established, who inherit little from their fathers ; and who, in consequence of the prejudices against trade, are prevented from employing the only effectual means of bettering their fortune.

In these circumstances, shall we conclude that the politician can do nothing ? That little can be expected from direct rewards to marriage, or from punishments inflicted on celibacy, has already been observed. If the evil is at all curable, the remedy *must* be applied to its source, by the gradual operation of those just and enlightened views of political economy, which tend at once to multiply the means of subsistence among the body of the people ; to inspire them with moderate and reasonable ideas of a competence, and to cherish that desire, so natural to a happy and uncorrupted mind, of transmitting to an offspring of its own, the same blessings which it has itself enjoyed. In proportion as these *general* causes operate, marriages will become more frequent; and in the same proportion in which they increase, the temptations to unlawful pleasure will diminish; for all these political evils hang together, and when once the remedy begins to take effect, the cure advances with an accelerated progress. Every person removed from the state of celibacy, weakens the influences of the causes which make celibacy common. In short, put an end, as far as possible, to every institution which counteracts the intentions of Nature; and without any ingenuity exerted on the part of the statesman, his wishes are accomplished. The ancient sanctity of domestic manners, and the ancient felicity of domestic life, will gradually revive; and men will look forward to the conjugal union as to the source of the purest and most exquisite happiness that the condition of humanity affords. "Atque adeo, nihil largiatur princeps, dum nihil auferat; non alat, dum non occidat: nec deërunt, qui filios concupiscant."[1]

In order, however, to prevent misapprehensions of my meaning, it is necessary for me, before I finish this head, to take notice of an important circumstance, which I shall have occasion afterwards to illustrate more fully; the essential difference in the relative place which *population* occupies in the *ancient* and in the *modern* systems of Political Economy. This difference arises chiefly from the civil and domestic liberty now enjoyed in this part of Europe by the industrious orders of the community, contrasted with that *slavery* which entered into the constitutions of those states which, in the old world, were understood to have accomplished, in the most effectual manner, the great ends of government. In consequence of this mighty change, produced by the dissolution of the *feudal system*, the care of the statesman (in so far as population is concerned) is necessarily transferred from the higher classes of the people to

[1] Plinii *Panegyricus Trajani.*

a description of men, whose numbers in the *free states* (as they were called) of antiquity, were recruited, as they are now in the West India Islands, by importations from abroad.* It is this description of men that forms the *basis* of that political fabric which Sir William Temple has so finely compared to a *pyramid;* and it is on their numbers, combined with their character and habits, that the stability of the superstructure depends. Their *numbers*, however, it is evident, can in the actual state of things be kept up only by such political arrangements as furnish them with the means of rearing families; and it is into the question concerning the comparative expediency of the various arrangements proposed for that purpose, that the problem of *population* ultimately resolves.

The efforts of Augustus and of the other statesmen of Rome to discourage celibacy, had in view the Citizens only, and more especially the *nobility;* of whose importance to the *military* strength of the country a judgment may be formed, from the rings which Hannibal is said to have sent to Carthage after the battle of *Cannæ.* To correct the extravagance and profligacy of this order of men was the great object of the laws formerly mentioned; and, accordingly, we are told that it was by the *knights* that the repeal of these laws was most loudly solicited.

In such a state of society as that in which we live, the prevalence of celibacy among those who are raised above the condition of the multitude, does not so *materially*, at least not so *immediately*, affect the *military* resources of a people, as it affects their general character and manners; partly by the contagion of their example, and partly by the extinction of the hereditary spirit and worth peculiarly characteristical of that rank of men, who, by their education and circumstances, are placed at an equal distance from the views of the great and of the vulgar.

* [See Note, p. 32.]

[SECT. III.—DEPENDENCE OF POPULATION ON THE MEANS OF
SUBSISTENCE ENJOYED BY THE PEOPLE.]

These remarks naturally lead me to consider how far the population of a country depends on *the means of subsistence* which the people enjoy.

[SUBSECT. I.—*Dependence of Marriage and Population on the Notion held in regard to the Competent Support of a Family.*]

That a country cannot be peopled beyond its resources, is almost an identical proposition; and, on the other hand, it is no less certain, that population (wherever things are left to their own course) *will* advance till checked by this limit. The natural inducements to marriage are so strong, that no encouragement on the part of the politician is required, provided the circumstances of the society are such as to present to all orders of men a reasonable prospect of their being able to rear and educate a family, *according to the ideas of competency which they have formed to themselves.* It appears to me to be necessary to modify in this way the general proposition, which is commonly stated in too unlimited terms; for, in order to engage a man to marry, he must not only have a prospect of being able to provide to his children the necessaries of life, but he must have a prospect of being able to rear his family, without lowering that rank to which he has been accustomed; or retrenching any of those articles of luxury which, by habit, he has been accustomed to consider as essential to his comfort. It is possible, therefore, that of two countries which afford the means of subsistence in equal abundance, the one may be much more populous than the other, in consequence of the *more moderate* ideas of a competency which the generality of the people entertain.

Of this last remark, no proof more satisfactory can be produced than what is furnished by a comparative view of the state of population in *England* and in *Ireland.* Without entering into any nice computations of the number of inhabitants in either country, we may venture to assert, that, in the latter, the population is incomparably greater in proportion to its extent than in the former,—due allowance being made for the defects under which it labours, of police, of commerce, and of both agricultural and manufacturing industry.—The numbers in England and Wales are very variously estimated by different writers, according to their political prejudices; by Dr. Price, (in 1777, [*Essay*, &c.]) at less than five millions; by Mr. George Chalmers, (in his *Political Estimate*, [about 1791,]) at more than eight millions. The former is of opinion that the population of the kingdom has suffered a great diminution since the Revolution in 1688: the latter asserts, that during this period it has received an augmentation of a million and a half.—With respect to our sister island, notwithstanding the powerful obstacles which retard its progress, all accounts agree in admitting a great increase of inhabitants since the end of the last century. In 1657, the number was computed by Sir William Petty to be 850,000; and in 1672, to be 1,100,000.[1] In 1688, it has been estimated at 1,200,000. At present different opinions have been adopted concerning its actual population, but all of them admit, that the augmentation has been remarkably rapid. Mr. Young states it in the year 1779 as under *three millions*, according to the *common* belief then entertained by those with whom he conversed in the course of his agricultural tour.[2] Mr. Howlett, from documents transmitted to him in 1786, by Mr. Beresford, then first Commissioner of the Irish Revenues, states it as amounting *at least* to *two millions and a-half;* and concludes that since the time of the Revolution it has nearly doubled.[3] Mr. Chalmers computes it, in 1791, at no less than 4,193,158, asserting that, during the last hundred years, Ireland has done much more than *trebled* its inhabitants.[4] From the Report of the Secret Committee of the Irish Parliament, published last summer,

---

[1] See Young's *Ireland*, p. 88 of Appendix to Vol. II.; and Chalmers's *Estimate*, p. 223.

[2] Young, ibid.

[3] *Essay on the Population of Ireland*, (Richardson, 1786,) pp. 15, 20.

[4] *Political Estimate*, p. 222.

(1798,) Dr. Emmet appears to have stated the actual population of that country at "*five millions*, whereas, at the time of the Revolution, it did not exceed *a million and a half.*" [Addition :]—Lord Castlereagh, in his speech, (February 5, 1800,) "on delivering to the House of Commons of Ireland the Lord-Lieutenant's message on the subject of a union with Great Britain," estimates the population of Ireland from 3,500,000 to 4,000,000. This he mentions as the common computation at present; and as he may be presumed, from his official situation, to have availed himself on such an occasion, of all the most authentic sources of information, I should be disposed amidst so great a diversity of statements, to adopt his *numbers* in preference to any of the others.

This very extraordinary increase in the population of Ireland, (admitted by writers of the most opposite political views,) is to be ascribed almost entirely to the peculiar habits of the lower orders, in consequence of which they find it so much easier than the English peasantry, to satisfy their wants in the two great articles of *habitation* and *food.* Something, undoubtedly, must be placed to the account of the comparative advantages they enjoy, in being free from the oppression of the English *Poor Laws*, and the consequent *Laws of Settlement;*[1] and also to the account of their common food, (potatoes,) which experience has shown to go much farther to the support of animal life than *wheat*, or any of the other sorts of grain employed for food in this part of the world that can be raised on the same extent of surface.[2] But that the circumstances I mention are by far the most important, may be inferred from the following statements, for which we are indebted to a very intelligent observer, (Mr. Young,) who made an agricultural tour in Ireland, in the years 1776, 1777, and 1778.

"In England, where the poor are, in many respects, in such a superior state, a couple will not marry unless they can get a house to build, which, take the kingdom through, will cost from twenty-five to sixty pounds; half the life, and all the

[1] Young's *Ireland*, Vol. II., Appendix, p. 86.
[2] Smith's *Wealth of Nations*, Vol. I. p. 240. Irish edit., [B. I. c. xi. First Part.]

vigour and youth of a man and woman, are passed before they can save such a sum; and when they have got it, so burthensome are poor to a parish, that it is twenty to one if they get permission to erect their cottage. But in Ireland, the cabin is not an object of a moment's consideration; to possess a cow and a pig is an earlier aim; the cabin begins with a hovel that is erected with two days' labour, and the young couple pass not their days in celibacy for want of a nest to produce their young in. If it comes to a matter of calculation, it will then be but as four pounds to thirty." . . . . " Of their food (*potatoes*) there is one circumstance which must ever recommend it, they have a *belly-full*, and that, let me add, is more than the superfluities of an Englishman leave to his family. Let any person examine minutely into the receipt and expenditure of an English cottage, and he will find that tea, sugar, and strong liquors can come only from pinched bellies. I will not assert that potatoes are a better food than bread and cheese, but I have no doubt of a *belly-full* of the one being much better than *half-a-belly-full* of the other, still less have I, that the milk of an Irishman is incomparably better than the small-beer, gin, or tea of the Englishman, and *this* even for the father, how much better must it be for the poor infants? Milk to them is nourishment, is health, is life.

" If any one doubts the comparative plenty which attends the board of a poor native of England and Ireland, let him attend to their meals. The sparingness with which our labourer eats his bread and cheese is well known: mark the Irishman's *potato bowl* placed on the floor, the whole family upon their hams round it, devouring a quantity almost incredible, the beggar seating himself to it with a hearty welcome, the pig taking his share as readily as the wife, the cocks, hens, turkeys, geese, the cur, the cat, and perhaps the cow,—and all partaking of the same dish. No man can have been often a witness of it, without being convinced of the *plenty*, and I will add, the cheerfulness that attends it."*

The same author adds in another passage:—" Marriage is

* [*Tour in Ireland.*]

certainly more general in Ireland than in England: I scarce ever found an unmarried farmer or cottar; but it is seen more in *other* classes, which with us do not marry at all; such as servants: the generality of footmen and of women servants in gentlemen's families, are married, a circumstance we very rarely see in England. Another point of importance is their children not being burthensome. In all the inquiries I made into the state of the poor, I found their happiness and ease generally relative to the number of their children, and nothing considered as such a misfortune as having none. Whenever this is the *fact*, or *the general idea*, it must necessarily have a considerable effect in promoting early marriages, and consequently population."*

It is not, however, by *preventing* marriages that the poverty of the lower orders chiefly obstructs population. The attachments of sex, and the fond hopes of domestic bliss which a youthful imagination inspires, are motives too powerful to be always regulated by the suggestions of prudence; and in the humbler walks of life, where vanity and ambition have little influence, they are sufficient to blind the judgment to all considerations of futurity. In such circumstances the indigence of the parents, while it renders the conjugal union a source of constant anxiety and despondence to themselves, is attended with consequences equally fatal to the community. " The tender plant," as Mr. Smith has observed, " is produced, but in so cold a soil, and so severe a climate, soon withers and dies. It is not uncommon in the Highlands of Scotland, for a mother who has borne twenty children, not to have two alive. Several officers," he continues, " of great experience, have assured me, that so far from recruiting their regiments, they have never been able to supply it with drums and fifes from all the soldiers' children that were born in it. A greater number of fine children, however, is seldom seen anywhere than about a barrack of soldiers. Very few of them it seems, arrive at the age of thirteen or fourteen. In some places, one-half the children die before they are four years of age, in many places before

* [Ibidem.]

they are seven, and in almost all places before they are nine or ten. This great mortality, however, will everywhere be found chiefly among the common people. Though their marriages are generally more fruitful than those of people of fashion, a smaller proportion of their children arrive at maturity."[1]

These observations will be found more peculiarly applicable to the very *lowest* order of the people. Those who have literally *nothing*, and who are beggars by profession, are very seldom unwilling to burden themselves with the cares of a family. Not to mention that a numerous offspring is rather an assistance to them in carrying on their trade, their ordinary habits gradually inspire them with a greater degree of confidence in looking forward to the future, than is felt by men who *exist*, but who are barely able to exist by their own industry. *That* beggary which appears to the bulk of mankind the most dreadful of all calamities they have already experienced; and by this experience they have learned what philosophy in vain attempts to teach others, to make the important distinction between the evils of reality and those of the imagination. Thoughtless of the future, they enjoy the little which the present moment affords them, and trust for to-morrow to that kind Providence which has hitherto supplied all their necessities.

What I have here remarked with regard to common beggars, is applicable also to those who have actually experienced the evils of want, and to whose imaginations the idea of beggary is become familiar. If this order of men contribute little towards the population of the State, it is not from their remaining in a state of celibacy, but from the little care they take in rearing and educating their children. The effects of an unequal distribution of property in discouraging marriage, are chiefly confined to the middling ranks of a people, who in consequence of those ideas which we imbibe in our earliest infancy, (particularly in the monarchies of modern Europe,) are led to form

---

[1] [*Wealth of Nations,* Book I. chap. viii.]—" La Mendicité," says the Maréchal de Vauban, [in his Dixme Royale,] " est un mal qui tue bientôt son homme."—Sir James Steuart, Vol. I. p. 72. [*Works,* Vol. I. p. 94. *Political Œconomy,* Book I. chap. xii.]

notions of a competency disproportionate to the state in which they are born, and to consider it as the great object of human life, to rise above the rank which they inherit from their forefathers.

From the observations already made, it appears that population does not depend solely on the fertility of the soil, and the industry of the inhabitants; but on these circumstances, combined with the *habits and ideas* which are generally prevalent concerning the necessaries and accommodations of life. Nor is this all. Much depends on the particular *kind of food* on which the great body of the people is accustomed to subsist. In the *savage* state, while men trust entirely to the fortunes of the *chase*, we find tribes consisting of a few hundreds, spread over regions equal in extent to the largest kingdoms in Europe. From this state to that of *pasturage*, the transition was of immense consequence in the *progress* towards improvement; but the *last* step is of all the most important, when human industry comes to be chiefly directed to the *cultivation of the soil*, with a view to the rearing of grains and of other esculent vegetables. In this form a given extent of land may be rendered incomparably more productive for the use of man, than in any other in which it can be employed; and it is fortunate, (at least in so far as *population* is concerned,) when the habits of a people dispose them to prefer that species of sustenance, which is so strongly recommended to them by the *economy* of nature; more especially when the kind of vegetable which is used for daily bread possesses the advantages which are experienced from *potatoes* in Ireland, and from *rice* in some eastern countries.

It is universally allowed that a rice-field produces a much greater quantity of food than the most fertile corn-field; and accordingly, in those countries where it is the common vegetable food of the people, the population is represented as immense. This is remarkably the case in Hindostan, where the natives are prohibited by the laws of their religion to eat the flesh of animals. *There* the population is great, notwithstanding all the disadvantages that the country labours under, in respect of government;—disadvantages of a peculiar description, as they unite all that is oppressive in a despotism, with all the instability and vicissitude which are commonly connected with popular constitutions.

The food produced by a field of potatoes is much superior to what is produced by a field of wheat, and (according to Mr. Smith) is not inferior in *quantity* (although not perhaps equal in *nutritious power*) to that produced by a field of rice. "Should this root," he observes, "ever become, in any part of Europe, like rice in some rice-countries, the common and favourite vegetable food of the people, so as to occupy the same proportion of the lands in tillage which wheat and other sorts of grain for human food do at present, the same quantity of cultivated land would not only maintain a much greater number of people, but the labourers being generally fed with potatoes, a greater surplus would remain after replacing all the stock, and maintaining all the labour employed in cultivation. A greater share of this surplus too would belong to the landlord. Population would increase, and rents would rise much beyond what they are at present." *

" It is difficult," the same author adds, " to preserve potatoes through the year, and impossible to store them like corn, for two or three years together. The fear of not being able to sell them before they rot, discourages their cultivation, and is perhaps the chief obstacle to their ever becoming in any great country, like bread, the principal vegetable food of all the different ranks of the people."†

It has been remarked by some late writers, that "in England, notwithstanding the produce of the soil has been in our times considerably increased by the enclosure of wastes, and the adoption, in many places, of a more successful husbandry, yet we do not observe a *corresponding* addition to the number of inhabitants ;" and this has been ascribed "to the more general consumption of animal food. Many ranks of people, whose ordinary diet was, in the last century, prepared almost entirely from milk, roots, or vegetables, now require every day a considerable portion of the flesh of animals: and hence a great

* [*Wealth of Nations*, Book I. chap. xi. Part First.] † [Ibid.]

part of the richest lands of the country are converted into pasturage. Much also of the bread-corn, which went directly to the nourishment of human bodies, now only contributes to it, by fattening the flesh of sheep and oxen.[1] The mass and volume of provisions are hereby diminished; and what is gained in the melioration of the soil, is lost in the quality of the produce." "This consideration," says Mr. Paley, "may satisfy us, that tillage, as an object of national care and encouragement, is *universally* preferable to pasturage; because the *kind* of provision which it yields, goes much farther in supplying the essential wants of human life."[1] "Indeed, pasturage," he adds, "seems to be the art of a nation, either imperfectly civilized, as are many of the tribes which subsist by it in the internal parts of Asia, or of a nation like Spain, declining from its summit by luxury and inactivity."[2]

It cannot be denied that there is some foundation for these remarks, but they are certainly expressed in too unqualified a manner. Whatever a people principally consume as the means of their subsistence, must necessarily be the great object of the husbandman in his culture. Thus, in France, where bread is said to form nineteen parts in twenty of their food, corn, and especially wheat, is the only great object of their cultivation. In England, on the contrary, the quantity of meat, and of the produce of the dairy consumed by all ranks, is immense. Hence, to *our* farmer, cattle is an object no less important than corn; and, accordingly, vast quantities are kept in proportion to what we find in France. It would be rash, however, to draw any inference from this fact in favour of French husbandry as compared with English. It leads, in truth, to a conclusion *directly opposite*, in the opinion of a very competent judge, Mr. A. Young, who has paid more attention than any other individual to the agriculture of both countries.

"Let us consider," says Mr. Young, "on what principles the farmers of England and of France must necessarily manage their lands. In England, they keep such parts of their lands

---

[1] Vol. II. pp. 361, 362.—[*Works*, Vol. II. p. 72, ed. 1819. *Moral and Political Philosophy*, Book VI. chap. xi.]   [2] Ibid.

in meadow and pasture as are by the nature of the soil so adapted; and throw their arable land into such courses of crops, that several are introduced, which are either summer or winter food for cattle." Upon this system, for the details of which I must refer to Mr. Young's work, a considerable part of the whole farm, and a large portion of what is arable, are employed for cattle; the quantity of dung raised is, of course, very great, which being spread, as it usually is, on the arable fields, insures great returns; so much better than if such stocks of cattle were not kept, that I question if three acres are not quite as productive as five would be. "Nay," says Mr. Young, "I have in this point no doubt but the barley and wheat in a farm thrown into a proper course, with a due proportion besides of meadow, yield a greater value than the corn in general would if one year was fallow, and the three following ones were wheat and barley;—of such importance is this system of manuring."*

In the French system of husbandry, (which Mr. Young has likewise described particularly,) much the greatest part of the farm is arable;—the meadow and pasture being very trifling, except in spots that cannot otherwise be applied, and near great towns. Thus very little cattle can be kept except for tillage; in very many farms no other. Here we find manuring cut off at once, almost completely, and consequently the crops must be poor. Besides this, one-half or one-third of the land is fallow, at a mere barren expense; a system, which we know from the experience of our own open fields, is miserable, and not to be compared for profit to those in which crops for cattle are made the preparation for corn.

"Wheat being in France the great object, all the expense of the farmer is applied to its production. A year's fallow is given, and what little dung they raise is all spread on it. This produces a middling, perhaps a good crop; and when the farmer reaps his wheat, he often finds himself out of pocket, and has to depend for his profit on a poor crop of spring corn. Thus the little demand for meat, and the produce of the dairy, obliges him to confine his views to corn alone. The conse-

* [*Political Arithmetic.*]

quence is, he pursues a bad course of crops; he raises no manure, his produce is small, and his profit comparatively nothing.

"It must surely be evident to every one, that there is a great advantage to the *English* farmer, from corn and cattle being in equal demand, since he is thereby enabled to apply all his lands to those productions only to which they are best adapted; while, at the same time, the one is constantly the means of increasing the produce of the other.

"To suppose, therefore," continues the same writer, "that we should be more populous, if we lived as much on bread as the French, is an idea that seems doubtful. It is a strange position at best, that bad husbandry should add to our population; and yet this is a necessary consequence of the proposition in question; for if the demand for meat is changed to an increased one for wheat, the farmers must change their good course to the bad one of the French, by abandoning those crops which form the best preparation for corn.

"In so far as population is concerned, the question comes to this, Whether a tract of land, applied to yielding bread, will yield more than if applied to bread and meat?" Mr. Young endeavours to show, that in the latter form it is far more productive than in the former. For the details of his argument, in support of this opinion, I must refer to his book, contenting myself with stating his general result; that "where tillage and pasturage are properly combined, so as to have the farms from one-third to half of meadow or pasture; and the other two-thirds or half thrown into a proper course for the winter support of the cattle, such a farm will be found to feed more men than if it is all ploughed up, and as much wheat as is possible raised upon the French system."[1]

Of the justness of Mr. Young's reasonings, in so far as they involve a knowledge of agricultural practices, I am not a competent judge. But *one* general conclusion may be safely deduced from them; that in this part of the world, if the use of animal food were abandoned, after the use of some Eastern

[1] *Political Arithmetic*, p. 158, *et seq*.

nations, the plan would at least *in part* defeat itself. In those climates where water alone renders the soil perpetually fertile in producing vegetable food, such habits are not disagreeable to the physical circumstances of the inhabitants, and an immense population is almost a necessary consequence. But *here* the physical economy of nature points out a mixture of animal and of vegetable food; the fertility of the soil failing when it is kept constantly in tillage, and cattle supplying that species of manure which is most effectual in adding to its produce.

After all, it is far from being impossible that the luxury of this country may have carried the demand for animal food beyond its due proportion.[1] . . . . .

[1] [It is doubtful, from the manuscript of these *Lectures*, whether what is placed in the following note, should not have constituted part of the text.]—It would be worth while to ascertain, by accurate experiments, the comparative nutritious power of a given extent of fertile land, when employed in raising *animal* and *vegetable* food. The only attempt of the kind that I have met with, (excepting some hints by *A. Young*,) is a letter addressed to Colonel Dirom, by Mr. William Mackie of Ormiston, in East Lothian, which is published at the end of an *Inquiry into the Corn Laws and Corn Trade of Great Britain*, 1796, by the late Mr. Dirom of Muiresk, in the county of Aberdeen. The result of Mr. Mackie's computations is, that 504 acres of fertile land (the garden ground not included) will maintain, when well cultivated, 1977 people, old and young; and if the population of Great Britain amounts to 9,000,000, it would require only 2,412,746 fertile acres, well cultivated, to maintain them, when living on the same portion of vegetable food as the common people do in Scotland. The *data* on which Mr. Mackie proceeded were some facts ascertained by an examination of several families in his neighbourhood; from which it appeared, that about 2¾ lbs., avoirdupois, raw potatoes, and 5½ oz. good oat-meal, when made into porridge, did actually maintain, for one day, in good health and condition for labour, on an average, each individual of a family, composed of two parents and three children, as long as their stock of potatoes lasted.

The same gentleman calculates, (upon *data* which appeared to him to be reasonable,) that the above farm of 504 acres, when employed in pasturage, will yield a produce competent only to the support of 103 individuals throughout the year; and that it would require 44,475,728 fertile acres to maintain the population of Great Britain; each individual consuming 2¼ lbs. of butcher meat per day. The same number of acres would support a population of 165,921,725 individuals of all ages, if the inhabitants lived on the same portions of vegetable food, which at present maintain the common labourers in Scotland.

"I have calculated," says Mr. Mackie, "these two extremes of the produce of land under the *plough*, or in *pasture*, merely for fattening cattle, without including a dairy in either case; in order to place this object in a strong point of view, and to show the different effects which living on vegetable or animal food will have in supporting an increased

But whatever opinion may be formed on this point, it is evidently a matter which no law should attempt to regulate; and the same observation may be applied to the complaints which have been founded on the cultivation of hops, and population, or in rendering sustenance plentiful or scarce in a country. Hence it may be inferred, that it was to encourage and preserve the immense population of the Eastern nations, the original lawgivers of India discharged the eating of animal food, and engrafted this political maxim upon the ancient stock of superstition in the country. The abstaining from animal food, however, seems best suited to those countries situated under a burning sun, where water alone renders the soil perpetually fertile in producing vegetable food for supporting the inhabitants. In more temperate climates, the soil cannot be kept in a constant state of producing bread for man, without materially injuring its fertility; a circumstance which renders occasional pasturage indispensably necessary. The beasts of the field are also the children of nature, and the land must be allowed to afford grass for their sustenance; and man being formed to live on a mixture of animal and vegetable food, avails himself of this economy of nature to add to his enjoyment.

"From this cause, agriculture, in temperate climates, will be carried to the greatest perfection in those countries where the inhabitants add a certain proportion of animal to their vegetable food. But there is a certain proportion from which, if, in the progress of luxury, they deviate, by increasing the quantity of their animal food, they will certainly feel the want of bread-corn, which appears to be one of the principal causes that, of late years, there is an evident deficiency in the growth of corn in Britain, or rather in England, to supply the inhabitants, and that we are every year becoming more and more dependent upon foreign nations for our daily support, in place of being able as formerly to spare a large surplus quantity annually for exportation."

In the further prosecution of the same interesting inquiry, Mr. Mackie sketches out for the same farm of 504 acres, a plan of cultivation suited more nearly to the average consumption and population of the country. From his computations founded on this plan, it appears "that a farm of 504 acres of very fertile land in a high state of cultivation, could maintain 392 people, old and young, living on a mixture of animal and vegetable food; and to maintain the inhabitants of Great Britain, computing the number at 9,000,000, and each individual to consume daily on an average the quantity of animal and vegetable food mentioned above, there would be occasion for 11,793,799 acres of very fertile land in a high state of cultivation. But if, at any time, from the increase of luxury in the nation, every inhabitant was to consume an ounce more of animal food per day, in that case it would require an additional 803,079 acres of fertile land, one half in rich pastures, and nearly the other half in turnip, to fatten and produce the necessary quantity; four-sevenths of which, or 458,900 were annually carrying luxuriant crops of corn. But even computing these crops at the low average of two quarters per acre, it would occasion an annual failure of 917,800 quarters, which will account for the difference between the most flourishing period of the corn trade, and the deficiency of latter times. Whoever, therefore, considers with attention the increased consumption of animal madder, and other crops which do not afford food for man. In all such cases the husbandman is the best judge of his own interest; and when he increases his private wealth, he employs the most effectual means in his power for advancing that measure of population which is useful to his country.

I cannot help remarking also in this place, (although the observation is not connected immediately with our present subject,) the inconsistency of the remonstrances which some avowed friends to agriculture have made against the waste of animal and vegetable food occasioned by modern cookery. The French economists expressly brand this species of luxury by calling it— "an inversion of the natural and essential order of national expenses, which increases the mass of unproductive expenses to the prejudice of those conducing to production." The true encouragement to agriculture, (as will afterwards appear,) is the extension of the market for the commodities it furnishes; and the effect is the same to the farmer, whether the market is opened by the necessities of the industrious orders, or by the extravagance of the opulent.

One *political* benefit, too, it must not be forgotten, arises

food in Britain within these last fifty years, and particularly since the peace of 1763, will see good cause for the growing scarcity of corn."

I shall only add to these extracts, a remark of the same author with respect to another effect of luxury in adding to the scarcity both of animal and vegetable food, and that is the great degree of fatness which the people of England now require in their beef and mutton. "There is reason to believe that half the quantity of land would feed cattle moderately fat, that is required to put them in condition for slaughtering in England; and it is more than probable, that the great noise that has been made of late years about increasing the size of live stock, is a species of quackery which is a real loss to the nation."

The observations which I have quoted from this intelligent writer, seem to me to be deserving of attention, although I would neither be understood to vouch for the accuracy of his results, nor to give any opinion on a subject which is so foreign to my own studies.

[In reference to this subject, I find from notes written by Mr. Bridges in a subsequent session, that Mr. Stewart farther observed,—" It ought also to be taken into account, that among other economical advantages obtained by attention to the breeds of cattle, the possibility has now been established of communicating to animals a constitutional propensity to a state of fatness; in consequence of which some become marketable at a much smaller expense than others of a more 'lean and hungry' habitude."—See Marshall's *Rural Economy of the Midland Counties*, &c., 1790; and Culley's *Observations on Live Stock*, 1786.]

from the waste of food in years of plenty, (however blameable this waste may frequently be on the part of *individuals*,) that by increasing the demand for the productions of the earth, it operates like a freedom of exportation, in securing a regular surplus to meet the occasional pressure of a scarcity.

It is with peculiar pleasure I add, that in such an emergency there is *now* every reason to hope that additional resources may be derived from the prosecution of such experiments as Count Rumford has lately begun with so much credit to himself, on the subject of *Nutrition*.

The reasonings which have been already offered, are sufficient to shew in general, how intimately the state of *population* in a country is connected with the state of its *agriculture*, and that the most effectual measure a lawgiver can employ for advancing the former, is to give every possible encouragement to the latter. I do not speak here of such *direct* rewards to the husbandmen as were held out by the legislators of antiquity, and which probably would not produce much effect in the present state of society. I have in view merely the care which the statesman should take to secure to the husbandman the complete and exclusive enjoyment of the fruits of his own industry; the only effectual and universal excitement in this or any other employment to human labour. All therefore that the laws can do, is to secure this right to the occupier of the ground; so that the full and entire advantage of every improvement go to the benefit of the improver; that every man may work for himself and not for another; and that no one share in the profit who does not contribute to the production.[1] These are advantages which, in former times, the husbandman enjoyed nowhere, and which, in many parts of Europe, he still enjoys in a very imperfect degree.

In order to illustrate this general and fundamental principle, it is necessary for me to take a pretty wide compass, and to treat at some length of *Agriculture and Manufactures, considered in their relation to Population.*

[1] Paley, Vol. II. p. 363.—[*Works*, Vol. II. p. 73, ed. 1819. *Moral and Political Philosophy*, Book VI. chap. xi.]

CHAP. II.—POPULATION POLITICALLY CONSIDERED. (§ 3.) 113

[SUBSECT. II.—*Of Agriculture and Manufactures, considered in relation to Population.*]

[i.—And *first*, of Population in connexion with *Agriculture.*] The various circumstances which conspired to discourage Agriculture in the ancient state of Europe after the fall of the Roman Empire, and the gradual steps by which the lower orders raised themselves from a servile condition to that comparative independence in which we now see them, have been very fully and ingeniously illustrated by Mr. Smith.*

[1. *Kinds of Farm Tenure.*]—In all the countries of Europe, during the eighth, ninth, and tenth centuries, slaves seem to have formed the most numerous part of the community. In France, about the time of the commencement of the third race of kings, *all* the ground was cultivated by slaves, and the towns were chiefly filled by people of the same description. It appears, from *Doomsday Book*, that the case was nearly the same in England at the time of the Conquest.

Among the causes which favoured, in the first instance, the rise of the lower orders, Lord Kames† lays particular stress on the extensive estates into which land property was divided; and which forced the proprietors, for their own interest, to encourage, by a more liberal policy, the industry of those cultivators whom they could not (as on a small farm) place under the immediate inspection of an overseer. This soon suggested the idea of making the bondman a *colonus partiarius*, by communicating to him a proportion of the product, in place of wages. The proprietor furnished him with the seed, cattle, and instruments of husbandry; and the tenant became bound to pay a certain proportion of the fruits. Tenants of this description are called in French, *Métayers ;* and we are told by M. Turgot, in a book published in 1766,‡ that at the period when he wrote, five parts out of six of the whole kingdom of France were thus cultivated. In Picardy, Normandy, the environs of Paris, and the greater part of the provinces of the

* *Wealth of Nations*, Book III. chap. ii.; Vol. II. p. 90, *seq.*, tenth edition, 1802.]
† [*Sketches of Man*, B. I. sk. ii. *et alibi.*]
‡ [*De la grande et de la petite Culture ; Œuvres*, Tom. IV.]

north of France, the ground was cultivated by farmers who employed their own stock, paying a certain rent to the landlord. In the south, the land was almost universally laboured by *métayers*. The same author adds, that "the different effects of the two modes of cultivation were such as to strike the most careless observer." And that this *must* have been the case, no person can doubt who has attended to the consequences produced by *tithes* in the other part of our island.

"It is evident," says Mr. Smith, "that it never could be the interest of a *colonus partiarius* to lay out in the farther improvement of the land, any part of the stock which he might save from his own share of the produce; because the proprietor who laid out nothing was to get one half of whatever was produced. In France, accordingly, it was a common complaint, that the *métayers* took every opportunity of employing their master's cattle rather in carriage than in cultivation; because in the one case they got the whole profit to themselves, in the other, they shared them with their landlord."*

To this species of tenantry succeeded, though by very slow degrees, *farmers* properly so called, who traded upon their own stock, and paid a fixed rent for the land they possessed. By this means the tenant came to be excited to yet greater industry, by having the whole benefit of it to himself; and the advantages experienced from this, naturally led the way to the last step of the progress, which was giving the tenant a lease for a certain term of years, and thereby encouraging him to undertake still more extensive and costly plans of improvement. It was long, however, before this progress was completed in any country of Europe; and in many parts of it much remains to be done at this day. Even in *England*, till the reign of Henry VII., a farmer could be legally outed of his lease before the expiration of his term, by the fictitious action of a common recovery; and it was not till the period now mentioned, that the lessee was protected against these contingencies, and his interest rendered secure and permanent. This security in the condition of the English farmers, together with some other

* [*Wealth of Nations*, Book III. chap. ii.; Vol. II. pp. 91, 92, tenth edition, 1802.]

circumstances peculiarly favourable to the yeomanry of that country, have (in the opinion of Mr. Smith*) contributed more to the present grandeur of England than all her boasted regulations of commerce taken together. When we reflect on these circumstances, it cannot fail to excite our surprise, that in a country so distinguished for liberality, and where the happy consequences resulting from an equitable system of laws have been so long experienced, there should still be found, among the English proprietors of land, so large a proportion of individuals, who either grant *no* leases, or grant them under such restrictions as defeat, in a great measure, the beneficial purposes for which they are calculated. This is the more wonderful, as the practice seems formerly to have been different; and that, even at present, the prevailing system is loudly condemned by all those whose opinions might be expected to possess any authority. It is reprobated *unanimously* by the respectable writers who have drawn up the county surveys for the Board of Agriculture; all of whom concur in ascribing to leases whatever *improvements* have been made by the farmers of England.

In the history of this part of rural economy among our southern neighbours, several stages are remarked by one of these writers. " The first," he observes, " was probably leases for lives, formerly it should seem very general, and still far from being uncommon. The second step seems to have been a transition into the opposite extreme of no leases at all, by far the most *general* tenure by which lands are rented at present. The third originated in an attempt to remedy the evils of the second, by granting leases (at first) for three years, and afterwards for five, seven, nine, eleven, and sometimes for fourteen years, loaded, however, with restrictions upon the management and culture of the lands. The fourth and last, is leases founded on more just and enlightened principles, extending to such a term as to give complete encouragement to the industry of the husbandman, by affording him a prospect of recovering before his removal all his advances with a competent profit. From a rough calculation, founded on an examination of the different

* [*Wealth of Nations*, Book III. chap. ii. ; Vol. II. p. 93, tenth edition.]

surveys, it has been inferred, that if we divide England and Wales into *five* parts, probably *two-fifths* are farmed by tenants at will,—that is, by tenants whose security is only from year to year; *one-fifth* by tenants for life; *one-fifth* by the owners themselves; and probably much less than the remaining *fifth* by tenants for a term of years. Of this last portion it should seem, besides, that there is hardly *one-fifth* (that is *one-twenty-fifth* of the whole) farmed in lease for twenty-one years; the rest being let from three to fourteen. Calculations of this sort, it is hardly necessary for me to observe, cannot fail, in the present state of our information, to be wide of the truth; but the data on which they proceed are sufficiently accurate, to evince the extent of the evil which led me to introduce these observations. It may be worth while to add, that the counties in which a refusal of leases appears to be most general, (and in some of them it is almost universal,) are Cumberland, York, Derby, Nottingham, Leicester, Rutland, North Wales, Salop, Worcester, Northampton, Cambridge, Berks, and Bedford. In a number of other counties, the same mischievous system prevails, though in an inferior degree, particularly in Westmoreland, Cheshire, Gloucestershire, Somersetshire, Monmouthshire, Kent, Essex, and probably several others."[1]

The fact is so curious, that I could not help mentioning it as an interesting subject of examination; but I am too imperfectly acquainted with the state of the other part of the island, to attempt any explanation of the circumstances which have occasioned it; nor do any of the *surveys* which I have looked into afford much satisfaction with respect to it.

In *Scotland,* where we fall short, in so many important articles of national improvement, of our southern neighbours, the ideas of our landed proprietors at present are certainly much more favourable to the progress of Agriculture, *in so far as it depends on the security of the farmer's tenure,* than those of the same order in England. Leases are now general in every part of this country; extending commonly to nineteen or twenty-one years. Formerly leases for *three* nineteen years

[1] See Robertson's *General Report.*

were frequent; and instances of them are still to be met with in several of the counties. Leases for such long terms are recommended by several of the surveyors, particularly in those counties which have not kept pace with the others in point of cultivation. They have certainly been attended with great advantages in many instances. It is observed in the *Survey of the County of Fife*, that "many entailed estates there, and indeed throughout Scotland, were tied down not to grant leases longer than nineteen years; but the proprietors considering that this had proved, in many cases, a bar to improvement, applied to Parliament, and were authorized to grant a lease of *thirty-one* years, upon certain conditions of improvement, which, it is believed, has proved, in general, to be for the benefit of the proprietors, the tenant, and the country at large : that other proprietors who were not restricted by entails, have sometimes granted leases of nineteen, twenty-one, twenty-five, thirty-one, thirty-eight years; and that leases of twenty-five, thirty-one, or two nineteen years, are *commonly* granted, where heavy advances, in the way of building, inclosing, or draining, are to be made by the tenant."

When I reflect on these facts, (combined with some others that will fall under our consideration afterwards, more especially our exemption from poor-rates and tithes,) I can scarcely bring myself to acquiesce in an assertion of Mr. Smith's, when applied at least to the two parts of the United Kingdom during the last forty years, that "Scotland is not only much poorer than England, but that the steps by which it advances to a better condition seem to be much slower and more tardy."*

It is observed by Mr. Smith, that "the law which secures the *longest* leases against successors of every kind is peculiar to Great Britain."† It was introduced into Scotland so early as 1449, by a law of James II., (a proof that the state of the peasants was then considerably improved ;) but its beneficial influence has been much obstructed by the restrictions with respect to the duration of leases which *entails* generally impose.

* [*Wealth of Nations*, Book I. chap. ix.; Vol. I. p. 137, tenth edition.] † [Ibid. Book III. chap. ii.; Vol. II. p. 94, tenth edition.]

In other parts of Europe tenants are secured against heirs and purchasers only for a short period. In France, for example, this period was limited to nine years from the commencement of the lease, till it was extended to twenty-seven, under the administration of M. Turgot. In Spain and Italy (according to Arthur Young) the sale of an estate vacates the lease.[1]

[2. *Farm Burthens.*]—Besides paying the rent, the farmers were anciently understood to be bound to perform a number of *services* to the landlord, not specified in the lease, but regulated by custom, and of consequence arbitrary and vexatious. They were also bound to many *public* services; such as making and repairing high roads, and providing horses, carriages, and provisions for the King's troops when they passed through the country. This last service was exacted in *England*, in consequence of what was called the Royal prerogative of *purveyance and pre-emption,*—a prerogative which was understood "to give the Crown a right of buying up provisions and other necessaries, by the intervention of the King's purveyors, for the use of his royal household, at an appraised valuation, in preference to all others, and even without consent of the owner; and also of forcibly impressing the carriages and horses of the subjects to do the King's business on the public roads, in the conveyance of timber, baggage, and the like, however inconvenient to the proprietor, on paying him a settled price."[2] The oppressions to which it gave rise in the golden days (as they have been termed) of Queen Elizabeth, may be judged of from a passage in Lord Bacon's *Speech touching Purveyors;* a passage which, though somewhat long, deserves to be quoted, as exhibiting a lively and authentic picture of the obstacles which then existed to agricultural industry. He says, speaking of the abuses of the Purveyors:—

"These do naturally divide themselves into three sorts: The first, they take *in kind* that they ought not to take; the second, they take *in quantity* a far greater proportion than cometh to

---

[1] *Political Arithmetic,* p. 189.
[2] Blackstone, [*Commentaries,* &c.] Vol. I. p. 287.

your Majesty's use; the third, they take in an *unlawful manner*, in a manner expressly prohibited by divers laws.

In the *first* of these, I am a little to alter their name; for, instead of *takers* they become *taxers*; instead of taking provision for your Majesty's service, they tax your people *ad redimendam vexationem;* imposing upon them, and extorting from them, divers sums of money, sometimes in gross, sometimes in the nature of stipends annually paid, *ne noceant,* to be freed and eased of their oppression. Again, they take trees, which by law they cannot do; timber trees, which are the beauty, countenance, and shelter of men's houses; that men have long spared from their own purse and profit; that men esteem, for their use and delight, above ten times their value; that are a loss which men cannot repair or recover. *These* do they take, to the defacing and spoiling of your subjects' mansions and dwellings, except they may be compounded with to their own appetites. And if a gentleman be too hard for them while he is at home, they will watch their time when there is but a bailiff or servant remaining, and put the axe to the root of the tree, ere ever the master can stop it. Again, they use a strange and most unjust exaction in causing the subject to pay poundage of their own debts, due from your Majesty unto them; so as a poor man when he has had his hay or his wood, or his poultry, which perchance he was full loth to part with, and had for the provision of his own family and not to put to sale, taken from him, and that not at a just price, but under the value, and cometh to receive his money, he shall have after the rate of twelve-pence in the pound abated for poundage of his due payment upon so hard conditions. Nay, farther, they are grown to that extremity, as is affirmed, though scarce credible, that they will take double poundage, once when the debenture is made, and again the second time when the money is paid.

"For the *second* point, most gracious Sovereign, touching the quantity which they take, far above that which is answered to your Majesty's use ... it is affirmed to me by divers gentlemen of good report and experience in these causes, as a matter which I may safely avouch before your Majesty ... that there is no pound profit which redoundeth unto your Majesty in this course, but induceth and begetteth three pound damage upon your subjects, beside the discontentment. And to the end they make their spoil more securely, what do they? Whereas divers statutes do strictly provide, that whatsoever they take shall be registered and attested, to the end, that by making a collation of that which is taken from the country, and that which is answered above, their deceits might appear; they, to the end to obscure their deceits, utterly omit the observation of this, which the law prescribeth.

"And, therefore, to descend, if it may please your Majesty, to the *third* sort of abuse, which is of the unlawful manner of taking, whereof this omission is a branch, it is so manifold, as it rather asketh an enumeration of some of the particulars than a prosecution of all. For their price:—by law, they ought to take as they can agree with the subject; by abuse, they take at an imposed and enforced price; by law, they ought to make but one apprizement by the neighbours in the country; by abuse, they make a second apprizement at the Court Gate; and when the subjects' cattle come up many miles, lean and out of plight, by reason of their great travel, then they prize them anew at an abated price. By law, they ought to take between sun and sun; by abuse, they take by twilight and in the night-time,—a time well chosen for malefactors. By law, they ought not to take in the highways, (a place by her Majesty's high prerogative protected, and by statute by special words excepted;) by abuse, they take in the ways," &c. &c.*

This branch of the King's prerogative and revenue was resigned by Charles II. at the Restoration. The oppressions similar to it which existed on the Continent have been likewise much moderated in later times. In Sweden they were abolished entirely by Gustavus Adolphus. They affected (as appears from what has been said) both landlords and tenants, but must have fallen more peculiarly hard on the latter.

The *public taxes* to which the farmers were subjected in

* [The *Speech touching Purveyors* is found in Montagu's edition of *Bacon's* Works, Vol. VI., and the passage in question at p. 7, *et seq.*]

these ancient times, were as oppressive as the *services*. Such, for example, was the *taille* in France. It was a tax upon the supposed profits of the farmer, estimated by the stock on his farm, and which (of consequence) prevented effectually whatever stock accumulated upon the land from being employed in its improvement. The ancient tenths and fifteenths in England seem, so far as they affected the land, to have been taxes of the same nature with the *taille*.

The ancient policy of Europe was farther unfavourable to the improvement of land. 1. By the prohibition of the exportation of corn; 2. By the restraints laid upon inland commerce; by the absurd laws against *engrossers, regrators,* and *forestallers;* and by the privileges of fairs and markets. For a complete illustration of these particulars, I must refer to Mr. Smith.*

In all the successive changes which have taken place in the system of rural economics over Europe, the landholder has uniformly found his advantage in communicating to the occupier of the ground, a greater and greater degree of security in his possession; and the public prosperity has kept pace with this good administration of the landholder's private estate.[1] Various suggestions for still farther improvements in this liberal and enlightened policy have been offered by different writers; but the consideration of these is foreign to our present object. One thing, however, is certain and indisputable:—that the actual cultivators of the soil are eminently entitled to the protection and encouragement of the Legislator; not only on account of the essential importance of this occupation to national prosperity, but because, with all the liberty and security which law can give, they must necessarily improve under great disadvantages. "The farmer," as Mr. Smith observes, "compared with the proprietor, is as a merchant who trades with borrowed money, compared with one who trades with his own. ... The station of a farmer besides, is, from the nature of things, inferior to that of a proprietor; and is even regarded, in modern Europe, as inferior to that of a great merchant or

---

* [*Wealth of Nations*, Book IV. chap. v.; Vol. II. p. 304, *seq.*, tenth edition.]

[1] Ogilvie's *Essay on Property*.

master manufacturer.... After all the encouragement, therefore, which agriculture has received from the policy of later times, little stock is likely to go from any other profession to the improvement of land in the way of *farming*."* Nor is this all. The nature of his profession precludes him from commanding at a reasonable price, like other artists, the rude materials on which his industry is to be employed. "He is confined in his inquiry and choice to that narrow district of country with which he is acquainted, and even to the small number of farms that may happen to fall vacant about the same time with his own: And in this narrow district a monopoly is established against him in the hands of a few landholders. In this respect, therefore, his situation is much inferior to that of the artist, who can go to a cheap market wherever it is found, and can bring his rude materials from a great distance to his home; while the cultivator," as an ingenious writer observes, "must carry his home to his rude materials when he has been so fortunate as to find them."

Among the actual discouragements to Agriculture still existing in Great Britain, none appears to claim the attention of the Legislature so strongly as that tax upon industry which is imposed by *tithes* in England.[1] The nature and extent of this grievance cannot be better stated than in the words of Mr. Archdeacon Paley, whose sentiments upon this subject, considering his professional rank, do great honour to his liberality. "A claimant," says he, "here enters into the produce, who contributed no assistance whatever to the production. When years, perhaps, of care and toil, have matured an improvement; when the husbandman sees new crops ripening to his skill and industry, the moment he is ready to put his sickle to the grain, he finds himself compelled to divide his harvest with a stranger. Tithes are a tax not only upon industry, but upon that industry which feeds mankind; and upon that species of exertion, which it is the aim of all wise laws to cherish and promote; and to uphold and excite which, com-

---

* [*Wealth of Nations*, Book III. chap. ii.; Vol. II. p. 97, tenth edition.]
[1] See Arthur Young's *Farmers' Letters*, p. 335, *et seq.*

poses the main benefit that the community receives from the whole system of trade, and the success of commerce. And together with the more general inconveniency that attends the exaction of tithes, there is this additional evil, (in the mode at least according to which they are collected at present,) that they operate as a bounty upon pasturage. The burden of the tax falls with its chief, if not with its whole weight, upon tillage; that is to say, upon that precise mode of cultivation which it is the business of the State to relieve and remunerate in preference to every other."*

Of the extent to which this grievance is actually felt in many instances, some very striking examples are given in the *View of the Agriculture of Middlesex*, lately published by Mr. Middleton. They would appear indeed scarcely credible to an inhabitant of this part of the island, were it not for the sanction which the Board of Agriculture gave to the general accuracy of the author's information, by presenting him with the first gold medal which they bestowed on any literary performance, as a mark of their approbation.

" In many parishes of this county," he observes, " the tithes are taken in kind; and, which is nearly the same, in others they are annually valued and compounded for. In several parishes a reasonable composition is taken; in some it has been very little advanced during the last twenty years; happily there are farms which pay a *modus*, and others that are entirely tithe free.

" I met with an instance, near Longford, of a farmer having, with great pains, and by an expensive culture, raised large crops. He offered a guinea an acre (which was exactly the rent he paid) as a composition for the tithe of his wheat; but it was refused, and taken in kind.

" A late rector of Kensington, after a lawsuit in the Court of Exchequer, obtained a decree that pine apples and other fruits which are raised at the expense of hot-houses, should yield their tithe in kind. .I have not heard how many hot-houses were

* [*Moral and Political Philosophy*, Book VI. chap. xi.; *Works*, Vol. II. p. 105, ed. London, 1819.]

pulled down on that occasion; but a very exorbitant composition was demanded and received from the inhabitants in lieu of actual payment.

" A gentleman was at the expense of making a hop plantation at Denbys, in Surrey. The vicar refused to compound on any reasonable terms, and insisted on taking the tithes in kind, and also on having them picked. A suit in the Court of Exchequer was litigated, and the decree going against the improver, he grubbed up his hops, sowed grass seeds, and made a pasture of the lands. Thus was a produce of upwards of thirty pounds reduced to three.

" A few instances equally oppressive with these have happened in every county of England; and the necessary consequence is, that they have put a stop to many expensive but promising improvements. Every matter of this kind becomes a subject of general conversation among farmers, and of course discourages similar attempts. In short, an Act of Parliament, to prohibit the improvement of land by any considerable expenditure, would not more effectually do it than the tithe laws.

" Within the narrow limits of my own knowledge," the same writer adds, " several premeditated bills of inclosure have been given up, rather than the land should be subjected to yield tithes in kind, after the great expense of the Act, the survey, the making of new roads, the building of bridges, the fencing and erecting of new buildings, and cultivating the land should be incurred."

To the same purpose it is observed, in the *Report of the County of Kent*, (the author of which has the reputation of great practical skill in agriculture,) that " nothing can be devised that would so much set *improvements afloat*, as a commutation for tithe."[1]

[3. *Size of Farms.*]—In the foregoing general conclusions concerning the protection and encouragement due by government to the immediate cultivators of the land, *all* the writers on population are unanimously agreed. There are, however, some

[1] See *Monthly Review* for December 1799.

other questions of a much more complicated nature, (relating to the same branch of rural economics,) on which there still subsists a wide diversity of opinion among our most respectable politicians. Such is the question which has given rise to so much discussion of late concerning the comparative effects on population produced by GREAT or by SMALL FARMS. It is proper for me in a general review of this sort, to take some notice of a controversy which has been carried on with so much warmth; and which (although from its nature incapable of being ever adjusted on any fixed general principles) has given occasion, not only to much ingenious argument, but to many important observations.

One of the first writers who distinguished himself by his zeal against the *engrossment of farms* in England, was Mr. Kent, in his *Hints to the Gentlemen of Landed Property*. "Those," says he, "who contribute towards the destruction of small farms, can have very little reflection. If they have, their feelings are not to be envied. Where this has been the practice, we see a number of families reduced to poverty and misery, the poor-rates much increased, the small articles of provision greatly diminished in quantity and number, and consequently augmented in price." . . . "There are thousands of parishes, which, since little farms have been swallowed up in greater, do not support so many cows as they did by fifty or sixty in a parish; and the inhabitants have decreased in proportion." . . . "Every speculative Englishman," he remarks in another passage, "who travels through the Austrian Netherlands, is astonished at the great population of that country, and at the sight of the markets, which are plentiful beyond description. Upon inquiring into the internal state and regulations of the country, he finds that there are no large farms; no class of men who pass under the character of gentlemen farmers, acquiring large fortunes merely by superintending the business of farming; but that the whole country is divided into much smaller portions than land is with us, and occupied by a set of laborious people, who in general work for themselves, and live very much on a footing of equality." He concludes his observations on this subject, with expressing his anxious wishes, that " the destructive practice of engrossing farms may be carried no farther ; the stab already given by it to plenty and population having greatly affected the population of this country."

The same argument has been much insisted on by Dr. Price, who expresses great apprehensions that the evil will go on increasing; "the custom of engrossing farms easing *landlords* of the trouble attending the necessities of little tenants and the repairs of cottages." "A great farmer," he observes farther, by having it more in his power to speculate and command the markets, and by drawing to himself the profits which would have supported several farmers, is capable, with less culture, of paying a higher rent." "But it is indeed," says he, "creating *private* benefit on *public* calamity ; and for the sake of a temporary advantage, giving up the nation to depopulation and distress."[1]

In confirmation of this conclusion, he quotes some observations from a *Memoir on the State of Population in the Pays de Vaud*, by M. Muret, Secretary to the Economical Society at Vevay This paper was published in 1766, and contains an enumeration of the principal causes which, in the judgment of the writer, obstruct population in that part of Switzerland. Among these, he insists particularly on engrossing farms ; remarking in support of his opinion, that "a large tract of land in the hands of one man, does not yield so great a return as when in the hands of several, and does not employ so many people." In proof of this, he mentions two parishes in the *Pays de Vaud*, one of which (once a little village) having been bought by some rich man, was sunk into a single *demesne;* and the other (once a single demesne) having fallen into the hands of some peasants, was become a little village.[2]

So prevalent were these ideas in France at the beginning of

---

[1] *On Annuities*, Vol. II. pp. 274, 275.

[2] A large farm has, on this account, been considered by some in the light of an *agricultural machine*, enabling the cultivators of the soil to do that with few hands which before they did with many ; resembling a stocking-loom, (for instance,) which enables the master manufacturer to turn off half his hands, and yet make more stockings than before.—Young's *Political Arithmetic*, p. 294.

the Revolution, that many of the *Cahiers* demanded a law to limit the size of farms, and to prevent their union. This request is to be found even in the *Cahier of Paris.*[1]

On the other hand, the advantages of *large farms* are maintained:—by Arthur Young in his *Political Arithmetic*, (published in 1774); in his various *Tours through England;*[2] in his *Travels through France* in 1787-88-89; and in the *Annals of Agriculture:*[3]—by Mr. Howlett in different political publications, particularly in an Essay, (published in 1788,) *On the Insufficiency of the Causes to which the Increase of our Poor and of the Poor-Rates have been commonly ascribed:*—by the authors of the French *Encyclopédie*, (Tom. vii.) :—by the Marquis de Mirabeau, in his *Ami des Hommes* :—by M. Herrenschwand, in his Discourses *Sur l'Economie Politique*, and *Sur la Division des Terres* :—and by many other authors at home and abroad.[4]

Mr. Smith, too, has laid it down as a general proposition, though without entering at all into the argument, that "*in every country*, after small proprietors, rich and great farmers are the principal improvers."[5] In another part of his work too, speaking of the great rise in the price both of hogs and poultry in Great Britain, he observes that "it has been frequently imputed to the diminution of cottagers, and other small occupiers of land; an event," he adds, "which has, *in every part of Europe*, been the immediate forerunner of improvement and better cultivation."[6]

Considerable additional light has been lately thrown on this subject in the *County Reports* drawn up for the consideration

---

[1] Young's *France*, p. 402.

[2] See in particular his *Six Months' Tour through the North of England*, Vol. IV. pp. 192, 251, 253, 264.

[3] Vol. VII. p. 510.

[4] Of one of the works now referred to, (Herrenschwand's *Essai sur la Division des Terres,*) I cannot speak from my own personal knowledge; but from what I know of his Treatise *Sur l'Economie Politique*, I should not be led to expect much from any of his performances. He appears to me to be an uncommonly vague and diffuse writer, although he is characterized by Mr. Young as "one of the greatest political geniuses of the present age."—*France*, p. 408.

[5] [*Wealth of Nations*, Book III. chap. ii.; Vol. II. p. 98, tenth edition.]

[6] [Ibid. Book I. chap. xi.; Vol. I. p. 354, tenth edition.]

of the Board of Agriculture. The arguments on both sides of the question will be found there very fully detailed; more particularly in favour of *large farms*, for which, with a very few exceptions, *all* the authors of the surveys are zealous advocates. Some of the reasonings in the papers, as well as in other publications of a similar nature, might perhaps have been spared, if the writers had explained with a little more precision the ideas they annexed to the words *large* and *small* as employed in this controversy; words which are not only indefinite in their signification, in consequence of the want of a given standard of comparison; but which must necessarily vary in their import, in different parts of the country, according to local circumstances. The advocates for small farms (for example) sometimes include under that denomination, farms from 150 to 200 acres, (which are far above the highest average of small farms in Great Britain,) contrasting these with farms of 1500 or 2000 acres, which are so very far above the highest average of large farms, that they should be considered as exceptions.[1]

Many of these writers, too, seem to have proceeded on the supposition, that the principles on which the size of farms ought to be settled, are of a much more universal application than they will be found to admit of in reality. A few of them, however, have been completely aware of this consideration, remarking that the size of farms must necessarily be regulated by a variety of local peculiarities, such as soil, situation, modes of husbandry, and the extent of capital possessed by the class of farmers; and that, admitting the general maxim,—*The best size of farm is that which affords the greatest proportional produce, for the least proportional expense*, the application of this maxim will be found to lead to widely different conclusions, in different districts.[2]

In general, it should seem, that in proportion as Agriculture advances, the size of farms should be reduced; or rather, that farms should divide themselves in proportion as the task of superintendence became more difficult. In the meantime,

[1] Robertson's *Report*, pp. 41, 42.   [2] Ibid. p. 48.

much praise is due to the authors who have exerted so much industry and ingenuity, in attempting to enlighten landlords and tenants with respect both to their own interests and those of the community. It is in this way alone, that any good can result from such speculations; for I take for granted, that, in the present state of Political Science, all idea of legislative interference in adjusting the terms on which farms are to be let or hired, is entirely out of the question.

With respect to the supposed tendency of small farms to promote population, I shall only remark before leaving this article, that it must not be judged of merely from the numbers which are subsisted on the spot. The idea that " the mode of culture which employs most hands, is most favourable to the population of the State," is justly reprobated by the author of *L'Ami des Hommes* [the elder Mirabeau] as a vulgar prejudice. " The surplus of produce carried to market," he observes, " is no less beneficial in this respect by feeding towns, than if eaten on the fields that produced it. The more, therefore, that the industry and riches of the farmer enable him to economize the labour of men, the greater is the surplus which remains for the subsistence of others."[1] To suppose, as some authors have done, that small farms add to the numbers of a people, while, at the same time, it is granted, that they neither yield an adequate produce nor rent, amounts very nearly to a contradiction in terms.

What can be so adverse to population as the high price of the necessaries of life ? And what circumstance can contribute more infallibly to augment this price, than to increase unnecessarily, by the multiplication of servants, labourers, and cattle, the expense of bringing the produce of the land to market ? Granting that in this way some small farmers may be converted into labourers, and some labourers thrown out of employment, the same cause which gives rise to large farms, (I mean the demand for workmen and the increased consumption produced by *flourishing manufactures,*) will furnish employment to these labourers elsewhere, while the part of the produce

[1] Tome V. p. 43, Tome VI. p. 79, (quoted by Young in his *France*, p. 408.)

which they formerly consumed *on the spot*, will be sold in the market at a price lower than the farmer could otherwise have afforded, contributing in a manner more advantageous to the general interest of the community, to the maintenance of a number of individuals equal to that of the labourers displaced.

It is thus that, in such a state of society as that in which we live, great farms not only supply, by an increased produce, the means of subsistence to an increasing population, but by economizing the expense of agricultural operations, have a tendency to keep down the price of provisions to those who are engaged in other kinds of industry.

It must not, however, be admitted as a *universal* fact, that the consolidation of farms has the effect of diminishing population *on the spot;* for although this is its natural and acknowledged effect, (the state of cultivation being supposed to remain the same,) the result will be directly opposite, if the capital of the great farmer, by extending the scale of his improvements, should enlarge the field of agricultural industry, in a greater proportion than that in which it economizes the mode of its employment. Nor is this reasoning merely hypothetical. In the agricultural reports, many instances occur of three or four small farms, after being thrown into one, having not only raised greater produce and paid a higher rent, but having added to the *population* maintained on the surface, by increasing the quantity of work, and of consequence, the demand for labourers.[1] Mr. Howlett affirms that this happens in nine cases out of ten.[2]

Even, however, where the case is otherwise, it remains to be considered, of what description the population is which small farms promote; and whether the real strength of a State is increased by multiplying mouths, without providing a proportional produce to feed them. Nor must it be forgotten that the same want of economy which on small farms multiplies unnecessary labourers, multiplies unnecessary horses, and thereby occasions a most ruinous waste of national produce. " I have found from a close inspection," says Mr. Young, speaking

[1] Robertson's *General Report.* [2] *Insufficiency of the Causes,* &c. [1788,] p. 85.

of the division of a country into small farms, "that the number of horses in such a country is treble and quadruple the number found on large farms. There was a farm in this parish (at present my property) of only sixteen acres of land, and yet the man kept two horses; no wonder he failed, notwithstanding the most intense industry. There is another remaining of twenty-eight acres, on which there are *three* horses kept. A contiguous one of three hundred and fifty has only ten upon it. Those who are advocates for little farms, in order that pigs and poultry may be plentiful, forget the swarms of horses that eat up what would feed myriads of pigs and chickens. I know," he adds, "little farmers that keep two horses, yet have not one cow."[1]

That the engrossment of farms has been a real grievance to many individuals is beyond all dispute; but the case is the same with every alteration in the policy of a State which obliges numbers to seek out a new employment. The same objection lies against every new mechanical contrivance for shortening labour, and even against the expediency of a peace at the close of a long and expensive war. In uniting small farms into larger ones, without any regard to the future provision of former possessors, much inhumanity, it is probable, has been displayed by particular proprietors; but in judging of the policy of such innovations in the habits of a country, it is absolutely necessary to abstract from the individual hardships that may fall under our notice, and to fix our attention on those general principles which influence the national prosperity.

It may be proper to add, before leaving this article, that in a considerable number of the *Surveys* very liberal ideas are suggested, with respect to certain appendages which ought to be connected with large farms, particularly an establishment for married servants or cottagers. Some striking instances are mentioned of the happy effects they have produced in different districts in lowering the poor-rates, and in promoting the industry and good order of the labourers.

[1] *Annals of Agriculture*, No. 42, p. 516.

[4. *Enclosures.*]—Nearly connected with this question concerning large and small farms, is another which has also given occasion to much controversy in England during the last thirty years; the question concerning the advantages or disadvantages of ENCLOSURES, considered in respect of their influence on *population*. On this subject, as well as on the former, it would lead me into details inconsistent with my general plan, if I were to attempt a particular discussion of the argument; and, indeed, I have introduced *both* into these lectures, not so much with the view of supporting any opinion concerning them, as in order to give some arrangement to your private studies in examining this branch of Political Economy, and to point out the principal authors from whom you may derive assistance in the prosecution of the inquiry. By following this plan, (which, as I hinted in my first lecture, I intend to do in various other parts of the course,) I am sensible that I must necessarily deprive my speculations of the systematic form affected by those writers, who bring every particular question (however complicated by existing institutions or by local peculiarities) to the test of a few abstract principles; but I flatter myself that this inconvenience will be in some measure compensated by the variety of matter which I shall be able to suggest for your future consideration. In truth, it is chiefly by thus marking out the field of inquiry, and by exhibiting such an outline of its principal parts, as may direct the attention of the student to a methodical survey of the whole, that academical lectures seem to me to possess much utility, when the subject treated of is so extensive and various as that which I comprehend under the title of *Political Economy*. At any rate, it is all that I would be understood to attempt at present, in mentioning such topics as those which are now under our review.

Dr. Price, who has distinguished himself so much by his zeal *against Great Farms*, has taken up the argument *against Enclosures* with no less warmth. "How astonishing is it," he observes, "that our Parliament should choose to promote depopulation, by passing every year, bills almost without number for new enclosures!"

In order to prevent misapprehensions of his meaning, he adds, that he " has here in view enclosures *of open fields and lands already improved.* It is acknowledged," he says, " by even the writers in defence of enclosures, that these diminish tillage, increase the monopolies of farms, raise the prices of provisions, and produce depopulation. Such enclosures, therefore, however gainful they may be at present to a few individuals, are undoubtedly pernicious. On the contrary, enclosures of *waste lands and commons* would be useful, if divided into small allotments, and given up to be occupied at moderate rents by the poor. But, if besides lessening the produce of fine wool, they bear hard on the poor by depriving them of a part of their subsistence, and only go towards increasing farms already too large, the advantages attending them may not much exceed the disadvantages."*

The argument on the *other side* of the question may be found in two pamphlets by Mr. Howlett, vicar of Great Dunmow, Essex. The one is entitled, " *An Enquiry into the influence which Enclosures have had upon the Population of this Kingdom,*" (1786.) The other, " *Enclosures a cause of improved Agriculture, of plenty and cheapness of Provisions, of Population, and of Wealth, both private and national,*" (1787.)

This writer, who has certainly treated of the subject with considerable ability and much candour, confesses after a review of the opposite representations and reasonings that have been laid before the public, that enclosures, according to particular circumstances, are attended with great advantages and great disadvantages, with respect to population, so that (although probability *seems* strongly on the favourable side) it does not appear merely from a *theoretical* view of the controversy, altogether indisputable, which of the two is prevalent in the vast number of enclosures which have taken place in this kingdom during the last twenty or thirty years. In order, therefore, to bring the question to the test of experience, he procured a list of the Enclosure Bills from the Journals of the House of Com-

* Price *On Annuities*, Vol. II. p. 292.

mons, (amounting to very near a thousand, between the years 1750 and 1781,) and applied to the clergy of the enclosed parishes for the annual register of baptisms. In this inquiry he omitted the counties of Nottingham, York, and Lancaster, because Dr. Price himself acknowledges *these* to be increased greatly. The result of the very extensive information he collected, was decidedly in favour of the enclosed parishes, and seems to amount to little short of demonstration of the beneficial influence of enclosures on the general population of the kingdom.

The prejudice against Enclosures is of a very early date in England, and has been sanctioned by the opinions of some very eminent writers; among others, by Lord Bacon, who expresses himself thus, in his *History of Henry the Seventh.** " Enclosures at that time, (1489,) began to be more frequent, whereby arable land, which could not be manured without people and families, was turned into pasture, which was easily rid by a few herdsmen. . . . This bred a decay of people. . . . In remedying this inconvenience, the King's wisdom and the Parliament's was admirable. *Enclosures* they would not *forbid*, . . . and *tillage* they would not compel; . . . but they took a course to take away *depopulating enclosures* and *depopulating pasturage*, . . . by consequence. The ordinance was, 'that all houses of husbandry, with twenty acres of ground to them, should be kept up for ever, together with a competent proportion of land to be occupied with them,' and in nowise to be severed from them. . . . By this means, the houses being kept up, did, of necessity, enforce a dweller; and the proportion of land for occupation being also kept up, did, of necessity, enforce that dweller not to be a beggar or cottager," &c. " The statute here mentioned was renewed in Henry Eighth's time, and every person who converted tillage into pasture subjected to a forfeiture of half the land, till the offence was removed."[1]

Mr. Hume, who, in his *History of England*, has interspersed

---

* [There being no general divisions of this book, I must refer to Montagu's edition of *Bacon's Works*, Vol. III. p. 234.]

[1] Price [*On Annuities,*] Vol. II. p. 292.

his narrative with many of the most important principles of *Political Economy*, dissents widely from Lord Bacon, in the judgment he pronounces on this part of Henry Seventh's policy. " The law enacted against Enclosures," he observes, " and for the keeping up of farm-houses, scarcely deserves the high praises bestowed on it by Lord Bacon. If husbandmen understand agriculture, and have a ready vent for their commodities, we need not dread a diminution of the people employed in the country. All methods of supporting populousness, *except by the interest of the proprietor*, are violent and ineffectual. During a century and a half after this period, there was a frequent renewal of laws and edicts against depopulation, whence we may infer that none of them were ever executed. The natural course of improvement at last provided a remedy."*

Another very curious document of the sentiments of former times on this subject, exists in a pamphlet first published in 1581, entitled " *A Compendium, or Brief Examination of certain ordinary Complaints of divers of our Countrymen in these our Days.*" The initials of the author's name are W. S.; from which circumstance, strengthened by some vague tradition, and probably also by the dramatic form of the work, it was long and very generally ascribed to *William Shakespeare*. But it appears from Wood's *Fasti*, and Farmer's book *On the Learning of Shakespeare*, that the real author was a person of the name of *Stafford*. The arguments both *for* and *against* Enclosures, are certainly stated in it with uncommon spirit and force, and anticipate the principal ones which have been brought forward in the course of the late discussions concerning them. The speakers in the dialogue are " a Merchant, a Knight, a Husbandman, a Capper, and a Doctor of Divinity."

I have dwelt longer on this article than I should have thought necessary on a question of so very local a nature, because it has formed one of the most conspicuous objects of internal policy under the present reign. During that of King William, not a single act was passed for enclosing wastes or dividing commons; and in the two succeeding reigns, only

* [*History of England*, Chap. xxvi., anno 1509.]

twenty-five in whole. In the reign of George II., (which lasted thirty-three years,) they amounted to a hundred and eighty-two; whereas they are said, during the first fourteen sessions of the present reign, to have exceeded seven hundred. "In this manner," says Mr. Chalmers, "was more useful territory added to the Empire, at the expense of individuals, than had been gained by all the wars since the Revolution. In acquiring distant dominions, through conquest, the State is enfeebled by the charge of their establishments in peace, and by the still more enormous debts incurred in war for their defence. In gaining additional lands by reclaiming the wild, improving the barren, and appropriating the common, the limits of our island are virtually extended, and a solid foundation is laid, in the additional produce of the soil, for the multiplication of the people."[1]

Impressed with these ideas, a variety of writers have for many years contended for the expediency of a *General Enclosure Bill*; and a bill for that purpose actually passed the House of Commons in the session of Parliament 1799, but was thrown out by the Lords. The Lord Chancellor, [Loughborough,] in his speech on the 3d of July *last*, (1800,)* when certain resolutions of the Commons concerning bills of enclosure were under consideration, stated that the Bill of 1799 had been rejected, *because it was loosely and vaguely drawn*, and expressed his doubts of the possibility of framing any *general law* which should not be liable to material objections. "If a canon could be devised, comprising all such provisions as by experience have been found necessary in most bills of enclosure, it would certainly have its use, but this he feared would be impracticable; and, (as in the case of the general Highway Act, which had not in the least tended to shorten private highway bills,) so a general canon of enclosure law might not in the least have the effect of shortening future private bills of enclosure." The Duke of Bedford expressed himself nearly to the same pur-

---

[1] *Estimate of the Comparative Strength of Great Britain during the present and four preceding Reigns.* By George Chalmers, pp. 145, 146.

* [This marks the year in which this part, at least, of the lecture was written.]

pose; avowing himself friendly to a system of general enclosure, but disapproving of the attempt to effect it by a general bill. Of the beneficial tendency of enclosures with respect to population, no doubt appears to have been suggested in the course of the debate. On the contrary, it was universally admitted that the population of the kingdom had of late years considerably increased; that the means of supplying that population had not increased in proportion; and that every measure which facilitated a general system of enclosure, was in a high degree wise and salutary in our present circumstances. The Chancellor alone doubted " whether any regulations adopted by the Legislature, could serve to promote the cultivation of waste lands and commons. He rather believed that enclosures in general must depend upon the spirit, the activity, and the ability of private individuals, who feel it their interest to set about enclosing, and apply to Parliament for bills of enclosure."

About one point, however, there can be no controversy, that if the multiplication of enclosures be a desirable object, it is the duty of the Legislature to remove as much as possible those obstacles to them which are created by the heavy expenses attending enclosure bills at present. The expense occasioned by fees to the officers of the two Houses, amounts to £209 per parish, however many there may be in an act; but this is, in many instances, trifling, in comparison of what is expended in paying solicitors and witnesses in London. Hence the *impossibility* of coming to Parliament for small enclosures; and the *discouragements* which oppose themselves even to more extensive projects of improvement.[1]

The expediency of reducing this expense as much as possible, is placed in a strong light by an acknowledged *fact*, on which has frequently been founded a plausible but very fallacious argument against the policy of enclosures in general. The great profit which speculations of this sort afford to individuals (it is well known) is derived from soils which are adapted to the purposes of the grazier. " Upon dry land well adapted to

[1] Young's Pamphlet, [*On the Question of Scarcity*, 1800,] p. 73.

corn, the advantage is far inferior. The consequence is, that immense tracts of this last sort of land remain open and waste; while the heavy, rich, deep soils that have been constantly yielding wheat under a low rent, are enclosed and converted into grazing land at double or treble the rents they formerly paid." "Such soils," says Mr. Young, "will bear any expense; and these have been thus taken from corn, which is the food of the poor, and thrown to bullocks to feed the rich."

It is acknowledged, however, by this writer, that these considerations afford no argument against the general encouragement of enclosures by the Legislature. The evil of which he complains is irremediable by legislative authority, being the natural consequence of the present circumstances of the country; and, so far from being diminished, it is *increased* by the existing impediments to enclosures,—impediments which, while insufficient to prevent enclosures where they are injurious to Agriculture, throw a bar in the way of improvement, in the case of those dry and poorer wastes, which might be converted into corn-fields for the benefit of the people.[1]

[5. *Size of Properties.*]—In the observations hitherto made on the relation between Population and Agriculture, I have had in view chiefly the effects produced on the latter, by the condition of those who *cultivate farms which do not belong to them in property*. It appeared to me to be the most natural arrangement, to *begin* with the consideration of this order of men, as it is chiefly by them that Agriculture is carried on in this part of the world. I now proceed to make a few remarks on the same subject, considered in its connexion with the *actual proprietors of the land*.

That the division and subdivision of landed property promote population in an eminent degree, is admitted as an indisputable maxim by political writers of all descriptions. "Only revive," says Mr. Suessmilch, "the laws of *Licinius*, forbidding any Roman to hold more than seven *jugera* of land; or that of *Romulus*, which limited every Roman to two *jugera*,

[1] Pamphlet *On the Scarcity*, p. 74.

and you will soon convert a barren desert into a busy and crowded hive." Ample illustrations of this proposition may be found in Dr. Wallace's *Dissertations on the Numbers of Mankind*, and in the *Political Tracts* of Dr. Price.

I shall have occasion to shew, in another part of this course, how much this equality in the distribution of landed property was favoured by all the ancient systems of legislation. I shall confine myself at present to the example of the Romans.

For about two hundred and fifty years after the foundation of Rome, during the monarchy, the whole land was divided into equal portions of two *jugera*,—that is, a little more than an English acre, and a little less than one Scotch; and each citizen had one of these portions assigned to him. Soon after the expulsion of the kings the quantity was increased, and inequalities of fortune arose; yet for about another two hundred and fifty years, the general size of a Roman farm was only seven *jugera*, or somewhat less than four and a half English acres. In the progress of luxury and avarice, however, so great an alteration took place in the manners of the people, that in the year of Rome 375, (under the tribuneship of *Licinius Stolo*,) a law was found necessary to limit estates to five hundred *jugera*, or about three hundred and twelve English acres. When the Roman Consuls and Dictators had only so small a portion of land which they laboured with the help of their slaves, and often with their own hands; it is easy to conceive with what frugality and simplicity they must have lived; how completely the ornamental arts must have been excluded; and how easy it must have been to support a family. In the family of such a Dictator or Consul, Dr. Wallace reckons the husband and wife, two or three children, and a slave or two; (which last allowance is probably under the truth, as slaves were very numerous.) A Roman family, therefore, which had not above seven *jugera*, or four and one-third English acres, to maintain them, might consist of seven persons or more, and had less than an acre, often perhaps not more than *half* an acre, for each individual: whereas, (according to Templeman's calculation,) the eight millions of inhabitants of England have very near thirty-two millions of acres to support them, or *four* acres per head.

In consequence of the influence of these laws, and the system of manners which they encouraged, the agriculture of the Romans appears to have been carried to a singular degree of perfection; and the effects continued for a long course of years after the causes had ceased to operate. Depending entirely on agriculture for the means of life, trained to it from generation to generation, cultivating every corner and inch of their little fields, the old Romans were not only distinguished above all other people for simplicity of manners, but set an example of economy, accuracy, and minute attention in the cultivation of land, which has never been equalled in this part of the world. It is observed by the author of one of the *Reports* presented to the Board of Agriculture, that the *Garden System* of Agriculture, which continued to be general for near five hundred years, probably laid the foundation of all that excellence to which Roman husbandry was afterwards carried; that the rural industry, practices, and ideas handed down from former times, long preserved their existence; and that the more extensive farms which afterwards took place, were cultivated with as religious and minute a care as the little allotments in earlier ages.[1]

In the pictures which have been transmitted to us of the old Roman manners, uniting in so wonderful a degree the simplicity and moderation of rural life, with all that is heroic and splendid in human character, there is undoubtedly something which is peculiarly interesting to the imagination. "Gaudente terra," as Pliny[*] expresses it, " laureato vomere et triumphali aratore." Nor is it surprising that they should be so often mentioned by way of contrast, to what the poet calls "The sober, gainful arts of modern days." The following stanza forms part of a beautiful *Ode* which he has addressed on this subject to the country gentlemen of England.

[1] Robertson's *Report*, pp. 71, 72.
[*] [*Historia Naturalis*, Lib. XVIII. cap. iii.]

> "Have ye not heard of Lacedæmon's fame?
> Of Attic chiefs in Freedom's war divine?
> Of Rome's dread generals? The Valerian name?
> The Fabian sons? The Scipios? matchless line!
> *Your* lot was theirs. The farmer and the swain
> Met his lov'd patron's summons from the plain.
> The legions gathered; the bright eagles flew;
> Barbarian monarchs in the triumph mourn'd;
> The conqu'rors to their household gods return'd,
> And fed Calabrian flocks, and steer'd the Sabine plough."*

When we indulge such ideas, we are extremely apt to forget the essential differences between the circumstances of mankind in ancient and in modern times. Granting the fact, that when a family has just land enough for its subsistence, that portion will be well cultivated, what deductions can be drawn from it applicable to the present policy of Europe? Of what use in a modern kingdom would be a whole province thus divided, except for the mere purpose of breeding men? A province of such farmers would consume nothing but the produce of their lands; they could neither possess the desire nor the ability to purchase manufactures; and they could pay no taxes without an oppression that would reduce them to misery. The case was widely different in the early times of the Roman Republic, for *then* the more abundant such population was, the more easily could the State levy that tax which consisted in personal service.[1] Hence an important distinction between the practice of agriculture as a *direct means of subsistence, and as a trade bearing a relation to the other trades and occupations which enter into the general system of Political Economy.* The former was exemplified in Rome, and in various other ancient republics. The latter is exemplified in Modern Europe, where it is the object of the farmer, by raising a surplus produce for the market, not only to provide a fund for the payment of taxes, but to acquire the means of purchasing from the artisan and manufacturer, whatever accommodations his habits may lead him to consider as contributing to his comfort. This distinc-

---

* [Akenside, *Odes*, XII. ix.]
[1] Young's *Political Arithmetic*, pp. 47, 48.

tion is much insisted on by Sir James Steuart in the Fourteenth Chapter of his First Book, [of *The Principles of Political Œconomy.*]

It is justly observed by the same writer, that "those passages of Roman authors which mention the frugality of that people, and the small extent of their possessions, cannot be rightly understood without the knowledge of many circumstances relative to the manners of those times. For if you understand such a distribution of lands to have extended over all the Roman territory, the number of the citizens would have exceeded what they appear to have been by the census, and even surpass all belief. But farther, I may be allowed to ask, Whether or not it be supposed that these frugal Romans laboured this small portion of lands with their own hands, and consumed the produce of it? If I am answered in the affirmative, (which is necessary to prove the advantages of agriculture's being exercised by all the classes of a people,) then I ask, From whence were the inhabitants of Rome and other cities supposed to come, who fed the armies when in the field? If these were fed by foreign grain imported, or plundered from their neighbours, where was the advantage of this subdivision of lands, and of this extensive agriculture which could not feed the inhabitants of the State? If it be said, that notwithstanding this frugal distribution of property among the citizens, there was still found surplus enough to supply both Rome and the armies, will it not then follow, that there was no necessity for employing all the people in agriculture, since the labour of a part might have sufficed?"*

I shall have occasion afterwards to take notice of some of the difficulties started in the foregoing passage, when I come to consider (in another part of the course) the immense *importations* of corn which, from the earliest times, were understood to be necessary for the subsistence of Rome. At present I shall only remark, (as I already hinted,) that whatever may be supposed to be the merits or defects of the agricultural policy of the Romans, considered in relation to the national objects

* [*Political Œconomy*, Book I. chap. xiv.; *Works*, Vol. I. p. 116.]

which *they* had in view, this policy is manifestly inapplicable to the present state of society in Europe. Mr. Hume, after acknowledging its tendency to promote that population which the exigencies of their state required, and even admitting that this population was partly to be ascribed to the want of commerce, (the small number of artisans who depended on the labour of the farmers leaving a greater share for the maintenance of the *soldiers*,) proposes the following question: " Whether sovereigns might not now return with advantage to the maxims of ancient policy ?" His answer is, " That it appears to be almost impossible ; and *that*, because ancient policy was *violent*, and contrary to the more natural and usual course of things."* It were to be wished, that Mr. Hume had explained a little more fully the idea suggested in the last clause of this sentence, but I presume his meaning was, that ancient policy aimed too much at modifying, by the force of positive institutions, the order of society, according to some preconceived notion of expediency, without trusting sufficiently to those principles of the human constitution, which, wherever they are allowed free scope, not only conduct mankind to happiness, but lay the foundation of a progressive improvement in their condition and in their character. The advantages which modern policy possesses over the ancient, (as I have elsewhere observed), arises principally from its conformity, in some of the most important articles of Political Economy, to an order of things recommended by nature; and it would not be difficult to show, that where it remains imperfect, its errors may be traced to the restraints it imposes on the *natural* course of human affairs.

The policy of the Romans, in the instance now under our consideration, " was," to use Mr. Hume's language, " *violent and contrary to the natural course of things*," inasmuch as it attempted, by the force of Agrarian Laws, to prevent that inequality in the distribution of landed property, which is plainly a part of the order of nature, and which (as I shall afterwards endeavour to shew) is intimately connected with the progres-

* [*Essays*, Vol. I., *Of Commerce.*]

sive improvement of the human species. Among *them*, it was the great object of State to keep up and to multiply the breed of soldiers; a narrow and oppressive scheme of Government, undoubtedly, when compared with that enlightened and generous system, which estimates national felicity, not merely by the register of births, but by the degree in which it distributes among all orders of the people, (together with the comforts connected with their animal existence,) all the gratifications of which man is susceptible as an intelligent and a moral being.

Conformable to this agricultural and military policy of the Romans, were the ideas imbibed by their youth from early infancy, and inculcated in the writings of all their most esteemed authors. From the most ancient period of their history descended that maxim which always continued to have a wonderful influence on their manners, that no employment was honourable but the plough and the sword; and hence, as both Pliny and Columella inform us, an enrolment into any of the Four *City* Tribes ("*sub umbra Civitatis intra mœnia desides cunctari*") was understood not to accord well with the spirit which became a Roman.*

In later times, an affectation of more effeminate habits seems to have gained ground even among their military characters, from the natural effects of a city life, and to have been regarded with some degree of jealousy and indignation by those who adhered to the occupation and sentiments of their ancestors. We are told by Valerius Maximus, that when *Scipio Nasica* (then a young man) was standing candidate for the office of Curule Ædile, this affectation defeated his hopes of attaining that dignity. "As he was passing," it is said, "where the tribes both of the city and country were assembled, (practising, it should seem, the same attentions which are usual among modern candidates for popular favour,) while he was squeezing the hand of a labouring man whom he knew, he could not forbear jesting with him on its hardness and callousness—" Joci gratia; interrogavit cum—Num manibus solitus esset ambulare?" "This jest," the writer adds, " cost him

* [*Hist. Nat.*, Lib. XVIII. cap. iii.—*De Re Rustica*, Præf.]

dear; for it was repeated immediately from one to another, and all the tribes offended with the *contumeliosa urbanitas* which it discovered, unanimously rejected a candidate whom the effeminacy of Rome had rendered so supercilious and petulant."[1]

While these ideas concerning the dignity exclusively attached to the professions of agriculture and of war maintained their influence, the mercantile and lucrative arts were entirely abandoned to aliens, slaves, and freedmen; and for a succession of ages not a citizen was found to practise them. In the time of Cicero other notions had begun to prevail, and these arts had risen considerably in the public estimation; and yet, what a contrast does the following passage present to the ideas now fostered by those establishments which have accomplished in the most effectual manner, and, in a far greater degree, than any of the ancient constitutions, all the most essential purposes of the political union!

" Concerning the arts, and the means of acquiring wealth, *which* are to be accounted *liberal*, and *which, mean*, the following are the sentiments usually entertained. In the first place, those professions are discreditable which are odious to mankind, such as the business of tax-gatherers and usurers. The arts of all hirelings, too, are illiberal and mean, who are paid for their labour and not for their skill. The wages they receive are the badges of servitude. They also are to be considered as dishonourably employed, who buy from merchants what they immediately retail. For they gain nothing unless they lie extravagantly, and, consequently, owe their profit to the basest of all the vices. All mechanics are occupied in mean employments; nor is it possible that anything liberal can be connected with a workshop. Least of all ought the arts to be esteemed which minister to pleasure, such as the arts of fishmongers, butchers, cooks, and confectioners. To these may be added, if you please, perfumers, dancers, and the whole tribe of such as administer to gaming.

[1] Valerius Maximus, [*De Dictis*, &c.] Lib. VII., cap. v. (Quoted in Postlethwayt's *Dictionary*, &c.; Article *Manufactures.*)

"But those arts which require a superior degree of skill, and from which arise a higher degree of utility, as medicine, architecture, instruction in liberal arts, are employments honourable to those with whose rank they correspond. As to commerce, it is mean, if it be inconsiderable; but if it be great and abundant, if it bring largely from every country, and without deceit supply an extensive market, it is an occupation not much to be censured, (*non admodum vituperanda ;*) nay, if the persons who follow it could be satiated, or rather be content with their profits, not making long voyages, but returning speedily to their farms and landed estates, they would deserve to be rather commended. But after all, among the various pursuits from which gain is derived, there is none which surpasses agriculture; none more profitable; none more delightful; none more worthy of a man who loves independence."[1]

I have quoted this passage as an additional illustration of the absurdity of drawing parallels between the condition of the ancient Romans and our own; and of imagining that the agricultural policy of the former is applicable to that state of society in which we live, I shall only add farther on the subject at present, that the *commerce* with which the Romans were acquainted, was essentially different, both in its nature and effects, from that which has changed the face of human affairs in Modern Europe. It was a saying of Manius Curius Dentatus, (and repeated by Cicero in the person of Cato,) that he thought it more glorious to conquer those who possessed gold, than to possess it himself.[2] The natural effect, however, of this spirit of conquest, (notwithstanding the disinterested views with which it was long connected in the case of many illustrious individuals,) was to bring immense sums of money into the city. Satisfactory proofs of this are produced by Dr. Wallace, (even in the early ages of the Republic,) from the high prices which were paid for things merely ornamental, at a time when all the ancient sim-

---

[1] Omnium rerum, ex quibus aliquid acquiritur, nihil est agricultura melius, nihil uberius, nihil dulcius, nihil homine libero dignius.—[*De Officiis*, Lib. I. cap. xlii.]

[2] Non enim aurum habere, præclarum sibi videri, dixit; sed iis, qui habuerunt aurum, imperare.—[*De Senectute*, cap. xvi.] Rollin, *Arts and Sciences*, I. p. 17.

plicity of manners remained, and the necessaries of life were to be purchased for a trifle. Towards the end of the Commonwealth, and afterwards under Augustus, riches and luxury increased to an extent unknown in the annals of the world. Julius Cæsar's debts, before he had been in any office, were, according to some, £2,018,229; according to others, £807,291. Crassus was his surety for £160,812. Mark Anthony owed on the Ides of March, £322,916 sterling, and paid it before the Calends of April. The *expenses* of these Romans were on a scale proportioned to their estates and debts, and far exceeded the most extravagant ideas of modern times. Much curious information concerning them may be found in Dr. Arbuthnot's *Treatise on Coins,* and in Wallace's *Dissertation on the Numbers of Mankind.* As this wealth was not acquired by commerce, it had no tendency to encourage a commercial spirit, excepting in so far as ministered to luxury. On the contrary, we find that commerce was dreaded on account of the obvious effect which it had to *drain* their riches; for as they had no commodity of their own to give in exchange for the luxuries which they imported at so immense a price from distant provinces, they must have paid for everything in silver and gold. " Hence it was, that the emperors forbid the people to send gold to the barbarians; which law appears (by the way) to have been in force before, from Cicero's *Oration for L. Flaccus:* '*Exportari Aurum* non oportere, cum sæpe antea Senatus, tum, me Consule, gravissime judicavit.'"[1]

The fatal consequences of this influx of wealth, and of the excessive luxury which attended it, (particularly after the conquest of Asia,) are sufficiently known. Juvenal has painted them strongly in a single line.

"Sævior armis
Luxuria incubuit; victumque ulciscitur orbem."[*]

The same remarks which have been now made with respect to Rome, are applicable, with some slight limitations, to most of the ancient republics. In States formed upon such a model, and in ages when commerce and manufactures were yet in their

---

[1] [? 28.]—Taylor's *Elements,* &c., p. 499.   [*] [*Sat.* vi. 291.]

infancy, a sudden influx of riches from abroad was justly dreaded as an evil alarming to the morals, to the industry, and to the freedom of a people. How different in its tendency is that wealth which, in a commercial country, is the gradual result of national industry! If we survey the countries around us, we uniformly find, that the most wealthy states are those where the people are the most laborious, and where they enjoy the greatest degree of liberty. Nay, it was the general diffusion of wealth among the lower orders of men which first gave birth to the spirit of independence in Modern Europe, and which has produced, under some of its governments, and more especially under our own, a more equal diffusion of freedom and of happiness, than took place under the most celebrated constitutions of antiquity.

I may perhaps appear to have insisted longer than was necessary, on institutions and manners so strikingly contrasted with those which exist at present. But it seemed to me to be of consequence to take the earliest opportunity which my subject afforded, of obviating some of the prepossessions which the study of the classics is apt to inspire in favour of agrarian regulations, to the prejudice of that more comprehensive and enlightened policy, which, giving full scope in all directions to human industry, allows agriculture and commerce to act and re-act on each other, in multiplying the comforts of human life, in developing all the capacities that belong to our nature, and in diffusing as widely as the imperfection of human institutions will permit, the blessings of knowledge and civilisation among all classes of the community.

Independently of the *violent* operation of Agrarian Laws, some authors have expressed their doubts, whether in some of the countries of Modern Europe, the subdivision of landed property has not been, in certain combinations of circumstances, carried to a pernicious excess, by the operation of *natural* causes. The following passage from Mr. Young's *Agricultural Survey of France,** (in the years 1787-89), will shew, that this doubt rests on something more than mere *hypothesis.* It is

* [That is, his *Travels in France during the Years* 1787, 1788, *and* 1789.]

proper for me to premise, that, according to his computation, the number of little farms in that kingdom belonging in property to the actual cultivators, was at that time so great as to occupy one-third of the whole territory.

"Before I travelled," says he, "I conceived that small farms in property were susceptible of good cultivation; and that the occupier of such having no rent to pay might be sufficiently at his ease to work improvements, and carry on a vigorous husbandry; but what I have seen in France has greatly lessened my good opinion of them. In Flanders I saw excellent husbandry on properties of thirty to one hundred acres; but we seldom find here such small patches of property as are common in other provinces. In Alsace, and on the Garonne, that is, on soils of such exuberant fertility as to demand no exertions, some small properties also are well cultivated. In Bearn I passed through a region of little farmers, whose appearance, neatness, and ease, charmed me; it was what property alone could on a small scale effect: but these were by no means contemptibly small; they were, as I judged by the distance from house to house, from forty to eighty acres. Except these, and a very few other instances, I saw nothing on small properties except a most unremitting industry." . . . "The circumstance which in France produces so immense a number of small farms in property, is the division which takes place after the death of the proprietor, commonly amongst *all* the children, but in some districts among the *sons* only. Forty or fifty acres in property are not incapable of good husbandry; but when divided, twenty acres *must* be ill cultivated; again divided, they become farms of ten acres, of five, of two, and even one; and I have even seen some of half, and even of a quarter of a rood, with a family as much attached to it as if it were an hundred acres. The population flowing from this division is, in some cases, great, but it is the multiplication of wretchedness. Couples marry and procreate, on the *idea*, not the *reality*, of a maintenance; they increase beyond the demand of towns and manufactures; and the consequence is distress, and numbers dying of diseases, arising from insufficient nourishment. Hence, therefore, small properties much divided, prove the greatest source of misery that can be conceived; and this has operated to such an extent in France, that" (in the opinion of Mr. Young) "a law undoubtedly ought to have been past, to render all division below a certain number of acres illegal."*

"If the industry of towns and manufactures were active enough to demand the surplus of all this population as fast as it arose, the advantages of the system would be clear. . . . It is idle to state in its favour the example of America, where an immensity of fertile land lies open to every one who will accept of it; and where population is valuable to an unexampled degree, as we see in the price of their labour. But what comparison between such a country and France, where the competition for employment is so great, (arising from too great a populousness,) that the price of labour is seventy-six per cent. below that of England, though the prices of provisions are as high in the former country as in the latter."†

These remarks of Mr. Young are chiefly levelled at some modern theories of Political Economy, according to which a country is flourishing in proportion to the equal distribution of the people over the territory; and "the greatest possible division of landed property is the best." That these maxims ought to be received with great restrictions appears obvious from this, that "on the supposition such a system were allowed time to operate, a nation would necessarily arrive at the limit beyond which the earth, cultivate it as you please, will feed no more mouths; yet those simple manners which instigate to marriage still continue. What, then, is the consequence, but the most dreadful misery imaginable! You soon would exceed the populousness of China, where the putrid carcases of domestic animals, and every species of vermin, are sought with avidity to sustain the lives of wretches who were born only to be starved."‡

* [*Travels in France during the Years* 1787, 1788, *and* 1789, *being an Agricultural Survey of the Kingdom*, p. 407, *seq.*]
† [Ibid. p. 410.] ‡ [Ibid. p. 409.]

Some of the foregoing remarks from Young have been suggested to him by the following passage in Sir James Steuart's *Political Œconomy*.

"I would recommend in countries where this minute subdivision of lands has taken place, that for the future none under a certain extent or value should be suffered to be divided among the children, but ordered to be sold, and the price divided among them, and that the same regulation should be observed upon the death of such proprietors where lands are not sufficient to produce three times the physical-necessary of the labourers. This would engage a people to exercise agriculture as a trade, and to give over that trifling husbandry which produces no surplus, and which involves so many poor people in the oppression of land-taxes. . . . The principle," he adds, " is so evident, that I never found any one who did not immediately agree to the justness of my observation; although in imposing land-taxes I have nowhere found it attended to."*

I have quoted these passages, because I am always much more anxious to suggest a variety of ideas for your examination, than to establish any particular system. I confess, for my own part, I have no doubt that, in so far as Agriculture and Population *alone* are concerned, *their* interests would be most effectually promoted by a perfectly free commerce of land. The evil complained of in France, plainly arose from the artificial value set on landed property, in consequence of prevailing institutions and habits. In a commercial country where there were *no* perpetuities, and *no* regard paid to primogeniture, the attachment to land would be nearly proportioned to its intrinsic value, and the *natural* course of things would bring small estates into the market, upon the death of every proprietor who left a numerous family. Nay more, this free commerce of land would put an end to that monopoly-price which it everywhere bears, and which, by diverting small capitals from such purchases, contributes perhaps more than any other cause to depress agriculture below the level of the commercial arts. In

* [Book V. Chap. xii.; *Works*, Vol. IV. p. 315.]

such a state of things, a law similar to that proposed by Sir James Steuart, would probably be found unnecessary; although I am far from asserting that in a country circumstanced as France *then* was, it might not have contributed to keep population more on a level with the means of subsistence.

The opinion, however, that we form on this point, is of little consequence, as the evils resulting from too minute a division of land must necessarily be confined to very unusual combinations of circumstances. Those which arise from the opposite extreme of an accumulation of this species of property in the hands of a small number of individuals, is a political disorder much more deeply rooted in our prevailing ideas and institutions, and affecting far more extensively and powerfully the general interests of society.

On this particular branch of our subject, which is perhaps the most important of all, I do not mean to enlarge at present, *partly* because it will again fall under consideration in the farther prosecution of my general plan; but *chiefly* because the effects of *Entails* and of the *Law of Primogeniture*, in checking the progress of agriculture, have been illustrated very fully by Mr. Smith. The remarks which this author has made on the circumstances from which these institutions naturally arose during the disorders and violence of the feudal times, are more especially deserving of attention, as they throw much light on the origin of that state of society, and system of manners, with which we are connected.

[ii.—*Second*, of Population (and Agriculture) considered in connexion with *Manufactures*.]

Having treated, at some length, [from p. 113,] of the *relation between Population and Agriculture*, in so far as it depends on the condition of the actual cultivators of the soil, and on the distribution of landed property, I proceed now to make some observations on the same subject, considered in connexion with the *influence of manufactures*.

"The proper and only right encouragement for agriculture," says Sir James Steuart, "is a moderate and gradual increase of demand for the productions of the earth; this works a natural and beneficial increase of inhabitants, and this demand must come from cities."* The author would, I think, have expressed his idea more unexceptionably, if he had contented himself with saying, that "the demand must come from *manufactures ;*" as the language he employs prejudges a much controverted question concerning the most beneficial form in which manufactures may be established, whether when collected into cities, or when scattered over a territory. In other respects, the observation is unquestionably just, and may be regarded as a fundamental principle in this inquiry. In truth, if we except the essential duty of protecting and maintaining the *rights* of the husbandman, the excitement of a spirit of manufacturing industry is the most effectual measure by which a statesman has it in his power, in the *actual* circumstances at least, of *this part of the world*, to influence the agriculture of his country. The seeming exceptions which may occur to this remark, (such as that of *Switzerland*, where, according to Mr. Hume, " we find at once the most skilful husbandmen and the most bungling tradesmen in Europe,")† do not in the least invalidate the general observation, as the effect, in all such instances, may be easily traced to some very peculiar and anomalous combinations of circumstances. And, at any rate, " Is it just reasoning," says Mr. Hume, " because agriculture may, in some cases, flourish without trade or manufactures, to conclude, that, in any great extent of country, or for any great tract of time, it would subsist alone ?" " The most *natural* way, surely, of encouraging agriculture, is, *first*, to excite other kinds of industry, and thereby afford the labourer a ready market for his commodities, and a return of such goods as may contribute to his pleasure and enjoyment. This method," he adds, " is *infallible* and *universal.*"‡

A few very slight remarks in illustration of this proposition will be sufficient for my present purpose.

Let us suppose then, a nation which practises no art but

* [*Political Œconomy*, Book I. chap. x.; *Works*, Vol. I. p. 70.]
† [*Essays*, Vol. I. Essay, *Of the Populousness of Ancient Nations.*]
‡ [Ibid.]

husbandry, and which subsists entirely on the rude produce of the soil. In such a situation, it is evident there would be no motive for the cultivator to increase his skill or industry beyond what is necessary for the bare support of himself and his family; for men will not labour merely from the patriotic view of increasing their numbers. The only thing that can quicken human industry, is the wants of men, real or imaginary; and these wants can be created only by the introduction of manufactures.

On a superficial view of the subject, it may perhaps appear that manufactures are rather the *effects* than the *causes* of that multiplicity of wants to which they are subservient; and that this has actually been the history of many of them, cannot be disputed. In general, however, it will be found, that refinements in the arts are more owing to the temptations held out by the industry and invention of the artists, than to the increased demand for the *novelties* they furnish, arising from the natural progress of luxury among their employers.

This has been well illustrated by the feelings which most persons must have experienced, *in some degree,* on visiting any of those shops which minister to the extravagance of a great city. Everything we see appears either necessary, or at least highly convenient; and we begin to wonder how we could have been so long without that which we never thought of before, and of which it is possible, after we are possessed of it, that we may never think again.[1]

A trifling anecdote mentioned by Dr. Franklin in one of his *Letters,* places the whole of this natural process in a stronger light than I can possibly do by any general observations. It exhibits at once the effects of imitation and fancy in creating a taste for superfluities, and the effect of this taste in stimulating human industry.

"The skipper of a shallop, employed between Cape May and Philadelphia, had done us some small service, for which he refused to be paid. My wife understanding that he had a

---

[1] Sir James Steuart, Vol. I. p. 178.—[*Political Œconomy*, Book II. chap. iii.; *Works*, Vol. I. p. 240.]

daughter, sent her a present of a new-fashioned cap. Three years after, this skipper being at my house with an old farmer of Cape May, his passenger, he mentioned the cap, and how much his daughter had been pleased with it. 'But,' said he, 'it proved a dear cap to our congregation.' 'How so?' 'When my daughter appeared with it at meeting, it was so much admired, that all the girls resolved to get such caps from Philadelphia; and my wife and I computed that the whole could not have cost less than a hundred pounds.' 'True,' said the farmer, 'but you do not tell all the story. I think the cap was nevertheless an advantage to us ; for it was the first thing that put our girls upon knitting worsted mittens for sale at Philadelphia, that they might have wherewithal to buy caps and ribbons there ; and you know that that industry has continued, and is likely to continue and increase to a much greater value, and answer *better purposes.*'"

In this simple narrative, we have a lively picture, in the first place, of the origin of *artificial wants ;* and, secondly, of their influence in encouraging that labour which multiplies the *necessaries and accommodations of life.* The same process is exhibited every day before our eyes in a thousand instances ; but in the *new world,* the political mechanism is less complicated, and its *principle* more obvious, while at the same time the rapidity with which the progress of improvement advances, magnifies the scale of observation. Nor must it be forgotten, that it is in consequence of the very peculiar circumstances in which mankind have there begun their career, that philosophers have been found whose attention was alive to such familiar incidents, and who were qualified to perceive the beautiful lights which they throw on the infancy of polished society.

While manufactures stimulate, in this manner, the industry of the husbandman, by multiplying his wants, they create, at the same time, a *market* for the rude produce of the earth, and communicating to him a portion of the commercial spirit, animate and enlighten his labours by the same motives to which the other lucrative arts owe their progress.

Hence it appears, that, in a civilized country, the importance of a great proportion of the people is to be estimated, not from the intrinsic value of what they produce, but from its subserviency to increase the industry of others. A hat, or a riband, or even a watch, may not in itself be very useful to a peasant, but if they lead him to increase his skill and his industry in order to be able to purchase them, and furnish employment to the artists who are to consume his surplus produce, an important advantage is gained. In this view manufacturers are useful members of the community, no less than husbandmen; and it may with truth be affirmed, that the artist who, in the centre of a populous town, is employed in polishing a button or a watch-chain, contributes to advance the agriculture of the state, as *really*, though not so immediately, as if with his own hands he threw the seed into the ground.

According to this view of the subject, it would appear that the great use of manufacturers in a State, is to set the husbandmen at work: and hence arises a most important distinction of labourers, into those who are *immediately* productive, and those who are instrumentally productive;—a distinction to which I shall have occasion to recur afterwards.

1. To prevent misapprehensions of what has been now stated, it is necessary to recollect, in the *first* place, that in these observations I confine my attention entirely to the policy of nations which *exclude the institution of Slavery*. If we appeal to the history of the ancient commonwealths, striking exceptions will immediately present themselves to our conclusions. But, as I have already repeatedly hinted, their systems of political economy were founded on principles, and had a reference to circumstances so essentially different from ours, that the consideration of the one can be of little use in illustrating the other, excepting in the way of contrast.

"In ancient times," says Sir James Steuart, "men were forced to labour the ground because they were slaves to others. In modern times, the operation is more complex; and as a modern statesman cannot make slaves of his subjects, he must engage them to become slaves to their own passions and desires. This is the only method to make them labour the ground; and provided this be accomplished, by whatever means it is brought about, mankind will increase."*

2. It must be remembered, also, that in the greater part of my reasonings, I have in view the *actual state of society in this part of Europe ;* that state of society I mean which resulted from the dissolution of the feudal system, and which (though on the whole more favourable to human improvement than any that ever existed before in the history of mankind) has been influenced by some powerful causes operating in a manner by no means agreeable to the general analogy of human affairs. Mr. Smith has shewn that, "according to the natural course of things, the greater part of the capital of every growing society is *first* directed to agriculture, *afterwards* to manufactures, and *last of all*, to foreign commerce. This order of things is so very natural, that in every society that had any territory, it has *always* perhaps been in some degree observed. Some of their lands must have been cultivated before any considerable towns could be established, and some sort of coarse industry of the manufacturing kind must have been carried on in these towns, before they could well think of employing themselves in foreign commerce.

"But though this natural order of things must have taken place in some degree in every such society, it has, in all the modern States of Europe, been in many respects entirely *inverted*. The foreign commerce of some of their cities has introduced all their finer manufactures, or such as were fit for distant sale; and manufacture and foreign commerce together, have given birth to the principal improvements of agriculture."† In what way things were forced into this unnatural and retrograde order by the manners and customs introduced by the feudal governments, Mr. Smith has explained with great ingenuity in the Third Book of his *Wealth of Nations.*

The case is very different in the States of America, the wealth of which is founded entirely on agriculture, and where (as one of their own writers [Franklin ?] expresses it) "the industry of

* [*Political Œconomy*, Book I. chap. xxi.; *Works*, Vol. I. p. 204.]   † [*Wealth of Nations*, Book III. chap. iv.]

man, in its first movements, attaches itself to the bosom of our common parent, as the infant hangs upon the breast of its mother."[1] In that quarter of the globe, besides, there are other circumstances which discriminate the condition of the inhabitants so essentially from that of European nations, that in speculations no parallel ought to be attempted between them. It is sufficient to mention the extreme cheapness of uncultivated land, and the extraordinary profits which may be made by the employment, either of a great or of a small capital in its improvement.

I thought it of particular consequence to state this last circumstance, because it has been frequently overlooked by very respectable political writers. Impressed strongly (it is probable) with the beauty and excellence of that *order* which (according to Mr. Smith) would everywhere have regulated the course of improvement, if it had not been disturbed by human institutions, they have indulged themselves in general unqualified maxims, the truth of which is obvious and striking wherever this order has been realized, but which are unfortunately not applicable, without many limitations, to that state of things in which we are more peculiarly interested. "Agriculture," says the anonymous author of a late *Essay on Taxation of Income*, "as the first and most important object with all nations of territory, should be carried to the greatest possible perfection, before any considerable encouragement is given to manfactures. It ought, indeed, to be considered as the life and soul of all manufactures, which will everywhere prosper and flourish, nearly in proportion as the agriculture of the country is more or less in a state of perfection."[2]

"Is there any profession or business," says Mr. A. Young, "which ought to be advanced to the height it is capable of, before others are encouraged which draw off the working hands from the former?" .... "The answer," he adds, "is clear, precise, and determinate. Agriculture, that greatest of all *manufactures*, ought to flourish to the full cultivation of the

---

[1] *Memorial addressed to the Sovereigns of Europe*, &c. Almon, 1780.

[2] *Three Essays*, &c. (London, 1799,) p. 116. [By Benjamin Bell, Esq.]

land, before what we *commonly call* 'manufactures' take place as articles of trade and commerce. And after cultivation is at its height, those manufactures ought first to be encouraged which work upon materials of our own growth ; and last of all, those which employ foreign materials."[1]

In this passage, Mr. Young has described exactly what Mr. Smith calls the *natural* progress of opulence in a country. This progress, however, it has been already observed, has been in a great measure *inverted* in Modern Europe; and the causes which have produced this effect are beyond the control of any statesman. If we wish our speculations, therefore, to be practically useful, we must attend to the actual circumstances of the case; applying our reasonings (if I may borrow the homely language of a very old English writer) "to the Common Wealth *as it is*, not as a philosopher may frame it by discourse, imitating herein, not a *breaker* of horses, whose part it is to perfect the horse in all his *natural* actions, but a good *rider*, who must strive to use him to the best advantage, such as he finds him."

The encouragement indeed which some modern statesmen have given to manufactures, has been founded on very partial and erroneous views, and has contributed powerfully to counteract that effect on agricultural improvement, which they are naturally calculated to produce, wherever their operation is not thwarted by injudicious systems of policy. Much, too, remains to be done in most countries to forward the progress of husbandry, by removing those obstacles which were thrown in its way during the ignorance and barbarism of former times, and which, however consecrated in the estimation of our ancestors by ancient prejudices, are widely at variance with the just and liberal ideas of the present age.

I have already hinted, that although manufactures and commerce have a more powerful tendency than any other cause whatever to quicken Agriculture, it is nevertheless possible, by an injudicious policy, to encourage the former at the expense of the latter. It has been supposed by the most

[1] *Farmers' Letters*, &c., [1767,] pp. 3, 4.

intelligent French writers, that this was the radical error in the administration of the celebrated *Colbert;* and the effects which it produced are represented as of the most ruinous nature. The subject is interesting, as it is intimately connected with the history of what has been since called the *Economical* or *Agricultural* System of Political Economy.

"*Colbert,*" says M. de Boulainvilliers, "to whom Lewis confided the care of augmenting his power by an augmentation of commerce, raised his edifice before he had laid the foundation. He saw the grandeur of the monarchy through the medium of manufactures, instead of viewing these in their due subserviency to the productions of the soil. He fixed his attention too much upon the Arts, and too little upon Agriculture; always fabricating, but never creating. His genius embraced every part of the detail, but was incapable of rising to the comprehensive views of a legislator. The minister was lost in the manufacturer. In spite of his high reputation, (a reputation acquired by all who make great changes in a government,) he projected none of those masterly designs" (those *coups d'état*) "which decide the fortune of a nation. He moved on in a beaten track without ever venturing to strike out a path of his own."*

The substance of various other censures bestowed by the French political writers on the administration of Colbert, is collected into one view in the following passage of [the Rev.] Mr. Harte's *Essays on Husbandry*, [1764.] My principal reason for transcribing it is, that the author (who was himself a practical farmer) had an opportunity in the course of his travels, of examining the agriculture of France with much accuracy; and, therefore, his judgment on this point possesses a weight which does not belong to the assertions of common observers.

"Colbert rather depressed than promoted the interests of his country, when he conceived a project of enriching it by establishing a vast number of manufactures; flattering himself, at the same time, that by making the productions of his

* [*Etat de la France*, &c.]

manufactures subservient to luxury and falsely refined elegance, he should multiply the wealth of his own nation by supplying and feeding the extravagance and vanity of other nations; but some part of the folly happened to stick where it took its rise, and became infectious at home; which shews that luxury is an unfortunate fashion in any country, though at the same time it prescribes the mode to foreigners, and induces them to purchase such merely ornamental elegancies as are the workmanship of our own artists. Under the idea of hoarding up great quantities of provisions for the support of his work-folks, (and that principally by obstructing the free vent and exportation of corn,) this minister had the applause of the poor, who naturally favour every scheme, real or imaginary, that promises to lower the price of bread; for their understandings can rarely see deeply into the truth of things, any more than the advantage of a nation in general, or of themselves upon the whole. In like manner the historians and poets loaded the Prime Minister with panegyrics, as the true father of the people, and made no ceremony to depreciate the wiser conduct of *Sully*. But, alas! it never truly appeared that trade and commerce, even in their most flourishing state, enriched a kingdom like the solid revenues that proceed from a right and effectual cultivation of the earth. Thus, though the French nation was intoxicated with the hopes of immense riches, and though they supplied all Europe with silks and embroideries and expensive trifles, yet the fund of real wealth was deficient at bottom; *famine made its appearance frequently and almost periodically*. The proprietors of landed estates (for they with others at first ran into the universal notion of admiring the project) thought themselves very happy, after a considerable tract of time, to advance their rents a *sixth* part, though money bore *one-third* a greater value than before; imposts and taxes were increased immoderately; and a considerable part of the lands (not being found, or at least not believed to answer the expenses of cultivation) was overlooked and neglected by little and little, and at length degenerated into waste and desolated tracts of country. All which may suffice to shew, that the cultivation of the earth ought not to be superseded by a passion for commerce."*

The great features of Colbert's policy are still more strongly and distinctly marked in the following slight outline of Mr. Smith.

" Accustomed by the habits of his education to regulate the different departments of public offices, and to establish the necessary checks and controls for confining each to its proper sphere, Colbert endeavoured to regulate the industry and commerce of a great country upon the same model; and instead of allowing every man to pursue his own interest his own way, upon the liberal plan of equality, liberty, and justice, he bestowed upon certain branches of industry extraordinary privileges, while he laid others under as extraordinary restraints. He was not only disposed, like other European ministers, to encourage more the industry of the towns than that of the country, but in order to support the industry of the towns, he was willing even to depress and keep down that of the country. In order to render provisions cheap to the inhabitants of the towns, and thereby to encourage manufactures and foreign commerce, he prohibited altogether the exportation of corn, and thus excluded the inhabitants of the country from every foreign market, for by far the most important part of the produce of their industry. This prohibition, joined to the restraints imposed by the ancient provincial laws of France, upon the transportation of corn from one province to another, and to the arbitrary and degrading taxes which are levied upon the cultivators in almost all the provinces, discouraged and kept down the agriculture of that country very much below the state to which it would naturally have risen in so very fertile a soil, and so very happy a climate. This state of discouragement and depression was felt more or less in every different part of the country, and many different inquiries were set on foot concerning the causes of it. *One* of those causes appeared to be the preference given by the institutions of *Colbert* to the industry of the towns above that of the country ;"† or, in other words, to Manufactures in preference to Agriculture.

* [L. l.]   † [*Wealth of Nations*, B. IV. c. ix.; Vol. III. pp 2, 3, tenth edition.]

The result of these speculations in France, was the *Economical system of M. Quesnai*, of which I shall have occasion to treat afterwards, and which Mr. Smith accuses of a fundamental error, the *reverse* of that which misled *Colbert*, but equally wide of the truth;—the error of undervaluing that species of industry to which Colbert had in a great measure confined his encouragement.

It is not necessary for me at present to inquire how far Mr. Smith's censure, in this instance, is well founded. I confess, for my own part, that he appears to me to have carried it *too far*, and that I think his criticisms apply rather to the *language* which the Economists have used, than to the substance of their doctrine when fully unfolded. *One* indisputable conclusion, at least, results from the facts which they have stated, that however powerfully manufactures may tend to stimulate agriculture under the influence of wise and equal laws, it is *possible*, not only for the former to flourish without a correspondent progress in the latter, but that the comparative encouragement which they receive from Government may be so great, as to withdraw from the other its natural share of capital and of industry.

It will appear afterwards, that the advantages of manufactures in encouraging agricultural industry, are *explicitly acknowledged*, and indeed strongly stated, by all the *Economical* writers; and therefore, their opinions must *not be confounded* with those maintained by *Mr. Arthur Young*, in his *Agricultural Survey of France*,* where he asserts that " there is something in manufactures *pestiferous to agriculture*." It is remarkable, indeed, of this author, (to whose industry and activity the public unquestionably lies under great obligations,) that notwithstanding the asperity with which he generally speaks, particularly in his later works, of the *Economists*, he has carried that part of their system which Mr. Smith considers as the most paradoxical of the whole, far beyond the limits assigned to it by their principles. As the illustrations, however, which Mr. Young has collected, are interesting and valuable, I shall (agreeably to my general plan) select some of the most strik-

* [That is, his *Travels in France*.]

ing facts which he has mentioned in support of his argument; although my knowledge of local circumstances is much too imperfect to enable me to remove completely the objections which they may suggest to some of the foregoing reasonings.

"The greatest fabrics of *France* are the cottons and woollens of Normandy, the woollens of Picardy and Champagne, the linens of Brittany, and the silks and hardware of the Lyonnais. Now, if manufactures be the true encouragement of agriculture, the vicinity of these great fabrics ought to be the best cultivated districts in the kingdom, whereas the fact is very strikingly the reverse. Considering the fertility of the soil, which is great, *Picardy* and *Normandy* are among the worst cultivated countries I have seen. The immense fabrics of Abbeville and Amiens have not caused the enclosure of a single field, or the banishment of fallows from a single acre. Go from Elbœuf to Rouen, if you would view a desert; and the *Pays de Caux*, possessing one of the richest soils in the world, with manufactures in every hut and cottage, presents one continued scene of weeds, filth, and beggary; a soil so villanously managed, that if it were not naturally of an inexhaustible fertility, it would long ago have been utterly ruined. The agriculture of *Champagne* is miserable, even to a proverb: I saw there great and flourishing manufactures, and cultivation in ruins around them. In *Brittany*, which affords but one spectacle, that of a dreary, desolate waste, you find yourself in the midst of one of the greatest linen manufactures in Europe, and throwing your eye around the country, can scarcely believe the inhabitants are fed by agriculture; if they subsisted by the chase of wild animals, their country might be as well cultivated. From hence across the kingdom to *Lyons*, all the world knows the immense fabrics found there; and yet we are told by a very competent judge, M. Roland de la Platiêre, 'de toutes les provinces de France le Lyonnais est le plus misérable.' What I saw of it gave me little reason to question the assertion. The remark of another French writer makes the experiment double. '*L'Artois* est un des provinces les plus riches du Royaume.—C'est une vérité incontestable . . . elle ne possède point de manufactures.'—I will not presume to assert that the agriculture of these districts is bad, *because* they abound with manufactures, though I believe it to be very much the case in the Pays de Caux; I merely state the facts. *The fabrics are the greatest in the kingdom, and certainly the agriculture is among the worst.*"*

In farther confirmation of the same view of the subject, Mr. Young refers to some facts stated in his *Tour through Ireland* many years ago,† with respect to the effects of the vast linen manufacture which spreads all over the north of that kingdom. "*There,*" says he, "I found the same spectacle that Brittany offers; husbandry so miserably, so contemptibly bad, that I have shewn by calculation the whole province converted into a sheep-walk, and feeding but two sheep per acre, would yield, in wool only, a greater value than the whole amount of the linen fabric; a circumstance I attribute entirely to the manufacture spreading into the country, instead of being confined to towns. ' *Wherever the linen manufacture spreads, there tillage is bad,*' said that attentive observer, the Lord Chief Baron Forster. The Earl of Tyrone has an estate in the county of Derry, amidst manufactures, and another in that of Waterford, where there are none; and he assured me that if the Derry land were in Waterford, or absolutely freed from fabrics, he should clear full one-third more money from it. If we pass into *England*, we shall find something similar, though not in an equal degree; the manufacturing parts of the kingdom being among the worst cultivated. You must not go for agriculture to Yorkshire, Lancashire, Warwickshire, or Gloucestershire, which are full of fabrics, but to *Kent*, where there is not the trace of a fabric; to *Berkshire*, *Hertfordshire*, and *Suffolk*, where there are scarcely any: *Norwich* affords an exception, being the only manufacture in the kingdom in a thoroughly well-cultivated district, which must very much be attributed to the fabric being kept remarkably within the city, and spreading (spinning excepted) not much into the country; a circumstance that de-

* [*Travels in France during the Years* 1787, 1788, *and* 1789; *being an Agricultural Survey of the Kingdom*, p. 507, *seq.*]

† [In 1776-1779.]

serves attention, as it confirms strongly the preceding observations. But the two counties of Kent and Lancaster are expressly to the purpose, because they form a double experiment: Lancaster is the most manufacturing province in England, and amongst the *worst* cultivated; Kent has not the shadow of a manufacture, and is perhaps the *best* cultivated.

"*Italy* will furnish instances yet more to the purpose than any yet cited. The richest and most flourishing countries in Europe, in proportion to their extent, are probably *Piedmont* and the *Milanese*. All the signs of prosperity are there met with; populousness well employed and well supported, a great export without, a thriving consumption within, magnificent roads, numerous and wealthy towns, circulation active, interest of money low, and the price of labour high. In a word, you can name no circumstance that shall prove Manchester, Birmingham, Rouen, and Lyons to be in a prosperous state, that is not found diffused throughout the whole of these countries. To what is all this prosperity to be ascribed? Certainly not to manufactures, because they possess hardly the trace of a fabric. There are a few of no consideration at Milan, and there are in Piedmont the silk-mills, to give the first hand to that product, but on the whole to an amount so very trifling, that both countries must be considered as *without* fabrics. They are equally without commerce, being excluded from the sea; and though there is a navigable river that passes through both these territories, yet no use is made of it, for there are five sovereigns between Piedmont and its mouth, all of whom lay duties on the transit of every sort of merchandise. As these two countries do not owe their riches to manufactures or commerce, so undoubtedly they are not indebted for them to any peculiar felicity in their governments. Both are despotisms; and the despot of Milan makes that country a beast of burden to Germany; the revenues are remitted to Vienna, and the clothes, even for the troops, paid by Milan, come from Germany. The origin and the support of all the wealth of these countries are to be found in agriculture alone, which is carried to such perfection, as to prove that it is equal to the sole support of a modern and most flourishing society, to keep that society in a state of great wealth, and to enable the governments to be, in proportion to their extent, doubly more powerful than either France or England. Piedmont supports a regal court, and pays 30,000 men. The same extent of country, or number of people, effect the half of this in any other dominion of Europe. But are these territories really without manufactures? No; nor is any country in the world: it is not possible to find a people totally exempt from them. The present inquiry demands no such exemption: it is only necessary to shew that the manufactures found in the Milanese and Piedmont, are such as arise absolutely in consequence of agriculture; that it is agriculture which supports and nourishes them; and that on the contrary these manufactures are so far from doing anything politically for agriculture, that they occasion the exposing of it to restrictions and monopolies; for the governments in these countries have been bitten by the same madness of commerce that has infected other kingdoms; and have attempted by such means to raise these trifling fabrics into foreign export. Happily they have never been able to do it; for there is reason to imagine, that success would have suggested other restrictions unfavourable to the great foundation of all their prosperity. Thus the instances produced are expressly to the purpose, as they exhibit two opulent States, supported by agriculture alone, and possessing no other manufactures or commerce than what every country must possess that enjoys a flourishing cultivation; for it is not to be expected that such great results are to be found attending common exertions only. On the contrary, those that have converted part of those noble territories into a garden, have been great and exemplary."*

These facts are certainly highly deserving of attention, and I have no doubt that, if they were accurately examined, they would throw much new and important light on this subject. It is indeed only by thus bringing fairly into view the apparent exceptions that occur to our general principles, that we can

* [Pp. 508-510.]

either hope to limit them with the necessary precision, when they have been stated in too unqualified terms, or can be enabled to exhibit in full force the important truths they may involve.

It seems to have been with the design of bringing this very subject under public discussion, that the Abbé Raynal, about ten years ago, [c. 1790,] remitted a sum of money to the Royal Society of Agriculture at Paris, as a prize for the best Dissertation on the following question:—" *Whether does a flourishing Agriculture tend more to promote the prosperity of Manufactures, or the growth of Manufactures to promote the prosperity of Agriculture?*" Of the *Essays* which appeared on this occasion, I have never heard any account.

A few very slight general remarks is all that I propose to offer at present on Mr. Young's statement. To examine it in detail, would lead me into a field of boundless extent, and would require a knowledge of local circumstances, not to be acquired but by personal observation. Of the inconclusiveness, however, of a beadroll of facts so loosely stated, a judgment may be formed by directing our attention to *one* of those instances on which Young lays the greatest stress, the flourishing state of agriculture in the county of *Kent*, in which he asserts *there is not a shadow of a manufacture.* How far this assertion is well founded, may be judged of from the statements of a very accurate and intelligent writer, whose observations were published more than twenty years before those of Mr. Young, —I mean Campbell [?] in his *Agriculture of Kent.* After remarking that " in respect of plenty, *Kent* is another Canaan, fruitful in all good things, and in which there are fewer forests and waste lands than in most other counties," he continues in the same tenor, through passages to which I shall only refer.[1]

I have no doubt that Young's other instances, if carefully examined, would be found equally irrelevant to the question now under consideration, but I must not prosecute this view of the subject any farther. My principal reason for referring to it

---

[1] Vol. I. pp. 386, 402, 408. But in regard to Kent, we ought also to take into account the vicinity of London, and the practice of Gavil Kind.

was to point it out as an object of curiosity, and to show that the question concerning the reciprocal effects of agriculture and of manufactures, is still far from being exhausted.

That Mr. Young's facts do not warrant the general conclusion, that "there is something *pestiferous* to agriculture in the neighbourhood of a manufacture," we may venture to assert with confidence. They prove, indeed, in a striking manner, the miserable effects produced in France, by the discouragements under which agriculture has laboured in that country; and that manufactures of themselves can do little where the rights of the husbandman are not only insecure, but systematically violated. Nay, farther, they prove that in such a state of things the encouragement which is given to the industry of towns may withdraw from agriculture some part of the capital which it would otherwise have employed even in its actual state of depression. Wherever this is the case, the effect may be expected to be most conspicuous in the *neighbourhood* of extensive manufactures; and, in fact, (as Mr. Young has hinted,) something of the same kind, though in a very inferior degree, has been remarked in England. Where large manufactures are established, yielding much more tempting profits than can be obtained by agriculture, the wages given to workmen will naturally attract the labourers from the surrounding districts, and its money capital will have a tendency to follow the same direction. Landholders and farmers will both be induced either to form mercantile connexions themselves, or to establish their sons in trade; and in this manner, notwithstanding the curious and refined husbandry exhibited on the small properties of a few individuals enriched by commerce, agriculture in general will languish, from the failure of the funds destined by the natural course of things for its support and encouragement.[1]

It does not, however, follow from all this, either that manufactures are unfavourable in their general tendency, or that they have, *even in France*, prevented agriculture from advancing so rapidly as it would have done, if they had not existed in

[1] Bell's Pamphlet, p. 119. [*Three Essays*, &c., 1799.]

that kingdom. They may have intercepted *part* of the industry and capital which would otherwise have gone to the improvement of land, without counterbalancing by this inconvenience their salutary effects on the agricultural industry of the whole territory.

It has been shewn by Mr. Smith, that " the greatest and most important branch of the commerce of every nation is, that which is carried on between the inhabitants of the town and those of the country. The inhabitants of the town draw from the country the rude produce which constitutes both the materials of their work, and the fund of their subsistence; and they pay for this rude produce, by sending back to the inhabitants of the country a certain portion of it manufactured and prepared for immediate use. The trade which is carried on between these two different sets of people, consists ultimately in a certain quantity of rude produce exchanged for a certain quantity of manufactured produce. The dearer the latter, therefore, the cheaper the former; and whatever tends in any country to raise the price of manufactured produce, tends to lower that of the rude produce of the land, and thereby to discourage agriculture. The smaller the quantity of manufactured produce which any given quantity of rude produce is capable of purchasing, the smaller the rude value of that given quantity of rude produce, the smaller, of consequence, is the encouragement which either the landlord has to increase its quantity by improving, or the farmer by cultivating his land." It has been shewn also, that " whatever tends in any country to diminish the number of artificers and manufacturers, tends to diminish the home market, the most important of all markets for the rude produce of the land, and thereby to discourage agriculture still farther."[1] That the only possible way to make a *manufacture* thrive, is to procure a ready vent for the goods it furnishes, was never once disputed; and why should we doubt that the same maxim applies to agriculture, which Young himself has repeatedly and justly called " the most important *of*

---

[1] *Wealth of Nations*, Vol. II. p. 286. [Book IV. chap. ix.; Vol. III. pp. 40, 41, tenth edition.]

all manufactures;" and which (as he has remarked after Sir James Steuart, in numberless parts of his works, [see above, pp. 141, 142]) is to be considered in Modern Europe not merely as a means of subsistence for the cultivators, but as one of the *trades* which enter into the general system of Political Economy?

On this point, indeed, we may fairly quote one part of Mr. Young's works against another. "The manufactures of the single city of Norwich (he observes in a book published in 1780) amount to as much as the whole linen export of Ireland, but it is very far from being the *whole* exported produce of the county of Norfolk. On the contrary, this county, besides feeding its capital, besides feeding Yarmouth and Lynn, two of the greatest ports in England, and a variety of other towns, exports, I believe, more corn than any other county in the kingdom; and whoever is acquainted with the supply of the London markets, knows that there are thousands of black cattle fattened every year on Norfolk turnips, and sent to Smithfield. What a spectacle is this! The most productive agriculture in the world, in the way of exportation, around one of the greatest manufactures in Europe. It is thus that manufactures become the best friends to agriculture, that they animate the farmer's industry by giving him ready markets, until he is able not only to supply them fully, but pushes his exertions with such effect, that he finds a surplus in his hands to convert into gold in the national balance, by rendering foreigners tributary for their bread. Examine all the other fabrics in the kingdom, you see them prodigious markets for the surrounding lands; you see those lands doubling, trebling, quadrupling their rents, while the farmers increase daily in wealth. Thus you see manufactures rearing up agriculture, and agriculture supporting manufactures. You see a reaction which gives a reciprocal animation to human labour: Great national prosperity is the effect. Wealth pours in from the fabrics, which, spreading like a fertilizing stream over all the surrounding lands, renders them, comparatively speaking, so many gardens, the most pleasing spectacles of successful industry."*

* [*Tour through Ireland*, &c.]

I cannot help adding to these extracts from Mr. Young, that I do not know of any author in our language whose writings abound more with inconsistencies and contradictions. This is more particularly remarkable in the general principles relating to Political Economy which he has interwoven with his different Agricultural *Tours*.

In the passages *now* under consideration, the inconsistency of his conclusions arises, in part, from his confounding together (in the extract which I quoted from his account of France) two questions which are essentially different. The *one* is the *general* question concerning the influence of manufactures on agriculture; the *other* is the question concerning the comparative effects of manufactures when confined to towns, and when spread over the country.

The confusion which runs through Mr. Young's *later* speculations on this subject, is the more remarkable, that in his *Tours through Ireland,* [1776, &c.] he has been at pains to distinguish these two questions, enlarging on the beneficial influence of manufactures in the *one* case, and on their ruinous effects in the *other*. I before remarked, (if I am not mistaken,) that this work bears fewer marks of haste and negligence, than most of his other publications.

"In the north of *Ireland* you behold a whole province peopled by weavers; it is they who cultivate, or rather beggar the soil, as well as work the looms. Agriculture is there in ruins; it is cut up by the root, extirpated, annihilated; the whole region is the disgrace of the kingdom. No other part of Ireland can exhibit the soil in such a state of poverty and desolation.

"But the cause of all these evils, which are absolutely exceptions to everything else on the face of the globe, is easily found;—a most prosperous manufacture, so contrived as to be the destruction of agriculture, is certainly a spectacle for which we must go to Ireland. It is owing to the fabric spreading over all the country, instead of being confined to towns. This in a certain degree is found in some manufactures in England, but never to the exclusion of farmers; whereas, literally speaking, there is not a farmer in a hundred miles of the linen country in Ireland. The lands are infinitely subdivided; no weaver thinks of supporting himself by his loom; he has always a patch of potatoes, of oats, or of flax, and grass or weeds for a cow; so that his time is divided between his loom and his farm. The land is sown with successive crops of oats, until it does not produce the seed again, and then left to become grass as it may, in which state it is under weeds and rubbish for four or five years. As land thus managed will not yield rent, they depend for that on their web. If linen sells indifferently, they pay their rents indifferently; and if it sells badly, they do not pay them at all: rents in general being worse paid there than in any other part of Ireland.

"But if instead of the manufacture having so diffused itself as absolutely to banish farmers, it had been confined to *towns*, the very contrary effect would have taken place, and all those vast advantages to agriculture would have followed, which flourishing manufactures in other countries occasion. The towns would have been large and numerous, and would have proved such ample markets to all the adjacent country, that *it could not have failed* to become well cultivated, and to let at double the present rent. The manfacturers would have been confined to their own business, and the farmers to theirs; and both trades would have flourished the better for this arrangement."[1]

If this reasoning of Mr. Young's be just, it will go far to account for the very extraordinary facts I quoted *on his authority*, with respect to the state of manufacturing and of agricultural industry in *France ;* for he tells us that the poor all over that kingdom abound with *domestic* manufactures. The culture of hemp or flax, in particular, for home uses, prevails (according to him) *universally :* And in so far as this is the case, no advocate for manufactures, however sanguine, could possibly expect from them any beneficial effects on husbandry. If every family in the country have a patch of flax or hemp for its own supply of all the articles manufactured from these

[1] [*Tour through Ireland,* &c.] Vol. II. p. 162.

materials, the exchanges between the country and the town are in the same proportion diminished; and if a similar practice were extended to every other article, the circulation would stop completely. The farmer would have nothing to *buy*, and would soon have nothing to *sell*. "A countryman thus living on his own little property, industriously employed with his family in manufacturing for all their own wants, exhibits, it must be owned, a pleasing spectacle of simple and sober manners, but of manners perfectly inconsistent with the prosperity of a great society in the actual circumstances of Modern Europe."[1]

Various other particulars, in Mr. Young's statement, which have a very paradoxical aspect at first view, would probably appear in a different light, if we were acquainted with all the circumstances. Thus, in the *Pays de Caux*, (the country, to wit, from Havre to Rouen,) upon which he has laid particular stress, the difficulty is completely explained by some facts mentioned by Young himself, on a different occasion. "The soil," we are informed, "is among the finest in France. The number of small properties, and consequently population, is very great, which is the reason for the price and rental of land through this country being vastly out of proportion to the products. Landlords also divide their farms according to the demand, as the rise of rent tempts it; but they often find themselves depending for the rent of their land on the prosperity of a fabric. Had the *Pays de Caux* been a miserably poor, rocky, or barren territory, the result would have been beneficial, for the fabric would have covered such a district with cultivation."[†]

Mr. Young informs us further, that the farmers in the *Pays de Caux* are not only manufacturers, but have an inclination also for trade. The large ones engage in commercial speculations at Havre, particularly in the cotton trade, and some even in that of the West Indies. "This," he adds, "is a most pernicious circumstance; the improvement of their cultivation being never the object or result of their growing rich, but merely the engaging more largely in trade or manufacture. If

---

[1] Young, [*Travels through France,*] p. 504.   † [Ibidem, p. 505, *seq.*]

they get a share in an American adventure, no matter whether docks and thistles cover their fields."* Such facts are abundantly curious; but it is surely unfair to state merely the general result, without any specification of the peculiarities of the case, in order to invalidate the important doctrine of the influence of manufactures on the improvement of a country.

I shall take this opportunity of remarking, (as a more convenient one may not occur afterwards,) that Mr. Young's assertions, with respect to the pernicious effects of domestic manufactures, (an opinion, by the way, in which he has persevered more uniformly than in most of his other general principles,) are stated in too unqualified a form. Dr. Crumpe, in an *Essay* which gained the prize from the Irish Academy, expresses strong doubts (founded on some observations communicated to him by Dr. Burrowes) whether Mr. Young's description of the farming manufacturers in Ulster is not highly exaggerated. And at any rate, the circumstances of that people are too peculiar, in many other respects, to authorize us to draw from them any general conclusions. The same remark may be applied to this opinion, in so far as it rests on the state of agriculture in France.

It is certainly true in general, that the two employments of a farmer and a manufacturer will be carried on to greater perfection when divided, than when united in one person. "A country weaver," as Mr. Smith observes, "who cultivates a small farm, must lose a good deal of time in passing from his loom to his field, and from the field to the loom. A man commonly saunters a little in turning his hand from one sort of employment to another; and this renders him almost always slothful and lazy, and incapable of any vigorous application even on the most pressing occasions."†

Although, however, it follows from this, that a domestic manufacture must *always* be a most unprofitable employment for an individual who depends chiefly for his subsistence on the produce of a farm, the converse of the proposition seems to

* [Ibidem, p. 506.]
† [*Wealth of Nations*, Book I. chap. i.; Vol. I. pp. 13, 14, tenth edition.]

require some limitations. A man, indeed, who exercises a trade which occupies him from day to day, must, of necessity, be disqualified for the management of such agricultural concerns as require a constant and undivided attention. But it does not appear equally evident, how the improvement of the country should be injured by his possessing a few acres as an employment for his hours of recreation; nor does it seem likely, on the other hand, that his professional skill and industry will be more impaired by his occasional labour in the fields, than by those habits of intemperate dissipation in which all workmen who have no variety of pursuit are prone to indulge.

The manufacture of our national broad-cloth, affords a contrast to some of the examples mentioned by *Young*. " This manufacture," as is remarked by a late writer *On Taxation of Income*,* " is almost everywhere carried on by unconnected workmen, who employ all the hours which they devote to relaxation and amusement, in the care of their garden and other small portions of ground which they happen to possess, to which they and their families become commonly so much attached, that they have been known to remain in them (small as their properties commonly are) for many generations. Nor does the possession of this variety make them worse tradesmen; on the contrary, this class of manufacturers are everywhere noted for their industry, and the article which they furnish, which has long been considered as the staple commodity of our country, is the best and most perfect of its kind that can anywhere be met with."†

The advantages to health and to morals attending manufactures of this description, when compared with the effects of manufacturing towns, are so great that some political writers have gone so far as to assert, that it is only when spread over the face of a country they can be considered as a public benefit. Mirabeau, [the son,] in his book *On the Prussian Monarchy*, maintains this opinion, and lays it down as a general

---

* [Mr. Benjamin Bell, the eminent Surgeon of Edinburgh, in *Three Essays*, &c., 1799.] † [*Three Essays*, &c., pp. 132, 133.]

proposition, "That great manufactures belonging to individuals who hire workmen by the day, can never form an object worthy of the attention of Government."[1]

In stating these considerations I would not be understood to deny the truth of Young's reasonings in favour of manufacturing towns compared with *scattered* manufactures; for I am sensible that much may be alleged in support of his system. But he has unquestionably carried it too far, by keeping completely out of view the arguments which favour the opposite conclusion. The fact is, that in all human establishments we may expect to find a mixture of good and of evil; and the only question is, which of the two preponderates? It is sufficient for me in the case of *this* incidental question, to have suggested some doubts in opposition to Mr. Young's unqualified assertions. The prosecution of the discussion would lead me too far aside from my principal subject.[2]

It is not, however, only by the peculiarity in the manufacturing establishments of France, which has occasioned this digression, that Mr. Young has complicated the general question concerning the influence of Manufactures on Agriculture. Much depends on the *species* of manufactures that are established in a country; and in this respect the choice of *Colbert* seems to have been guided by narrow and erroneous principles. The manufactures which he encouraged were chiefly those which minister to luxury and to elegance; the demand for which depending to so great a degree on fashion and caprice cannot be so constant and steady as for articles which are subservient to the real wants and necessities of mankind. It has been observed in our own country, that the manufacturers of Norwich, who deal in fine crapes and other delicate stuffs, are laid idle three times for once that the Yorkshire manufacturer, who deals chiefly in low-priced serviceable cloths, experiences a similar misfortune.[3] The disturbances which have so often

---

[1] Tome III. p. 109. Young, [*Travels in France*,] p. 505.

[2] Some important remarks on the disadvantages of cities are made by Sir James Steuart, [*Political Œconomy,*] Book I. chap. x.; [*Works*, Vol. I. p. 65, *seq.*]

[3] Anderson, *On National Industry*, p. 57.

been occasioned by the silk-weavers of Spitalfields, and which have exceeded any that have taken place among the other classes of our manufacturers, have been ascribed partly to the same circumstance. This error, however, has been long perceived and corrected in France; and, under the old government, a variety of the most useful manufactures were advancing rapidly to perfection.

The Manufactures that, in addition to their other advantages, draw from the farmer the materials on which they depend, and thereby present a new *stimulus* to Agriculture, possess undoubtedly great advantages over those that work up materials imported from abroad. Some remarks on this subject that deserve attention, blended with other speculations of less consequence, may be found in Dr. Anderson's *Observations on the Means of Exciting a Spirit of National Industry in Scotland.*

I have been led into these observations (which have extended to a much greater length than I expected) by the passage quoted from Mr. Young's *Account of France*, in which he has plainly lost sight of some important general principles, to the truth of which he has, on other occasions, borne ample testimony. If I should be thought, in stating them, to have sometimes forgotten the general title under which they were introduced, I have only to remark, by way of apology, (in the words of Sir James Steuart,) "that the complicated mechanism of society in modern times, (so different from the simplicity of ancient manners,) has rendered almost every disorder in the political body an obstacle to that useful *population* that constitutes national strength."* This, it is evident, holds more particularly true of every disorder which affects agricultural industry.

Before concluding my observations on Agriculture and Manufactures considered in their relation to population, I cannot help remarking once more, the extravagance of general decla-

* [*Political Œconomy*, Book I. chap. xii.; *Works*, Vol. I. p. 91; the meaning, but not the words, identical.]

mations in favour of Agriculture when accompanied with invectives against those employments from which the farmer derives his market. It is very justly observed by Mr. Smith, that those systems which, in order to promote Agriculture, would impose restraints upon manufacturing and foreign trade, act contrary to the very end which they propose, and indirectly discourage that very species of industry which they mean to promote. They are so far more inconsistent than even the system which would encourage manufactures and foreign trade in preference to Agriculture; inasmuch as the latter, while it turns a certain portion of the capital of the society from supporting a more advantageous, to support a less advantageous species of industry, really accomplish their favourite object. Those agricultural systems, on the contrary, in their ultimate tendency, discourage that very species of industry which it is their professed aim to animate.*

Mr. Smith (as I already hinted) accuses the French *Economists* of this very inconsistency, of proposing to advance agriculture by depressing manufactures.† I am doubtful if in this charge he has treated them with his usual candour; but the remarks he has made on this alleged imperfection of their system, are just and profound, and are strictly applicable to the reasonings of Mr. Young, and of various other later writers.

If, indeed, by *depressing manufactures* be understood the abolition of all those institutions which have hitherto given the industry of towns an advantage over that of the country, so as to allow the industry and capital of the society to follow as much as possible its natural course, without receiving any particular determination on the part of Government; it must be owned that the *Economists* are, *in this sense*, advocates for agriculture in preference to manufactures. But this is equally the tendency of Mr. Smith's own system, which seems to me, so far as the present question is concerned, to differ from that which he criticises only in its phraseology; according to both systems, the perfection of policy consists in abolishing all re-

---

* [*Wealth of Nations*, Book IV. chap. ix.; Vol. III. p. 41, tenth edition.]
† [Ibidem, p. 3.]

gulations which tend either to preference or to restraint; and in allowing every man to bring both his industry and his capital into competition with those of any other man or order of men, so long as he confines himself within the limits of justice.

After all, in the present circumstances of Europe, allowances ought to be made for the zeal with which some writers have taken up the argument in favour of Agriculture, when we consider the discouragements under which it has so long laboured, and which still contribute so powerfully to retard its progress. Nothing indeed could be so absurd as to think of advancing it, by depressing that species of industry to which it owes its chief improvements; but still it must be owned, that it stands in need, in a very peculiar degree, not only of the protection, but of the fostering care of Government. Mr. Smith has himself, in another part of his work, made some observations which tend strongly to confirm this conclusion. "With all the liberty and security which law can give, the occupiers of land must always improve under great disadvantages. The farmer, compared with the proprietor, is as a merchant who trades with borrowed money, compared with one who trades with his own. The stock of both may improve, but that of the one, with only equal good conduct, must always improve more slowly than that of the other, on account of the large share of the profit which is consumed by the interest of the loan. The lands cultivated by the farmer must, in the same manner, with only equal good conduct, be improved more slowly than those cultivated by the proprietor, on account of the large share of the produce which is consumed in the rent, and which, had the farmer been proprietor, he might have employed in the further improvement of the land. The station of a farmer besides, is, from the nature of things, inferior to that of a proprietor. Through the greater part of Europe, the yeomanry are regarded as an inferior rank of people, even to the better sort of tradesmen and mechanics, and in all parts of Europe to the great merchants and master manufacturers. It can seldom happen, therefore, that a man of any considerable stock should quit the superior to place himself in an inferior station;

and therefore, even in the present state of Europe, little stock is likely to go from any other profession to the improvement of land in the way of farming. More does perhaps in Great Britain than in any other country, though even there the great stocks which are in some places employed in farming, have generally been *acquired* by farming, the trade, perhaps, in which of all others stock is commonly acquired most slowly."*

Nor is this all. The education and habits of a husbandman, his solitary life and stationary residence, naturally attach him to the practices with which he is familiar, and prevent, in this order of men, the possibility of a mutual communication of lights analogous to what exists all over the commercial world, among tradesmen and artists of every description.[1]

Hence the duty of Government to give every possible assistance to Agriculture by promoting the circulation of useful knowledge; and the duty of those who fill the higher stations in society, to instruct and animate their inferiors by the influence of example. In the various departments of *Trade*, individuals may be safely left to themselves, and are most likely to advance both the public interests and their own, when they exercise freely their private judgment concerning the most effectual means of bettering their fortune. But experience shows that this maxim does not apply in its full extent to the cultivators of the soil, whose situation precludes them, in a great measure, from all information but what is supplied by the narrow circle of their professional employments. The general progress of improvement, therefore, in this most important of all arts, is likely to be extremely slow, where it does

---

* [*Wealth of Nations*, Book III. chap. ii.; Vol. II. pp. 97, 98, tenth edition.]

[1] The *Reports* presented to the Board of Agriculture are full of complaints against the inveteracy of local prejudices and practices, and the repugnance with which farmers listen to any ideas that are new. In remote situations, such as Wales, (we are told,) the people will not adopt English improvements, because their neighbours would laugh at them; and in some districts (such as Bedfordshire) it is stated, that the art of husbandry is a century behind the nearly adjoining counties. Some very striking facts in illustration of this remark are mentioned by *Harte* in his *Essays on Husbandry*, [1764,] p. 222; Second Edition. "Nothing shows more strongly the inattention and indolence of Mankind," &c.

not engage the superintending care of Government, and is not aided by the enlightened example of landed proprietors; and it is pleasing to reflect on the attention which begins to be paid to it, in our own country, as a national object. The rapid progress which the more refined systems of modern husbandry have made in some districts, in consequence of the exertions of a few leading individuals, is a satisfactory proof, that however difficult it may be to struggle with ignorance and prejudice, these obstacles are by no means insurmountable.

Justice, too, and humanity, as well as sound policy, plead strongly in favour of a class of men, who, while they are employed in laying the only solid foundation of national greatness, are necessarily, in the present circumstances of the world, left behind by those who follow the commercial arts. Nor ought we to forget what is due to the simple and interesting virtues which seem, in every age, to be attached to this primitive occupation of man; and on which, in a far greater degree than on the arithmetical numbers of a people, the prosperity and the resources of a country essentially depend. They are beautifully described in the following fragment of *Old Cato:*—

"Majores nostri. . . . virum bonum cum laudabant, ita laudabant:—'*bonum Agricolam, bonumque Colonum.*' Amplissime laudari existimabatur, qui ita laudabatur. Mercatorem autem, strenuum studiosumque rei quærendæ existimo; verum (ut supra dixi) periculosum et calamitosum. At ex agricolis, et viri fortissimi et milites strenuissimi gignuntur; maximeque pius quæstus stabilissimusque consequitur, minimeque invidiosus. Minime quoque male cogitantes sunt, qui in eo studio occupati sunt."*

In some of my last lectures, I have enlarged, at considerable length, on the essential importance of Manufactures as a *stimulus* to Agriculture, in the present circumstances of Modern Europe: and I have also touched slightly on the incidental disadvantages attending them, when established on erroneous principles. The subject, I am sensible, is far from being

* [M. Cato, *De Re Rustica*, cap. i.]

exhausted; and, indeed, the new views of it which open upon us at every step of our progress, are so various, that I find it extremely difficult to proceed with steadiness towards those general conclusions which I wish to establish. Some of these views, I flatter myself, I may be able to prosecute hereafter, when I shall have leisure to survey more comprehensively, the whole field of inquiry. *At present*, the multiplicity of other articles to which I am anxious to direct your attention, compared with the limited extent of the course, obliges me to hasten to speculations of a different nature.

[1.—*On the Employment of Children in Factory Work: its Advantages and Disadvantages.*]

I cannot, however, bring to a close the discussions in which we have been last engaged, without taking notice of a *new form* in which manufacturing labour has lately appeared in this country,—I allude to those establishments which, by *employing crowds of children separated from the inspection of their parents, appear to threaten* (at least on a superficial view of the subject) *the most fatal consequences to the health and to the morals, as well as to the numbers, of the rising generation.* The following statement of *the fact*, as it is exemplified on a very great scale, in Lancashire and some of the neighbouring counties, I borrow from Dr. Aikin's *Description of the Country round Manchester.*

" In the cotton mills, children of very tender age are employed; many of them collected from the workhouses of London and Westminster, and transported in crowds, as apprentices to masters resident many hundred miles distant, where they serve, unknown, unprotected, and forgotten by those to whose care Nature or the laws had consigned them. These children are usually too long confined at work, in close rooms, often during the whole night; the air they breathe, from the oil, &c., employed in the machinery, and other circumstances, is injurious; little regard is paid to their cleanliness; and frequent changes from a warm to a cold atmosphere are predisposing causes to sickness and debility, and particularly to the epidemic fever which so generally is to be met with in these factories. It is also much to be questioned, if society does not receive detriment from the *manner* in which children are thus employed during their early years. They are not generally strong for labour, or capable of pursuing any other branch of business when the term of their apprenticeship expires. The females are wholly uninstructed in sewing, knitting, and other domestic affairs, requisite to make them notable and frugal wives and mothers. This is a great misfortune to them and to the public, as is sadly proved by a comparison of the families of labourers in husbandry, and those of manufacturers in general. In the former, we meet with neatness, cleanliness, and comfort; in the latter, with filth, rags, and poverty, although their wages may be nearly double to those of the husbandman. It must be added, that the want of early religious instruction and example, and the numerous and indiscriminate association in these buildings, are very unfavourable to their future conduct in life."

These facts seem abundantly to justify the *quære* of a late humane and liberal writer, (Sir Frederick Morton Eden,) " Whether any manufacture, which, in order to be carried on successfully, requires that cottages and workhouses should be ransacked for poor children ; that they should be employed by turns during the greater part of the night, and robbed of that rest which, though indispensable to all, is most required by the young ; and that numbers of both sexes of different ages and dispositions, should be collected together in such a manner, that the contagion of example cannot but lead to profligacy and debauchery, will add to the sum of national felicity ?"*

The subject, undoubtedly, even when viewed in the most favourable light, is far from being pleasing ; nor is it possible for any views of remote expediency to reconcile the mind to commercial projects, which are not only injurious to the *morals* of the community, but which require a sacrifice of the happiness attached by nature, to the gaiety, the freedom, and the innocent activity of childhood. As most political subjects,

* [*State of the Poor*, &c. Lond. 1797.]

however, may be considered under different aspects, and as it is more useful to attempt the melioration of unavoidable evils than to indulge ourselves in declamations against what it is beyond our power to remedy, it may be worth while to employ a few moments in examining, *first*, Whether the misery and profligacy described by Dr. Aikin be *necessarily* connected with these establishments, in the extent which he has stated; and, *secondly*, Whether they may not have their use in palliating some other disorders of a still more alarming nature, in a commercial and luxurious society, such as that in which they have arisen.

In answer to the first of these inquiries, it gives me great pleasure to mention the following particulars, which evince, in a very striking manner, how much may be effected by the active zeal of private humanity when wisely and systematically directed to its object, in alleviating those evils which, as they seem to originate in causes intimately connected with national wealth and prosperity, it is scarcely possible for the Legislator to remedy. The particulars I am to state relate to the *Cotton Manufactory* in the neighbourhood of Lanark, lately the property of Mr. Dale at Glasgow.*

The supply of workers for this establishment comes either from the native inhabitants of the place; from families who have been collected about the works from the neighbouring parishes, and more distant parts of the country; or, lastly, from Edinburgh and Glasgow, both of which towns constantly afford great numbers of destitute children.

The period during which they are engaged varies according to the circumstances of their situation. Those who receive weekly wages (the greater part of whom live with their parents) are commonly engaged for four years; while such as are sent from the workhouse in Edinburgh, or who are otherwise without friends to take the charge of them, are bound four, five, six,

* [The same philanthropic care of these factory children, in relation to their comforts and education, was, after Mr. Dale's death, continued and extended by his son-in-law, Mr. Robert Owen; whose theories though we must reject, we cannot but admire the benevolence of his intentions.]

or seven years, according to their age; their service continuing until they have completed their fifteenth year. Children of this last description receive, instead of wages, their maintenance and education.

The hours of labour are eleven and a half each day, from *six* in the morning till *seven* at night, with half an hour of intermission at nine o'clock for breakfast, and a whole hour at *two* for dinner.

Seven is the hour for supper; in half an hour after which the children go to school, where they continue till nine o'clock. In 1796, (after which period I cannot speak on the subject with the same accuracy,) the schools were attended by five hundred and seven scholars; in instructing whom in reading, writing, and the principles of arithmetic, besides the common branches of education appropriated to females, sixteen teachers, with two occasional assistants, were employed. Besides these *night* schools, there were two *day* schools for children too young for work; all of them unattended with any expense to the scholars. The utmost attention was paid, at all times, to the purity of their morals, and to their religious instruction.

Of the attention given to cleanliness, diet, and everything else connected with health, the following statement of the number of children in the boarding-house at different periods, compared with the annual deaths, affords the most satisfactory evidence. The *greatest* part of the workers, it is to be observed, are lodged with their parents, who reside either in the village, in the immediate neighbourhood, or in the town of Lanark, one mile distant; and, therefore, this statement is to be understood as applying to those who receive their maintenance instead of wages, and who are all lodged together in one house. This number, in 1796, amounted to 396 boys and girls.

In 1792, ... 270 Boarders,	 2	Deaths.
„ 1793, ... 288 „	 1	„
„ 1794, ... 306 „	 0	„
„ 1795, ... 384 „	 5	„
	8	

With respect to their aptitude for other employments and the general state of their bodily strength, when their size disqualifies them for this species of labour, we are assured by Mr. Dale, in a printed letter addressed to Mr. Bailey of Hope, near Manchester, that "the workers, when too big for spinning, are as stout and robust as others of the same age. The male part of them are fit for any trades; a great many, since the commencement of the war, have gone into the army and navy, and others are occasionally going away as apprentices to smiths or joiners, but especially to weavers; for which last trade, from the expertness they acquire in handling yarn, they are particularly well fitted, and of course are taken as apprentices on better terms. The females very generally leave the mills and go to private family service, when about sixteen years of age. "Were they disposed to continue at the mills," Mr. Dale adds, "*these* afford abundant employment for them, as well as for many more young men than ever remain at them."

I shall only observe farther, before concluding this article, that if it were possible to restrain the unjustifiable practice of ransacking cottages and dissolving family connexions, by carrying away children to a distance from their homes; and if such establishments as have been now under review were confined to the orphan and destitute, supplied in such abundance by our great cities, their evil consequences would be much diminished; and they might even be considered as a salutary provision for some political disorders inseparably connected with our present system of manners. It will appear, in another part of the course, that the poverty and beggary which has prevailed so much in these last ages among the lower orders, arose necessarily from that important change which has gradually taken place in this part of Europe; the decrease of *villainage*, and the dependence of the body of the people on their own industry. This evil, therefore, is *necessarily* connected (although I am far from thinking that it is so to the extent in which it exists) with the manufactures and commerce to which this nation owes so much of its prosperity. In such a state of society, the number of destitute children cannot fail to be great; and it is increased to a wonderful degree by the licentious morals so prevalent in all our towns, but more especially in the capital. The condition of the unfortunate objects of manufacturing speculation cannot, therefore, be fairly compared with that of the young who enjoy the inestimable advantages of parental care and tenderness, but with what their own situation would probably have been if they had not found such an asylum.

From some facts, indeed, that have been very strongly stated in the other part of the island, it would appear that the protecting interference of the Legislature is loudly called for, in the case of parish children transported, as is often the case, from workhouses in the metropolis, to factories in distant counties. A late writer of most respectable character, [the Rev.] *Mr. Gisborne,** assures us, that he has known, from indisputable authority, cruel punishments inflicted on such as have found the means of representing the hardships they suffered, in order to deter them and their companions from similar attempts ;— an abuse which cannot be checked while magistrates have no power of entering the workshops of manufacturers for the purpose of inquiring into the treatment of the children whom they employ. Government, certainly, can never be better occupied than in measures, which, by promoting the comforts, the health, and the morals of those whom Providence has deprived of their natural guardians, re-establish, in some measure, those ties which the unfortunate accidents of life have broken, and give vigour to the first principles on which the political fabric depends.

[2.—*On Machinery as a Substitute for Labour : its Advantages and Disadvantages.*]

To the same branch of our subject belongs another question, which has not only occasioned much discussion among speculative politicians, but has given rise to frequent insurrections among the labouring classes of the people. The question con-

* [*Inquiry into the Duties of Men,* &c. Lond. 1794, 1795.]

cerning the *tendency of mechanical contrivances for superseding or for abridging labour*, to increase or to diminish the *population* of a country, in consequence of their tendency to increase or to diminish the quantity of employment to those whose subsistence depends on their own industry.

On this question I must confine myself, at present, to a few imperfect hints. I shall begin with stating the opinion of *Montesquieu*, whose sentiments coincide with those of some other very distinguished writers of the same country.

"Where there is an Agrarian Law," he observes, "and the lands are equally divided, the country may be well peopled though there are but few arts; because every citizen receives from the cultivation of his land whatever is necessary for his subsistence; and all the citizens together consume all the fruits of the earth. Thus it was in some of the ancient republics.

"In our present situation, in which lands are so unequally distributed, they produce much more than those who cultivate them can consume; and consequently, if the arts should be neglected, and nothing attended to but Agriculture, the country could not be peopled. Those who cultivate, having corn to spare, nothing would engage them to work the following year. The fruits of the earth would not be consumed by the indolent, for these would have nothing with which they could purchase them. It is necessary then that the Arts should be established, in order that the produce of the land may be consumed by the labourer and the artificer. In a word, it is now proper that many should cultivate much more than is necessary for their own use. For this purpose they must have a desire of enjoying superfluities, and these they can receive only from the artificer.

"Those machines which are designed to abridge art are not always useful. If a piece of workmanship is of a moderate price, such as is equally agreeable to the maker and buyer, those machines which render the manufacture more simple, or in other words, diminish the number of workmen, would be pernicious. And if water-mills were not everywhere established, I should not have believed them so useful as is pretended, because they have deprived an infinite multitude of their employment, a vast number of persons of the use of water, and the greater part of the land of its fertility."[1]

I recollect few passages in the writings of this very eminent author in which he appears to me to have reasoned in so loose and slovenly a manner. The chapter which I have now quoted is entitled, "Of the Number of Inhabitants with relation to the Arts." From the scope of the argument in the first part of it, we are naturally led to expect that the author is pointing at a distinction formerly illustrated, between that state of society in which Agriculture was practised as *a means of subsistence*, and the state of society in Modern Europe, in which it is practised as a *trade*, with a view of shewing *the disadvantages of machines in the former case, and their utility in the latter.* Of this speculation, however, he makes no use whatever in the concluding paragraph ; but, on the contrary, seems to call in question the expediency of water-mills even at present. —" If water-mills were not everywhere established, I should not have believed them so useful as is pretended, because they have deprived an infinite number of hands of their employment, a vast number of persons of the use of water, and a great part of the land of its fertility." Of these three considerations, the last two, it is evident, are perfectly inapplicable to the general question, as they would only prove, even if they were admitted as just, the inferiority of *water*-mills to *wind*-mills. I shall confine myself, therefore, to the *first ;* the tendency of such contrivances to diminish the quantity of employment in a manufacturing and commercial country.

Before entering on the argument, it may not be a disagreeable relief to the attention, in the midst of these discussions, to quote a very beautiful Greek epigram, occasioned by the invention here objected to by Montesquieu, and which has frequently struck me as bearing a strong resemblance to the general strain of Dr. Darwin's Imagery in the *Botanic Garden.* The ancients, (it may be proper to premise,) during many ages, knew nothing

[1] *Spirit of Laws,* Book XXIII. chap. xv.

CHAP. II.—POPULATION POLITICALLY CONSIDERED. (§ 3.) 191

but *hand-mills* ;* and in Greece the labour of turning them was committed to the women. The case would appear to have been the same among the Egyptians, from the following passage of Scripture :—" All the first-born of Egypt shall die, from the first-born of Pharaoh that sitteth upon the throne, even to the first-born of the maid-servant that is behind the mill."[1] I shall quote the Epigram, (which is ascribed to Antipater,) in an elegant Latin version by *Boivin*.†

---

* [*Ass-mills* (Molæ Asinariæ) were long as well known in antiquity as *Hand-mills*, (Molæ Manuariæ, Trusatiles.)]

[1] The mechanism of the machine is still more explicitly alluded to in that prohibition, where Moses forbids the Israelites " *to take the upper or the nether mill-stone in pledge.*"

† [The author of this Epigram is Antipater of Thessalonica, not Antipater of Sidon. He flourished during the Augustan age, and was a contemporary of Vitruvius, who notices the introduction of Water-Mills as then recent. (*Architectura*, X. x.) The reference to Ceres in the Epigram is appropriate ; that goddess being commemorated as the inventor of Corn-Mills in general. (Pliny, *H. N.* VII. lxvi.) The Epigram is not contained in the *Planudian Anthology* or *Collection of Greek Epigrams*, but is preserved, with many other *anecdota*, in the famous *Palatine Codex*, or *Heidelberg Manuscript*. From thence it was first published by Sulmasius in a note on the Augustan History. (Lampridii, *Heliog.*, cap. xxiv.) *John* Boivin (M. Boivin le cadet) afterwards published the original, with French and Latin versions, in his "*Remarques Historiques et Critiques sur l'Anthologie manuscrite qui est à la Bibliothèque du Roy.*" (*Mém. de l'Acad. des Inscript.*, T. ii. p. 279, seq.) The manuscript there quoted was a copy derived from that of Heidelberg, through the transcript of Salma-

sius ; of whose publication of the Epigram, in his note upon Lampridius, Boivin was, however, unaware. (*Ibid.* p. 316.) The original is subjoined, with an emendation of two corrupted places. The first and more obtrusive is indeed silently made by Boivin. I give the Epigram as it appears in the *Mantissa Quarta*, p. 426 of the third volume of De Bosch's *Anthologia;* and annex the version of Grotius to compare with Boivin's. I have not, on this occasion, looked into the collection of Brunk or of Jacobs.

" Ἴσχιτι χεῖρα μυλαῖον, ἀλιτρίδις, εὐδιτι
μακρὰ,
Κἢν ὄρθρον προλίγῃ γῆρυς ἀλικτρυόνων.
Δηὼ γὰρ' Νύμφαισι χορῶν [l. χερῶν] ἐπιτείλατο μόχθους.
Αἱ δὲ κατ' ἀκροτάτην ἀλλόμιναι τροχιήν,
Ἄξονα δινεύουσιν· ὁ δ' ἀκτίνεσσιν ἑλικταῖς
Στρωφᾶται τισύρων [l. Στρωφᾷ τῶν τισύνων] κοῖλα βάρη μυλάκων.
Γευόμισθ' ἀρχαίου βιότου πάλιν, εἰ δίχα μόχθου
Δαίνυσθαι Δηοῦς ἔργα διδασκόμεθα."

" Parcite pistrices manibus, longumque soporem
Carpite, mane licet gallus adesse canat.
Flava Ceres choreas [?] en Nymphis imperat:
illæ
Saltantes summo molliter orbe super
Circumagunt axem : radii momenta sequuntur,
Bis duo [?] versantes concava saxa molæ.
Vita redit veterum, quando Cerealia nostro
Dona frui nobis absque labore datur."]

> "Stertite jam famulæ; cesset mola; brachia cessent:
>   Stertite, dum gallus provocat ore diem.
> Alma Ceres liquidas operi succedere vestro
>   Naiadas, et manuum jussit obire vicem.
> Scandit Nympha rotam celeri pede; vertitur axis,
>   Versatur celeri turbine rapta mola.
> Rursum ævi veteris fruimur bona. Dat sua nobis
>   Munera non ullo parta labore Ceres."

I have alluded to this Epigram, not merely as an object of curiosity, but as it exhibits a picture of a state of society which, when contrasted with that of the more polished nations in modern Europe, affords of itself, without any comment, a strong general presumption against Montesquieu's conclusion. How have mankind been enabled to emerge from barbarism to civilisation, but by the introduction and the progressive improvement of machinery? It is by these that all human arts are carried on, and that the condition of the citizen is distinguished from that of the savage; a fact so striking and so important in the history of human affairs, that *Franklin* has somewhere fixed on it as the best foundation for a definition of *Man*. And, undoubtedly, if all such definitions were not absurd, that of being a *tool-making animal*, or *engineer*, which he has humorously substituted instead of some of those proposed by the philosophers of antiquity, must be allowed to possess considerable merit, inasmuch as it turns upon one of the most essential characteristics by which our species is discriminated from the brutes. How intimately it is connected with the progress of mankind, more especially in the advanced stages of their improvement, will appear more fully hereafter. In the meantime, the experience of the past is sufficiently decisive on the subject, to discourage all attempts to fetter human ingenuity and invention. The simplest machines and implements, without which we now should be at a loss how to subsist, were new in their day; and, in many instances, the invention of them undoubtedly diminished, perhaps annihilated, the demand for some species of labour which was before in request. In what situation would the world now be had these inventions been proscribed, out of tenderness to the old workmen; and who will venture to pronounce, that human life has *yet* attained to its highest degree of refinement?[1]

It is hardly possible to introduce suddenly the smallest innovation into the Political Economy of a State, let it be ever so reasonable, nay, ever so profitable, without incurring some inconveniences. But temporary inconveniences furnish no objection to solid improvements. Those which may arise from the sudden introduction of a machine cannot possibly be of long continuance. The workmen will, in all probability, be soon able to turn their industry into some other channel; and they are certainly entitled to every assistance the public can give them, when they are thus forced to change their professional habits. "An advantageous and honourable peace," as Sir James Steuart well remarks, "at the end of a long and destructive war, is attended with the same inconvenience as the invention of a machine. A number of soldiers are disbanded, and become burdensome to the public; but the evil is of short duration, and bears no proportion to the extensive and solid advantages of which peace is productive."[2] At the end of the war before last, more than a hundred thousand soldiers and sailors were all at once thrown out of employment,—a number equal to what is employed in the greatest manufactories; and yet (according to Mr. Smith*) no sensible inconvenience happened to the country. Many of the seamen probably betook themselves to the merchant service, while the rest, with the soldiers, (adverse as the habits of both are to manufacturing industry,) were very soon absorbed in the great mass of the people.

In what I have hitherto said, I have taken for granted, that the invention of a machine must necessarily diminish the quantity of employment in that particular branch of industry which it is its object to facilitate; and that it is necessary, upon such an occasion, for those who are deprived of their former

---

[1] See Gisborne, [Paley's *Critic.—An Inquiry into the Duties of Men in the Higher Rank and Middle Classes of Society in Great Britain, resulting from their respective Stations, Professions, and Employments.* Lond. 1794.]

[2] *Political Œconomy*, Book I. chap. xix.; [*Works*, Vol. I. p. 161.]

* [*Wealth of Nations*, Book IV. chap. ii.; Vol. II. p. 204, tenth edition.]

mode of subsistence, to betake themselves to some *other* trade or manufacture, in which the demand for labourers still continues. But this is by no means a *necessary* consequence of such inventions; for it is far from being impossible, that by lowering the price of commodities, and improving their quality, they may increase the demand for work in a greater proportion than that in which they diminish the number of hands by which it is carried on. By lowering the price, they may open new markets abroad, or place the commodities within the reach of a lower class of people at home; or, on the other hand, by improving the fabric, they may bring them into request, both at home and abroad, among the higher orders; and, in this manner, a larger quantity wrought in a more compendious manner, may employ as many hands as a less quantity in a way more laborious. In fact, this can scarcely fail to be the consequence, inasmuch as the demand for labour has no other limit than the extent of consumption; and in the present state of the world, consumption may be fairly said to have no limit which may not be extended by a reduction of price. When such an effect has once taken place, its operation increases and extends beyond calculation; for the increased demand for the commodities produced by the assistance of the machine, increases the demand for all the various materials and all the various trades which are subservient to the manufacture, and which furnish perhaps employment to an immense number of hands without admitting of a mechanical abridgment.

It may be worth while to add, that the same state of society which multiplies these compendious processes in the old and established trades, is continually multiplying the number of pursuits and occupations, and enlarging our prospect of that boundless field which will never be exhausted by human industry.

Another consideration, too, which adds much force to the foregoing reasonings, may be deduced from the effect of mechanical abridgment of labour, in disengaging corresponding quantities of the manufacturing capital of the country. In proportion as this happens, the funds destined for the maintenance of labour receive a virtual augmentation; and, in a nation such as ours, cannot fail to find immediate employment either in extending the scale of old establishments, or in striking out new channels of industry. In truth, all that has been alleged by Turgot, Smith, and Bentham, in proof of the astonishing effects produced by the accumulation of capital, may be fairly urged in favour of those machines which render a given quantity of capital more productive.

These observations, however, relate only to the *eventual* or *possible* advantages of machines in increasing employment, and, by no means, do justice to the present argument. Their infinite importance, or rather, indeed, *their absolute necessity* to maintain the national prosperity of a commercial country like Great Britain, will appear from the following considerations.

"The Russians," we are told,* "had no other way of making planks, till near the end of the last century, but by hewing or chipping away a whole tree to the necessary thickness; notwithstanding which, they could afford to sell them cheaper than their neighbours. Suppose that two Russians could, in this manner, finish a plank in a day, and that in the same time two common sawyers could cut out twenty, it follows that the Russians must work for one-twentieth part of the sawyers' wages. If a sawyer in Sweden can get tenpence a day, the Russian must be paid with a halfpenny." ....

"In Sweden," Postlethwayt adds, "there are a kind of mills turned by water, and so contrived as to take in large trees on the upper side of the stream, and deliver them out on the lower, sawed into planks in a few minutes." One of these mills will make at least five hundred planks, whilst the Russian could make a single one by hewing; and consequently, with the attendance of a single person, it performs the work of a thousand men labouring with the axe.

It is only by such contrivances, combined with that division of labour which is intimately connected with them, that nations, among whom the wages of labour are comparatively high, can maintain the competition in foreign markets; and to what an

* [Postlethwayt's *Dictionary*, &c.; Article, *Machine*.]

extraordinary extent the productive powers of industry may thus be multiplied, the commercial history of our own island affords a proof hitherto unequalled among mankind.

In a country where, by increase of money, by a load of taxes, and by various other causes, the price of labour has risen higher than among its commercial competitors, its trade must necessarily go to decay, unless this circumstance is counteracted by others of an opposite tendency. So strongly does this remark apply to our own case, that many of our manufacturing towns must long ago have given up all thoughts of foreign commerce, if they had not been constantly struggling against the advancing price of manual labour, by those astonishing combinations of mechanical ingenuity which nothing but necessity can account for. It is a fortunate arrangement in human affairs, that the same circumstances which create the evil should thus furnish the remedy. When demands from abroad slacken, and foreign rivals, in consequence of the cheapness of labour, are on the point of securing the prize, the pressure of necessity awakens invention; and by the seasonable introduction of a new machine, re-establishes the manufacture, lowered in its price or improved in its quality. The competition, in truth, among commercial nations at present, is not merely a competition of *industry*, but of *ingenuity* and *skill;* and it is likely to become so in a greater and greater degree, as the progress of Science and of Art advances. It is this inexhaustible fund of mechanical invention, in which we have now left all our competitors far behind, aided by the division of labour arising from mercantile opulence, and protected by civil liberty, which is the great foundation of our commercial prosperity.

The foregoing observations, while they appear to me to go far to *justify the general principle on which mechanical abridgments of labour* proceed, suggest, at the same time, if I am not mistaken, an *additional* confirmation of some reasonings formerly stated in *vindication of the consolidation of farms*. [P. 124, *seq*.]

It was long ago observed by Mr. Jenyns,* (and, indeed, the remark must have occurred to every person who has bestowed

* [*Thoughts on the present High Price of Provisions*: 1767.]

a moment's consideration on the subject,) "That although no tax is *immediately* laid, in Great Britain, on corn, it is taxed as *effectually* as if a duty by the bushel had been primarily laid upon it; inasmuch as out of its price, all the innumerable taxes drawn from the farmer on windows, soap, candles, malt, hops, leather, salt, and a thousand others, must be repaid." . . . "*The price of corn, therefore*," he concludes, "*must necessarily be advanced.*"[1] Since the time he wrote, how astonishingly have taxes increased and multiplied on the farmer's articles of consumption; and yet the price of corn has not, certainly, risen in the same proportion. Indeed, under all this weight of taxation, its price, at an average, appears to have *fallen* in the course of the present century.

To what cause can we ascribe this very important fact, but to the accumulation of agricultural capital in the hands of those men who are accused of *consolidating farms?* and who, in consequence of the circumstances which have been already explained, are enabled to bring their grain to the market at a reduced expense. The advantages which manufacturers derive from the division of labour, and from the use of machinery, cannot be attained, but in a very inconsiderable degree, by the husbandman; and hence the inestimable value of every arrangement which, by economizing his operations, prevents the price of the necessaries of life from keeping pace with the growing weight of taxation. These circumstances, it must be confessed, render agriculture less profitable than formerly to small farmers, and they have, perhaps, a tendency unfavourable to the agricultural population of the country. But although this must be allowed to be an evil, it is not to be compared in magnitude with a dependence on foreign nations for the means of subsistence. From the increasing importations of grain, for a good many years past, there is but too much reason to apprehend that the remedy is not altogether adequate to the disorder; but the efficacy of the remedy, to a certain extent, is unquestionable; and if it had not operated very powerfully indeed, the mischief would long before now have been incalculable in

[1] See Davies, [Rev. David,] *The Case of Labourers*, &c., [1795,] p. 51.

its consequences. Could we suppose it possible that, by an increase of taxes, wheat might be imported at a less expense than that at which it can be raised, on how precarious a foundation would the grandeur of this empire rest!

It affords some consolation, under the impression of these gloomy ideas, to reflect, that the discouragements to agriculture, and the checks to agricultural population, are consequences, not of the natural progression of things, but of those accidental causes which have produced our public burdens; and that, therefore, if we could indulge the prospect of a short respite from the calamities of war, a reduction of taxes might gradually operate in placing agriculture more upon a level with the other branches of national industry.

[SUBSECT. III.—*Is the Density of Population in Proportion to the Extent of Country, a certain Index of National Prosperity?*]

In the course of the foregoing Lectures, I have repeatedly intimated my dissent from a very common opinion, that *the number of a people compared with the extent of their territory, furnishes the most unequivocal of all the tests that can be appealed to, in our inquiries concerning national prosperity.* That in order to ascertain in how far a country is flourishing, nothing more is necessary than to examine this *proportion*, is by many writers assumed as a fundamental maxim; and yet the slightest consideration may satisfy us, that it is the *industrious* alone who constitute the strength of a nation, and that a population composed of the idle and the indigent is to be dreaded as one of the greatest of political evils.*

(*Interpolation from Notes.*)—One of the first writers who seems to have become aware of this important truth, was Sir James Steuart, who clearly pointed out the essential differences

* [In the manuscript Lectures several blank pages are here left, and there is subjoined the following memorandum:—" See Volume marked POL.—Paley, vol. ii. p. 348; Townsend; Arthur Young; Sir James Steuart." There is no volume in my possession marked POL; and I have endeavoured to supply the lacuna here left from the notes taken of the course in 1809 by Mr. Bridges, and by the late Mr. Bonar.]

between a population of industrious citizens, and a population of idle men and of beggars.* The same distinction was taken about the same time by several French writers, and from them was adopted by Mr. Arthur Young. In his Survey of the Agriculture of France, he states it explicitly as his opinion, that the population of that country was too great, in consequence of the excessive subdivision of land in many districts, and that the prosperity of the nation would be greatly enhanced if the inhabitants could be reduced by five or six millions at least. He founds particularly on the remarks made in an excellent *Report on Beggary*, drawn up by M. de la Rochefoucauld Liancourt.†

In some other countries of Europe, we find population forced beyond its natural limit, by expedients expressly and avowedly intended for this purpose. Such was the policy which induced the Spanish Government to establish a colony of Germans in the Sierra Morena, though every province in Spain swarmed with vagrants, who owed their support to the hierarchy and monasteries. Of this attempt and its ill success, a very interesting account is given by Mr. Townsend.‡ The failure of the whole project might indeed have been anticipated. Where a country has already a greater population than the State can govern well, public evils are not to be remedied by the introduction of new settlers. A cure for these must be found nearer home, in a melioration of the government and of the condition and circumstances of the people.

The policy adopted in some nations, of increasing population by holding out inducements to marriage, has been suggested by the same views as the expedient of inviting foreign settlers. No maxim can be more certain than this,—that *marriages will take place in every instance where they ought to do so.* There is no example of a country furnishing regular employment to industry where these are not entered into. The policy, therefore, is at best useless; but it can scarcely fail to be hurtful. In

---

* [*Political Œconomy*, Book I. chap. xiv.; *Works*, Vol. I. p. 117, *et alibi*.]
† [*Travels in France*, p. 409.]
‡ [*Journey through Spain in the years* 1786, 1787, &c. Vol. II. p. 266, *seq*., first edition.]

Spain such an expedient was tried by Charles IV., who extended the privileges of nobility to married men for a certain number of years, and to the father of six children, for life; whilst, on the contrary, those nobles who continued bachelors after twenty-five years of age, were deprived of all the immunities of their order. This edict was without effect; and it was in vain that attempts were made to enforce it.—(*End of interpolation from Notes.*)

In all such cases as have now been under consideration, where the numbers of a people have increased steadily for a length of time, without a proportional increase in the means of subsistence, alarming consequences may be apprehended to follow sooner or later: and although this might be the *ultimate* result of the most perfect model of human policy, (were it possible to realize it,) at least in so great a degree as ought to lower the pride of philosophical speculation, yet if it appear that the same evil may be produced without adding, in the meantime, to the sum of national happiness, the political arrangements in which it originates cannot be too anxiously avoided as sources of an unmixed accumulation of mischiefs. In China, where population has been forced by a variety of unnatural expedients, by the permission which parents have to expose their children, by the singularly abstemious habits of the people, and by the indiscriminate use they are led to make of everything through which life can be supported,—the fatal effects of a policy, artificially contrived to extend the multiplication of the race beyond its just limits, are seen in all their magnitude. In such circumstances, any deficiency in the ordinary produce, arising from an unfavourable season, cannot fail to be followed by the horrors of famine. The miseries which have so often been experienced from this in Hindostan are, in like manner, the obvious consequences of a population pushed to its utmost possible limit, relatively to the means of subsistence. The ordinary habits of frugality to which the people are accustomed, leave no superfluities to be retrenched in a year of scarcity.

The conclusion to which these considerations lead is manifest,—that the only equitable and beneficial means which can be employed for the advancement of population, suppose a corresponding increase in the funds necessary to support it; and that every project to encourage it in any other way, can only add to the number of human creatures born to poverty, to vice, and to wretchedness. To consider population merely in the narrow commercial view, of producing men who are to be subservient to the fortunes of the opulent, and who, by their increasing numbers, are to lower the reward of labour, and to favour the competition of our manufacturers in foreign markets, is a policy not only inexpedient, but unjust and inhuman, and dictated by the same spirit which has led men, in so many other instances, to overlook, in the eagerness of mercantile speculation, the rights, the feelings, and the morals of those who are doomed to be the instruments of their avarice.

This general principle furnishes an infallible criterion for adjusting the *relative claims of Agriculture and of Manufactures* to the attention of the statesman. The powerful stimulus which manufactures give to agriculture has been already illustrated; and in so far as this operates without any check from adventitious causes, their tendency is wholly beneficial, inasmuch as they at once multiply the numbers of the people and provide the additional food by which they are to be supported. It must however be remembered, that although this is a *natural* effect, it is not the *necessary* effect of manufactures, and that it is possible for them to advance population in a far greater degree than that in which they add to the produce of the earth. It has been shewn, that in the actual history of modern Europe, the spirit of the prevailing systems of legislation has obstructed, in a variety of ways, the natural and salutary operation of manufacturing upon agricultural industry, more particularly by the encouragement which they have given to the labour of *towns* in preference to that of the *country;* and wherever this has been the case, although the lower orders may have *multiplied*, and may even, in consequence of collateral circumstances, have increased the sum of their enjoyments, yet a large proportion of them must have been deprived of their full share of those progressive advantages which Nature, if not thwarted by human policy, would not fail to distribute, with an equitable hand, among all her industrious children.

The legal provision which is made for the *poor* in the other part of the island, although originating in motives which reflect the highest honour on the benevolence of our countrymen, is obviously liable to this objection, that while it tends to increase population by encouraging marriage, it has no tendency to provide additional food for the people. Nor is this all: the population it increases is chiefly that of idle consumers; and, therefore, it not only diminishes the quantity of provisions which the labour of the industrious man can command, but abridges *his* share of the comforts of life, to feed those who are a burden on the community. The evils occasioned by all such expedients cannot fail to be progressive; for whatever depresses the condition of the labouring classes must eventually multiply the objects of charity.[1] But of this subject I shall have occasion to treat afterwards.

The *agricultural* improvements of which this country is susceptible, present immense resources both for meliorating the state of the lower orders, and for adding to the numbers of the most valuable part of its inhabitants. That its produce might be easily doubled, or even trebled, has been affirmed by very competent judges;[2] but without aiming at arithmetical precision on this point, it may be confidently asserted, that the present population of our island is far short of what the territory, if properly cultivated, would be able to maintain. It is not merely the *commons* and the *waste lands*, (the extent of which in Great Britain has been computed[3] to amount to twenty-two millions of acres,—that is, to more than one-fourth of the whole

---

[1] *Essay on the Principle of Population.* [In 1798, by Malthus.]

[2] Bell's Pamphlet, p. 119. [According to the notes of the later Courses of Political Economy, Mr. Stewart quotes Mr. Benjamin Bell by name, and with approbation; and in Watt's *Bibliotheca* there are given to him, as author,— 1*. *Three Essays, on Taxation of Income*, &c., Edin., 1799;—2*. *Essays on Agriculture*, &c., Edin., 1802.]

[3] *Essential Principles of Wealth of Nations*, [1797, by Grey,] p. 130. In the Report of the Committee on *Waste Lands*, it is stated that there are throughout the kingdom no less than 7,800,000 acres in a perfectly uncultivated condition.— *Lord Carrington's Speech in the House of Lords*, July 3, 1800.

kingdom ;) it is not merely *these*, which open a field for future exertions in husbandry ; but, if we except a few districts where the soil is naturally rich, and which have been long in a state of high cultivation, scarcely a farm is to be found, of which the occupier will not readily grant, that the produce might be greatly augmented. Nor is there the smallest reason to doubt, in a country so eminently distinguished by enterprising and enlightened industry, and which enjoys so many advantages over neighbouring states, that the natural course of events, aided by such laws as *now* unite the suffrages of politicians of all descriptions, would advance both its agriculture and population with a rapidity equal to our most sanguine wishes, if the circumstances of Europe should ever enable us to enjoy, undisturbed, for a course of years, the blessings of peace.

In order to damp the exertions inspired by such prospects, it has been frequently urged, that supposing them to be attended with complete success, and a similar spirit to animate the legislators of other countries, the globe would, at no very distant period, be overstocked with inhabitants, and would be rendered a scene of incalculable misery. An idea of this kind serves as the ground-work of a late very ingenious and candid Essay, "*On the Principle of Population as it affects the Future Improvement of Society ;*"*—an Essay distinguished by originality of thought, and which (among some general speculations, more plausible, perhaps, than solid) contains a variety of acute and just reflections of a practical nature. A remarkable passage, too, of a similar tendency, forms the conclusion of Pinto's Treatise, *On Circulation and Credit.*† Nor has this calamitous consequence of the natural course of events been altogether overlooked by the romantic authors of some late political theories. It was plainly perceived in its full force by Godwin, when he had

---

* [By Malthus. The Essay, as noticed, was originally published anonymously, in 1798. It will be seen that this speculation from the first strongly excited the attention of Mr. Stewart. See pp. 62, 64, 205, *seq.* If these Lectures were written in 1800, Mr. Malthus had not as yet acknowledged the publication. See p. 64.

† [Pinto's *Essay on Circulation and Credit* was not only published in French in Holland, but translated into English, if I recollect aright, in 1774. See App. I. p. 429, *seq.*]

recourse (in order to solve the difficulty) to the most paradoxical of all his hypotheses, that in consequence of the intellectual and moral improvement of man, the passion between the sexes will be gradually extinguished, and that, while the period of human life will, in the case of *individuals*, be indefinitely prolonged, the *species* will cease to propagate.* The same difficulty led Dr. Wallace, fifty years ago, to conclude much more philosophically, "that the existence of perfect governments (even though they were consistent with the human passions and appetites) is physically inconsistent with the circumstances of mankind upon the earth."[1]—(*Interpolation from Notes.*)—" How happy," he also says, " would be the consequences of such an excellent government! Every discouragement to marriage would be effectually removed. Wise regulations would be established to gratify the natural passion of love, in an easy and agreeable manner. No false maxims which corrupt the taste in this grand concern would be in vogue, nor any temptation from interest to mislead the choice. Poverty being effectually banished, and every one upon an equal footing, the numerous impediments arising from an inequality of rank, estates, or other circumstances, would be wholly removed. In this situation, according to the original blessing and command, mankind would be fruitful, and multiply, replenish the earth, and subdue it." . . . " How long the earth, with the best culture of which it is capable from human genius and industry, might be able to nourish its perpetually increasing inhabitants, is as impossible as it is unnecessary to be determined. It is not probable that it could have supported them during so long a period as since the creation of Adam. But whatever may be supposed of the length of this period, of necessity it must be granted, that the earth could not nourish them for ever, unless either its fertility could be continually augmented, or by some secret in nature, like what certain

---

* [*Inquiry into Political Justice*, &c., 1793, B. VIII. chap. vi.]
[1] *Prospects of Mankind*, &c. [1761, Pr. iv. p. 125.]

[The following memorandum is at this place appended:]—" Introduce here, by way of Appendix, an examination of the *Essay on the Principle of Population.*"

enthusiasts have expected from the philosopher's stone, some wise adept in the occult sciences should invent a method of supporting mankind quite different from any thing known at present. Nay, though some extraordinary method of supporting them might possibly be found out, yet if there was no bound to the increase of mankind, which would be the case under a perfect government, there would not even be sufficient room for containing their bodies upon the surface of the earth."
. . . . " It would be impossible, therefore, to support the great numbers of men who would be raised up under a perfect government; the earth would be overstocked at last, and the greatest admirers of such fanciful schemes must foresee the fatal period when they would come to an end." . . . . " During all the preceding ages, while there was room for increase, mankind must have been happy; the earth must have been a paradise in the literal sense, as the greatest part of it must have been turned into delightful and fruitful gardens. But when the dreadful time should at last come, when our globe, by the most diligent culture, could not produce what was sufficient to nourish its numerous inhabitants, what happy expedient could then be found out to remedy so great an evil ?"*

In one very important respect, indeed, Dr. Wallace has misapprehended the subject, in supposing that the evils of an overgrown population were placed at a great and almost immeasurable distance, and that they could not be realized till the whole world was cultivated like a garden. In opposition to this idea, Mr. Malthus has shown, and I think with demonstrative evidence, that the evils in question would be imminent and immediate; and that in every period of the progress to the time when the whole earth should be cultivated like a garden, the distress for want of food would be constantly pressing on all mankind, supposing them all on a footing of equality. Though the produce of the earth might be increasing every year, the population would advance much faster, and the redundance must be reduced by the return of periodical disease, or the constant action of misery.

* [*Prospects*, &c., Prs. iii. iv. pp. 104, 115-117. Dr. Robert Wallace was one of the Ministers of Edinburgh.]

The following curious Apologue from Mr. Townsend's *Dissertation on the Poor Laws*, [1780,]* as it so well illustrates the relation of human society to population, I shall present without any comment.

" Navigators relate, that in the South Seas there is an island, which, from the first discoverer, is called Juan Fernandes. In this sequestered spot, John Fernando placed a colony of goats, consisting of one male, attended by his female. This happy couple finding pasture in abundance, could readily obey the first commandment, to *increase and multiply;* till in process of time they had replenished their little island.[1] In advancing to this period they were strangers to misery and want, and seemed to glory in their multitude; but from this unhappy moment they began to suffer hunger: yet, continuing for a time to increase their numbers, had they been endued with reason, they must have apprehended the extremity of famine. In this situation the weakest first gave way, and plenty was again restored. Thus they fluctuated between happiness and misery, and either suffered want or rejoiced in abundance, according as their numbers were diminished or increased; never at a stay, yet nearly balancing at all times their quantity of food. This relation of equipoise was from time to time disturbed, either by epidemical diseases or by the arrival of some vessel in distress. On such occasions their numbers were considerably reduced; but to compensate this alarm, and to comfort them for the loss of their companions, the survivors never failed immediately to find a return of plenty. They were no longer in fear of famine; they ceased to regard each other with an evil eye; all had abundance, all were contented, all were happy. Thus, what might have been considered as misfortunes, proved a source of comfort; and, to them at least, " partial evil" was " universal good."

" When the Spaniards found that the English privateers

---

* [Sect. viii. p 37, *seq.*—In this little work, (*passim*,) to say nothing of his other books, (See his *Free Thoughts*, chap. ix.; *Journey through Spain*, Vol. I. 383, *seq.*; II. 269, *seq.*; 361, *seq.*; III. 107, *seq.* Mr. Townsend, who was an Anglican clergyman, has anticipated his brother divine, Mr. Malthus, in the most important doctrines touching Population.]

[1] Dampier, Vol. I. part ii. p. 88.

resorted to this island for provisions, they resolved on the total extirpation of the goats; and for this purpose they put on shore a greyhound dog and bitch.[1] These in their turn increased and multiplied, in proportion to the quantity of food they met with; but in consequence, as the Spaniards had foreseen, the breed of goats diminished. Had they been totally destroyed, the dogs likewise must have perished. But as many of the goats retired to the craggy rocks, where the dogs could never follow them, descending only for short intervals to feed with fear and circumspection in the valleys, few of these, besides the careless and the rash, became a prey; and none but the most watchful, strong, and active of the dogs could get a sufficiency of food. Thus a new kind of balance was established. The weakest of both species were among the first to pay the debt of nature; the most active and vigorous preserved their lives.—It is the quantity of food which regulates the numbers of the human species," &c.—But to return:

The reasonings of Mr. Malthus, therefore, in so far as they relate to the Utopian plans of Wallace, Condorcet, and Godwin, are perfectly conclusive, and strike at the root of all such theories. But they do not seem to justify those gloomy inferences which many persons are disposed to draw from them concerning the established order of nature. And the very ingenious and liberal author has assured us explicitly, that he did not mean, when he stated these considerations to the public, to insinuate any argument against the expediency of meliorating, to the utmost of our power, the real imperfections of our existing institutions. In one point only, I am disposed to differ from Mr. Malthus. He seems to me to lay by far too little stress on the efficacy of those arrangements which nature herself has established for the remedy of the evils in question, and to trust too little to that *vis medicatrix naturæ*, which is not less susceptible of an application to the political than to the natural world. But these remarks I shall have occasion to illustrate more fully when I come to treat of the Economical system.—(*End of interpolation from Notes.*)

[1] Ulloa, Book II. chap. iv.

I shall not enter into the argument at present, although I am fully persuaded that the subject is still unexhausted, and that if prosecuted with a dispassionate love of truth, it would open an interesting and not unpleasing field of speculation. It is sufficient for my purpose to observe, that whatever opinion we may form concerning it, no solid reason *can* be suggested, which ought to have any practical effect in diminishing our zeal to advance, to the utmost of our power, the prosperity of that society with which we are connected. For, although the greater that prosperity, the sooner must population arrive at that ultimate limit where it ceases to be a blessing, yet it belongs not to us, in the contemplation of a remote contingency, to supply what appears to our limited faculties an imperfection in the arrangements of Providence, by neglecting those duties to which we are called in the present moment. The field which yet remains to employ the labours of ourselves and our children, is sufficiently ample to animate the exertions of the most sanguine beneficence; and it is a miserable misapplication of the time and talents which are now in our possession, to waste them in fruitless anticipations of the condition of remote ages, while so much may be done to lighten the pressure of actual evils. The article of Political Economy to which I have now been directing your attention, illustrates, with peculiar force, the truth of these remarks, when we compare, in the *first* place, the actual population of the globe with the prolific powers of the sexes, and still more when, in the *second*, we reflect on the importance of that sublime function entrusted to the legislator, of being able eventually to bestow not only *existence* but *happiness* on millions who would never otherwise have seen the light.

(*Interpolation from Notes.*)—These general principles coincide, in most essential respects, with the system of the Economists and of Quesnai; one of whose fundamental maxims is, that the statesman should fix his attention rather on the increase of national wealth than on the increase of population, that is, aim at the advance of population only through the medium of agriculture, and consider manufactures and commerce as useful only in so far as they tend to augment the territorial produce by the stimulus of an extended market.

This view of the subject may perhaps enable us to clear up an inconsistency formerly referred to, (p. 65,) which occurs in the work of the very ingenious author of the *Ami des Hommes*. The change of opinion which this author acknowledges, may easily be accounted for by the varying point of view in which he considers his subject. The two opinions, when stated with proper limitations, will both be found agreeable to truth. That population is the consequence of riches, is a maxim which, I believe, holds true without any exception, and no illustration of it can be more striking than what is afforded by the progress of population in America. On the other hand, when we cast our eyes on what has happened in modern Europe, we find riches to be the consequence of an increasing population.

It is to this last state of society that it is necessary for us to confine our attention, if we wish our speculations to be practically useful ; I mean, to that state of society where there are no laws favouring the division of landed property, as in the ancient republics, or an open field for agricultural enterprise, as in the New World ; but where a great accumulation of land in the hands of a few proprietors is the necessary consequence of existing institutions, while, at the same time, the lower orders are left dependent on the free and voluntary exertions of their own industry. The question is not how a speculative politician should regulate the course of human affairs; but in what manner, subject to existing conditions, the peace of society may be effectually maintained, and the greatest amount of happiness secured. But how this is to be accomplished, independently of Manufactures and Commerce, I confess myself unable to form even an idea. The writers who, in their zeal for agriculture, have been led to declaim against manufactures and commerce, placing to their account all the evils which result from the mutual jealousy of nations, seem to have entirely lost sight, not only of the causes which have brought agriculture to its present state, but of the operation of commerce and manufactures in applying a cure to the anarchy which prevailed for ages after the abolition of villanage.

The existence of many poor was in reality the necessary effect of breaking down this institution established by the feudal system. By that revolution, all those who had formerly been serfs to the proprietors of land, were left to depend on their own industry for subsistence, instead of receiving, directly or indirectly, maintenance from their feudal lord. Hence, in the progress of human affairs, it could not but ensue that a great number became indigent. Not many years ago the condition of the poor in Scotland, in consequence of scarcity, was undoubtedly distressing; but how limited and transitory was the suffering at that time, compared with what was here chronically prevalent towards the end of the seventeenth century? This contrast may be seen from the statement made by Mr. Fletcher of Saltoun, in a Discourse addressed to the Scottish Parliament in 1698.* He estimated the number of beggars then in Scotland at no fewer than 200,000. The only remedy he, a Republican by principle, could suggest, was to restore the ancient state of villanage, and to make slaves of all those who were unable to provide for their own subsistence.

In England, although from various causes the career of improvement began at an earlier period, a similar progress of order and regular police accompanied the advancement of national industry; and it is not a little remarkable how completely the licentiousness and insubordination of the lower classes bid defiance to the authority of the wisest and most vigorous princes, till a gradual extension of the field of employment insensibly converted the multitude to better habits. During the sixteenth century, the police of England does not appear to have been better than that of Scotland at the end of the seventeenth. In proof of this I may refer to Harrison's account of the state of England in the reigns of Henry VIII. and of Queen Elizabeth, [in his *Historical Description*.] The most satisfactory proof that I know of the disorderly condition of England, is a statement preserved in Strype's *Annals*, drawn up in 1596, by a justice of peace in Somersetshire.

* [*Discourses;* Second Discourse concerning the Affairs of Scotland.]

Against such a state of anarchy there are only two remedies. The *one* is a return to the institution of Villanage of the feudal ages, or to the Agrarian policy of the Roman Commonwealth; the *other* is the operation of Manufactures and Commerce, which have already accomplished such wonders in this part of the world, and not yet occasioned any general inconvenience which may not be traced to the caprice of that policy diverting them from their natural channels, or to those accidents, perhaps inseparable from the lot of humanity, which occasionally disturb those pacific relations on which the prosperity of nations depends. The facts, accordingly, which I have borrowed from Mr. Fletcher, led him not unnaturally to regret the emancipation of the lower orders, and to recommend strongly the revival of such a policy as subsisted in the ancient republics. The same ideas have plainly warped the speculations of Dr. Wallace.* The disorders which appeared to this author so formidable as to require the violent and cruel laws of antiquity, must be admitted by those who were not affected by the same classical prepossessions, to afford a strong confirmation of what has been already urged in favour of the remedy which the natural course of things in modern Europe has provided for the gradual extirpation of these evils. All that it is necessary for the statesman to remember, is—that the care of population belongs exclusively to nature, and that it is his peculiar business, by securing employment to all ranks of the people, and by directing all the various kinds of industrious speculation, to bestow due encouragement on that art which alone can render an increasing population the source of an increasing fund for its own subsistence.—(*End of interpolation from Notes.*)

[APPENDIX.—OF THE MEANS WHICH HAVE BEEN EMPLOYED TO ASCERTAIN THE STATE OF POPULATION IN PARTICULAR INSTANCES.]

In entering on this article, it may be proper to remark in general, that it is obviously one of those where mathematical accuracy cannot possibly be attained. Even supposing an actual

* [See his books; *On the Numbers*, and *On the Prospects of Mankind.*]

numeration to be made of all the inhabitants of a country, the result would not be consistent with truth, unless the observations were carried on in all the different parts of it at the same time; nor would *this* result, however correctly it might state the fact at the moment when it was ascertained, afford anything more than a single measurement of an object, which, from its nature, is always varying, less or more, in its dimensions. Such a method, however, of ascertaining the number of a people is unquestionably susceptible of a greater degree of precision than any other, although, in most cases where it has been attempted, numerous errors have been committed in the execution; partly from the want of *method* in those to whom the details have been entrusted; and partly from the prejudices which dispose the more ignorant classes of the community to distrust the views of Government in proposing such a measure.

In by far the greater number of instances, inquiries concerning Population have been conducted on a plan much more indirect, and affording a still less accurate approximation to the truth. In order to shorten the labour necessarily attending an operation of so great a magnitude, certain *facts* have been fixed upon which are supposed to have a constant relation to the whole number of the people, and from these (by an application of general rules founded on experience) this number has been inferred or computed. Such, for example, is the number of *Houses*, the quantity of *Consumption;* and, above all, the state of *Births, Deaths,* and *Marriages.*

The first person who led the way in this department of political science was Sir William Petty; and it was by him that the phrase *Political Arithmetic* was introduced. The idea which he annexed to the term may be judged of from the explanation he gives of it in the title of one of his books: "*Political Arithmetic;* or, A Discourse concerning the Extent of Land, People, Buildings, Husbandry, Manufacture, Commerce, Fishery, Artisans, Seamen, Soldiers, Public Revenues, Interest, Taxes, Superlucration, Registries, Banks, Valuation of Men, Increasing of Seamen, of Militias, Harbours, Situation, Shipping, Power at Sea, &c., as the same relates to every

Country in general, but more particularly to the territories of his Majesty of Great Britain, and his neighbours of Holland, Zealand, and France." This book was presented in manuscript to King Charles II., but was not printed till the year 1690. Lord Shelborne, the author's son, in his dedication of it, observes, "that it was styled by his father *Political Arithmetic*, inasmuch as things of Government, and of no less concern and extent, than the glory of the Prince, and the happiness and greatness of the People, are by the ordinary rules of arithmetic, brought into a sort of demonstration. He was allowed by all," it is added, " to be the *inventor* of this method of instruction, where the perplexed and intricate ways of the world are explained by a very mean part of science." On the same subject, Sir William Petty himself writes as follows:—" The method I take is not very usual; for, instead of giving only comparative and superlative words and intellectual argument, I have taken the course (as a specimen of the *Political Arithmetic* I have aimed at) to express myself in terms of *number, weight,* or *measure,* to use only argument of *sense,* and to consider only such causes as have visible foundations in nature; leaving those that depend on the mutable minds, opinions, appetites, and passions of *particular* men to the consideration of others. . . . . Now, the observations or positions expressed by number, weight, and measure, upon which I bottom the ensuing discourses, are either true, or not apparently false; and which, if they are not already true, certain, and evident, yet may be made so by the sovereign power, (nam id certum est quod certum reddi potest;) and if they are false, not so false as to destroy the argument they are brought for, but at worst are sufficient as suppositions, to show the way to that knowledge I aim at. . . . Which, if it shall be judged material and worthy of a better discussion, I hope all ingenious and candid persons will rectify the errors and imperfections which may probably be found in any of the positions on which my ratiocinations are grounded. Nor would it misbecome authority itself, to clear those matters which private endeavours cannot reach to."[1]

[1] Preface to *Political Arithmetic.*

I have quoted these passages at greater length than I should otherwise have thought necessary, in order to show, with how little reason the German writers value themselves as the authors of that science to which they have given the name of *Statistics*. "It is now about forty years ago," says Zimmermann in his *Political Survey of Europe*, "that a branch of political knowledge, which has for its object the actual and relative power of the several modern states, the power arising from their natural advantages, the industry and civilisation of their inhabitants, and the wisdom of their governments, has been formed, chiefly by German writers, into a separate science. It used formerly to be improperly connected with geography; and it was but superficially treated amidst the topographical and descriptive details of the larger geographical works. By the more convenient form it has received, and by its growing importance, this science, distinguished by the new-coined name of *Statistics*, is become a favourite study in Germany."[1] The Baron de Hertzberg informs us, in one of his *Academical Discourses*, that since the middle of the present century it has been gradually supplanting among his countrymen, what used formerly to be the principal object of attention, in the German system of academical education, the system of *Natural Jurisprudence*.

With respect to Sir William Petty, however, whatever his merits were in opening this new field of political research, it must be owned, that in the execution of the plan, he did little more than set an example to his successors. His object was to compute the number of the people from the trade and consumption of the nation, and from the number of houses in the kingdom. For the former branch of information he trusted to the accounts of the Excise and the Customs, and for the latter to the gross produce of the hearth-money. But on none of these articles did he possess the means of ascertaining the truth;

---

[1] Sinclair's *Account of the Origin and Progress of the Board of Agriculture*, (p. 34.) [Denina, in his *Prusse Littéraire*, vindicates, as I recollect, the invention of this branch of science to Italy and to his countryman Botero, who lived long before Petty.]

and, accordingly, his computations often proceed on erroneous or uncertain data. His most valuable reasonings are founded on the bills of mortality and the registers of births, which he appears to have studied with great care, with a view to the population both of this and of other countries. A spirit of theory, however, runs through all his speculations, calculated to flatter the wishes and prejudices of government; and hence his anxiety to overrate the resources of England, and to undervalue those of our neighbours. It is thus only we can account for such assertions as the following:[1]—" That France exceeded Great Britain very little in point of territory; that our numbers approach near to those of the French, and, in point of strength, are as efficient; that France was under a natural and perpetual incapacity of being powerful at sea; and that it had not above fifteen thousand seamen to manage its trade, out of which not above ten thousand could be spared for a fleet of war."

" Every good Englishman," says Postlethwayt, " does undoubtedly wish all this had been true ; but we have since had manifest proofs that this great genius was mistaken in all these assertions, for which reason we have ground to suspect, he rather made his *court* than spoke his *mind.*"

Researches similar to those which Sir William Petty had recommended and exemplified, were afterwards prosecuted (about the end of last century) by Mr. Gregory King, whose results are to this day much valued for their accuracy ; and by Dr. Davenant, " the best," (according to Dr. Price,) " *while not venal*, of all political writers."[2]

The greatest step, however, that has ever been made in this branch of science, by any *one* individual, was undoubtedly by the original and inventive genius of *Dr. Halley*, whose observations (of which I shall afterwards have occasion to take notice) have not only contributed much to correct the ideas of political writers on the subject *now* under our consideration, but have led the way to all the improvements which have since been made in the doctrine of *annuities*,—a doctrine which forms the

[1] Postlethwayt's *Dictionary;* Article, *Political Arithmetic.*

[2] Price, *On Annuities,* Vol. II. p. 275.

basis of an immense branch of commercial speculation in this country, and which proceeds on one of the most refined general principles that have yet been applied successfully to human affairs, the possibility of counteracting the inconveniences resulting from the precarious duration of life in the case of *individuals*, by the uniformity of those *general laws* by which those events that appear the most accidental on a superficial view, are found to be regulated in the order of nature.

Among the different methods which have been employed for estimating the state of population, one of the most simple is founded on the supposed *proportion* between the number of *houses* and that of the *inhabitants*. In order, however, to employ this method with advantage, in particular instances, much attention is necessary to the circumstances of the case.

The proportion between the number of houses and that of their inhabitants must vary widely, it is evident, according to the opulence or poverty of the people; according to their habits of living; according to their residence in towns or in the country; according to the *size* of towns, their commercial or dissipated manners, and many other accidents.

The calculations of Gregory King on this subject are founded on an examination of the *hearth-books*, and of the assessments on marriages, births, and burials, and (in the opinion of Dr. Davenant) "are more to be relied on than anything of the same kind that had ever been attempted."

According to these calculations,—

London within the walls produced almost	$5\frac{1}{2}$ per house.
Sixteen Parishes without, full	$4\frac{1}{2}$,,
The rest of the bills of mortality, almost	$4\frac{1}{2}$,,
The other cities and market towns,	$4\frac{3}{8}$,,
The villages and hamlets,	4 ,,

Upon the whole, (making allowance for *divided houses*, occupied by different families, for *uninhabited houses*, &c.,) he was led to conclude, that in England and Wales the people answer to four and a half per house and four per family.[1]

---

[1] Chalmers's *Estimate*, pp. 54, 56.

Subsequent inquirers have enumerated the houses and the inhabitants of various villages, towns, and cities, instead of relying on the defective returns of tax-gatherers; and from their researches it appears, that *King's* estimates of the number of dwellers which he allowed to every house, and to every family, were considerably under the truth.

From a table published by Dr. Price in his *Treatise on Annuities*, containing the results of actual surveys of the number of inhabitants, houses, and families in many different places, that ingenious writer was led to conclude, " That *six* to a house was probably too large an allowance for London, and that *five* to a house was certainly an allowance sufficiently large for England in general."[1] The same Table (although not quite so complete) is inserted in Morgan's *Doctrine of Annuities and Assurances*. Mr. Howlett, [*Examination*, &c.] from a still more extensive series of observations, insists for *five and two-fifths*, which, in the opinion of Mr. Chalmers, we may reasonably conclude to be the smallest number which dwells in every house, on an average of the whole kingdom.[2] M. Moheau, in his *Researches concerning the Population of France,* (published in 1778,) allows only five inhabitants to a house, on a general average of the population, both in towns and in the country.

Another principle from which conclusions have sometimes been deduced on the subject of population, is the quantity of *consumption* in the article of *food.* Supposing the mean consumption of individuals in bread-corn to be known, and also the annual produce of the national territory, with the imports and the exports, the population of the State would of consequence be determined; or, *vice versa*, the mean consumption might be ascertained on converting the *hypothesis.* The quantity of wheat, in like manner, imported into a town during a year, compared with the mean annual consumption of an individual, would determine the population of the town, and, in the opinion of a very competent judge, M. Paucton, would afford one of the nearest approximations to the truth that can be obtained in an inquiry of this nature.[3]

[1] Vol. I. p. 247.   [2] *Estimate,* p. 57.   [3] *Métrologie,* [1780,] p. 507.

The state of manners, however, (it must be remembered,) in the country where he wrote, rendered researches of this sort much more practicable than in others where the habits of living are different. *Bread* is, in France, a universal article of consumption among all classes of the people; to a very great proportion of individuals the *only* means of subsistence, and to the whole nation a most important part of diet. Even in France, however, the rate of consumption must vary greatly according to circumstances; according to the temperature of the climate (for example) which differs considerably in the northern and in the southern provinces, and according to the species of grain which the province produces. The results, besides, must vary in towns where flour is manufactured into various forms by the arts of cookery, and in villages where it is all converted into bread; in districts where wine and animal food are within reach of the lower orders, compared with others which are destitute of these resources; and in numberless other cases which may be easily imagined. The consumption, too, of individuals in the same family is extremely unequal; diversified as these individuals are by age, by sex, or by habits of indolence, or of bodily exertion. In founding calculations accordingly on data of this description, it is necessary, not only to make allowances for all the varieties of local peculiarities, but in examining any particular city or district, to conduct our observations on so great a scale that circumstances may fully compensate each other, and enable us to ascertain, within as narrow limits as possible, the mean consumption which falls to the share of individuals.[1]

It would be perfectly superfluous to enter into any particular statement of the French calculations on this subject, more especially as their results vary very considerably. In *one* conclusion indeed, they are pretty generally agreed, that the consumption of the people in wheat (one with another) may be rated at three *setiers* a year. This is the opinion of the author of the *Essai sur les Monnoies*, [M. Dupré,] printed at Paris in 1746; and most of the later writers on Political

---

[1] Moheau [*Recherches*], pp. 57, 58.

CHAP. II.—POPULATION POLITICALLY CONSIDERED.—APP. 219

Arithmetic have adopted his determinations. The *setier* is equal to something more than four Winchester bushels; and *three setiers* will be found rather to exceed one quarter, four bushels, three pecks, London measure.[1] This conclusion agrees very nearly with the result of the most accurate researches that have been made in England, with respect to the consumption of the labouring classes; and is strongly confirmed by a remark which the ingenious author of the *Corn Tracts* deduces from an extensive induction, "that the quantity of corn consumed by those who derive their means of subsistence from the work of their hands, has been in *all times*, and in *all places*, nearly the same, varying only according as the quantity of other food was more or less."[2]

Although, however, facts of this sort may have their use in comparing together the population of such cities as London and Paris, they can lead to no conclusion concerning the general population of an extensive country, without a knowledge of particulars, which it would be as difficult to ascertain as to accomplish an actual *census* of the people. In the year 1784, when M. Necker published his work *On the Administration of the Finances*, he there asserts, that the quantity of consumption in *wheat* over France was still unascertained; and he adds, that "the most accurate idea of it is to be formed from the state of population." Some of his conclusions, indeed, he founds on the consumption of *salt*, which, next to grain, was, in France, the most universal article of domestic expenditure. To this inquiry concerning the relation between consumption and population a greater degree of attention has been paid in France than in any other country. Some interesting facts with respect to it may be found in Moheau's *Researches on Population*, and in a useful work, entitled *Métrologie*, [by M. Paucton;] but it has, of late years, been treated with far greater accuracy than before by two celebrated writers, Lavoisier and Lagrange. Their calculations, with some others of a similar description, have been collected into

[1] *Corn Tracts*, [by Charles Smith, published in 1758 and 1759, and reprinted in 1804, with a life of the author, by George Chalmers, p. 190.] [2] Ibidem, p. 196.

a small pamphlet by Rœderer. The Essay, by Lavoisier, is more particularly valuable, and cannot fail to excite in those who read it, the deepest regret that the author should have fallen a victim to the ferocity of his countrymen, at a moment when he was beginning to divert his profound and original genius from those physical pursuits which have immortalized his name, to speculations still more immediately connected with the happiness of society. The slight sketch which he published a short time before his death, of his intended labours, is sufficient to show what light he was qualified to throw on some of the most important questions of Political Economy.

The plan which he has sketched for ascertaining with a precision hitherto unattempted, from time to time, the agricultural produce of France in all its different branches, the state of its commerce, and the state of its population, if it were actually carried into execution, would exhibit (as he has observed) in a few pages, the most important results of that science ;—" or rather," he adds, " Political Economy would, on that supposition, cease to be a science. Such statements would form an accurate *Thermometer* of public prosperity, and would afford a palpable standard for estimating the expediency or inexpediency of existing institutions."

With respect to the quantities of the several sorts of grain consumed annually in England, there is a very valuable collection of facts and observations in the supplement to an accurate and useful work, entitled " *Tracts on the Corn Trade and Corn Laws,*" first published in 1758, and reprinted, with additions, in 1766. [See p. 219.]

From these speculations, which afford but a feeble and uncertain light where questions concerning national population are under discussion, I proceed to another source of information, from which far more authentic and accurate documents may be derived. The registers which are kept in most civilized countries (with greater or less degrees of exactness) of *Births, Deaths,* and *Marriages.*

In my Lectures on Moral Philosophy, I have founded several important arguments on the uniformity which takes place in events depending on contingent circumstances; on the wonderful balance (for instance) which is everywhere preserved between the *two sexes*, and the proportion which the number of *births* and of *deaths* bears to the whole inhabitants of a country.* I may add, as another illustration of the same remark, the proportion which *marriages* bear to the number of a people who possess the means of subsistence in abundance, and whose manners have not been corrupted by luxury.

Some general rules relative to these proportions are collected in a book which I have repeatedly quoted, (entitled *Métrologie,*) but I learn from one of the Baron de Hertzberg's *Academical Discourses*, that the subject has been much more fully discussed by a German writer (Mr. Suessmilch) in a work entitled, "*The Divine Order in the Population and in the Revolutions of the Human Race.*"

" In this work," says the author from whom I borrow my information, [Hertzberg,] " Mr. Suessmilch has collected together, with as much judgment as erudition, almost everything which can be said upon the subject of population, giving the justest rules and the most accurate modes of calculation, for estimating the population of nations; shewing the best means of advancing population, and of removing the obstacles to it; illustrating the favourable tendency, in this respect, of the Christian religion, and demonstrating that Providence has established an admirable order for the continuance of the human race, by a certain proportion of births, of deaths, and of marriages, which is nearly equal throughout the world." I do not know that this book has been yet translated into our language, nor am I at all acquainted with its merits, except from the account given of it by the Baron de Hertzberg, Dr. Price, and some French writers, who all unite in bearing testimony to the industry, the accuracy, and the ingenuity of the author.

The regular proportions which have now been mentioned, can only obtain, or at least can only be observed, in a district where there are no settlers or emigrants. Thus, " in France,"

* [*Works*, Vol, VII. pp. 108-119, 380-382; and these *Lectures*, *supra*, pp. 87-92.]

Necker informs us, "that the number of births is in proportion to that of the inhabitants as one to twenty-three and twenty-four; in the districts which are not favoured by nature, nor by moral circumstances, this proportion is as one to twenty-five, twenty-five and a half, and twenty-six in the greater part of France; lastly, each birth corresponds with twenty-seven, twenty-eight, twenty-nine, and even thirty inhabitants in cities, proportionably to their extent and their trade. They even exceed this proportion in the metropolis." He adds, indeed, that "the difference arising from settlers and emigrants, and many other causes, acquires a kind of uniformity, when collectively considered, and in the immense extent of such a kingdom as France."*

The number which Necker fixes on, (in his work on the French Finances,) is twenty-five and three-fourths, by which he multiplies the births, in order to form an estimate of the population of that kingdom. The multiplier fixed on by Moheau for the same purpose is twenty-five and a half. The grounds on which he proceeds in making this choice are particularly stated in the *Treatise* already referred to.

The results of these writers receive considerable confirmation from the observations made in other countries. In Sweden, the number of inhabitants was found, by an actual survey, to be, in 1763, 2,446,394. The average of annual births for nine years ending in 1763, was 90,240, or a twenty-seventh part and a tenth of the inhabitants. These facts are stated on the authority of M. Wargentin, whose memoir is published in the fifteenth volume of the *Collection Académique*, printed at Paris in 1772.[1] In the kingdom of Naples, (where there is a survey made every year, and published in the *Court Calendar*,) the number of inhabitants was in 1777, 4,311,503. In the same kingdom, the average of annual births for five years ending in 1777, was 166,808, or a twenty-fifth part and four-fifths of the inhabitants.

From a great number of very accurate documents relative to the Prussian dominions, Mr. Suessmilch (as we are informed by

* [*De l'Administration des Finances.*]   [1] Morgan, *On Annuities*, [1779,] p. 291.

the same Baron de Hertzberg) was led to reckon *one* birth for every *twenty-six* living persons. The coincidence of these different results, *on the whole*, is not a little remarkable, when the nature of the subject is considered.

Of the *three* tests of population which I mentioned in entering upon this article, (*Births, Deaths*, and *Marriages*,) the first is that which is chiefly to be relied on. The last depends so much on the state of manners, that in the present circumstances of society in Europe, it can scarcely be assumed as a principle of reasoning.

[In regard to the second,] the Bills of *Mortality* are often appealed to in speculations of this kind; and they are certainly applicable (as will hereafter appear) to most important purposes. When considered, however, as a *direct* measure of population, they are obviously much more uncertain than the register of *Births*, the waste of life being influenced by a variety of accidental causes; such as epidemical disorders, healthful or sickly seasons, which do not affect the constant and regular supplies which nature secures to the human race. If, in order to compensate these irregularities, we extend our observations over a greater number of years, the *data* we assume become less and less applicable to the circumstances which determine the *present* population. It is not therefore surprising, that the results of calculations upon *this* head should vary more widely than on the former.[1]

Under the present division of our subject, it may not be improper to mention, that, according to *Dr. Halley*, the number of persons in a country able to bear arms may be computed at a little more than one-fourth of the whole inhabitants, more accurately at nine thirty-fourths of the whole.[2] Of this class he reckons all males betwixt eighteen and fifty-six, preferring these numbers to the limits of sixteen and sixty, which other authors have fixed on; because, "at the former age," he observes, "men are generally too weak to bear the fatigues of

---

[1] See Moheau, Paucton, Price, Morgan.

[2] *Miscellanea Curiosa*, Vol. I. p. 286.

war, and at the latter too infirm, notwithstanding particular instances to the contrary." As great use has been made of this rule by later writers, I think it of importance to add, that it is not only confirmed by modern observations, but by two passages (quoted by Dr. Wallace) from *Cæsar* and *Strabo*, who may be justly ranked among the most authentic authors of antiquity.

"The first of these relates, that after he had conquered the *Helvetii*, who had abandoned their country to seek new habitations, and in this view had carried their wives and children along with them, he found in their camp, rolls of all who had undertaken this expedition, distinguishing such as could bear arms, and the old men, women, and children separately.

" In the rolls the number stood thus,—

Of the Helvetii,	263,000
Tulingi,	36,000
Latobrigi,	14,000
Rauraci,	23,000
Boii,	32,000
Sum,	368,000

" And of the whole number, those who could bear arms were 92,000, which is the fourth part, and agrees perfectly with Halley's computation.

" The same rule is confirmed by a passage in Strabo.

" When Augustus Cæsar rooted out the nation of the *Salassii*, who dwelt upon the *Alps*, he sold 36,000 persons for slaves, of whom 8,000 were able to bear arms. And though by Halley's rule there ought to have been a few above 9000, this inconsiderable difference may be reasonably accounted for, by the number whom we may presume to have been killed before they were subdued."*

I shall conclude this article with a slight outline of the principles on which calculations concerning Population are founded on *Bills of Mortality*, combined with *Registers of Births*.

* [*A Dissertation on the Numbers of Mankind*, 1753, second edition, 1809, p. 40, *seq.*]

CHAP. II.—POPULATION POLITICALLY CONSIDERED. (APPEND.) 225

It is evident, that in so far as population depends on mere procreation, it is regulated by *two* circumstances.—1°,) By the number of *births;* and 2°,) By the *expectation* of a child just born. The one circumstance determines the rate at which population receives its fresh *supplies;* the other determines the number of *co-existent* individuals. It may not perhaps be superfluous to add, that by the *expectation of life*, is to be understood the number of years which mankind, taken one with another, enjoy, either from birth or any age proposed; the excess in the life of those who survive it being exactly equal to the deficiency in the life of those who do not reach it.

The manner in which the probabilities of life are ascertained is equally simple and ingenious.

Supposing the number of inhabitants in a city or country to be nearly equal for a course of years, and the number of settlers and of emigrants to be either inconsiderable in respect of the whole, or to balance each other, it would be manifestly an easy matter to find the probabilities of life from an exact register of the deaths, specifying the respective ages of the dead.

As the population of the place in question is supposed to remain nearly *constant*, the whole number of births must be equal to the whole number of deaths. If the births and deaths, therefore, of the infants who die in the first year be subtracted, both the remainders will be equal, or the numbers who live to the end of the first year will be equal to the number of persons dying annually above the age of *one*. For the same reason, the number of persons who live to ten, or any other age, is equal to the number of annual deaths above that age; therefore, if we add the numbers in the bills of mortality from any age upwards, the sum is the number of those born in one year who attain that age; and thus a table may be composed, exhibiting the rate of mortality at every age, and consequently the probability of living to any age proposed.

It is convenient to reduce these tables to the proportion of *one thousand* persons, and to mark both the number alive at the end of each year, and the number that die during the year.

[1] Price, *On Annuities*, Vol. I. p. 278.

Such tables, accordingly, consist of *three* columns; the first exhibiting the years of life in their natural order, 1, 2, 3, 4, 5, &c., continued to the utmost probable extent of life; the second exhibiting the numbers alive at the end of each year, (the number at the end of the first year being stated at 1000;) the third exhibiting the number of annual deaths. Hence the *probability*, that a person whose age is given shall reach any age proposed, may be found by mere inspection; that is, by comparing the numbers alive at these two periods of life. According to the practice of mathematicians, in similar cases, it is expressed by a fraction, the numerator of which is the number in life at the age proposed, and its denominator the number in life at the age given. In the doctrine of chances, it is to be observed, *certainty* is represented by one, and any degree of *probability* by a fraction; the denominator expressing the number of *possible* cases, and the numerator the number of cases in which the proposed event is found by experience to *succeed*.

The first table of this kind was constructed by *Dr. Halley*, whose thoughts appear to have been turned towards the subject by the obvious defects in the deductions drawn by Sir William Petty from the bills of mortality in London and Dublin. In these bills he remarks *three* imperfections:—" First, the *number* of the people is wanting; secondly, the ages of the people dying is not mentioned; lastly, both London and Dublin, by reason of the great and casual accession of strangers, (as appears in both from the great excess of the *funerals* above the *births*,) are rendered unfit to be employed as standards for the purpose, which requires, if it were possible, that the people should not at all be changed, but die where they were born, without any adventitious increase from abroad, or decay by migration elsewhere."

"This defect," continues Dr. Halley, "seems in a great measure to be rectified by the curious tables of the bills of mortality at the city of *Breslau*, wherein both the ages and sexes of all that *die* were monthly delivered, and compared with the number of the *births*, for five years, viz., 1687, 1688, 1689,

1690, 1691, the statement appearing to be made with all the exactness and sincerity possible."*

As this city (the capital of *Silesia*) has acquired a considerable degree of celebrity among writers on Political Arithmetic, in consequence of the important conclusions deduced from its bills of mortality by Dr. Halley, it may be worth while to observe, that it is situated on the western bank of the river Oder, near the confines of Germany and Poland, and very near the latitude of London. It is at a great distance from the sea, and as much a mediterranean place as can be desired, so that the confluence of strangers is but small; and the manufacture of linen, which is the chief, if not the only merchandise of the place, gives employment to the poor people of the town as well as of the adjacent country. "For these reasons," says Dr. Halley, "the people of this city seem most proper for a standard, and the rather, for that the births do a small matter exceed the funerals. The only thing wanting is the number of the whole people, which, in some measure, I have endeavoured to supply, by the comparison of the *mortality* of the people of all ages, which I have from the said bills traced out with all the accuracy possible."†

Dr. Halley's tables, constructed from these *Silesian* observations, have been found to correspond nearly with the bills of mortality of some manufacturing towns in England. Others in a still more correct form have been composed from the London Bills by Mr. Simpson; and of late, many important suggestions, tending to farther improvement in the practical application of them, have been offered by *Dr. Price*.

In order to understand the use of these tables, in calculations concerning *population*, it is necessary to consider, first, that if all the births happened on the *first* day of the year, and all the deaths on the *last*, the sum of the table of probabilities would be equal to the whole number of inhabitants. This is obvious; since the table of probabilities, as *directly inferred from the bills of mortality*, (that is, without being reduced to the proportion of 1000 persons, in the manner already mentioned,) consists of

* [*Miscellanea Curiosa*, 1708, Vol. I.]   † [Ibid.]

the number of inhabitants alive at birth, and at the end of the first, second, and following years. On the other hand, if all the births happened on the last day of the year, and the deaths on the first day, the number of inhabitants would be less than on the former supposition by the whole number born in one year. As the truth, therefore, lies in the middle, between these two suppositions, (the births and deaths neither happening all at the beginning, nor all at the end of the year, but occurring equally during the whole course of it,) the true number constantly alive together will be the arithmetical mean between the hypothetical results, and, consequently, may be found by subtracting half the sum of the annual births from the sum of the table of probabilities.

What has been hitherto said proceeds on the supposition, that the place whose bills of mortality are given supports itself by procreation only, unaided by recruits of settlers, and undiminished by the migrations of natives.

This is seldom or never the case with great cities, where, as the burials always exceed the births, the population would necessarily decline if they were not constantly supplied with recruits from the country. The age at which these recruits generally settle may be inferred from the bills of mortality. In these circumstances, in order to find the true number of the inhabitants, from bills of mortality containing an account of the ages at which all die, it is necessary that the proportion of the annual births to the annual settlers should be known, and also the period of life at which the latter remove. The following considerations will convey a general idea of the principles which afford, in such cases, an approximation to the truth.

In London, the burials are about one-fourth more than the births; and the bills of mortality from the age of ten to twenty, correspond nearly with others; but after twenty, the proportion of burials compared with those under twenty, is twice as great as in other places. This is occasioned by the number of strangers who resort to the capital about that age, whose deaths, as well as those of the natives, are inserted in the bills; and although no register of births were kept, we might infer from that sudden increase in the number of burials above twenty, that the population of London was supported by strangers who flocked to it about that age. In order to reduce the London bills to a useful form, we must divide the deaths *above* twenty into two parts, distinguishing those of the natives and settlers; and the burials *under* twenty, (which includes few settlers,) being completed by such a proportion of the burials above twenty as arise from the natives only, may be safely used for forming tables of probabilities.

Without this correction, the number of inhabitants would be overrated, the tables giving the probabilities of life, and consequently the expectation of life, too high in all ages under twenty. The true probabilities and expectations may be calculated from the corrected tables, and the true number of inhabitants is found, by multiplying the number of births by the expectation of life at birth, and the number of settlers by the expectation at the age of settlement.

An objection indeed obviously occurs to this correction, that it proceeds on a supposition (not strictly true) that all the settlers in London resort to it at the age of twenty. As this is not the case, the correction instead of being made at once, should be introduced at different ages, in proportion to the numbers that settle at each age. But the bills, when corrected as above, come pretty near the truth; and in inquiries of this sort, mathematical precision is out of the question.

The country is so favourable to population, that though many of the inhabitants remove to cities and foreign countries, the number of inhabitants remains undiminished. In this case, the bills of mortality give the probabilities of life and number of inhabitants too low. In order to calculate the true probabilities, the bills must be corrected, by adding the deaths of the emigrants, supposing them to waste at the same rate as the natives. To calculate the number of inhabitants, we multiply the number of births by the expectation of life at birth, computed from the true probabilities, and subtract from the product the number of emigrants, multiplied by their expectation of life at the time of their removal.

*In some countries, there is a rapid increase of the number of inhabitants from the stock of natives. In this case the bills will also give the probabilities of life too low; for the first effect of the increase is to enlarge the number of children beyond the due proportion of adults, and consequently enlarge the number of burials in the first stage of life.

Some cities, on the contrary, increase rapidly by reason of a resort of strangers, though the numbers be not maintained from the original stock. In this case, the bills must give the probabilities of life much too high, and much too low about that period of life when the strangers in general settle, and somewhat but not so much too low in the latter stages of life, providing the place has been in that situation for a course of years.

On the same principles, we might trace the effects of a decrease in the number of inhabitants, whether occasioned by a defect in the births, by extraordinary mortality, by migrations, or by a combination of these causes.

It appears, from the comparison of tables, that the duration of life is greatest in the country, shorter in towns, and still shorter in great cities. This may be accounted for from the circumstance of great numbers being crowded in a small compass, by which the air is rendered unwholesome, and infectious diseases more prevalent; the sedentary employments and want of exercise in the open air, and especially from the luxury and excess which prevails in cities. The difference is greatest in infancy, and very considerable in the first years of manhood, and becomes gradually less in the more advanced stages of life. In old age, the waste of life is as slow, or perhaps slower, in cities than in other places; the reason of which probably is, that all persons of weak constitutions are cut off in earlier years, and none but those who possess an uncommon share of natural vigour ever reach that period. It is also observed, that the lives of women, especially after the middle period of life, waste more slowly than those of men. "In general," Dr. Price observes, "there seems reason to think that in towns (allowing

* [The *three* following paragraphs are ambiguously deleted in the manuscript.]

for particular advantages of situation, trade, police, cleanliness, and openness, which some towns may have) the excess of the burials above the births, and the proportion of inhabitants dying annually, are more or less as the towns are greater or smaller. In London itself, about 160 years ago, when it was scarcely a fourth of its present bulk, the births were much nearer to the burials than they are now. But in country parishes and villages, the births almost always exceed the burials; and I believe it never happens, except in very particular situations, that more than a fortieth part of the inhabitants die annually. In the four provinces of New England, there is a very rapid increase of inhabitants; but notwithstanding this, at *Boston*, the capital, the inhabitants would decrease, were there no supply from the country ; the burials from 1731 to 1762, having all along exceeded the births. So remarkably do towns, in consequence of their unfavourableness to health, and the luxury which generally prevails in them, check the increase of countries." *

For a full illustration of these particulars, I must refer to Dr. Price, who has treated it with great ability and accuracy.

Some of Dr. Price's statements with respect to the progressive unhealthiness of London, have been disputed upon very plausible grounds by Mr. Wales.†

Having treated, at considerable length, of the general principles which influence *population*, I shall now take leave of the subject, after stating a few remarks more peculiarly applicable to our own country, and some other miscellaneous particulars which I could not easily refer to any of the foregoing heads, or which escaped my attention when considering the articles with which they are connected.

Before entering into any details concerning the population of particular countries, it may not be improper to premise the statement of M. Paucton, with respect to the total population

---

* [*Observations*, &c.]
† [*An Inquiry into the Present State of Population in England and Wales, and the Proportion which the present Number bears to the Number at Former Periods.* London, 1781.]

of the globe. It proceeds, as may be supposed, on very vague *data;* but it derives some authority from the general accuracy of the author, and from the near coincidence between his result and that of Dr. Wallace.

In this computation, the population of Asia is stated at 650,000,000
Of Africa, at 150,000,000
Of America, at . . . 150,000,000
Of Europe at . . . 130,000,000
———————
1,080,000,000[1]

The number is probably *below* the truth, as the writer certainly underrates the population of this part of the globe, in various instances. The population of China, too, is stated by him only at two hundred millions; although (from later accounts to be mentioned afterwards,) it appears to amount to three hundred and thirty-three millions.

It is not a little curious, that this population of China exceeds considerably that of the whole earth, according to Sir William Petty's estimate, which supposes the number of mankind now existing, not to exceed three hundred and twenty millions. Even according to Paucton and Dr. Wallace, the Chinese form, in point of numbers, *one-third* of the *human race*. But this subject I shall have occasion to resume in another lecture.

The question concerning the actual population of Great Britain, and its progress and decline since the period of the Revolution, has been at different times very keenly agitated by political writers, whose opinions on the point in dispute have been, in general, not a little biassed by their favourable or unfavourable sentiments of the system of policy pursued by our Government in the course of the present century. During the war in 1756, the controversy was carried on by Dr. Brackenridge on the one side, and by Mr. Forster on the other; the former contending for an increase, the latter for a decrease in the number of the people. The American war revived the

---

[1] The superficial extents of Europe, Africa, Asia, and America, are, according to *Paucton*, respectively as the numbers 1, 4, 5, and 7.

contest in a form still more interesting to the public; some writers of distinguished abilities having espoused opposite sides of the argument, resting their conclusions not merely on the details of *Political Arithmetic,* but on those general principles which regulate the multiplication of the species. A few years before the commencement of hostilities, Dr. Price had opened the discussion in his *Observations on Reversionary Payments,* published in 1769; but he afterwards entered into it much more fully in an *Appendix* to Mr. Morgan's Essay *On Annuities,* in which he attempted to prove, by a comparison of the number of houses in 1690 and 1777, a gradual decline in the population of England and Wales. At Lady-day 1690, the number of houses in England and Wales was (according to the Hearth-books, as examined by Dr. Davenant) one million three hundred and nineteen thousand two hundred and fifteen. In 1777, the total of houses charged, chargeable, and excused, (according to the returns of the surveyors of the house and window-duties,) was only nine hundred and fifty-two thousand seven hundred and thirty-four.* The population of England and Wales, therefore, Dr. Price concluded, must have decreased since the Revolution near *a quarter;* †—an effect which appeared to him to result naturally and necessarily from a variety of causes which have been operating during that period. Among these he insists chiefly on the following:—

1. "The increase of our Army and Navy, and the constant supply of men necessary to keep them up.

2. "A devouring Capital, too large for the body that supports it.

3. "Three long and destructive Continental Wars, in which we have been involved during the present century.[1]

4. "The migrations to our settlements abroad, particularly to the East and West Indies.

5. "Engrossing of Farms.

6. "Inclosing of Commons and Waste Grounds.

* [*Essay* appended to Morgan, *On Annuities,* p. 288, first edition.]
† [Ibid. p. 293.]

[1] Dr. Price's Essay (it must be remembered) was published in 1779.

7. "The high price of Provisions.
8. "The increase of Luxury, and of our Public Debts and Taxes."*

In support of the same opinion, several other considerations are suggested by Price, particularly the decrease of burials in the London bills of mortality, and the decrease in the hereditary and temporary excise.

One of the earliest opponents of Dr. Price was Mr. Arthur Young, whose arguments in proof of an increased population, rest chiefly on the progressive improvements of the country in Agriculture, in Manufactures, and in Commerce. He was soon followed by Mr. Eden, (now Lord Auckland,) whose observations on Dr. Price's statements may be found in a collection of [*Four*] *Letters to Lord Carlisle*, published in 1779. They relate chiefly to Price's reasoning, founded on his comparative view of the number of houses at the Revolution, and at present.

The most formidable of Dr. Price's antagonists, however, were indisputably Mr. Wales and Mr. Howlett. The former (who had previously distinguished himself as a practical mathematician and astronomer in the course of his voyage with Captain Cook) published his *Inquiry* in 1781. In reply to Price's fundamental argument founded on the comparison of houses at different periods, he shews,—1°· That the returns of houses to the tax-office are far from being always precise; 2°· From actual enumeration of a great variety of places taken indiscriminately, he proves a progressive population during the period in question. The present number of inhabitants (for example) in thirty-eight parishes in different parts of England, (according to the register of births and burials in these parishes,) was found to be to the number which was in the same thirty-eight parishes at the Revolution, as eight to three nearly. The present number of inhabitants in one hundred and forty-two parishes, taken in the same manner as in the former instance, is to the number which were in the same parishes between the years 1740 and 1750, as ten to seven nearly.

* [Ibid. p. 305.]

Many other facts leading to a similar conclusion are stated by the same writer, and certainly form a mass of evidence of great importance in determining the general question.

"In every instance," says Mr. Wales, " the places have been taken indiscriminately, that is, just as I could procure them, and I have omitted no place which I could procure; it may, therefore, be concluded, that they represent justly the state of the kingdom in general, and this argument cannot be overturned but by producing a greater number of parishes which tend to prove the contrary, or an equal number of facts of a more certain nature."[1]

Mr. Howlett's *Examination of Price's Essay* followed immediately after, [1781.] It was written without any communication with Mr. Wales, and corroborates strongly his reasonings and statements. Both writers adopt the same mode of investigation, appealing to the testimony of parochial registers, in a variety of places, at distinct periods; and as their researches were, in general, directed to different quarters, each of them has furnished a separate contribution of facts leading to the same conclusion.

It is impossible for me, in this place, to enter into so extensive and complicated an argument, as that which relates to the present population of Great Britain. One consideration, however, mentioned by Mr. Howlett in a pamphlet[2] published two years ago,* deserves notice on account of the stress laid on it by so very intelligent a writer, and I shall accordingly state the fact particularly, although I am far from thinking it so decisive as he conceives it to be. It is founded on the flourishing and increasing state of our hop plantations.

The annual average number of bags of hops, two hundredweight two quarters to the bag, grown in this kingdom during four successive periods of twenty-one years each, has been nearly as follows:—

---

[1] *Inquiry into the State of Population,* published 1781.

[2] *Dispersion of the Gloomy Appre-* *hensions occasioned by the Present State of our Corn Trade:* 1797.

* [This Lecture thus apparently written in 1799.]

Annual average of number of bags during the twenty-one years,

ending with 1731,	36,527
Ditto, ending with 1752,	50,752
Ditto, ending with 1773,	65,799
Ditto, ending with 1794,	77,195

In the opinion of Mr. Howlett, a great increase of population can alone account for this great increase in the growth of hops. Fifty years ago, the majority of our peasants brewed each of them a cask or two of good ale every year. Now a very small proportion of them, from a deficiency of wages, are able to purchase either hops or malt. Our tradesmen, our farmers, and in general all of the middle classes, drink more wine and spirits than they formerly did, and, of course, a less quantity of beer; and yet, notwithstanding these deficiencies, the total consumption of hops is amazingly increased. What is the plain inference, but that the number of our inhabitants must have augmented with a correspondent rapidity? For can it be imagined that the increased exportation of ale, beer, and porter, great as it has been, can have equalled the increased produce? especially when it is remembered that the exportation of any article of home-production is comparatively nothing to that applied to domestic use. This is strikingly exemplified by the trifling exports of cloth and of leather from our manufactures of wool, of skins, and of hides, in proportion to what they afford for the home market.

Besides, however, the increased population of the country, various other obvious causes might be mentioned which must have contributed greatly to increase the consumption of hops in the home market; and, therefore, the fact, although extremely worthy of examination, affords very little additional light with respect to the question at issue. But I must not dwell any longer on the details of this controversy.

The arguments founded on the general state of the country as affecting the acknowledged causes of population, are of a much more interesting nature; and it is here that Dr. Price appears to the greatest disadvantage. In the investigation and analysis of *facts*, his experience and skill in Political Arithmetic have given him, in various instances, a superiority over his opponents, but when he attempts to reason from general economical principles, his views are often confined and erroneous. It is but justice to him, however, to add, (what has not been always attended to by those who have combated his reasonings,) that, after a long and minute investigation of the subject, he requested " it might be remembered, that his opinion in this instance was by no means a clear and decided conviction;" and that he candidly allowed " there was a probability that in continuing to support his former arguments, he might be influenced too much by a desire to maintain an assertion once delivered."[1]

In reflecting on the general causes which have an immediate influence on population, our attention is led in the first instance to the quantity of *employment* which the country affords. " The demand for men," says Mr. Smith, "like that for any other commodity, necessarily regulates the production of men, quickening it when it goes on too slowly, and stopping it when it advances too fast. It is this demand which regulates and determines the state of propagation in all the different countries of the world; in North America, in Europe, and in China, which renders it rapidly progressive in the first, slow and gradual in the second, and altogether stationary in the last."* It may be laid down, therefore, as a first principle on this subject, that population will keep pace with employment; that where hands are wanted, hands will be found; that an increasing demand for agricultural labour will multiply the number of those who cultivate the earth, and an increasing demand for manufactures will swell our towns and cities.

The progress which agriculture, and manufactures, and foreign commerce, have made during the course of the present century, is well known, more particularly the two last, which have increased with a rapidity of which history does not furnish a

[1] *Monthly Magazine* for September 1796.

* [*Wealth of Nations*, B. I. c. viii.; Vol. I. p. 122, tenth edition.]

parallel instance. The progress, however, *even* of agriculture, must have been very great, as we may infer from an acknowledged fact, that " during the course of the last century, taking one year with another, grain was dearer in both parts of the United Kingdom than during the present."* At least on an average of the sixty years which terminated the last century, it was dearer than during the *first* sixty years of the present.[1] To whatever cause the effect be ascribed, whether to the bounty on exportation as some have supposed, or (according to the opinion of others) to collateral circumstances wholly unconnected with this regulation, it is a *fact* that from nearly the commencement of the present century, our exports of grain continually increased, and our imports as constantly diminished till about 1750, when the former exceeded the latter by an annual average of about 800,000 quarters. Since that time, indeed, a striking reverse has taken place; our imports constantly gaining on our exports, till at length the balance of importation against us has amounted to an enormous value. Of this last circumstance I shall have occasion to take notice afterwards. In the meantime, I would only remark the evidence we have in proof of the progress of agriculture during the *first* half of this century; and, accordingly, even those writers who have expressed the greatest alarm about its late decline, acknowledge its prosperous state till about the year 1750. This is repeatedly and strongly asserted by Mr. Dirom in his *Inquiry into the Corn Laws;* and Dr. Price himself admits, that from the Revolution till the period now mentioned, tillage seems to have been increasing over the kingdom.[2]

It is, however, unquestionably *since* that period that agriculture has advanced with the greatest rapidity. Of this, presumptive evidence is afforded by the rise of rents both in England and Scotland. In the latter part of the island the fact is sufficiently known; and in the former, Mr. Howlett asserts, that in most places they have been increased one-fourth, in many one-third, in some one-half; and that in the

* [Ibid. p. 115.]   [1] Townsend, [*On the Poor-Laws,*] p. 10.
[2] [*On Annuities ?*] Vol. II. p. 289.

neighbourhood of large manufacturing towns, they have been trebled and quadrupled. In the meantime, rates, taxes, and the expenses of farming and of living have been increasing so fast, that a diminution of rents must necessarily have followed, had not their effects been counteracted and greatly overbalanced by a more spirited, and more extended, and a more skilful cultivation.[1]

A still more palpable proof, if possible, of a general spirit of agricultural improvement during the period in question, may be derived from some facts mentioned in the *First Report* from the Committee on Waste Lands. In the reign of Queen Anne, it appears that there were only two bills of enclosures; in that of George I. sixteen; in that of George II. two hundred and twenty-six; whereas, during the present reign, there have been one thousand five hundred and thirty-two. The increase in the extent of land, or number of acres enclosed, has been vastly greater than the increased number of enclosures. The number of acres enclosed in the former periods of sixty years, was only 33,676; but in the latter of only thirty-six years, there have been 2,770,521; that is, there has been an absolute increase of more than eighty to one in the total quantity; and the medium annual increase above one hundred and fifty to one. The enclosure of almost 3,000,000 of acres whether of wastes and commons, or of open fields under prior cultivation and management, must have occasioned great expense to the proprietors of the land, and this expense they must necessarily have redeemed by an increase of rent. Accordingly the increased rent of the enclosures, even of common fields, under previous but imperfect culture, is stated to have been seldom less than one-fourth, sometimes one-third, and not unfrequently one-half; while the advanced rents of wastes and commons have been from the merest trifle to 15s. or 20s. an acre. In order to pay these increased rents, the tenants must necessarily, from an improved and extended cultivation, have raised a produce of value equivalent to three, four, or even five times the increased rent;

[1] *Dispersion of the Gloomy Apprehensions occasioned by the Present State of our Corn-Trade:* 1797.

and that they have actually done so, is evident from their increased opulence and prosperity.

I am abundantly sensible that doubts may be entertained how far the demand for agricultural labour increases *in the same proportion* with the general improvement of the country; and whether the prevalence of large farms, and the increase of pasturage occasioned by the progress of luxury, may not operate in the opposite direction. But granting this to be the case, (which, however, is far from being admitted by some of the more sanguine advocates for our increased population,) it can scarcely be doubted, that the demand for agricultural labour has increased *on the whole*. Something, indeed, more than mere conjecture may be offered in proof of this. By inquiries made in the different counties of England in 1770, by Mr. A. Young, and by calculations founded by him on *data*, (which Mr. Chalmers considers as *sufficiently accurate*,) he was led to conclude, that the persons engaged in farming alone amounted to two millions eight hundred thousand; besides a vast number of people who are as much maintained by agriculture as the ploughman that tills the soil. Whereas in an account which Gregory King has left of the number of all the ranks of the people, from the highest to the lowest, the two orders at the bottom of his scale, including labourers and out-servants, cottagers, paupers, and vagrants are estimated only at two millions six hundred thousand.[1]

Calculations of this sort, however, must necessarily be extremely vague; nor is it material to the present argument what judgment we pronounce on their accuracy. It is one great advantage (as I have repeatedly observed) of our modern systems of Political Economy, that they have converted agriculture into *a trade*, clearing the country of superfluous hands, and providing *employment* for those who would otherwise have added to the number of idle consumers. The great question is, What is the state of our population *on the whole?* And, therefore, even if we should suppose a diminution in the numbers who derive their subsistence *immediately* from hus-

[1] Chalmers, [*Estimate*, &c.] p. 207.

CHAP. II.—POPULATION POLITICALLY CONSIDERED. (APPEND.) 241

bandry, it remains to be considered, whether this may not be far overbalanced by the increased population which it supports at a distance. On this point there can scarcely be a diversity of opinion, after the statements given by Mr. Chalmers of the progress of our manufactures, commerce, and navigation during the present century,—a progress which necessarily implies an increasing demand for labourers in these various departments of national industry.

The woollen manufacture of Yorkshire alone, appears from documents mentioned by Mr. Chalmers to be, in the present day, of equal extent with the woollen manufactures of England at the Revolution. Since that era, too, we may be said to have gained the manufactures of silks, of linen, of cotton, of paper, of iron, of glass, of the potteries, besides many others.

Of the increased demand for labour occasioned by our extended *commerce*, some interesting proofs are to be found in Mr. Chalmers's *Estimate*, to which I must beg leave to refer for more particular information on the subject.

The public works, too, and private enterprises which have been carried into execution during the last fifty years, such as high-roads, navigable rivers, canals, bridges, harbours, &c., while they furnish the most unequivocal proofs of general prosperity, must have added greatly to the amount of national *employment*, not only by the labour to which they necessarily gave occasion, but by their effect in extending that commercial intercourse from which they derived their origin.

Among these, the system of inland navigation, now extended to every corner of the kingdom, is, in a more peculiar degree, characteristical of the opulence, the spirit, and the enlarged views which distinguish the commercial interest of this country. "The town of Manchester," says Dr. Aikin,* "when the plans now under execution are finished, will probably enjoy more various water communications than the most commercial town of the low countries has ever done. And instead of cutting them through level tracts, so as only to make a wider ditch, its coals are situated in mountainous districts,

* [*Description of the Country about Manchester*, &c., 1795.]

where the sole method of avoiding the difficulties of steep ascent and descent has been to perforate hills, and to navigate for miles within the bowels of the earth. At the beginning of this century, it was thought a most audacious task to make a *high-road* practicable for carriages over the hills and moors which separate Yorkshire from Lancashire; and now they are pierced through by *three* navigable canals." . . . "Nothing but highly flourishing manufactures can repay the vast expense of these undertakings; and there is some reason for thinking, that in the other part of the United Kingdom, the spirit which still prompts to their *unbounded* extension, originates in that passion for bold and precarious adventure, which scorns to be limited by reasonable calculations of profit."[1]

The effects, however, of these artificial navigations, which join the Eastern and Western Seas, and connect almost every manufacturing town in England with the capital, together with that of our multiplied highways, must be incalculably great on the *internal* commerce of the country. It is this branch of our trade which, in point of extent, is the most important of any, and which, at the same time, rests on the most solid foundation; *the best customers of Britain* (according to an old observation) *being the people of Britain.*[2]

As I cannot, at present, prosecute this discussion any farther, I shall only state the results of the opposite calculations which it has suggested. According to Dr. Price, the number of inhabitants in England and Wales must be short of five millions. His calculation proceeds on the number of houses as collected from the Returns of the surveyors of the house and window-duties. From these it appears that the number of houses in England and Wales in 1777, was 952,734. Supposing it, however, to amount to a million, and reckoning five persons to a house, which (according to Price's observation) is a high allowance for England in general, this gives only five millions for the whole number of people in England and Wales. The inhabitants of Scotland, Price supposes to be more than a *fifth* part of Britain.

[1] Pp. 136, 137.   [2] Chalmers, *Estimate*, p. 125.

On the other hand, it is contended by Mr. Chalmers in the edition of his *Estimate* published in 1794, from *data* which he has particularly stated, that the present population of England and Wales exceeds eight millions; and that since the Revolution there has been an augmentation of a million and a half.[1] *Mr. Howlett, in a pamphlet published in 1797, states the augmentation at a little less than two millions.[2] According to some later writers, even Mr. Howlett's computations fall greatly short of the truth. In a pamphlet (for example) published a few months ago (1800) by Arthur Young, entitled " *The Question of Scarcity plainly stated,"* I find the following passage:—
" Some years ago, I calculated that England and Wales contained ten millions of souls. This was the result of comparing the population as estimated by Dr. Price, from the houses returned to the tax-office, with the errors discovered in these lists by actual enumeration; and it ought farther to be observed, that the indefatigable researches of Sir John Call, Bart., in every county of the kingdom, have proved fully to his satisfaction, that the people have increased one-third in ten years,—that is, from 1787 to 1797."

If this very astonishing fact should be admitted, the people of England and Wales (as Mr. Young remarks) cannot be short of twelve millions.

I confess, for my own part, I have no great faith in the accuracy of any of these results; and my scepticism on the subject is not a little increased by observing at the end of Mr. Middleton's *View of the Agriculture of Middlesex*, (published 1798,) a letter from Mr. Howlett, (a very able writer on Population, and formerly extremely dogmatical in his assertions,) a frank avowal of the exaggerations into which he had inadvertently been led in the course of his controversy with Dr. Price.

" In my *Examination*," he observes, " *of Dr. Price's Essay*, I made the population of the kingdom to be between eight and nine millions. This estimate was formed upon principles so

[1] Chalmers, [*Estimate,*] p. 221.

* [From this to the end of the reference to Middleton's *Report*, (*infra*, p. 245,) added in 1800.]

[2] *Dispersion,* &c., p. 9.

extremely unfounded, which I did not then know, *but very soon discovered*, as rendered the final result utterly erroneous. From a more minute and accurate investigation of the subject, about fourteen or fifteen years, (which I intended to publish, but did not, and I believe never shall,) I am nearly confident our population did not then amount to seven millions and a half, and that at present it does not exceed eight millions. It is somewhat extraordinary that the fallacy which misled me, neither the public nor the keen penetrating eyes of Dr. Price, ever saw. The Doctor, indeed, pointed out an apprehension which he supposed me to be under; but that was entirely groundless."

The difference in these statements will appear the less wonderful when we consider the difficulty which has been experienced in arriving at anything like certainty with respect to the population of *London*. The inquiry has of late years occupied the industry of a number of writers of acknowledged abilities, and yet their results vary from each other by more than 400,000.

Dr. Price published very plausible reasons in support of the opinion, that about one in twenty and three-fourths died annually in London between the years 1758 and 1769. And, taking the interments at 29,000, it produced him the number 601,750, as the amount of the whole population within the bills of mortality.

Mr. Wales, in 1771, states them at 625,131. Dr. Fordyce within these few years states them at 1,000,000; and still more lately, Mr. Colquhoun asserts that the inhabitants of the Metropolis amount to 1,200,000.

Mr. Howlett, in a pamphlet published about 1782, computed the number of inhabitants within the bills of mortality at between eight and nine hundred thousand. In his late letter, however, addressed to Mr. Middleton, he confesses that the *data* on which the reasonings and deductions, which appear in his pamphlet in answer to Dr. Price, were founded, are too vague and precarious to be safely depended on, and that he has long been inclined to think that the number of inhabitants within the bills have never yet amounted to 700,000.

Mr. Middleton, from a calculation founded on some suggestions of Mr. Howlett's, computes "the total present population within the bills to be 628,484."[1]

During the last hundred years, Mr. Chalmers thinks that *Ireland* has done more than treble its inhabitants. And although this computation may perhaps be somewhat exaggerated, yet the data on which he proceeds sufficiently demonstrate a great progressive population, and afford a strong collateral argument against the reasonings of those who are of opinion that the population of England has been decreasing during the same period. According to some late statements, Mr. Chalmers's estimate falls short of the truth. From the *Report of the Secret Committee of the Irish Parliament*, published in 1798, Dr. Emmet appears to have stated the actual population of Ireland "at five millions," whereas, "at the time of the Revolution, it did not much exceed a million and a half." (The same gentleman is said to have acknowledged that this symptom of national prosperity had grown out of the connexion of Ireland with Great Britain.)

The progressive population of *Scotland*, from the year 1755, is demonstrated by very authentic documents. In the year 1743, Dr. Webster, an eminent clergyman of this city, and distinguished for his accuracy and skill as a political arithmetician, established a general correspondence over the country, both with clergy and laity, *one* object of which was to procure lists, either of individuals, or of persons above a certain age, in the different parishes of Scotland. When the lists contained only those above a certain age, he calculated the amount of the whole inhabitants, by the proportion which they might be supposed to bear to the number of souls, according to the most approved tables, compared with *the fact* in many parts of Scotland, where the ministers, at his desire, not only numbered their parishioners, but distinguished their respective ages. This inquiry was completed in 1755, at which period Dr. Webster

---

[1] Middleton's *Report*, p. 451.
[2] Lord Castlereagh in his speech on the Union, (1800,) estimated it from 3,500,000 to 4,000,000.—(Added Note.)

computed the number of souls in this part of the United Kingdom at 1,265,380.[1]

From the statistical accounts published by Sir John Sinclair, it appears, that a very great augmentation has taken place since that period, although, perhaps, not so immense a one as that gentleman at one period apprehended.

In the Statistical Table of Scotland, lately drawn up by Mr. Robertson of Granton, (from the *Agricultural Surveys*, the *Statistical Accounts*, and whatever other sources of information on the subject the public is as yet possessed of,) the population of Scotland is stated at 1,227,892. As the principal documents, however, on which he proceeds have been collected during a period of six years, (from 1792 to 1798,) his result, when applied to the population of the country *at the present moment*, must be understood with a certain degree of latitude. According to these computations, the increase of population from 1755 to 1798 would appear to be 262,512.[2]

A remarkable illustration of the natural bias even of *enlightened* minds in favour of times past, is mentioned by Sir John Sinclair, in one of his publications relative to this subject. "I have found the clergy," says he, "in *guessing* the population in 1755, *exceed in every instance* the number stated by Dr. Webster, and that they have *almost uniformly fallen short of the truth*, if they made a rough guess of the number of their parishioners at the time, before undertaking the trouble of an actual enumeration."

I mentioned in a former part of this Lecture, a very curious fact with respect to the state of our corn trade since about the year 1750, [see p. 238,] of which, however, I made no use in the course of my subsequent reasonings. It has, indeed, been often appealed to, by *one* set of writers, as a palpable proof of an increased population, while *others* have concluded from it, that the agriculture of the country is going fast to ruin. The truth is, that when considered abstractedly from other circum-

---

[1] Chalmers, *Estimate*, p. 224.

[2] The population of Edinburgh is stated in the same Table at 68,045; that of Leith at 13,241; that of Glasgow at 64,743.

stances, it neither justifies the former inference nor the latter, as the effect is manifestly influenced by a great variety of causes combined together. It may be proper, however, *now* to state it more particularly.

"From a representation drawn up in the year 1790 by the Lords of the Committee of his Majesty's Council for Trade, ' upon the present State of the Laws for regulating the Importation and the Exportation of Corn,' it appears, that this kingdom which, in former times, used to produce more corn than was necessary for the consumption of the inhabitants, has of late years been under the necessity of depending on foreign countries for a part of its supply." In proof of this their lordships state, " that while, upon an average of nineteen years, from 1746 to 1765, the nett returns to the nation from the grain exported is supposed to have been no less than £651,000 per annum, so great is the subsequent change of circumstances, that on an average of eighteen years, from 1770 to 1788, it appears that this country paid to foreign nations no less than £291,000 per annum to supply its inhabitants." I am not in possession of the latest information on the subject; but from a statement some years posterior to the former, it appears that the annual value of imported corn has amounted to about a million sterling.[1]

In one of the printed reports of the Chamber of Commerce at Glasgow, this change in the circumstances of the corn trade is placed *solely* to the account of a rapidly increasing population; while a late very respectable writer, *Mr. Dirom of Muiresk*, ascribes it to the alterations in our old Corn Laws, which began to take place about 1750. " In consequence of these alterations," he observes, " our agriculture, which gradually advanced, from the commencement of the present century, out of the lowest state of depression, till it arrived, between the years 1730 and 1750, at the highest degree of prosperity, has ever since been rapidly declining." He adds, that " the principal increase of our population in the course of this century was prior to 1750, and that 137,256 persons were employed in

[1] See Robertson's *Report on the Size of Farms*.

the cultivation of our lands, between the years 1741 and 1750, *more* than between the years 1773 and 1784.*

This work of Mr. Dirom, which was published a few years ago, [1796,] with some additional tracts by Mr. Mackie of Ormiston, gave occasion to a pamphlet by Mr. Howlett, entitled, *Dispersion of the Gloomy Apprehensions, of late repeatedly suggested from the Decline of our Corn Trade;* [1798.] The great object of the author is to show, that various other causes have been operating to produce the necessity of an importation, and which are fully adequate to the effect, without supposing the agriculture of the kingdom to be in a state of decline. I shall touch slightly on the most important of these, referring to Mr. Howlett's Essay for the particular results of his calculations.

1. The first of these is, the increased consumption arising from the vast increase of our population. The reality of the *cause* is here assumed as sufficiently established by other proofs; and supposing it to amount (as Mr. Howlett does) to two millions and a half within the compass of the last forty or fifty years, it certainly goes a considerable way to remove the difficulty.

2. Immense numbers now consume the finest wheat, whose ancestors were confined to oats and barley.

In a book formerly referred to, entitled *Corn Tracts*,† (published about fifty years ago,) the author, after estimating the actual population of England and Wales at six millions, computes the number of persons who used wheaten bread to be 3,750,000. The increase since that period must have been very great, from its gradual introduction among the labouring classes in various parts of the kingdom, where it was formerly, in a great measure, unknown. In the northern counties of England it was scarcely an article of food; at present its consumption must be considerable, from the vast augmentation of manufactures and of opulence.

The following fact I mention on the authority of Sir F. M. Eden, whose information with respect to the *North* of England

* [*Inquiry into the Corn Laws and Corn Trade*, &c.]
† [By C. Smith, see p. 219.]

seems to be more particularly correct. "About fifty years ago, so little was the quantity of wheat used in the county of Cumberland, that it was only a rich family that used a peck of wheat in the course of a year, and that was at Christmas. An old labourer of eighty-five, remarks, that when he was a boy he was at Carlisle market with his father, and wishing to indulge himself with a penny loaf made of wheat-flour, he searched for it for some time, but could not procure a piece of wheaten bread at any shop in that city."[1]

Of the increased consumption of wheat in some parts of Scotland, a very striking proof occurs in the *Agricultural Survey of Mid-Lothian.* "About the year 1735, (we are told,) the total annual consumption of wheat did not much exceed 25,000 bolls; whereas, at present it amounts to about 144,540, a quantity nearly six times greater than was consumed only sixty years ago."

The same writer informs us, that "the whole country fifty years ago did not sow above a thousand acres of wheat, and about the year 1727, not above five hundred, but that there are now seven or eight thousand;" he adds, that "the total consumption of the country is estimated to be three times its produce."

3. Another consideration on which Mr. Howlett lays great stress, is the increased consumption of the fruits of the earth occasioned by the immense multiplication of oxen, sheep, hogs, and above all of *horses.*

The multiplication of this last species of animal is beyond all accurate calculation, in consequence of the increased demand occasioned, not only by the ostentation and luxury of the great, but by carriers' waggons, post-chaises, mail, stage, and hackney coaches.

The increase of these several denominations, Mr. Mackie estimates at 400,000; and he allows three acres of fertile land for the maintenance of each horse, which allowance requires 1,200,000 acres for the support of the whole number. Mr. Howlett thinks this allowance much too little for those descriptions of horses which have been chiefly multiplied. It is cer-

[1] [*State of the Poor,* &c., 1797,] Vol. I. p. 564.

tainly much under the common computation. Mr. Kent states the quantity of land of the common medium quality as necessary for the support of a horse at seven acres; and Mr. Howlett thinks this statement not extravagant, if confined to horses destined for continual and vigorous exertion. Mr. Townsend, in his *Dissertation on the Poor Laws*, observes, that a horse to be fully fed, requires five tons of hay, and from thirteen to three-and-twenty quarters of oats, per annum, according to his work. Some farmers, he says, allow the former, and the latter is given by the great carriers on the public roads, which would bring the computation to about eight acres each for horses used in husbandry; whichever of these estimates we adopt, the consumption by horses must be enormous. Allowing five acres for the average of the horses which enter into Mr. Mackie's computation, these additional animals will require the produce of 2,000,000 of acres, which might otherwise have been applied to the cultivation of wheat.

When these different causes are combined, they go far to justify Mr. Howlett's conclusion, that the balance against us in the article of importation, is so far from being wonderful by its *magnitude*, that it is truly astonishing it should not be much greater. It certainly leads to no inference to the disadvantage of our national prosperity, and indeed the progress of our *agriculture*, and in a far greater degree that of our *trade* and *manufactures*, is a fact for which we almost appeal to the evidence of the senses.

In what I have hitherto said upon this subject, although I have in general *leaned* to the side of Dr. Price's opponents, I have avoided as much as possible to express a decided opinion. That an increase, however, has taken place in the number of inhabitants in this Island since the end of last century, I confess appears to me to be established by a mass of evidence direct and presumptive, which is almost irresistible. At the same time I do not, with the greater part of these writers, consider this increased population as an *unequivocal* proof, that the sum of our national happiness has increased exactly in the same proportion. On the contrary, a variety of considerations conspire to render it doubtful, whether the comforts of the labouring poor are now greater than they were a century ago.

That the comforts of the labouring poor depend upon the increase of the funds destined for the maintenance of labour, and that they will be exactly in proportion to the rapidity of this increase, may be assumed as fundamental, and almost as self-evident propositions. The demand for labour which such increase would occasion, by creating a competition in the market, must necessarily raise the value of labour; and till the additional hands required were reared, the increased funds would be distributed to the same number of persons as before the increase, and therefore every labourer would live comparatively at his ease. It does not, however, follow from this, (as Mr. Smith has concluded,*) that *every* increase in the revenue or stock of a society, may be considered as an increase of those funds. Such surplus stock or revenue will, indeed, be always considered by the *individual* possessing it, as an additional fund from which he may maintain more labour; but it will not be a real and effectual fund for the maintenance of an additional number of labourers, unless a great part of this increase of the stock or revenue of the society be convertible into a proportional quantity of provisions; and it will not be so convertible where the increase has arisen merely from the produce of *labour,* and not from the produce of *land.* The fact is, Mr. Smith seems to have confounded together two things which are essentially different; the number of hands which the stock of the society can employ, and the number which the territory can maintain.

Supposing a nation, for a course of years, to add what it saved from its yearly revenue to its *manufacturing* capital solely, and not to its capital employed on *land,* it is evident it might grow *richer* (according to the common use of language) without a power of supporting a greater number of labourers, and, therefore, without an increase in the real funds for the maintenance of labour. There would, notwithstanding, be a *demand* for labour, from the power which each manufacturer

* [*Wealth of Nations,* Book I. chap. viii.; Vol. I. p. 131, tenth edition.]

would possess of extending his old stock in trade, or of setting up new undertakings. This demand would, of course, raise the price of labour; but if the yearly stock of provisions in the country was not increasing, this rise would soon turn out to be merely *nominal*, as the price of provisions must inevitably rise with it. Nothing can be plainer than this, that any general rise in the price of labour, the stock of provisions remaining the same, can only be a *nominal* rise, as it must very shortly be followed by a proportional rise in the necessaries of life.

Something of this kind appears to have taken place, in this island, during the course of the present century, in consequence of a system of policy which has considered manufactures and commerce as *ultimate* objects, instead of regarding them in their due *subserviency* to agricultural improvement. The exchangeable value in the market of Europe of the annual produce of our land and labour has increased greatly; but the increase has been chiefly in the produce of labour, and not in the produce of land; and, therefore, though the wealth of the nation (according to Smith's definition of it) has been advancing rapidly, the effectual funds for the *maintenance* of labour have been increasing much more slowly, as I shall have occasion to show more fully when I come to consider the state of the *poor*.*

These considerations suggest a doubt whether Mr. Smith's definition of *national wealth* (according to which it consists in the annual produce of its *land and labour*) be equally just with that of the French Economists, who measure it by the *rude produce;* excluding completely from this definition, the results of manufacturing industry. But this inquiry properly belongs to the *second* branch of the course.

* [From the *Notes* taken of these Lectures in 1809, it appears there are here wanting the more recent returns of the population of *Great Britain* and *Ireland*, and likewise estimates of the population of *France, Spain, Russia, United States of America, China,* and *Holland*. But the same is shown, though less fully, by the " *Plan of Lectures on Political Economy for winter* 1800-1801," which is found among Mr. Stewart's papers. As, however, the parts deficient seem not essential to an understanding of the more authentic lectures, it has not been thought necessary to interpolate from the notes, which, at best, are comparatively old, and often hardly to be relied on for numerical details.]

[BOOK SECOND.]

[OF NATIONAL WEALTH.]

[CHAPTER I.*]

[OF PRODUCTIVE AND UNPRODUCTIVE LABOUR.]

(*Interpolation from Notes.*)—In the occasional use which I have hitherto made of the phrase *National Wealth*, I have employed these words in that general and popular sense in which they are commonly understood. But in analyzing the first principles of Political Economy, it is proper to ascertain, with as much accuracy as possible, the precise meaning of this expression; for which purpose I shall introduce this Second Part of the Course with an examination of the different definitions of the phrase *National Wealth*, which have been proposed by different writers, and with a comparative view of their advantages and disadvantages. The prosecution of this subject will lead me to an illustration of some of the characteristic peculiarities of language and doctrine by which Mr. Smith's system is distinguished from that of the French Economists. In considering, in the former part of my course, the effects of agriculture and the appropriation of land on general improvement, I have endeavoured to illustrate their tendency to excite a commercial spirit, and their connexion with the origin of most of the useful arts. It would furnish a curious subject of

---

* [The commencement of this Book and Chapter not being extant in Mr. Stewart's manuscript of these Lectures, the want is supplied, as far as possible, from the very copious notes of Mr. Bridges, occasionally supplemented, especially in regard to quotations, by those of Mr. Bonar. The beginning and end of this, as of similar interpolations, are carefully marked.]

speculation to examine this beautiful progress in detail, studying the mechanism of civilized society in that grand outline which Nature has sketched, and for the execution of which she has provided in the constitution of man, when combined with his physical circumstances.

It is evident that, in the profession of Agriculture itself, abstracting from the other arts to which it gives occasion, the foundation is laid for many exchanges which had no existence in the former stages of society; such, for instance, as the exchanges which arise from the difference of soil and exposure which distinguish different districts of the same country. The proprietors of each of these districts have their peculiar advantages, which would invite them to a friendly intercourse, by uniting them by the ties of their common interest. Experience would soon teach each individual to what kind of produce his land is best adapted, and would suggest the expediency of turning it to that kind of produce, in hopes of procuring, by an exchange with his neighbours, those articles of which he stood in need. The exchange, therefore, of the productions of one district for those of another, results necessarily from the physical situation of the husbandman, and will advance with the increasing multiplicity of his wants and desires.

The exchange of productions for labour is necessarily occasioned by the long and difficult preparation which most of the fruits of the earth require, in order to be fit for the use of man, and by the impossibility of the husbandman performing this task himself, without a ruinous waste of time and distraction of attention. The same motives, accordingly, which have established the exchange of commodities between the cultivators of different kinds of soil, introduces an exchange between the cultivators and a new order of men in the social system,—men who are induced by inclination, or compelled by circumstances, to betake themselves to the occupation of preparing for use those productions which the cultivator supplies in a rude form. By this means, the success of each party is obtained by the simplicity of his pursuits. The husbandman draws from his field the greatest quantity it can produce, procuring to himself,

CHAP. I.—OF LABOUR PRODUCTIVE AND UNPRODUCTIVE. 255

by an exchange of his surplus, the means of gratifying all his other wants, with far greater facility than he could by his own labour. Thus the shoemaker secures to himself a portion of the harvest; and every workman labours for the wants of the others, all of whom, in their turn, labour for him.

In this circulation of labour, it cannot fail to occur, that the husbandman possesses a distinguished pre-eminence over the other classes of the community, as observed by Turgot.* On this essential distinction between these two kinds of labour, the system of Political Economy proposed by Quesnai and his followers in a great measure hinges; and the distinction seems to me, under some slight limitations and corrections, to be not only just and important, but to hold a conspicuous rank among the fundamental principles of the science. I shall endeavour to illustrate it as fully and clearly as I can, and to vindicate it from some of the objections to which it is supposed to be liable. This appears the more necessary, as, though I agree with some of Mr. Smith's criticisms, I think he has not in this instance placed the doctrine of the Economists in a just point of view.

According to Mr. Smith, the wealth of a country is in proportion to the exchangeable value of the annual produce of its Land and Labour, comprehending, evidently, under the word labour, both manufacturing and agricultural industry. To this position I do not mean to object at present, nor am I disposed to limit in all conceivable cases the application of the phrase National Wealth to agricultural produce. It would be manifestly an abuse of language to deny that the Dutch are a wealthy people, because the means of their subsistence are entirely derived from abroad, or because the same system of policy would be impracticable in a different country. In consequence of these circumstances, their wealth, undoubtedly, is much less independent than that of an agricultural country; and it is evident that their example is totally inapplicable to the general condition of mankind. But as long as they continue to possess a complete command of the productions of other regions, the wealth of Holland differs from that of other coun-

* [*Sur la Formation et la Distribution des Richesses*, 2 v.; *Œuvres*, Tome V. p. 6.]

tries only as the wealth of the monied capitalist differs from that of the cultivator of the ground. The difference, indeed, in a national point of view, will be found to be great and essential; but as far as appears hitherto, it would be improper to cavil at Mr. Smith's expression, when it is possible by any restriction to reconcile it to a just way of thinking.

Of these two sources of national wealth, Land and Labour, the latter is by far the most considerable, or rather, in comparison with it, the former is of trifling moment. For although the difference between one country and another, in respect of natural advantages, be not inconsiderable, it requires the exertion of human skill and industry to render these subservient to the condition of man, as Locke has observed.*

In so far as the wealth of a country arises from manufactures or commerce, the argument is still clearer and more indisputable. Indeed, as Mr. Hume [in his *Essay on Commerce*] has remarked, trade, artisanship, and manufactures, are nothing more than the public storehouses of labour.

Since, therefore, the great source of national wealth is human industry, the opulence of every society must be regulated by the two following circumstances: first, by the proportion which the number of those employed in useful labour bears to those who are not so employed; and, secondly, by the skill, dexterity, and economy by which this labour is applied. It is justly observed by Mr. Smith, that it seems to depend more on the latter than the former.†

These considerations naturally suggest the inquiry to what causes this difference in the effective powers of labour is owing. I have substituted this word *effective*, instead of the term *productive*, employed by Mr. Smith, for a reason which will afterwards appear. On examination, it appears to be chiefly owing to the division of labour, the effects of which Mr. Smith has very beautifully and happily illustrated. One of the instances which he mentions, places the subject in a peculiarly striking point of view.

" To take an example," he says, "from a very trifling manu-

* [*Of Civil Government*, Book II. chap. v. §§ 41, 43.]
† [*Wealth of Nations*, Introduction, Vol. I. p. 2, tenth edition.]

facture, but one in which the division of labour has been very often taken notice of, the trade of the pin-maker; a workman not educated to this business, (which the division of labour has rendered a distinct trade,) nor acquainted with the use of the machinery employed in it, (to the invention of which the same division of labour has probably given occasion,) could scarce, perhaps, with his utmost industry, make one pin in a day, and certainly could not make twenty. But the way in which this business is now carried on, not only the whole work is a peculiar trade, but it is divided into a number of branches, of which the greater part are likewise peculiar trades. One man draws out the wire, another straights it, a third cuts it, a fourth points it, a fifth grinds it at the top for receiving the head; to make the head, requires two or three distinct operations; to put it on is a peculiar business; to whiten the pins is another; it is even a trade by *itself* to put them into the paper; and the important business of making a pin is, in this manner, divided into about eighteen distinct operations, which, in some manufactories, are all performed by distinct hands, though in others the same man will sometimes perform two or three of them. I have seen a small manufactory of this kind where ten men only were employed, and where some of them consequently performed two or three distinct operations. But though they were very poor, and therefore but indifferently accommodated with the necessary machinery, they could, when they exerted themselves, make among them about twelve pounds of pins in a day. There are in a pound upwards of four thousand pins of a middling size. Those ten persons, therefore, could make among them upwards of forty-eight thousand pins in a day. Each person, therefore, making a tenth part of forty-eight thousand pins, might be considered as making four thousand eight hundred pins in a day. But if they had all wrought separately and independently, and without any of them having been educated to this peculiar business, they certainly could not each of them have made twenty, perhaps not one pin in a day; that is, certainly, not the two hundred and fortieth, perhaps not the four thousand eight hundredth part of what they are at present capable of performing, in consequence of a proper division and combination of their different operations."*

Before, however, I proceed to follow Mr. Smith through his very ingenious speculations on the subject, it appears to me that some attention is due to the previous question concerning the relative importance of the different modes in which labour may be employed, more particularly concerning the relative importance of Agricultural and Manufacturing industry. This inquiry will lead to a comparison of the different sources of national wealth and revenue.

The remarks of Mr. Smith on this subject are not introduced in his system till he has finished not only the exposition of his elementary principles, but the discussion of various interesting and complicated questions connected with the science. But I must confess, it appears to me that it would greatly improve the arrangement of his work, and add to the precision of our ideas on the subject, if he had begun first with fixing his ideas, and defining his language with respect to the different employments of labour. Such, at any rate, is rendered necessary by the general plan which I have formed for these lectures, as the questions to which I am now to attend, are the link which is to connect our speculations concerning National Wealth with what has already been advanced on the subject of Population.

In illustrating the distinction made by the Economists between Productive and Unproductive Labour, I shall intersperse, as I proceed, a few strictures on such of Mr. Smith's criticisms on their doctrines as do not seem to me to be well founded. Those which I shall hazard on the system of the Economists I shall reserve for another lecture. In the sketch, therefore, which I am now to offer, I wish to be considered, in a great measure, only the expounder of a system proposed by others, without acquiescing implicitly in its details, excepting in those instances where I shall have occasion to mention my own opinion. The statements I am to give, will express, to the best of my judgment, the meaning of the authors by whom the phrase, *productive* and *unproductive* labour, was first

* [*Wealth of Nations*, B. I. chap. i.; Vol. I. p. 7, *seq.*, tenth edition.]

CHAP. I.—OF LABOUR PRODUCTIVE AND UNPRODUCTIVE. 259

introduced. But I have thought it advisable, for the sake of perspicuity, to aim rather at a faithful exposition of their general doctrines, than to give any full transcript of their writings. How far I have succeeded in simplifying the subject, I am not a competent judge; but I am particularly aware, after all that I have done in freeing it of the prolixity and technical phraseology of its authors, that my speculations with regard to it must necessarily appear, at first, to be expanded beyond what the importance of the subject can well justify. Those, however, who reflect on the advantages which, in some other parts of human knowledge, have been derived from a scientific arrangement of known truths unfolded in a natural order, and the substitution of appropriate and definite terms, instead of the looseness of common language, will not be apt to form conclusions to the prejudice of the very ingenious theory from which they are borrowed.

As the existence of the human race, even when limited to the necessaries of life, supposes a constant consumption of food, it supposes also some fund from which this expense is to be defrayed.

The fund which supplies this annual expense to any individual or community, constitutes a stock or revenue essential to their preservation, and without which all other possessions are useless. When this fund is once secured, the objects of their desires are multiplied, and a more ample revenue provided, if that is possible, the extent of revenue being everywhere measured by the possession of those articles of subsistence or accommodation which either furnish the means of gratifying those desires, or enable the possessor to command the labour of others. It is further obvious, that everything we are possessed of comes originally from the *earth*, including under that term the two great divisions of our globe into land and sea; and that its productions, variously modified, must supply all the wants of man, and furnish the means of defraying all his expenses.

The Labour of man can be employed to increase this fund only in *two* ways; by adding to the quantity of those productions, or by making such alterations on their form as may render them either more useful in themselves, or more valuable in exchange. The first of these is the object of Agriculture, the second of Manufactures.

In whatever manner the industry of man is employed, the produce of his labour is necessarily burdened by the consumption of the labourer. In estimating, therefore, the productive power of any species of industry, before inquiring whether it adds to the quantity, utility, or exchangeable value of the possessions of the society, the first question that presents itself is, Whether it supplies the means of defraying the necessary consumption by which it is maintained? In this respect, the pre-eminence of Agriculture is evidently conspicuous; the fund employed not only continuing without any diminution, but being more than replaced by the additional produce which it can draw from the earth. In consequence of the production of this surplus, the general revenue is augmented, and can defray expenses to which it was not equal before. Therefore, the epithet *productive* is most justly applied to that labour and expense by which it is raised. With respect to Manufacturing labour, the case is different; for though by the operations of the manufacturer the materials of his trade become much more useful, it does not follow that he thereby increases the national revenue. This revenue is the fund of national consumption; and it is not increased by any operation which does not supply the means of a greater consumption. That the work of the artificer yields no such supply is manifest. He adds nothing to the materials of his labour but the value of his own subsistence; and only changes the form of the materials so as to adapt them to the purposes of life. In this respect, therefore, the labour of the artificer, however useful, does not add to the general revenue *in the same sense* with the labour of the husbandman.

It is probable, however, that those writers who contend that the labour of the artificer is really productive, mean only, that it increases the exchangeable value of the productions of the earth. It is in this sense plainly that Mr. Smith employs the term, when speaking of the probable effects of foreign commerce in increasing the *productive* powers of manufacturing industry. I shall, therefore, consider how far the proposition is true, when taken with this limitation.

The exchangeable value of everything manufactured by human industry depends on *two* circumstances ; the price of the original raw material, and that of the labour which has been employed on it. The price of this labour arises altogether from the expense occasioned by the necessary consumption of the labourer ; and this expense is all the exchangeable value which the artificer can add to the raw materials, the competition of others restraining him from demanding more. Therefore, whatever value he adds to these materials, he destroys as much of the other funds of the society, and leaves the whole of the exchangeable revenue no greater than it otherwise would have been. For the illustration of these reasonings, no example can be more in point than that mentioned by Mr. Smith in the manufacture of lace.—" The person," he says, " who works the lace of a pair of fine ruffles, for example, will sometimes raise the value of perhaps a pennyworth of flax to thirty pounds sterling. But though at first sight he appears thereby to multiply the value of a part of the rude produce about seven thousand and two hundred times, he in reality adds nothing to the value of the whole annual amount of the rude produce. The working of that lace cost him perhaps two years' labour. The thirty pounds which he gets for it when it is finished, is no more than the repayment of the subsistence which he advances to himself during the two years that he is employed about it. The value which, by every day's, month's, or year's labour, he adds to the flax, does no more than replace the value of his own consumption during that day, month, or year. At no moment of time, therefore, does he add anything to the value of the whole annual amount of the rude produce of the land ; the portion of that produce which he is continually consuming being always equal to the value which he is continually producing."*

It is agreeably to these principles of the Economists that Dr.

* [Ibid. Book IV. chap. ix. ; Vol. III. p. 9, *seq.*, tenth edition.]

Franklin, in one of his political fragments, considers manufactures as " subsistence metamorphosed."*

In opposition to the reasonings already stated against the productive powers of manufacturing industry, Mr. Smith argues thus:—" It seems, upon every supposition, improper to say, that the labour of artificers, manufacturers, and merchants, does not increase the real revenue of the society. Though we should suppose, for example, as it seems to be supposed in this system, that the value of the daily, monthly, and yearly consumption of this class was exactly equal to that of its daily, monthly, and yearly production ; yet it would not from thence follow that its labour added nothing to the real revenue, to the real value of the annual produce of the land and labour of the society. An artificer, for example, who, in the first six months after harvest, executes ten pounds' worth of work, though he should in the same time consume ten pounds' worth of corn and other necessaries, yet really adds the value of ten pounds to the annual produce of the land and labour of the society. While he has been consuming a half-yearly revenue of ten pounds' worth of corn and other necessaries, he has produced an equal value of work capable of purchasing, either to himself or to some other person, an equal half-yearly revenue. The value, therefore, of what has been consumed and produced during these six months is equal, not to ten, but to twenty pounds. It is possible, indeed, that no more than ten pounds' worth of this value may ever have existed at any one moment of time. But if the ten pounds' worth of corn and other necessaries which were consumed by the artificer, had been consumed by a soldier or by a menial servant, the value of that part of the annual produce which existed at the end of the six months, would have been ten pounds less than it actually is, in consequence of the labour of the artificer. Though the value of what the artificer produces, therefore, should not at any one moment of time be supposed greater than the value he consumes, yet at every moment of time the actually existing value

---

* [*Positions to be examined concerning National Wealth*, 1769, § 5; *Works*, by Sparks, Vol. II. p. 374.]

of goods in the market is, in consequence of what he produces, greater than it otherwise would be."*

If I understand completely the face of this argument, it means only, that the values of what had been consumed are equal to twenty pounds. But the question is, Whether the nation has been benefited? The ten pounds' value of corn consumed cannot be again employed in any expense, and therefore cannot be said to constitute any addition to the revenue of the nation, which is only another expression for the quantity of expense which the nation is able to defray. Mr. Smith contends farther, that the labour of artificers produces a value equal to its expense, and continues the capital which employs it,—in this respect differing essentially from that of menial servants, which produces no revenue. This, however, I cannot help thinking is a fallacy to which this profound writer has been led, by the use of money as a medium of exchange. The artificer sells the produce of his labour, and, on a superficial view, appears to replace his capital as effectually as the farmer by reaping his crop; and, in truth, they are perfectly similar, as far as the individual is concerned; but they are very different in their relation to the community in general. The corn which the farmer produces is the free gift of nature, and costs nothing to the society; the manufacturer only changes the form of his commodity, converting what formerly was useless to purposes of general accommodation. When he does so, however, he derives the means of his subsistence from the general stock. He is not supported immediately by the produce of his own labour; and if he were cut off from all communication with others, he could do nothing to renew the capital by which he is to be maintained. His work is of no absolute value to himself, and is only the means of procuring subsistence from others, who exchange their superfluities for the gratification of their secondary wants. The capital of the artificer, therefore, is replaced by some other person, who thereby spends some part of his revenue. Suppose, for instance, I reap a crop of corn, of which, after deducting all expenses, there remain twenty bushels,

* [Ibid. p. 23, *seq.*]

which I exchange for a quantity of lace. These twenty bushels are very little more than equal to the consumption of the lace manufacturer while employed in the production of his article. His subsistence, therefore, is supplied, not by his labour, but by the produce I have drawn from the ground. He has lived during that time at my expense, as much as if I had advanced to him the wages of his labour. In fact, the capital which employs him is not the lace which he has made, but the twenty bushels of corn which I have paid him for it; and, therefore, it does not follow, that because his advances have been repaid, his labour replaces the capital which has been employed. The question is, Whether it replaces the capital I have employed, and pays the expenses I have incurred in raising these twenty bushels? This it certainly does not do. The expense, indeed, which I have laid out has procured me something, more or less useful, which I consider as an equivalent. But if the lace be an equivalent, so also is the labour of menial servants. The lace wears as the servant perishes; neither the one nor the other leaves anything behind; and if they differ somewhat in the length of their duration, the difference is only in degree, and not the consequence of any essential distinction between them. Suppose, now, the same quantity of corn had been applied to sow and reap a field; in this case the corn expended would not only be replaced, but there would be a clear addition to the revenue not only of the individual, but also of the community. In both cases, the expense laid out is replaced; but in this instance, it reproduces a surplus in addition to its value.

The difference now stated between these two kinds of expenses is essential and sufficiently great to authorize the distinction between them which has now been insisted on. This distinction, it must always be carefully remembered, has no reference whatever to the utility of the different employments now mentioned. The labour of a soldier, for instance, is perfectly unproductive; yet the defence of a State is an object of no less importance than the encouragement of commerce and manufactures; and, like manufactures, the labour of the soldier is useful, in some cases even necessary. But still there is an essential distinction between labour which is merely *useful*, and that which is also *productive*.

According to Mr. Smith, the true characteristic of productive labour is, that it fixes itself on some vendible commodity, the sale of which replaces the capital employed in it; whereas unproductive labour consists in services which perish almost in the time of performance. This distinction of Mr. Smith's appears to rest on an accidental and very unimportant circumstance, according as the subsistence of the workman is advanced by his employer, or is repaid through the medium of some third person, who has advanced his wages. If his wages are advanced by an employer, his labour necessarily consists in personal services; and it is a matter of indifference what these services are if they equally accommodate his employer. If, on the other hand, his wages are to be repaid by another, no person will be induced to do so unless that expense is replaced by some commodity which may be useful. This circumstance, therefore, is sufficient, in many cases, to determine whether labour, according to Mr. Smith's doctrine, shall be held productive or unproductive. A distinction resting on a circumstance so very slight, cannot surely be of very great moment in a system of political economy.

From what has been already said, it appears, that the process of manufactures can only be viewed in the light of a salary paid by the proprietors of land to those who are willing to employ their labour for their accommodation, and that the wages of artificers are a mere *transference of wealth*. Here, then, say the Economists, is the whole society divided, by a necessity founded on the nature of things, into two classes, both of them reciprocally useful to each other; one of which, by its labour, forms, or rather draws from the earth, riches continually new, which supply the whole society with the means of subsistence, and the materials for all their wants; while the other is employed in giving to the rude materials such preparations and forms as render them of a greater exchangeable value. He sells his labour to the former, and receives in return his subsistence. The first may be called productive, the second stipendiary.

We have hitherto proceeded on the supposition, that the

wages of the workman are merely sufficient for his subsistence, a result which must hold in most cases, as the amount of wages is necessarily limited by the number of those who work for a livelihood. This supposition, however, I apprehend, is not necessary for establishing the general conclusion. If, in consequence of any particular circumstances, the labourer should receive wages greater than his consumption, this would in no respect add to the revenue of the society. If, for instance, one half of the labourers of a country should be carried off by a plague, the price of their labour would be doubled. But though, in such a case, it may appear, on a superficial view, that the manufacturer adds to the value of his work a greater quantity than he consumes, yet it is plain, that nothing is added to the productions of the earth, either in quantity or value, so as to enable the society to supply a greater portion of subsistence to its inhabitants. It is the exchangeable value of commodities only that is increased. The difference is, that the proprietor of land is obliged to consider the same quantity of subsistence as an equivalent for a smaller quantity of labour. Labour gets a greater share of the revenue; but the revenue is in no way altered. Any saving a manufacturer makes from his wages is so much taken out of the hands of another person, and can no more be said to increase the funds of the society, than the gains made at a gaming table.

The same observations apply, with equal force, to the profits of merchants and master manufacturers. It is easy to conceive a State in which there should be no such persons, in which the proprietors of the land should superintend the labourers employed in manufactures, and transport the goods to the market from the place where they are produced. The trouble and waste which would attend such a mode of proceeding induce them to give a higher price for the goods to those who will undertake this branch of business, and make the necessary advances. This increase, evidently, is a salary, and the gains of the merchant are but a transference, not a production of riches. The same thing may be said of every species of industry, the object of which is to modify the productions of the earth, without increasing their quantity. They all agree in this circumstance, that they make no increase to the general revenue, though in the highest degree useful, and many of them absolutely necessary. They effect the important purpose of distributing the national riches; but they are totally unproductive. They add nothing to the revenue, but, on the contrary, draw the means of their support from those who are in possession of the fruits of the earth. These fruits, therefore, according to the Economists, are the only riches of a nation; and the labour which produces them is the only productive labour, and the only source of revenue.

Among those writers, however, who dispute the doctrines of the Economists, there are some who acknowledge the unproductive nature of manufacturing labour and expense, when considered in relation to the world in general; while they deny that the doctrine is applicable to the case of a particular country pursuing a separate interest of its own. As the inhabitants of a town, by applying to manufactures, find means to appropriate a part of the productions of the earth raised by the cultivators of the ground, so may a nation procure a part of the subsistence of other nations. Thus, manufactures and foreign trade add all the fund of subsistence which is drawn from abroad. In answer to these objections, the Economists state the following reasonings, on which I shall have occasion afterwards to offer some criticisms. If the trade of two nations consists in the exchange of production for production, whether rude or manufactured, it is evident that the exchanges must be equal, each giving as much as it receives. The only species of commerce, say they, in which a nation can be said to add to the national fund, is the exchange of productions on the one side for labour on the other. In such a case, manufacturing industry may be considered as productive to the nation which, by its superior ingenuity, thus lays its neighbours under contribution. If a landed nation supplies the rude materials and the subsistence of the labourers, to a manufacturing country, and brings back the manufactured article, these artificers certainly carry on a trade which is productive, and the expense of the one country is an addition to the revenue of the other. The artificers of the commercial nation are, in fact, those of the agricultural country. They have the same relation to it as if they had lived in it; and the only difference is, that their place of residence is at a distance from the market. The manufacturers settled in the agricultural country itself, would be on a level in the market with the commercial nation, even though they should add to their profits a sum equal to the whole expense of carriage. The necessary consequence is, that they would undersell the commercial nation; and nothing could prevent such manufactures from rising in the country itself, except the most essential defects in their system of Political Economy; and it is owing to such defects alone, they tell us, that a merely manufacturing country can exist at all; and the establishment of a more liberal system would necessarily raise up a competition which it could not withstand. In an age, therefore, add the Economists, when the minds of men begin to be enlightened, this is a most precarious resource; and a nation which relies on it entirely, sees in the improvement of its neighbours the presages of its own decline. Nor is this all. It is but a very few articles that can bear the expense of a long carriage; and these are not objects of a general consumption. This, therefore, may support a very small state; but it necessarily forms a very trifling object to a great agricultural nation. We may therefore conclude, that the labour of the agriculturist is the only productive labour, and that the rude produce of the soil is the only revenue of a nation,—the only fund out of which all its expenses must be defrayed.

In entering on the discussions which I now have in view, with respect to the Economical system, it seemed proper for me to begin with a general outline of its fundamental principles, delineated as faithfully as possible, after the ideas of its original authors. Something of this kind seemed to be necessary, in order to correct those misapprehensions of its nature which have prevailed to a considerable degree, in consequence of the account of it given by Mr. Smith. I now proceed to consider, at some length, those points in which the doctrines of Quesnai and his followers appear to me to differ from those stated by Mr. Smith in the *Wealth of Nations*, endeavouring, as far as I can, to separate real diversities of opinion from mere disputes about words, and to combine what appears to be valuable in both, without adopting implicitly the opinions of either.—(*End of Interpolation from Notes.*)

[SECT. I.—SPECIALLY ON THE SYSTEM OF THE ECONOMISTS.]

I made some observations at our last meeting, on the distinction between *productive* and *unproductive labour*, according to the doctrine of the Economists, with a view chiefly to a vindication of their language on this subject, against the criticisms of Mr. Smith. Of the particulars in which this part of his system differs from theirs, some of those which appear at first view the most striking, will be found to resolve ultimately into a question concerning the propriety of certain technical modes of speaking which they introduced ; and in so far, the dispute may be considered as amounting merely to a verbal controversy. It must, however, be remembered, that in inquiries of so difficult a nature, the choice of phrases is by no means a matter of indifference ; particularly when a want of coincidence between their technical and their ordinary acceptations may have a tendency to mislead our reasonings. In the present instance, this is remarkably the case ; for the epithets *productive* and *unproductive*, as they are commonly employed, being as precise and significant as any which the language furnishes, can scarcely fail to have some effect on the estimate we form of the comparative importance of the two kinds of labour to which we are accustomed habitually to appropriate them. The truth is, that the influence of these epithets may be distinctly traced in various instances, on the conclusions of Quesnai, on the one hand, and of Mr. Smith on the other ;—I mean the influence of the *popular* meaning of these epithets, as contradistinguished from the *technical* acceptations in which they have thought proper respectively to define them. The difference of opinion, however, between Smith and Quesnai concerning productive and unproductive labour, does not turn entirely on the meaning of words. It turns also *in part on a fact* which they have apprehended very differently, and which it is of great consequence to view in its proper light. I shall make no apology therefore for offering here, (even at the risk of appearing somewhat prolix and tedious,) a few additional illustrations and proofs of the remarks which I have already stated on this fundamental article of Political Economy.

It will contribute to render some of the following reasonings more clear and satisfactory, if it is distinctly remembered, that in the *first* part of the argument we abstract entirely from the effects of *foreign* commerce, and confine our attention to those which result from the operations of the different descriptions of labour in a separate and independent society. The fact is, that in a great agricultural country like Great Britain, and still more in a territory like France, where the importation of necessaries cannot possibly bear any great proportion to the consumption of the inhabitants, the conclusions I have in view will hold, in every essential respect, even although the operations of foreign commerce be admitted into the supposition. But it may obviate some difficulties and objections which might otherwise present themselves, to begin with stating the argument in its simplest form.

That Mr. Smith's opinion with respect to *the fact* on which the Economists lay the principal stress was the same with theirs, appears (among various other acknowledgments in different parts of his *Wealth of Nations*) from the following passage in the fifth chapter of the Second Book, entitled, "Of the different Employments of Capital."

"In agriculture, nature labours along with man; and though her labour cost no expense, its produce has its value, as well as that of the most expensive workman. The most important operations of agriculture seem intended, not so much to *increase*, though they do that too, as to *direct* the fertility of nature towards the production of the plants most profitable to man. A field overgrown with briars may frequently produce as great a quantity of vegetables as the best cultivated vineyard or corn-field. Planting and tillage frequently *regulate* more than they animate the active fertility of nature; and, after all their labour, a great part of the work remains to be done by her. The labourers, and labouring cattle, therefore, employed in agriculture, not only occasion, like the workmen in manufactures, the reproduction of a value equal to their own consumption, or to the capital which employs them, together with its owner's profits, but of a much greater value. Over and above the capital of the farmer, and all its profits, they regularly occasion the reproduction of the rent of the landlord. This rent may be considered as the produce of those powers of nature, the use of which the landlord lends to the farmer. . . . It is the work of nature that remains after deducting or compensating everything which can be regarded as the work of man."*

These observations, although by no means unexceptionable, in so far as they relate to *manufacturing* industry, not only coincide in the main with the opinions of the Economists, but express in strong and explicit terms one of the fundamental principles on which their system rests. It is a principle, indeed, so perfectly obvious and indisputable, that it is almost as painful to peruse their prolix elucidations of it, as the reasonings of those who have had the *appearance* of disputing its solidity: I say the *appearance* of disputing its solidity; for I know of no writer who has directly called in question *the principle itself*, whatever diversity of judgment may exist about the remoter consequences to which it necessarily leads, or the form of words in which it ought to be expressed.

In this last respect Mr. Smith's system differs widely; and accordingly, in the sentence which immediately follows the sentence just quoted, he speaks of agricultural and manufacturing labour as being both *productive*, though not in an equal degree. " No equal quantity of productive labour employed in manufactures can ever occasion so great a reproduction as in agriculture. In them nature does nothing, man does all; and the reproduction must always be in *proportion* to the strength of the agents that occasion it. The capital employed in agriculture, therefore, not only puts into motion a greater quantity

* [Vol. II. pp. 52, 53, tenth edition.]

of productive labour than any equal quantity employed in manufactures, but in proportion too to the quantity of productive labour which it employs, it adds a much greater value to the annual produce of the land and labour of the country; to the wealth and revenue of its inhabitants. Of all the ways in which a capital can be employed, it is by far the most advantageous to the society."*

In Mr. Smith's account of the Economical system, he has entered into a particular statement of the reasons which induce him to reject, as improper and inaccurate, the application which it makes of the epithet *unproductive* to manufacturing industry. He regards this indeed as the *capital error* of its authors. " Their capital error," he observes, " seems to be in considering the class of artificers, manufacturers, and merchants, as altogether unproductive and barren." In confirmation of this remark he reasons as follows:—

" It is acknowledged of this class, that it *reproduces* annually the value of its own annual consumption, and *continues*, at least, the existence of the stock or capital which maintains and employs it. But upon this account alone the denomination of barren or unproductive should seem to be very improperly applied to it. We should not call a marriage barren or unproductive, though it produced only a son and a daughter to replace the father and mother, and though it did not increase the number of the human species, but only continued it as it was before."

" Farmers and country labourers, indeed, over and above the stock which maintains or employs them, reproduce annually a neat produce, a free rent to the landlord. As a marriage which affords three children is certainly more productive than one which affords only two, so the labour of farmers and country labourers is certainly more productive than that of merchants, artificers, and manufacturers. The superior produce of the one class, however, does not render the other barren or unproductive."†

According to *this* statement of Mr. Smith, his objection to

---
* [Ibid., p. 53.]
† [Ibid., Book IV. chap. ix.; Vol. III. pp. 21, 22, tenth edition.]

the doctrine of the Economists turns entirely on a philological question, Whether the epithets *barren* and *unproductive* could in strict propriety be applied to anything which merely continues or replaces what existed before, without yielding any increase; whether, for example, the labour of the husbandman could be said to be barren, on the supposition that his harvest was barely sufficient to restore to him the seed which he sowed in the spring? That his labour, in such a case, might be said to be *productive*, in a particular sense of that word, cannot, I apprehend, be disputed; but surely *not* in the sense in which it is commonly applied in the operations of agriculture.

The example of a *marriage*, referred to by Mr. Smith, is not altogether a fair one, for when applied to this connexion, the word *barren* has a specific and appropriate meaning, implying a complete negation of the power to procreate. A marriage which produces a *single child*, could no more be said to be barren, than one which produced *two;* and therefore, if we were to argue from this case to that of manufacturing industry, it would follow, that the latter might with propriety be called *productive*, even although it did not reproduce annually the value of its own annual consumption.

This, however, as I already said, is but a dispute about words, although, even according to this statement, I must confess, the advantage seems to me to be on the side of the Economists. It may at the same time be fairly questioned, whether Mr. Smith has not gone too far, when he has stated it as a fact acknowledged by all parties, that "the class of artificers, manufacturers, and merchants, reproduces annually the value of its own annual consumption, and continues the existence of the stock or capital which maintains and employs it." For, so far as I am able to perceive, this proposition applies only to the wealth of *the individual*, but not in the least to that species of wealth about which the present argument is alone concerned, the wealth of the nation. This consideration, however, I shall reserve for future discussion; and in the meantime shall admit as correct, the account which Mr. Smith has given of the doctrine of his antagonists.

In the farther prosecution of the same subject, Mr. Smith has attempted to convict these writers, not only of an abuse of language, but of an inattention to a most important distinction in point of *fact*, in the classification they have proposed of the different kinds of labour.

" It seems," he observes, " to be altogether improper to consider artificers, manufacturers, and merchants, in the same light as menial servants: the labour of menial servants does not continue the existence of the fund which maintains and employs them. Their maintenance and employment is altogether at the expense of their masters, and the work which they perform is not of a nature to repay that expense. That work consists in services which perish generally in the very instant of their performance, and does not fix or realize itself in any vendible commodity which can replace the value of their wages and maintenance. The labour, on the contrary, of artificers, manufacturers, and merchants, naturally does fix and realize itself in some such vendible commodity. It is *upon this account*," Mr. Smith adds, " that I have classed artificers, manufacturers, and merchants, among the productive labourers, and menial servants among the barren and unproductive."*

Before I proceed to make any remarks on this passage, it is necessary for me to observe, in justice to the Economists, that although they rank artificers and manufacturers, as well as menial servants, in the class of sterile labourers, they do not confound these different descriptions of men together, or view them in the same light. On the contrary, a particular illustration of the stations which they occupy respectively in the social system, and of their comparative importance as members of it, may be found in various works published by these writers; among others, in a valuable book published by the Marquis de Mirabeau in 1763, entitled *Philosophie Rurale.* The sterile class is there divided into the *Classe Stérile Industrieuse,* the *Classe Stérile Soudoyée,* and the *Classe Oisive.* The *Classe Stérile Soudoyée* is farther subdivided into different orders of

* [Ibid. pp. 22, 23.]

men, the nature and effects of whose functions are illustrated by the author with much ingenuity.—P. 55.

In reply to the reasonings last quoted from Mr. Smith, in proof of the essential distinction between the labour of artificers and that of menial servants, the following observation is stated by the anonymous author of a pamphlet printed a few years ago, under the title of *The Essential Principles of the Wealth of Nations illustrated, in opposition to some False Doctrines of Dr. Adam Smith and others.*[1]

" The labour of artificers and manufacturers differs from that of menial servants in this, that the former yields an equivalent for expenditure, the latter *no* equivalent. Still, however, they are both with the greatest propriety termed *unproductive*, though the one be much more so than the other." To explain this difference, the author has recourse to an illustration or comparison:—" It will be allowed," says he, " that a field which returns only the seed sown into it is a barren field. But some ground, such as the sea-beach, may possess no vegetative power at all, and may not even return the seeds sown into it, consequently, would be much more barren than the other. The labour of menial servants is aptly compared to this completely sterile ground. But will the greater sterility of one spot entitle ground to be called productive, that actually only returns the seed, but gives no increase. This difference is only a greater or less degree of a *minus*, but will never give a *plus.*"[2]

This answer to Mr. Smith does not seem to me to be at all satisfactory, nor even to proceed on an accurate conception of the circumstances of the case. Perhaps the following considerations may be of some use in removing the obscurity in which the subject has been involved by these contradictory statements.

In order to remove, as much as possible, in the examination of this question, those biasses which the mind is apt to receive from accidental associations founded on familiar phrases or examples, it may not be improper to remark, that *the labour of*

[1] Printed for Becket, 1797. [According to Watt, the author's name seems to have been Grey.] [2] Pp. 11, 12.

a menial servant is employed by Mr. Smith, as well as by the Economists, to represent a great variety of other kinds of labour, which he considers as equally unproductive, although he differs from them in the principles on which his classification is made. " The labour of some of the most respectable orders in the society," he observes, " is, like that of menial servants, unproductive of any value, and does not fix or realize itself in any permanent subject or vendible commodity, which endures after that labour is past, and for which an equal quantity of labour could afterwards be produced. The *Sovereign*, for example, with all the officers both of justice and war who serve under him, the whole army and navy, are unproductive labourers. They are the servants of the public, and are maintained by *a part of the annual produce of the industry of* the people. Their service (how honourable, how useful, how necessary so ever) produces nothing for which an equal quantity of service can afterwards be procured. The protection, security, and defence of the commonwealth, the effect of their labour this year, will not purchase its protection, security, and defence for the year to come. In the same class must be ranked some, both of the gravest and most important, and some of the most frivolous professions, churchmen, lawyers, physicians, men of letters of all kinds, players, buffoons, musicians, opera singers, opera dancers, &c. The labour of the meanest of these has a certain value, regulated by the very same principles which regulate that of every other sort of labour, and that of the noblest and most useful, produces nothing which could afterwards purchase or procure an equal quantity of labour. Like the declamation of the actor, the harangue of the orator, or the tune of the musician, the work of all of them perishes in the very instant of the production."*

I thought it of importance to state this fully, because in consequence of the constant reference which is made to the case of *menial servants*, the labour of artificers and manufacturers seems, on a superficial view, to be degraded in the economical system below its just level; while, on the other hand,

* [*Wealth of Nations*, Book II. chap. iii.; Vol. II. p. 3, tenth edition.]

the mind more easily reconciles itself to the superiority ascribed by Mr. Smith to manufacturing industry over menial services, than it would do if the reader were always to recollect, that, according to his arrangement, menial services are classed along with the labours of the most useful and honourable orders in society.

Mr. Smith himself has, if I am not mistaken, been more than once misled by this very circumstance; as when he remarks, for example, in order to contrast the more strongly what he calls *productive* with what he calls *unproductive labour*, that "a man grows rich by employing a multitude of manufacturers, but he grows poor by maintaining a multitude of menial servants."* An inference by the way from which no inference can be drawn applicable to Mr. Smith's purpose; for when a man ruins himself by the multitude of his menials, it is not owing to the nature of the labour in which they are employed, but to the excess of their number above the reasonable demand which he has for their services; and a master manufacturer might ruin himself exactly in the same way, if he were to engage more workmen than the extent of his trade called for, or enabled him to support.[1]

In another passage, too, he observes of the Economical system, that "as *men are naturally fond of paradoxes, and of appearing to understand what surpasses the comprehension of ordinary men*, the paradox it maintains concerning the unproductive nature of manufacturing labour, has not perhaps contributed a little to increase the number of its admirers."† Now, I confess, for my own part, that to affirm of manufacturing labour, that the epithet *productive* cannot be applied to it *in the same sense* in which it is applied to agriculture, so far from having the air of a paradox, strikes me as bordering upon a self-evident proposition; nor can I easily conceive how this most profound and ingenious writer could consider such a proposition as more repugnant to the common apprehensions of mankind, than a distinction which represents the productive

* [Ibid. p. 2.]
[1] See *Edinburgh Review*, Vol. IV. p. 355, [July, 1804. Review of Lauderdale *On Public Wealth*, by Brougham.]
† [Book IV. chap. ix.; Vol. III. p. 28, tenth edition.]

power of agriculture and of manufactures as differing only *in degree;* while it classifies the labour of the Sovereign, of the officers of the army and navy, of churchmen, lawyers, and men of letters, with those of musicians, opera singers, and buffoons. To this last classification I do not in the least object; although I am much mistaken if it has not, at first view, somewhat of a *paradoxical* appearance to persons unaccustomed to the technical arrangements of speculative politicians. I only differ from Mr. Smith in this, that I think the labours of all the various kinds of artificers, manufacturers, and merchants, should have been included in his enumeration; and I am not without hopes, that the observations I have now quoted from him may tend to reconcile the mind more easily to the doctrine he combats; inasmuch as it appears to be so clearly acknowledged *on both sides*, that the question concerning the productiveness or unproductiveness of any species of labour is altogether unconnected with any consideration of its dignity, or of its utility, or even of its necessity to the existence of the social order. The Abbé Baudeau, in his *Exposition of the Economical Table*, places this in a very strong light, when he observes, that "even the plough-wright, although he makes the instrument with which the husbandman carries on his operations, is no more to be considered (according to the definition of that system) as a productive labourer, than a lace-maker or an embroiderer."[1]

In the reply formerly quoted [p. 275] to Mr. Smith's reasonings, the labours of artificers and manufacturers are compared to what the labour of the husbandman would be, if he were only to reap the same measure he had sown; the labour of menial servants is compared to that of a man who should sow his seed on the sea-beach, or on a rock without any return whatever. "The labour of artificers and manufacturers," it is said, "differs from that of menial servants in this, that the former yields an equivalent for expenditure, the latter yields *no* equivalent." This view of the matter (as I formerly hinted) does not seem to me to be just; and I think the author has been led into it, partly

[1] P. 98.

by the representation which Mr. Smith has given of this doctrine of the Economists; and partly by the imperfect and indistinct manner in which it is stated in their own writings.

"It is acknowledged," says Mr. Smith, "that the class of artificers, manufacturers, and merchants, reproduces annually the value of its own annual consumption, and continues, at least, the existence of the stock or capital which maintains and employs it; differing in this respect essentially from that of menial servants, who produce no value to repay the expense of their maintenance."*

I observed, in my last Lecture, [p. 263,] that there seems to be a fallacy in this distinction, and that its plausibility arises from the use of *money* as a *medium* of exchange, which keeps the real similarity of the two cases a little out of view. The artificer *sells* the produce of his industry, and at first sight appears to replace his capital as effectually as the former by reaping his crop. In truth, the effects are the same in both instances, so far as the individual is concerned; but they are very different when considered in relation to the community. The corn which the husbandman reaps is a free gift of nature, and costs nothing to the rest of the society. The manufacturer *changes the form* of his materials, converting, in many cases, what was formerly useless, to purposes of general commerce and accommodation. While he does so, however, he derives the means of his subsistence from the general stock. He is not supported immediately by the produce of his labour; and if he were cut off from communication with others, could do nothing to renew the capital by which he is maintained. His work is of no absolute value to himself; and it is only the means of procuring the subsistence from others who exchange their superfluities for the gratification of their secondary wants. The capital, therefore, which the artificer has consumed, is replaced by some other person who thereby spends part of his revenue. Hence it appears, that if the labour of a menial servant may be aptly compared to that of a man sowing grain on a rock, or on the sea-coast, the very same comparison will apply to the labour of an artificer or

* [Book IV. chap. ix.; Vol. III. p. 21, tenth edition.]

manufacturer. The truth is, that in both cases the simile *holds* in so far as the *productiveness of labour* is alone concerned; but that in both cases it *fails upon the whole*, and precisely from the same reason,—inasmuch as it has the appearance of implying an analogy between an operation expressive of folly or insanity, and two kinds of industry which, though equally barren, are essentially subservient to the comfort of human life.

According to Mr. Smith, the true characteristic of productive labour is, that it fixes itself in some *vendible* commodity, the sale of which replaces its expense; whereas unproductive labour consists in services which perish almost at the instant of performance.

In this distinction of Mr. Smith's, there are two different considerations involved. *First*, the *vendibility*, if I may be allowed the word; and, *secondly*, the *durability* of the fruits of productive labour. Productive labour, he observes, fixes itself in some vendible commodity, the sale of which replaces its expense; whereas unproductive labour consists in services which *perish* almost at the instant of performance. From the manner in which the observation is stated, Mr. Smith seems to have considered these two circumstances as coinciding; or, in other words, he seems to have considered the want of *vendibility* in the fruits of unproductive labour, as a consequence of their want of *durability*. If this was *not* his meaning, it is manifest that the two clauses of the sentence are not accurately contrasted; the *perishable* nature of menial services being stated in direct opposition to the *vendibility* of the commodities furnished by productive industry.

In order, however, to do all justice to the definition in question, I shall consider *separately* the *two* circumstances which have just been mentioned, as the distinguishing tests or characteristics of productive and of unproductive labour.

With respect to the *first*, that " productive labour fixes itself in some *vendible* commodity, the sale of which replaces its expenses;" it is obvious that it depends in many cases on the accidental manner in which the subsistence of the workman is advanced; whether by the person who ultimately consumes or enjoys the fruits of his labour, or by a *third person*, who is to re-imburse himself by the sale of what the labourer has manufactured. If the wages are advanced by the person who is to enjoy the fruit of the labourer's industry, the labour consists in *personal service*, never fixing itself in a commodity which is to become an object of commerce, or to repay its expense by a sale. In this case I presume it will be readily granted to be a matter of indifference what these services are, provided they contribute equally to the accommodation of the employer. The labour of a housemaid, for example, when employed (according to the old practice of this country) in spinning flax for her master's convenience, could not be supposed to differ essentially in its nature from her services in making the beds, or in sweeping the apartments. If her labour, in the former way, save him from an expenditure which he must otherwise have incurred to procure the same accommodation, her services in the latter way have an effect precisely similar, by relieving him from the personal execution of a task which would otherwise have interfered with more profitable or more agreeable engagements.

If, on the other hand, we suppose that the wages of the workman are to be repaid by the sale of the commodity he has manufactured, the fact is in all essential respects the same. The end is accomplished in a way more circuitous, and with a different effect to the income of the person who thus replaces his capital; but that these circumstances cannot alter the nature of the labourer's employment, when considered in relation to the community of which he is a member, might almost be assumed as a self-evident proposition; inasmuch as the expense of his maintenance must, in some way or other, be derived ultimately from the general fund or revenue.

In the *second* place, Mr. Smith observes of *unproductive* labour, that "it consists in services which perish almost at the instant of performance." If this characteristic of unproductive labour be considered as coinciding with the other; that is, if the *perishable nature* of these services be supposed to render them *unproductive only* by preventing their fruits from ever becoming the objects of commerce, the same remarks which have been made on the former characteristic, are exactly applicable to the latter: and that this *was* Mr. Smith's meaning cannot, I apprehend, be reasonably doubted; because, on the supposition that the *unproductiveness* of menial, or any other services, were a consequence of the *perishable* nature of their effects, the absurd conclusion would follow, that the productiveness of labour is proportioned to the *durability* of the object it fabricates; and that it admits of all possible *degrees* according to the quality of the materials upon which it is employed.

From what has been already said, it would appear that the price of manufactures is to be considered in no other light than as a *salary* paid by the proprietor of land to those who are willing to employ their labour in his service. The wages of artificers are mere transferences of riches; and the result of their industry, *not* the production or the continuation of a part of national stock, but the means of procuring a portion of the produce of the soil.

The indistinct manner in which some of the economical writers have explained this article of their system, has contributed to occasion these misapprehensions with respect to the nature of manufacturing industry. From the particular stress they lay on the general principle, that "the consumption of manufacturers and artificers is equal to the (exchangeable) value of what they produce," it has been assumed by their opponents, and among others by Mr. Smith, as an admitted truth, that this class by reproducing annually the value of its own consumption, continues the existence of the stock or capital which maintains and employs it. And, indeed, this idea seems frequently to be implied in their reasonings. It is, however, obvious, with respect to this favourite principle of the Economists, concerning the exchangeable value added to commodities by manufacturing industry, that although it is of great importance in the argument, concerning the effects of manufactures *when combined with foreign commerce*, it has no immediate connexion with that part of their theory which asserts the unproductive nature of this species of labour *in an independent and insulated society*. To say that "the labour employed on land is productive, because (over and above completely paying the labourer and the farmer) the produce affords a clear rent to the landlord; and that the labour employed in a piece of lace is unproductive, because it merely replaces the provision that the workmen has consumed, is to rest this important distinction on a fact very different from that on which it really hinges."[1] Supposing the value of the wrought lace to be such, as that besides paying in the most complete manner the workmen and his employer, it would afford a clear rent to a third person, the reasonings which have been already stated against the productive power of manufacturing industry would still remain in full force.

This I endeavoured to shew as clearly as I was able at our last meeting; and I have now only to add, that the converse of the proposition is no less certain; that as a capital employed in manufacturing speculations may often be highly productive to the individual, while it must be ever *unproductive* to the community, so a capital employed in agriculture may be highly productive to the community, while the individual accomplishes his own ruin.

In considering the effects of manufactures *as combined with foreign commerce*, the Economists have expressed themselves in terms much more liable to objection, (as I shall endeavour afterwards to shew,) although even on this head their reasonings may suggest conclusions of great practical importance to the rulers of nations. As I must not, however, at present prosecute this subject any farther, I shall confine my attention to the *obvious fact*, (which cannot be better stated than in the words of Mr. Smith,) " that by means of trade and manufactures, a greater quantity of subsistence can be annually imported into a particular country, than what its own lands in the actual state of cultivation could afford. The inhabitants of a town, though they frequently possess no lands of their own, yet draw to themselves by their industry such a quantity of the rude produce of the lands of other people, as supplies them not only with the materials for their work, but with the fund of

[1] *Essay on the Principle of Population*, p. 430. [By Malthus, 1798.]

their subsistence. What a town always is with regard to the country in its neighbourhood, one independent state or country *may frequently* be with regard to other independent states and countries. It is thus that Holland draws a part of its subsistence from other countries; live cattle from Holstein and Jutland, and corn from almost all the different countries of Europe."*

With this observation of Mr. Smith I perfectly agree, and I think it calls our attention to a principle too much overlooked or slurred over by most of the Economists, in the statement of their *theory*. On the other hand, I agree with the general doctrines of this sect so far, as to feel it incumbent on me to remark, that in a great agricultural country such as ours, too much stress ought not to be laid on the passage which has now been quoted, as a ground for abating the efforts of our statesmen, to advance to the utmost possible extent our independent agricultural resources. The example of Holland itself which Mr. Smith has quoted, (the happiest undoubtedly for his purpose which the world affords,) is the best illustration of this that can be mentioned. It forms, in truth, one of those extreme cases in human affairs, (cases from which it is always dangerous to apply our inferences to the general condition of mankind,) of which I formerly took notice, when contrasting the policy of this singular district with that of the Empire of China. The grain raised in Holland is said to be scarcely sufficient to maintain the labourers employed on the dykes; and yet it is mentioned by St. Pierre as a subject of doubt, whether there is not more Polish corn in its granaries, than that country retains for the subsistence of its own inhabitants.† How totally inap-

---

* [*Wealth of Nations*, Book IV. chap. ix.; Vol. III. pp. 26, 27, tenth edition.]

† [This suggests an Epigram of Joseph Scaliger, written in Greek and Latin, *On the Marvels of Holland*, and addressed by the "Dictator" to the celebrated Janus Dousa, (1600.) The following is the Latin version:—

"DE MIRANDIS BATAVIÆ.

"Ignorata tuæ referam miracula terræ,
Dousa, peregrinis non habitura fidem.

Omnia lanitium hic lassat textrina Minervæ.
Lanigeros tamen hinc scimus abesse greges.
Non capiunt operas fabriles oppida vestra.
Nulla fabris tamen hæc ligna ministrat humus
Horrea triticeæ rumpunt hic frugis acervi.
Pascuus hic tamen est, non Cerealis ager.
Hic numerosa meri stipantur dolia cellis.
Quæ vineta colat nulla putator habet.
Hic nulla, aut certe seges est rarissima lini.
Linificii tamen est copia major ubi?
Hic mediis habitatur aquis, quis credere possit?
Et tamen hic nullæ, Dousa, bibuntur aquæ."]

CHAP. I.—OF LABOUR PRODUCTIVE AND UNPRODUCTIVE. 285

plicable to the general state of the world must those speculations be, which are founded on the policy of a people so peculiarly circumstanced! Of the absurdity of applying them to our own country, no stronger proof can be adduced than what I shall have occasion to state more particularly afterwards, that, notwithstanding the advantages it derives from its insular form, and the extent of its inland navigation, the greatest importation of grain which ever took place in one year, previous to the late years of scarcity, did not exceed a *thirtieth* part of our annual consumption; and that even in the course of the year 1801, notwithstanding the enormous expense of £15,000,000, it did not exceed an *eighteenth* part of that quantity.[1]

In a great agricultural territory, not enjoying the same easy intercourse with other parts of the world, the comparison must fail to a proportionally greater degree; and, in general, as different countries approach more nearly to this last description, Mr. Smith's remarks become inapplicable to the physical condition of their inhabitants.

Still, however, it must be granted, that manufacturing industry (though invariably the same in its nature when considered in relation to the whole world) may be justly said to be productive in its effects *to the nation*, which, by superior ingenuity or industry, thus lays its neighbours under contribution; however precarious and liable to interruption so circuitous a channel of revenue must always be, when compared with that resulting from the productive labour which depends on ourselves. In justice, at the same time, to a former part of my argument, I must take the liberty to add, that while I grant that in the case which has been just stated, the epithet *productive* may be justly applied to the industry of *manufacturers and artificers*, this affords no reason for distinguishing them from those other classes of labourers who are considered as *unproductive* in Mr. Smith's argument. A celebrated University which should attract a concourse of students from other countries, the public spectacles of a great capital, where the

[1] Bell, p. 454. [See above, p. 202.]

"declamations of the actor, the tune of the musician, and the grimace of the buffoon," contribute to swell the crowd of opulent and prodigal foreigners; the exertions of those who carry their talents and enterprise to the splendid markets which ambition opens to them in every quarter of the globe, and who afterwards return to enjoy their acquisitions in their native land; are all productive in the same sense with the manufacturers of a trading nation. They introduce into the country a fund which would not otherwise have existed in it, and which *may* be eventually productive, either by supplying the means of importing rude produce from abroad, or by adding to the number of productive labourers at home.

A still closer resemblance may be remarked between the labour of *manufacturers* and that of *authors*, abstracting altogether from the effect of foreign intercourse, and adopting Mr. Smith's own definition of productive labour. What inestimable and what extensive utility, not only to his own country, but to the whole human race, did *his* genius and information communicate to the blank paper, to which was intrusted the original copy of the *Wealth of Nations!* Or, laying aside all considerations of *this* kind, and viewing merely in a commercial light the exchangeable value of his labour, in what respects did the productiveness of this labour to the author differ from that of the workman who spends a year in fabricating a pennyworth of flax into a costly piece of lace? In the one case as well as in the other, is not labour *fixed and realized* in a vendible commodity?

In *one* particular respect, I do not think that Mr. Smith has done complete justice to manufacturers and artists. "They reproduce," he says, "annually the value of their own annual consumption, *continuing* at least the existence of the stock or capital which maintains them."* And that their labour has *this* effect, *in as far as they themselves, or the individual who advances their wages are concerned*, I have already acknowledged. But, if this is to be considered as a test of productiveness, the argument might be pushed much farther, by

* [*Wealth of Nations*, Book IV. chap. ix.; Vol. III. p. 21, tenth edition.]

examining the effects of *experience* and *habit* in rendering the workman's *skill and dexterity*, no less than the *articles he fabricates* vendible commodities, which he may carry to a profitable market. In this case, the labour he employs, during his years of apprenticeship, does a great deal more than replace to the individual the expense of its maintenance. It even affords him a *nett produce*, analogous, in some respects, to that which the husbandman enjoys.

If this view of the subject be admitted, the parallel between manufacturers and those who devote themselves to labour purely intellectual, will be found still to hold without any disadvantage to the latter. The harangue, indeed, of the orator, the declamation of the actor, and the tune of the musician, (to borrow Mr. Smith's own instances,) "may perish in the very instant of the production."* The labour is coexistent with the effects. But although this may be the case with the *particular exertions* of all their labours, the observation will not apply to the labour directed to the acquisition of the *talents* which are thus displayed; and which by converting these talents into a source of revenue to the possessors, has fixed and realized itself into a vendible and durable commodity. When the labour is at all successful, the sale not only replaces to the employer the expense incurred during the tedious process of preparation, it generally does a great deal more; and in no case is it necessarily subjected to any such limitation. I cannot help taking this opportunity to add, that the labour which is employed in the cultivation of the *understanding* approaches more nearly, (in the harvest which it yields,) than anything else which can be specified, to the labour of the husbandman; and the creative powers of human industry are, in both instances, founded on the combination of its effects with that *bounty of nature*, which, in the moral not less than the material world, rewards in due season with its plentiful increase the toils of the spring.

To this analogy, Lord Bacon had manifestly a reference when, in his usual figurative style, he bestowed on education the

* [Ibid. Book II. chap. iii.; Vol. II. p. 3, tenth edition.]

significant title of "*the Georgics of the Mind.*"[1] Intimating to legislators this important truth, that of all the means they have in their power to employ, to increase the sum of public happiness, none can so amply and so infallibly reward their benevolent exertions, as the encouragement which is afforded to Agriculture, and the attention which is bestowed on the Instruction of the people. In both instances the legislator exerts a power which is literally *productive* or *creative*, compelling, in the one case, the unprofitable desert to pour forth its latent riches; and, in the other, vivifying the dormant seeds of genius and virtue, and redeeming from the neglected waste of human intellect a new and unexpected accession to the common inheritance of mankind.

A few additional observations on the fundamental principles of the *Economical System* still remain, which I shall reserve (with some critical remarks on the improprieties of its phraseology, and on certain errors into which its authors appear to have been led by mistaken views of philanthropy) to be the subject of another lecture.

My two last Lectures were employed in examining Mr. Smith's criticisms on the doctrine of the Economists, concerning productive and unproductive labour. The subject, after all I have stated, is, I am sensible, very far from being exhausted; and when I recollect the different lights in which it has been viewed by so many eminent men, it is impossible for me not to feel a certain degree of hesitation about the strictures which I have occasionally hazarded on their conclusions. The truth is, that on this, as on most other occasions, I should wish to be understood as aiming rather to suggest matter for future consideration, than to support any particular system; and I am never more anxious that this should be kept in view, than when I happen to dissent from the deliberate and decided opinions of Mr. Smith. On the other hand, if authority is to be allowed any weight in such inquiries, it will be readily acknowledged

---

[1] [*Advancement of Learning;*—Of the nature of Good.] *De Augment. Scient.* Lib. VII. [cap. i.]

that the most careful examination is due to every part of a theory recommended by such names as those of Quesnai, Morellet, and Turgot ; and of which the fundamental principles (at the distance of forty years from its original publication) were adopted, after mature deliberation and long discussion, by the late celebrated Lavoisier; a philosopher equally distinguished by the correctness of his judgment, and the extent and accuracy of his political information.

That the writings of the authors by whom the system was first explained ; those of Quesnai (in particular,) of Turgot, and of the Marquis de Mirabeau, will amply repay the labour of a very diligent perusal to all who turn their attention to these studies, I can venture to pronounce with confidence : and it is only after examining the different parts of the system in their relation to each other and to the whole, that a correct judgment can be formed of their scope and of their importance. In this view, I am somewhat afraid, that by dwelling so long on a detached and preliminary article, I may have created a prejudice against a doctrine, about which I was anxious to excite your curiosity, more especially as it is a doctrine to which the following remark of Lord Bacon applies with peculiar force : " Theoriarum vires in apta et se mutuo sustinente partium harmonia, et quadam in orbem demonstratione consistunt ; ideoque per partes traditæ, infirmæ sunt."*

I am sensible that this acknowledgment forms but an awkward introduction to a farther prosecution of the same subject ; but having already said so much, I am unwilling to leave it without stating a few considerations, which appear to myself to throw some light on the circumstances which have produced this diversity of opinion on a question apparently of so simple a nature.

Among the objections which naturally present themselves against the *Economical system*, one of the most obvious is founded on the restricted sense in which it employs the phrases *productive labour* and *national revenue*. The latter of these

* [The " *Demonstratio in orbem* " is to be here taken in a favourable meaning ; not as reasoning in a circle, but as an exhaustive proof.]

Mr. Smith charges the Economists with supposing to consist *altogether* in the quantity of *subsistence* which the industry of the people can procure. This statement, however, is not accurate. It would be nearer the truth to say, that they suppose it to consist in the *rude produce* ;[1] for although by far the greater part of this is destined for the subsistence of man, it is not on *that* account that the epithet *productive* is applied to the labour employed in raising it; but because this labour, in consequence of being associated with the genial powers of nature, augments the national stock, by an accession or creation which would not otherwise have existed. According to this idea, the labour which is employed in raising *hemp* or *flax*, is no less productive than that which brings *wheat* or *barley* to market; and the former articles, as well as the latter, are to be considered as forming part of the national revenue.

In offering this explanation, I would not be understood to vindicate the *language* employed by the Economists, but only to shew, that there is a solid foundation for the distinction which they have endeavoured to establish between the nature and effects of agricultural and of manufacturing labour. That the epithets *productive* and *unproductive* were not very happily chosen to express this distinction, appears sufficiently from the criticisms which have been made on them by different writers, as being at variance with the common apprehensions and common modes of speaking among mankind. But if, on the one hand, it be granted to be an abuse of words to bestow the epithet *unproductive*, on any species of labour which contributes essentially to the happiness of society, and to exclude from the national revenue the result of those arts which multiply so wonderfully the accommodations of human life; it must, in my opinion, be admitted, on the other hand, that an objection still stronger applies to the language introduced by Mr. Smith, according to which we are led to rank the most honourable and useful members of the community among its *unproductive labourers*: "the sovereign, for example, with all the officers both of justice and war who serve under him; the

---

[1] Malthus, [Book III. chap. viii.]

whole army and navy; churchmen, lawyers, physicians, and men of letters of every denomination;"* while the national revenue is measured exclusively by the exchangeable value of those *vendible* commodities which compose the annual produce of the land and labour of the country. Perhaps a mode of expression on this subject might be devised, less exceptionable than either of those which have been now under our review; marking, on the one hand, with precision the essential distinction which the Economists are so anxious to establish; and avoiding on the other, that paradoxical appearance which a proposition is apt to assume, when the meaning of the technical terms in which it is stated does not coincide exactly with their ordinary acceptations in popular discourse. The history of modern chemistry affords a sufficient proof, how much the progress of knowledge depends on the logical propriety of the terms employed in our reasonings. The *Economical* system seems to me to have been partly suggested by the same general views which gave rise to the new *nomenclature;* and in this respect it reflects the highest credit on the ingenuity and sagacity of its authors. Considered as a first attempt, it is much more wonderful that it should have been carried so skilfully and plausibly into execution, as to divide the opinions of the best judges in Europe to the present day, than that some faults should have occurred in the details of so vast and complicated an undertaking. A few of them, I suspect strongly, will be found to vitiate that very part of it which I have been attempting to illustrate; and, if I do not deceive myself, they might be completely corrected, by slight alterations in certain technical terms which confound together things which ought to be distinguished. From this confusion arises entirely whatever *obscurity* appears at present to involve the subject; and various difficulties connected with the details of the system may be traced to a similar cause. These imperfections it is certainly of consequence to remove; for in the same proportion in which a technical vocabulary, founded on the principles of a sound logic, facilitates the discovery of truth, it must have a tendency,

* [*Wealth of Nations,* Book II. chap. iii.; Vol. II. p. 3, tenth edition.]

wherever it violates these principles, to add to the difficulty of detecting error, by the systematical form in which it is exhibited.

I cannot help taking this opportunity of adding, that a scientific language appropriated to Political Economy (if successfully executed) would be still more useful than in Chemistry; because the subjects of our reasonings entering more constantly and familiarly into popular discussion, give rise to a far greater number of absurd associations to perplex the ordinary vocabulary. The task, however, is proportionally more arduous, inasmuch as it is necessary to unite, along with precision, a certain deference for the usual modes of expression. In chemistry, the novelty of the phenomena reconciles us to the use of whatever technical terms our instructors find necessary to employ; but in Political Economy, which is, more or less, a subject of daily speculation to all classes of men, an appropriate vocabulary is apt to convey the idea of pedantry or of affected mystery; and, in truth, this circumstance will be found, more than anything else, to have revolted the public taste at the speculations of *Quesnai*. How far it may be possible to combine that precision of language which he had in view, with a diction more simple and more familiar to the ear, is a question upon which I cannot at present hazard an opinion.

In the view which has been given of the Economical system concerning *productive* and *unproductive labour*, I have endeavoured to vindicate it against Mr. Smith's very ingenious criticisms; not because I think it unexceptionable, but because these criticisms, if I am not much mistaken, have betrayed that profound writer into an indistinctness of language which has obscured his reasonings in some instances, and misled his conclusions in others: and, indeed, one of my chief objects in dwelling so long as I have done on a controversial discussion of this kind, was to direct your attention to a careful and scrupulous examination of those parts of the *Wealth of Nations* where the phrases *productive labour* and *productive expenses* appear to have any connexion with the argument.

For my own part, so far from considering it as the fault of *Quesnai's* phraseology, that it confines our attention too much to the labour and expenses employed in producing the means of subsistence, I think its chief indistinctness arises from the tendency which its language has to *confound*, in our apprehensions, that part of the rude produce which furnishes the *means of subsistence*, and that part of it which is subservient to the *arts of accommodation*. If the Economists had actually restricted the phrase *National Revenue* (according to Mr. Smith's *supposition*) to the means of *subsistence* alone, their language, although liable to censure on account of its obvious inconsistency with their fundamental and very important doctrine concerning the peculiar characteristics of *agricultural labour and expenses*, would have possessed, in some respects, an advantage over the mode of expression adopted in their theory. I shall mention one instance of this which will both illustrate the meaning of the remark, and confirm its truth.

Of the two different parts of rude produce which have now been distinguished, it is manifest, that although they agree in the circumstance of rewarding the labourer with *a free gift* derived from the bounty of nature, they differ in one very essential particular, that while the agricultural labour employed in providing the means of subsistence, renders the cultivator independent of all the other classes of the community, the agricultural labour employed in ministering to the arts of accommodation or of ornament, possesses only an *exchangeable value*, agree *in* this respect with the labour employed in manufactures. The Economists were evidently led to confound these together under the same epithet, by the application which they were to make of this part of their theory, to their favourite object of a *territorial tax ;* but it is of consequence to keep the distinction steadily in view, in order to direct the attention of the statesman to that species of revenue which can alone afford a solid basis for a *useful population*, and through the *medium* of which the encouragement to population should, in a great agricultural country, be exclusively directed.

Would it not obviate, in some degree, these different objections, (after stating in as unexceptionable language as could be devised, the radical distinction which the Economists express by the words *productive* and *unproductive*,) to subdivide what they call *productive labour* into two kinds,—that which affords the means of *subsistence*, and that which supplies the *arts of accommodation with their rude materials*, marking each by some appropriate and convenient epithet? Such a subdivision, while attended with the practical advantage just alluded to, would keep in view the principle on which the radical distinction really hinges, and would prevent those misapprehensions of its import which are apt to arise, *partly* from the associations established by ordinary speech between the ideas of *productive* and of *useful*, and *partly* from the bias which we naturally have to consider the *means of subsistence* as the *only* objects of agriculture. The illustrations of some of the Economical writers are extremely apt to encourage those misapprehensions, as they frequently blend with the argument in proof of that peculiarity in agricultural labour which I have been endeavouring to explain, a variety of other considerations which have no connexion with this particular conclusion: such, for example, as the *independence* of the husbandman, when compared with that of the other members of the social system; or the impossibility, in a great agricultural country, of importing to any considerable amount the necessaries of life. That both of these considerations are of the highest importance, when *National Revenue* is considered in reference to *Population*, I flatter myself I have sufficiently shewn when contrasting the policy of *China* with that of *Holland*, [p. 284.] And it was on this account chiefly, that I was led to object to Mr. Smith's definition of *productive labour* and of *national riches*, as tending by their latitude to keep out of view the peculiar characteristics of that species of *revenue*, to the increase of which alone the attention of the statesman may be, at all times, with safety directed, as necessarily implying a correspondent increase in the abundance and comforts enjoyed by the people. In the Economical system, on the other hand, the *practical* inconvenience of the indistinctness in question, is comparatively trifling, as the *objects of agriculture* and the *means of subsistence* are expressions which, in an extensive territory, must always coincide pretty nearly in their meaning. In studying, however, this system, it will contribute greatly to the precision of our ideas, to draw the line distinctly between these two different parts of the *rude produce,* so as to keep constantly in our recollection that the epithet *productive* or *creative* is not less applicable to what is to furnish the manufacturer with the materials of his web, than to that which is to furnish him with articles of the *first necessity.*

The indistinctness which, in this instance, I have ventured to ascribe to some of the Economical writers, may be perceived, if I am not mistaken, even in M. Turgot's excellent *Reflections on the Formation and Distribution of Riches.* It arose, indeed, not unnaturally, from the two different objects which these writers had principally in view. The first was the encouragement of *agriculture,* as the source of national subsistence; the second, the establishment of a *territorial tax* to be levied on the *nett produce.* As the arguments in favour of the latter apply equally to *all* the operations of husbandry, it was of consequence to establish, in the clearest manner, the distinction between *productive* and *unproductive labour,* upon which this speculation turns entirely. While engaged, however, in the illustration of this point, they have often been led by their agricultural enthusiasm, to embarrass their reasonings with a statement of some of the *other* characteristics or advantages of agricultural industry, altogether foreign to the purpose, and thereby to confirm their readers still more in the apprehension, that the word *productive,* as employed in the Economical system, has somehow or other a reference to the *utility,* or *necessity,* or *independence* of the occupation in which the husbandman is employed.

Having mentioned the subject of the *territorial tax,* it may be of some use to add, that, according to the principles of the Economists, all taxes fall ultimately on that part of the annual reproduction of the ground which remains after defraying all the expenses incurred to obtain it. They further hold, that the only just principle on which a tax can be imposed, is by proportioning the burden to the *surplus,* which, in the language of the Economists, is called the *nett produce*. In the last place they assert, that the only possible way to carry this principle into effect, is to levy the tax *directly* on that fund, which, by its nature, is inevitably destined to pay it in the end.

" It is with taxes," says one of these writers, " as with the operation of blood-letting on the human body. Puncture its various members in a hundred different places, and you only torment the patient, without obtaining the quantity which he ought to lose. Fix on a single vein, and the slightest incision will at once accomplish your purpose." The Economists flatter themselves with being the first who discovered that vein in the political body, by opening which the State may obtain what it desires with the least possible inconvenience to its subjects. This vein is the *nett produce of the land*, to which (according to them) all the operations of the legislator, in the way of taxation, should be directly and immediately applied.

The advantages which the Economists ascribe to such a tax, are, 1*st*, its *equality*, (the only fund which pays taxes ultimately being assessed with perfect exactness); 2*d*, its *certainty*, (nothing being left to arbitrary imposition); 3*d*, the *economy* with which it might be levied, (hardly anything being taken out of the subject's pocket but what is to go into the public treasury.) The circumstance, however, on which they dwell chiefly, is the accurate scale it would afford for exhibiting the proportion between public burdens and the national revenue; and for marking the limit beyond which they cannot be carried without injury to cultivation, and a decline of national prosperity,—points, which it is difficult, or rather impossible to ascertain, amidst the infinite complications of the established system.

With a view to demonstrate their fundamental principle, that all taxes fall ultimately on the *nett produce*, the Economists have been led to analyze the complicated mechanism of civilized society, and to examine in what manner the funds which the rude produce of the soil supplies is distributed among the different classes or order of the nations. The result of the investigation is, that from the nature of the distribution, the tax, in whatever manner imposed, must be paid, in the last

CHAP. I.—OF LABOUR PRODUCTIVE AND UNPRODUCTIVE. 297

result, out of this fund; and that it is beyond the power of the financier to contrive a tax which shall ultimately fall on any other.

It is with a view to the establishment of this important conclusion, that the Economists have been at so much pains to mark the respective characteristics of *productive and unproductive labour and expense;* and hence the stress they have been induced to lay on a distinction which must be acknowledged to have at first sight, somewhat of the appearance of idle and scholastic refinement. It was *partly* in order to obviate this impression, that I was led to introduce the subject of the territorial tax; but my chief object in this short digression was to reflect some additional light on the distinction which suggested it, by pointing out the result to which that distinction is subservient. As I have very little doubt that the Economists were, in this instance, conducted to their definitions by an *analytical process,* directly the reverse of that order which they have followed in their publications, I was induced to think that a general conception of the conclusion which they had in view might be of some use in ascertaining the import of those technical expressions, in the interpretation of which there might be any ground for hesitation or controversy.

If this view of the question had occurred to Mr. Smith, it could not have failed to suggest a correction of one of his statements concerning the Economical system which I formerly objected to, [p. 290]; that it limits the epithet *productive* to that labour alone which is directed to the increase of the *means of subsistence;* and that it considers these articles of *first necessity* as the sole constituents of *national revenue.*

In what I have now said, I would not be understood to insinuate any opinion with respect to the theory of the *territorial tax.* The discussion belongs properly to the article of *Taxation,*—a branch of Political Economy of which (as I hinted in my first lecture) I propose to delay the consideration till some future occasion. In the meantime, it may gratify the curiosity of such of my hearers as may wish to examine the theory of the territorial tax, to observe that, although it was by Quesnai and his followers that the first attempt was made to demonstrate it rigorously from first principles, to unfold its manifold supposed advantages, and to suggest the means of carrying it gradually into execution, the original idea was borrowed from this island. I do not know if it occurs in any writer prior to Locke; but the following passage from his *Considerations on the Lowering of Interest and Raising the Value of Money*, (published in 1691,) is abundantly explicit.

"When a nation is running into decay and ruin, the merchant and monied man, do what you can, will be sure to starve last. Observe it where you will, the decays that come upon and bring to ruin any country, do constantly fall first upon the land; and though the country gentleman be not very forward to think so, yet this is, nevertheless, an undoubted truth, that he is more concerned in trade, and ought to take a greater care that it be well managed than even the merchant himself. For he will certainly find, when a decay of trade has carried away one part of our money out of the kingdom, and the other is kept in the merchants and tradesman's hands, that no laws he can make, nor any little art of shifting property amongst ourselves, will bring it back to him again; but his rents will fall, and his income every day lessen, till general industry and frugality, joined to a well-ordered trade, shall restore to the kingdom the riches it had formerly.—This, by the way, if well considered, might let us see that taxes, however contrived, and out of whose hand soever immediately taken, do, in a country when their great fund is in land, for the most part terminate upon land. . . . A tax laid upon land seems hard to the landholder, because it is so much money going visibly out of his pocket; and, therefore, as an ease to himself, the landlord is always forward to lay it upon commodities. But if he will thoroughly consider it, and examine the effects, he will find he buys this seeming ease at a very dear rate. And although he pays not this tax immediately out of his own purse, yet his purse will find it by a greater want of money there at the end of the year than that comes to, with the lessening of his rents to boot, which is a settled and lasting evil that will stick upon him beyond the present payment."

After a long argument in support of this opinion, (for which I must refer to the Essay already mentioned,) Mr. Locke concludes thus:—" It is in vain in a country whose great fund is land, to hope to lay the public charge of the government on anything else. *There at last* it will terminate. The merchant, do what you can, *will* not bear it, the labourer *cannot*, and therefore the landholders *must.* And, whether it were not better for him to have it laid directly, where it will at last settle, than to let it come to him by the sinking of his rents, which when they are once fallen, every one knows are not easily raised again, let him consider."

A still more elaborate argument in favour of the same projects, may be found in a pamphlet, published in 1734, by Jacob Vanderlint,* an author whose merits have been in general strangely overlooked by our modern writers on Political Economy. For my own part, I was entirely unacquainted with them till his Essay was put into my hands a few years ago by Lord Lauderdale. Of Vanderlint's history, either as a man or an author, I know nothing; but he seems, from his own account, not to have enjoyed the advantage of a liberal education. " I am sorry," he observes in his preface, " that I am not in all respects equal to this most important undertaking; yet I doubt not, that I have sufficiently made out what I have undertaken, and though not with the accuracy of a scholar, yet with that perspicuity and evidence which may be expected from an ordinary tradesman." A few sentences, extracted from this performance, will sufficiently shew its coincidence, both in doctrine and in language, with the works of the Economists.

" If all taxes were taken off goods, and levied on lands and houses only, the gentlemen would have more *nett rent* left out of their estates than they have now, when the taxes are almost wholly levied on goods."

* [*Money answers all things*, &c. Mr. Stewart also speaks of Vanderlint in his *Memoir of Adam Smith*, as of Asgill, &c.]

"That the land *gives* all we have, would be self-evident, if we did not import many goods which are the produce of other nations. But this makes no alteration in the case, since the quantity of foreign goods which we import cannot continually be of greater value than the goods we export; because this in the end must exhaust our cash, and so put an end to that excess. Therefore, the goods we import stand only instead of those we export; and, consequently, the land gives not only all we have of our own produce, but virtually all we receive from other nations."

After these observations, which the author illustrates with considerable ingenuity, he proceeds to shew, "that the land must pay all taxes, in what manner soever they may be levied; a proposition," he remarks, "which might perhaps be assumed as virtually implied in a self-evident truth, *that what gives all must pay all.*" For the satisfaction, however, of the reader, Vanderlint here enters into a particular explanation of the *process* by which he conceived the effect to be accomplished; and although some of his reasonings on this point are liable to obvious objections, they must be allowed (more especially when we consider at what period he wrote, and what disadvantages, as an author, he laboured under) to bear the strongest marks of originality and refinement of thought. The investigation is much too long to admit of an abstract in this Lecture.

The same opinion with respect to the peculiar advantages of a *territorial tax,* appears to have been held by a Mr. [John] Asgill, who, about the end of the seventeenth, or the beginning of the eighteenth century, published a Treatise entitled, *Several Assertions Proved, in order to create another species of Money than Gold or Silver,* [1696.]

The object of the Treatise is to support the proposition of Dr. Hugh Chamberlayne for a land bank, which he laid before the English House of Commons in 1693, and before the Scotch Parliament in 1703.

I have not had an opportunity of perusing this performance, but the following very curious extract, which breathes the very spirit of Quesnai's philosophy, has been communicated to me by Lord Lauderdale, to whose researches and speculations concerning the history and principles of the Economical system, (more particularly concerning those parts of it which have been derived from old English writers,) I am indebted for much important information.

"What we call commodities is nothing but LAND SEVERED FROM THE SOIL. The owners of the soil, in every country, have the sale of all the commodities of the growth of that country, and, consequently, have the power of giving credit in that country; and, therefore, whatever they will accept for their commodities is money. MAN DEALS IN NOTHING BUT IN EARTH. The merchants are the factors of the world, to exchange one part of the earth for another. The king himself is fed by the labours of the ox; and the clothing of the army, and the victualling of the navy must all be paid for to the owner of the soil as the ultimate receiver."

I shall only add further on this subject at present, that the argument in support of the territorial tax may be found at length in the works of the Marquis de Mirabeau,—in the Treatise of Le Trosne, *On Provincial Administrations,*—and in various memoirs, published by Dupont, in the collection entitled, *Ephémérides d'un Citoyen.* The principal writers on the other side are Necker, Sir James Steuart, Pinto, Adam Smith, the Marquis de Casaux, and the author of a Treatise entitled, *Essai Analytique sur la Richesse et sur l'Impôt.* This last writer has entered into a more methodical and accurate examination of the Economical system, in all its parts, than any other I know; and has certainly displayed great acuteness and ability in the course of his discussion. His publication is anonymous; but it appears from a passage in the *Life of Turgot,* compared with a passage in the *Ephémérides,* &c., to have been the work of M. Graslin, a gentleman who held an important situation in the revenue department of Nantes.

From this digression with respect to the *territorial tax,* I now return to the elementary principles of the *Economical System,* concerning the nature of *National Wealth ;* with a view to the illustration of which principles I was led to introduce, somewhat out of place, a faint outline of the practical conclusion to which they are subservient. As the establishment of this conclusion was manifestly the *primary* object of the Economists, it seemed reasonable to think, that the consideration of the practical result might assist us in entering into the train of thought by which the preparatory parts of their system were suggested. And, if I do not deceive myself, this *analytical* view of their investigations has conducted us to a more precise conception of *some* of their principles and definitions than is commonly entertained.

To the criticisms which I have already offered on these principles and definitions, I have yet to add another, which is more general in its aim, and which leads to consequences affecting still more deeply the justness of the Economical system, as a theory practically applicable to the existing state of society in this part of the world.

I have observed in the *Philosophy of the Human Mind*,* that the leading object of the earliest and most enlightened patrons of the Economical system, seems to have been " to delineate that state of political society to which the social order may be expected to approach nearer and nearer as human nature is gradually matured by reasoning and reflection. I have observed, at the same time, that it is the height of enthusiasm and absurdity to suppose that the period is ever to arrive when this state of things will be realized in its full extent ; yet many of the most zealous advocates of the Economical system have so completely lost sight of this consideration, that they have formed many of their particular conclusions, on the supposition that it was already accomplished.

(*Interpolation from Notes.*)—Of this remark various illustrations occur in the works of the Economists. Thus, for example, they uniformly take it for granted, as an established principle, that the revenue or fund employed in the support of manufacturers, is always equal in its exchangeable value to the commodities which they produce. That this is the ultimate

* [*Supra, Works,* Vol. II. p. 236.]

tendency of things in all the employments of human industry, is unquestionably true ; and it is no less certain, that it has been already realized in various branches of trade. This, for instance, is the case in all those arts which are so well understood, that one class of workmen cannot be supposed to possess any advantage over another. In the manufacture of lace, for instance, of the workmen employed in which, it approaches nearly to a mathematical truth to assert, that at no moment of time do they add anything to the value of the whole annual amount of the rude produce of the land, the portion of that produce which they are continually consuming being always equal to the value of what they have produced. Notwithstanding, however, of this circumstance, it is certainly going a great deal too far to assert, that it will ever afford any universal principle with respect to that order of things which actually exists in such countries as France or England. The high wages which are occasionally given in some new arts, compared with the poverty of those who are engaged in the manufacture of lace, to borrow the instance of which the Economists are so fond, affords a demonstrative proof that, whatever may be the ultimate tendency of a general competition in all the various branches of manufacturing industry, the fact is, at present, in numberless instances, at variance with that result. To these observations I beg leave to add, that the fact in question is totally irreconcilable with the advantages which one manufacturer possesses over another, in consequence of the expedients which his skill and capital enable him to employ for abridging or superseding manual labour, and no less inconsistent with the advantages derived from secret processes in manufactures or the arts, which are sometimes transmitted as an inheritance in the same family for a succession of generations.

A similar paralogism occurs in the reasonings of the Economists concerning the effects of manufacturing industry when combined with foreign commerce. A detailed statement of their opinion upon this point has been already given, [pp. 267, 268.] We may therefore conclude, say the Economists, that that labour alone is productive which adds to the rude produce of the ground. With regard to this reasoning, I need hardly say, that however important the lesson is which it conveys, with respect to the independence and permanent stability of agricultural wealth, when compared with that which arises from commerce and manufactures, it leads to no just inference unfavourable to the latter as long as they continue to flourish. The following passage from one of Dr. Franklin's political tracts, by pushing these doctrines of the Economists a little too far, affords the best proof which I know of something radically defective in the system from which his arguments are borrowed.

"Where the labour and expense of producing commodities are known to both parties, bargains will generally be fair and equal. Where they are known to one party only, bargains will often be unequal, knowledge taking its advantage of ignorance.

"Thus, he that carries one thousand bushels of wheat abroad to sell, may not probably obtain so great a profit thereon, as if he had first turned the wheat into manufactures, by subsisting therewith the workmen while producing those manufactures, since there are many expediting and facilitating methods of working, not generally known; and strangers to the manufactures, though they know pretty well the expense of raising wheat, are unacquainted with those short methods of working, and thence being apt to suppose more labour employed in the manufactures than there really is, are more easily imposed on in their value, and induced to allow more for them than they are honestly worth.

"Thus the advantage of having manufactures in a country does not consist, as is commonly supposed, in their highly advancing the value of rough materials, of which they are formed; since, though sixpenny worth of flax may be worth twenty shillings, when worked into lace, yet the very cause of its being worth twenty shillings is, that, besides the flax, it has cost nineteen shillings and sixpence in subsistence to the manufacturer. But the advantage of manufactures is, that under their shape provisions may be more easily carried to a foreign market, and, by their means, our traders may more easily cheat strangers. Few, where it is not made, are judges of the value of lace. The importer may demand forty, and perhaps get thirty shillings, for that which cost him but twenty."*

The conclusions which are drawn from these reasonings are, —that there are only three ways of increasing the riches of a state; the first is by war: this is robbery; the second is by commerce: this is cheating; and the third is by agriculture: this is the only honest way. It seems abundantly evident, that the tone of morality here assumed is much too elevated for the actual condition of the human race. Indeed, it does not appear to be very consistent with itself; for where is the injustice in the advantage which the knowledge and skill of one set of persons give them over the ignorance of others, if it be allowed to be fair and equitable in industry to avail itself of its natural superiority over idleness?

But whatever opinion we may adopt on this abstract question, there can be no doubt that such as I have now described are the actual circumstances of mankind, producing everywhere, in a greater or less degree, a competition among nations, in which each makes the most, not only of its natural advantages, but of the superiority which it enjoys in consequence of its industry, skill, and accumulated stock. Nor is it difficult to trace in the operation of the latter, the provision for that commercial fraternity among nations, the foundation of which is laid in the diversity of the productions of different countries. It is here, I apprehend, that the characteristical excellence of Mr. Smith's work is to be found; that abstracting entirely from that ideal perfection to which it is possible that things may have a tendency, he adapts his speculations to the present state of this part of the world, and has demonstrated, with irresistible perspicuity, that even while this competition among nations continues, honesty forms the best and surest policy; and that the general prosperity of the globe, as well as the individual welfare of nations, is best consulted when each endeavours to

* [*Positions to be examined concerning National Wealth*, §§ 9-11.—*Works*, by Sparks, Vol. 11. pp. 375, 376.]

turn its own peculiar advantages to the best account, and leaves the same liberty to others. In these particulars, the doctrines of Mr. Smith coincide entirely with those of the economical system, over which they certainly possess one important advantage, that they are deduced from a view of nations as they actually exist, and that they are susceptible of an easy application to their present circumstances.

The result of the parallel, then, which I have been so long preparing to draw between these two great systems, is, that if, on the one hand, the language of the Economists be more precise and definite, and the result of a more accurate metaphysical analysis than that of Mr. Smith, and if some of the fundamental principles of the former are of a more scientific nature, and more universal application, the doctrines inculcated in the *Wealth of Nations* are, on the other hand, with a very few exceptions, of greater practical utility to those who are to engage in the general business of the world, especially to those whose views have a more particular reference to the business of political life. I speak at present of his doctrines with regard to the freedom of commerce; in which, indeed, both systems agree, though I must be allowed to remark, that in one important point the Economical system is eminently deserving of praise; I mean in that part which, by explaining so fully and so beautifully the peculiar productiveness and independence of agricultural labour, cannot fail to have a powerful tendency to prevent statesmen from ever mistaking the means for the end; or, as I have expressed the same idea in the *Philosophy of the Human Mind,* "from ever being led astray by more limited views of temporary expediency."* On this pre-eminence of agriculture, Mr. Smith has certainly enlarged too little, nor is his phraseology always sufficiently marked to keep it constantly in the view of the student. This is the more remarkable, as Mr. Smith seems to have been fully aware of the general tendency of the doctrines of the Economists. Thus, in one remarkable passage, after stating that the system of Quesnai forms a nearer approximation to a just system of political economy than

* [Above, *Works,* Vol. II. p. 240.]

any theory that had gone before it, he adds, "that it had a sensible effect in influencing the measures of the French Government in favour of agriculture. It has been in consequence of their representations, accordingly, that the agriculture of France has been delivered from several of the oppressions which it before laboured under. The term during which such a lease can be granted, as will be valid against every future purchaser or proprietor of the land, has been prolonged from nine to twenty-seven years. The ancient provincial restraints upon the transportation of corn from one province of the kingdom to another, have been entirely taken away, and the liberty of exporting it to all foreign countries, has been established as the common law of the kingdom in all ordinary cases."*

There are few speculative systems which can boast of practical effects equally calculated to advance national prosperity; more especially when I add the tendency which, in this particular instance, the doctrines of the Economists had to bring into disrepute the policy of Colbert on the subject of Population, which had long been acted upon in France, in recommending to statesmen to invert the order proposed by Colbert, and to encourage Population through the medium of Agriculture. It was Quesnai who first unfolded this important and fundamental truth; and it is only to be regretted, that in applying the maxim to the actual circumstances of the world, he has not always stated this doctrine with the proper limitations, too often overlooking altogether those circumstances so finely illustrated by Mr. Smith, which in this part of the world have forced into a retrograde order the natural course of things, and thus rendered all deductions drawn from that course inapplicable to the present state of things in the modern world.

Before leaving this subject, I think it proper to observe, that wherever I have mentioned the system of the Economists in terms of approbation, I would be understood to refer solely to their doctrines on the subject of *Political Economy* proper. "*The Theory of Government* which they inculcate," as I have

* [*Wealth of Nations*, Book IV. chap. ix.; Vol. III. p. 28, *seq.*, tenth edition.]

observed in the *Philosophy of the Human Mind*, " is of the most dangerous tendency, recommending in strong and unqualified terms an unmixed despotism, and reprobating all constitutional checks on the sovereign authority. Many English writers, indeed, with an almost incredible ignorance of the works which they have presumed to censure, have spoken of them, as if they encouraged political principles of a very different complexion; but the truth is, that the disciples of *Quesnai* (without a single exception) carried their zeal for the power of the monarch, and what they called the *Unity of Legislation*, to so extravagant a length, as to treat with contempt those mixed establishments which allow any share whatever of legislative influence to the representatives of the people. On the one hand, the evidence of this system appeared to its partisans so complete and irresistible, that they flattered themselves monarchs would soon see, with an intuitive conviction, the identity of their own interests with those of the nations they are called to govern; and, on the other hand, they contended that it is only under the strong and steady government of a race of hereditary princes, undistracted by the prejudices and local interests which warp the deliberations of popular assemblies, that a gradual and systematical approach can be made to the perfection of law and policy. The very first of *Quesnai's* maxims states as a fundamental principle, that the sovereign authority, unrestrained by any constitutional checks or balances, should be lodged in the hands of a single person; and the same doctrine is maintained zealously by all his followers—by none of them more explicitly than by *Mercier de la Rivière*, whose treatise on *The Natural and Essential Order of Political Societies*, might have been expected to attract some notice in this country, from the praise which Mr. Smith has bestowed on the perspicuity of his style, and the distinctness of his arrangement."*

* [Above, *Works*, Vol. II. pp. 240, 241.]

[SECT. II.—ON THE CIRCUMSTANCES WHICH RENDER LABOUR MORE EFFECTIVE.]

I proceed now to illustrate the general principles on which the effective powers of labour depend; or, in other words, to illustrate the circumstances which tend to economize the exertions of human power in accomplishing the purposes to which it is directed. The speculation, certainly, is one of the most curious which the mechanism of a commercial society presents to a philosopher; and it leads to many consequences of a very general and important application. From the observations already made, it appears that man is forced, in every situation in which he is to be found, by the necessities of his nature, to employ some degree of art in order to obtain the means of subsistence and safety. It appears farther, that it is to these necessities he is indebted for the development and improvement of those faculties by which he is distinguished from the brutes; and that, excepting in a few districts, where the preservation of his animal existence occupies his whole attention, and leaves him no leisure for the arts of accommodation, his intellectual attainments are, in general, proportioned to the number of his wants, and to the difficulties with which he has to struggle. As Rousseau observes:—" Chez toutes les nations du monde, les progrès de l'esprit se sont précisément proportionnés aux besoins que les peuples avaient reçus de la nature, ou auxquels les circonstances les avaient assujettis, et par conséquent aux passions qui les portaient à pourvoir à ces besoins. Je montrerais en Egypte les arts naissants et s'étendants avec les débordemens du Nil; je suivrais leurs progrès chez les Grecs, où l'on les vit germer, croître, et s'élever jusqu'aux cieux parmi les sables et les rochers de l'Attique, sans pouvoir prendre racine sur les bords fertiles de l'Eurotas."*

As soon as the situation of an individual is rendered easy

---

* [*Origine de l'Inégalité parmi les Hommes*, Partie I.—But the "*gaudent sudoribus artes*" had been long proverbial; it may be traced higher than Hesiod, and far lower than Baptista Mantuanus.]

and comfortable, with respect to the necessities of life, he begins to feel wants of which he was not conscious before, and his imagination creates new objects of pursuit to fill up his intervals of leisure. It seems to be the intention of Providence, that as soon as one class of our wants is supplied, another, whether real or imaginary, makes its appearance; and it is this, that as no limit can be stated to our desires, so there seems to be no limit to the improvement of the arts and the progress of refinement.

In the rudest state of society, in which all the members of a tribe are occupied in procuring subsistence, each individual will appropriate to himself the various objects of pursuit by his own personal exertions. He will form his own habitation, secure his prey by his own strength or agility, and be the artificer of those instruments which are employed in the simple arts which minister to his safety or accommodation; and thus his occupations, however limited in number, will be at least as various as the arts which he exercises; and the opportunities of intellectual improvement, however scanty, will be nearly the same to all the members of the community.

[SUBSECT. I.—*On the Division of Labour.*]

As society advances, the different tastes and propensities of individuals will give rise to a variety in their pursuits, and in their habits and attainments. In such circumstances, a very small degree of experience or reflection will satisfy them, that it would be for the advantage of all if each should confine himself to his own favourite occupation, cultivating to the utmost of his ability those mechanical habits which are connected with its exercise, and exchanging the surplus produce of his industry for what he may want of the commodities produced by the labour of his neighbours. Thus trades and separate professions will arise, which, in consequence of the operation of the same causes, will continually multiply and be divided and subdivided as society advances in wealth and refinement. The observation, that " *A Jack of all trades is master of none,*" is one of those maxims of common sense which the slightest survey of human life forces on the most careless observer.*

It is on this separation of trades and professions, and on this division and subdivision of labour, that the progress of the arts, according to Mr. Smith, in a great measure, depends; the effective powers of labour being, in general, proportioned to the degree in which these are divided and distributed.† The same idea had, before Mr. Smith's time, been adopted by various modern writers; particularly by Mr. Harris in his *Dialogue concerning Happiness*, 1741;‡ and by Dr. Ferguson in his *Essay on Civil Society*.§ The fact, too, has been very strongly stated by different writers of a much more early date; particularly by Sir William Petty and Dr. Mandeville; nor did it escape the notice of the ancients, as appears among various other documents, from a very curious passage in the *Cyropædia* of Xenophon, in which he compares the distribution of employments in Cyrus's kitchen to the division of trades in a populous city. This passage states the doctrine so circumstantially, and with a simplicity of detail so characteristical of this inimitable writer, that I shall make no apology for quoting the passage at length:—

" For as other arts are wrought up in great cities to a greater degree of perfection, in the same manner are the meats that come from the king dressed in greater perfection. For in little cities the same people make both the frame of a couch, a door, a plough, and a table; and frequently the same person is a builder too, and very well satisfied he is, if he meet with customers enough to maintain him. It is impossible, therefore, for a man that makes a great many different things, to do

* [" *Propre à tout, propre à rien.*" Indeed, all languages have a corresponding proverb. In Latin:—" *Cuncta nihilque sumus,*"—" *Nusquam est, qui ubique est,*"—" *In omnibus aliquid, in toto nihil,*" &c. In the *Margites*, a kind of Dunciad, attributed to Homer, it is said of the hero in a line preserved in the *Second Alcibiades*, one of the spurious dialogues of Plato,—

Πόλλ' ἠπίστατο ἔργα, κακῶς δ' ἠπίστατο πάντα.

And to this line, certainly, Mr. Stewart here makes reference.]

† [*Wealth of Nations*, Book I. chap. i.; Vol. I. p. 9, tenth edition.]

‡ [Part I. sect. xii.]

§ [Part IV. sect. i.]

them all well. But in great cities, because there are multitudes that want every particular thing, one art alone is sufficient for the maintenance of every one; and frequently not an entire one neither, but one man makes shoes for men, another for women. Sometimes it happens, that one gets a maintenance by sewing shoes together, another by cutting them out; one by cutting out cloths only, and another without doing any of these things is maintained by fitting together the pieces so cut out. He, therefore, that deals in a business that lies within a little compass, must of necessity do it the best. The case is the same with respect to the business of a table, for he that has the same man to cover and adorn the frame of a couch, to set out the table, to knead the dough, to dress the several different meats, must necessarily, in my opinion, fare in each particular as it happens. But where it is business enough for one man to boil meat, for another to roast it; for one to boil fish, and for another to broil it; where it is business enough for one man to make bread, and that not of every sort neither, but that its enough for him to furnish one sort good, each man, in my opinion, must of necessity work up the things that are thus made to a very great perfection."*

From this passage of Xenophon it is evident, that the effects of the division of labour, in contributing to the improvement of the arts, furnished a subject of speculation in ancient as well as in modern times. It is very observable, however, in the foregoing quotation, that what Xenophon lays the chief stress on, is the effect of this division in improving the *quality* of the articles produced, whereas the circumstance which has chiefly attracted the attention of Mr. Smith and other modern writers, is its astonishing effect in increasing their *quantity*. In proof of this, Mr. Smith has entered into some very interesting details with regard to the trade of the pin-makers.†

The effect of the division of labour in increasing its effective powers, is chiefly owing, according to Mr. Smith, to the three following circumstances :—

* [In the original, Lib. VIII. cap. ii. § 4.—The translation is by the Honourable Maurice Ashley.] † [See *supra*, p. 256, *seq*.]

CHAP. I.—OF LABOUR PRODUCTIVE AND UNPRODUCTIVE. 313

"*First*, The improvement of the dexterity of the workman necessarily increases the quantity of the work he can perform; and the division of labour, by reducing every man's business to some one simple operation, and by making this operation the sole employment of his life, necessarily increases very much the dexterity of the workman. . . .

"*Secondly*, The advantage which is gained by saving the time commonly lost in passing from one sort of work to another, is much greater than we should at first view be apt to imagine it. It is impossible to pass very quickly from one kind of work to another, that is carried on in a different place, and with quite different tools. . . . A man commonly saunters a little in turning his hand from one sort of employment to another. When he first begins the new work he is seldom very keen and hearty; his mind, as they say, does not go to it, and for some time he rather trifles than applies to good purpose. . . .

"*Thirdly*, and *lastly*, Everybody must be sensible how much labour is facilitated and abridged by the application of proper machinery. It is unnecessary to give any example. I shall only observe, therefore, that the invention of all those machines by which labour is so much facilitated and abridged, seems to have been originally owing to the division of labour."[*]

"1st, Greater skill and dexterity are acquired by each workman." Of the effects of practice in increasing the rapidity and address of the hand in performing mechanical operations, no proof more striking can be mentioned than the feats of legerdemain exhibited by jugglers. Some of these, indeed, are so astonishing, and evince a degree of dexterity so much before anything else that we know, that they appear to deserve a much more accurate investigation than philosophers have hitherto bestowed on them. Other examples of the same kind will readily occur to any person who has been accustomed to frequent the workshops of manufacturers. The following facts are mentioned in the *Wealth of Nations*:—" A common smith, who, though accustomed to handle the hammer, has never been used to make nails, if upon some particular occasion he is obliged to

[*] [*Wealth of Nations*, Book I. chap. i.; Vol. I. pp. 12-14, tenth edition.]

attempt it, will scarce, I am assured, be able to make above two or three hundred nails in a day, and those too very bad ones. A smith who has been accustomed to make nails, but whose sole or principal business has not been that of a nailer, can seldom with his utmost diligence make more than eight hundred or a thousand nails in a day. I have seen several boys under twenty years of age, who had never exercised any other trade but that of making nails, and who, when they exerted themselves, could make, each of them, upwards of two thousand three hundred nails in a day."*

The conclusion which Mr. Smith deduces from these and some similar statements is,—that as the subdivision of labour limits the attention of every different workman to a very simple operation, it must proportionally increase the dexterity of all; and consequently, their joint labour will, in a given time, be more effective, and their workmanship will be more perfect in its kind, than if each singly had attempted to perform all the different operations thus parcelled out.

In this view of the subject, there is unquestionably a great deal of truth. But it may, I think, be reasonably doubted, whether Mr. Smith has not laid too much stress on it, in accounting for the advantages gained from that astonishing division and subdivision of labour which takes place in some of the arts. That the rapidity of the hand in executing a mechanical operation, may be increased by practice to a very great degree, is an acknowledged fact. But there is obviously a limit, beyond which this rapidity cannot possibly be carried; and I am inclined to think, that in such very simple operations as drawing out a wire, &c., it is not very long before this ultimatum in point of rapidity is reached by the workman. Nor can I bring myself to believe, that after it is attained, the dexterity of the workman in performing this one operation would be at all impaired, though he should also have acquired a few other accomplishments of a similar nature: that the drawer of the wire would be less fitted for his employment, if he changed occupations for a day or two with the cutter or pointer of the

* [Book I. chap. i.; Vol. I. p. 12, tenth edition.]

pin. Indeed, I know of few manufactures where great manual dexterity is less required, than in that of pin-making. Even in those establishments which employ the labour of the hand to perform various operations, which in richer manufactures are accomplished by means of machinery, a very considerable part of the work is executed by children. Hence I am led to conclude, that though one of the advantages of the division of labour be to increase the rapidity of manual work, yet this advantage bears so very small a proportion to that which is gained in the last result, that it is by no means entitled to stand at the head of the enumeration; and certainly goes a very little length in accounting for that minute division and subdivision of labour which has been introduced into some of the most prosperous manufactures of this country. On this head, therefore, I entirely agree with a remark of Lord Lauderdale in his *Inquiry into the Nature and Origin of Public Wealth*, where he observes, that even in the trade of the pin-maker, without the use of machinery to supersede the work of the hand, no great progress could have been made in the rapidity with which pins are formed.

In the *second* place, says Mr. Smith, "when a man leaves off one employment, and begins another, he is always disposed to trifle for some time, &c. All this time is saved by the division of labour." The observation seems to be perfectly just, so far as it goes; but the economy of time gained in this way, must plainly bear a still more inconsiderable proportion than the former, to the magnitude of the effect which it is brought to explain.

It may perhaps be worth while to remark here in passing, that something similar to this effect in mechanical operations takes place with respect to the intellectual powers. When we pass suddenly from one speculation, and still more from one study to another, some time always elapses before the attention is completely engaged, and before the new set of ideas and facts is fully brought under our view. If I am not mistaken, this consideration affords an unanswerable objection to a practice which has been recommended by many authors, of making a regular distribution of the day into different portions, allotted to the study of different branches of literature and science. Where mere accomplishment is the object, this plan may contribute to its attainment better than any other, but with those who have in view the investigation of truth, and the acquisition of scientific knowledge, I am persuaded that much more intellectual work (if I may use the expression) will be performed, and much more successfully, in a given time, by preserving the train of thought, so as to bring one speculation completely to a close, before beginning another. Indeed, it would not be difficult to shew that the observation applies far more forcibly to intellectual exertion than to mechanical labour.

[SUBSECT. II.—*On the Use of Machinery as a Substitute for Labour.*]

In the *third* place, the division of labour, according to Mr. Smith, increases its effective powers by promoting the invention of useful machines. In illustration of this remark, he reasons as follows:—

" Men are much more likely to discover easier and readier methods of attaining any object, when the whole attention of their minds is directed towards that single object, than when it is dissipated among a great variety of things. But in consequence of the division of labour, the whole of every man's attention comes naturally to be directed towards some one very simple object. It is naturally to be expected, therefore, that some one or other of those who are employed in each particular branch of labour, should soon find out easier and readier methods of performing their own particular work, wherever the nature of it admits of such improvements. A great part of the machines made use of in those manufactures in which labour is most subdivided, were originally the inventions of common workmen, who, being each of them employed in some very simple operation, naturally turned their thoughts towards finding out easier and readier methods of performing it. Whoever has been much accustomed to visit such manufactures, must frequently have been shewn very pretty machines, which were the inventions of such workmen, in order to facilitate and quicken their own particular part of the work."*

Before I proceed to make any remarks on this reasoning of Mr. Smith, I think it necessary to observe, that even if it were perfectly just, it would not be at all applicable to the present question. His professed object is to explain in what manner the division of labour increases its effective powers. The two first reasons are certainly legitimate and satisfactory, so far as they go; but in his third reason, Mr. Smith has plainly departed from his usual logical accuracy. The tendency of the division of labour to promote the invention of useful machines, cannot with propriety be said to render that labour more effective, so long as it continues to be exerted; for as soon as the machine is invented, the labour is superseded altogether. The effects, therefore, of the division of labour, and of the use of machines, though they both derive their value from the same circumstance, their tendency to enable one man to perform the work of many, are produced on principles essentially different; nor is it more correct to resolve the advantages of machinery into the effects produced by the division of labour, than it would be to resolve the latter into the former. Indeed, in my opinion, the last theory might be easily rendered the more plausible of the two.

But, passing from this objection to Mr. Smith's reasoning, let us consider how far it is true, that workmen occupied from morning to night in repeating the same simple operation, are likely to be more fortunate than others in falling on mechanical inventions. The only proof of this produced by Mr. Smith, is the improvement of the steam-engine, said to be owing to the ingenuity of a boy engaged in the work. This account of the matter, I must own, has always appeared to me extremely unsatisfactory. That in some accidental cases the distribution of labour may have produced such effects, is possible. But it surely is an event not to be expected in the ordinary case, inasmuch as the workman has no motive to exert his ingenuity

* [*Wealth of Nations*, Book I. chap. i.; Vol. i. p. 14, *seq.*, tenth edition.]

in multiplying machines, as in doing so, though he may accelerate the progress of the manufacture, yet he does not abridge his own day's labour ; and indeed there is even a probability that he may throw himself and his companions out of employment. Nor is this all ; the division of labour tends to confine the attention, and of consequence the knowledge of the workman to the performance of one simple operation; whereas the perfection of manufacturing machinery consists in the combination of the greatest possible variety of operations in one machine. The habits of thinking, therefore, which the division of labour tends to generate, are adverse to that comprehension of mechanical contrivance on which the perfection of machinery depends. In confirmation of this reasoning, it may be worth while to remark, that among the many complicated machines which the manufactures of this country exhibit, while many of them may be traced to men who never entered the workshop, but in order to gratify a mechanical curiosity, hardly one can be mentioned which derives its origin from the living automatons, who are employed in the details of the work. With such fortunate inventors, the hope of reward operates in calling forth all their faculties ; and as their studies embrace a general view of the subject, instead of dwelling upon its detached parts, their success, notwithstanding their total ignorance in many cases, has been greater than could have resulted from the highest efforts of a more circumscribed ingenuity.

I am far at the same time from denying, that the division of labour has a powerful effect to promote the invention of machines. But where it has this effect, it appears to operate, not on the inventive powers of the workman, but on those of his employer, or of the speculative observer. As to the former, his inventive powers will be always on the stretch to economize time and labour ; and it is only where such a stimulus exists, that we can look with confidence to a perpetual succession of progressive improvement. In almost every instance the proverb will be found to hold true, that "Necessity," or what amounts to the same thing, some urgent motive leading to the accomplishment of some desirable object, "is the mother of invention."

CHAP. I.—OF LABOUR PRODUCTIVE AND UNPRODUCTIVE. 319

As to the principle on which the division of labour tends to multiply mechanical contrivances, this seems to me to be a good deal more refined than Mr. Smith appears to have thought. The obvious effect of the division of labour in any complicated mechanical operation is, to analyze that operation into the simplest steps which can be carried on separately. Of these steps, there may probably be some which can only be performed by the human hand, while others, either in whole or in part, admit of the substitution of machines. Now, it is only by resolving an operation into its simplest elements, that this separation can be made, so as to force on the attention of the mechanist, in their simplest forms, those particular cases where his ingenuity may be useful. It is thus, too, that the advantages arising from the aid of machinery become so apparent and palpable, as to excite the efforts of inventive genius; a machine which supplies the labour of the hand, superseding of course a particular description of workmen, and thereby exhibiting the utility of the invention on a scale proportioned to the number of individuals whose labour it supersedes. While thus it enables one man to perform the work of many, it produces also an economy of time, by separating the work into its different branches, all of which may be carried into execution at the same moment. While one man is employed in drawing out the wire, from which a multitude of pins are to be simultaneously cut by some analogous expedient, another is employed in pointing them, &c. The obvious effect of this arrangement is, in the first place, to enable one workman to cut or point a multitude of pins as easily as he could have done a single one; and in the second place, by carrying on all the different processes at once, which an individual must have executed separately, to produce a multitude of pins completely finished in the same time as a single pin might have been either cut or pointed. As the division of labour on the one hand, appears thus to be favourable to mechanical invention; so, on the other hand, it is probable that the general experience of the utility of machines has led ingenious men to push, in some cases, the division of labour to a far greater length than was useful. If I am not mistaken, a remarkable instance of this occurs in that very trade, so often referred to, of the pin-maker; the very minute analysis of work there carried into effect having originated, not in any views of increasing the dexterity of the workmen, but in an attempt to make machinery practicable in that manufacture. The foregoing remarks establish fully the truth of an assertion which was formerly made, [p. 317,] that the effects of the division of labour, and of machinery in the manufacturing arts, are produced on principles entirely different, though the objects of both are to accomplish the same purpose—the economy of labour and time; and although in doing so they are often so combined as to render it difficult to draw the line between their respective functions.

It is not, however, by means of these two expedients alone, that labour and time may be economized. The astonishing effects produced, in consequence of a skilful application of chemical principles, to shorten the tedious processes formerly practised in various branches of the arts, are universally known. The use of the oxy-muriatic acid in bleaching, is only one instance out of many, of the beneficial effects thus produced. Of the extent of the advantage to be gained by mere skill and activity, when prompted by the hope of gain, and aided by mechanical contrivance, no instance more curious can be mentioned than what is afforded by the history of the Scotch distilleries. In the year 1785, a proposal was made to collect the duties on distillation by way of license, to be paid annually on every still in proportion to its size, at a fixed rate per gallon, in place of all other taxes. The London distillers, who agreed to the proposal, declared themselves satisfied, from experience, that the time of working stills to advantage was limited to an extent perfectly well known, and that whoever exceeded this limit, would infallibly lose on his materials, and in the quantity of his goods, what he gained in point of time; and in conformity to their opinion, the duty was settled on a supposition that a still could be discharged about seven times in a week. Two years after this, in a petition to Parliament, the same men alleged, that the Scotch distillers had found means to discharge their stills upwards of forty times a week; and we since know, from a report made to the Lords of the Treasury in the year 1799, that a forty-three gallon still was brought to such perfection, as to be discharged at the rate of once in two minutes and three quarters. It appears also from this report, that the operation of distilling is capable of being performed in a still shorter time; and that the quality of the spirit is in no ways injured by the rapidity of the operation. On reflecting on the history of these astonishing exertions of human ingenuity, it cannot fail immediately to occur, that whatever advantages have been gained by mechanical contrivances, have derived their origin, not from the concentrated ingenuity of workmen eager to accomplish their own ruin by the invention of machinery, but from the comprehensive skill of the undertaker, stimulated to economize time to the utmost limit, by the pressure of the new difficulties with which he had to struggle.

Various other illustrations to the same purpose may be drawn from the improvements which have taken place in other arts within the narrow compass of our own times. It is necessary for me, however, to confine myself to the statement of general principles, without making a farther reference to facts than may be necessary to render these more intelligible and impressive. To those who wish to prosecute the speculation, it may be sufficient to mention the late improvements introduced into the manufacture of iron and copper, and the still more familiar improvements in spinning and weaving; to which we may add the prodigies effected in bleaching and dying, by the application of chemical principles to those arts. It may not, however, be superfluous to remark, before dismissing this subject, that the advantages derived by society from the facilities afforded by roads, canals, bridges, the establishment of regular posts, by safe and convenient harbours, and everything which tends to improve the art of navigation, are all illustrations of the same doctrine, evincing the powerful and manifold influence of those expedients which economize labour and time on the commercial interests of a country.

The author of the *Inquiry into the Nature and Origin of Public Wealth,* has chosen to express this general principle in a different way. What I would ascribe to the division of labour, he ascribes to the operation of capital; qualifying his statement by calling it the operation of capital *in superseding labour.* I confess, I do not think that the consideration of capital should enter at all into this general view of the subject; for though almost all the expedients alluded to, do imply the possession of capital, more especially those expedients which consist in the use of machinery, yet that they do not imply it necessarily, appears sufficiently from those compendious and cheap processes which chemistry has suggested in various arts. Nor is this all: Even in the most expensive machines, capital forms only one of the conditions to their establishment. Capital, of itself, can do nothing, unless directed by skill. Why, therefore, should this last circumstance be overlooked? Are not the advantages that have been derived from the improved steam-engine, due as much to the genius of Watt as to the capital of Boulton? On the whole, therefore, I am inclined to prefer the statement which I have now proposed, to either of the others which have been under consideration. Of these statements, that given by Mr. Smith is plainly defective, inasmuch as it embraces a very partial view of the subject; while the other is exceptionable, by clogging the correct statement of the principle by which the effect is produced, with a specification of the means by which it is accomplished, which specification, certainly, does not include all the possible ways by which labour can be encouraged by human ingenuity.

In the course of Mr. Smith's illustrations on this article of Political Economy, he takes occasion to remark, that "it is the great multiplication of the productions of all the different arts, in consequence of the division of labour, which occasions, in a well-governed society, that universal opulence which extends itself to the lowest ranks of the people. Every workman has a great quantity of his own work to dispose of beyond what he himself has occasion for; and every other workman being in exactly the same situation, he is enabled to exchange a great quantity of his own goods for a great quantity, or, what comes to the same thing, for the price of a great quantity of theirs. He supplies them abundantly with what they have occasion for, and they accommodate him as amply with what he has occasion for, and a general plenty diffuses itself through all the different ranks of the society."*

The same observation, too, occurs in some other writers of an earlier date. Thus Mandeville says:—" What a bustle is there to be made in several parts of the world before a fine scarlet or crimson cloth can be produced, what multiplicity of trades and artificers must be employed! not only such as are obvious, as wool-combers, spinners, the weaver, the cloth worker, the scourer, the dyer, the setter, the drawer, and the packer; but others that are more remote and might seem foreign to it, as the mill-wright, the pewterer, and the chemist, which yet all are necessary, as well as a great number of other handicrafts to have the tools, utensils, and other implements belonging to the trades already named. All these things are done at home; the most frightful prospect is left behind, when we reflect on the toil and hazard that are to be undergone abroad, the vast seas we are to go over, the different climates we are to endure, and the several nations we must be obliged to for their assistance."†

This quotation from Dr. Mandeville, appears to me to be interesting, as it has plainly suggested to Mr. Smith the idea of one of the finest passages in the *Wealth of Nations*:—

" Observe the accommodation of the most common artificer or day-labourer in a civilized and thriving country, and you will perceive that the number of people of whose industry a part, though but a small part, has been employed in procuring him this accommodation, exceeds all computation. The woollen coat, for example, which covers the day-labourer, as coarse and rough as it may appear, is the produce of the joint-labour of a great multitude of workmen. The shepherd, the sorter of

---

* [*Wealth of Nations*, B. I. chap. i.; Vol. I. p. 16, *seq.*, tenth edition.]
† [*The Fable of the Bees*, &c., with an *Essay on Charity and Charity Schools, and a Search into the Nature of Society*. Lond. 1714, 1723, 1732.]

the wool, the wool-comber or carder, the dyer, the scribbler, the spinner, the weaver, the fuller, the dresser, with many others, must all join their different arts in order to complete even this homely production. How many merchants and carriers, besides, must have been employed in transporting the materials from some of those workmen to others who often live in a very distant part of the country.; how much commerce and navigation in particular, how many ship-builders, sailors, sail-makers, rope-makers, must have been employed in order to bring together the different drugs made use of by the dyer, which often come from the remotest corners of the world! What a variety of labour too is necessary in order to produce the tools of the meanest of those workmen. To say nothing of such complicated machines as the ship of the sailor, the mill of the fuller, or even the loom of the weaver, let us consider only what a variety of labour is requisite in order to form that very simple machine, the shears with which the shepherd clips the wool. The miner, the builder of the furnace for smelting the ore, the feller of the timber, the burner of the charcoal to be made use of in the smelting-house, the brick-maker, the brick-layer, the workman who attends the furnace, the mill-wright, the forger, the smith, must all of them join their different arts in order to produce them. Were we to examine, in the same manner, all the different parts of his dress and household furniture, the coarse linen shirt which he wears next his skin, the shoes which cover his feet, the bed which he lies on, and all the different parts which compose it, the kitchen-grate at which he prepares his victuals, the coals which he makes use of for that purpose, dug from the bowels of the earth, and brought to him perhaps by a long sea and a long land carriage, all the other utensils of his kitchen, all the furniture of his table, the knives and forks, the earthen or pewter plates upon which he serves up and divides his victuals, the different hands employed in preparing his bread and his beer, the glass window which lets in the heat and the light, and keeps out the wind and the rain, with all the knowledge and art requisite for preparing that beautiful and happy invention, without which these northern parts of the world could scarce have afforded a very comfortable habitation, together with the tools of all the different workmen employed in producing those different conveniences; if we examine, I say, all these things, and consider what a variety of labour is employed about each of them, we shall be sensible that without the assistance and co-operation of many thousands, the very meanest person in a civilized country could not be provided, even according to what we very falsely imagine, the easy and simple manner in which he is commonly accommodated. Compared, indeed, with the more extravagant luxury of the great, his accommodation must no doubt appear extremely simple and easy; and yet it may be true, perhaps, that the accommodation of a European prince does not always so much exceed that of an industrious and frugal peasant, as the accommodation of the latter exceeds that of many an African king, the absolute master of the lives and liberties of ten thousand naked savages."*

These illustrations of Mr. Smith's are so happily and beautifully expressed, that I thought I could not do them justice in any other way than by transcribing them at length from his work. From the view of the subject which has been given, some of Mr. Smith's expressions will require correction; and his picture, if less pleasing in its colouring, might have been brought nearer to an exact resemblance to the truth, had he insisted less on his favourite topic, and enlarged more on the prodigious effects produced by machinery. On this last head, an anonymous author, who published a pamphlet soon after the riots in Lancashire, occasioned by the introduction of Sir Richard Arkwright's machinery, has made some very judicious observations, which, though not expressed with all the eloquence of Mr. Smith, may form no inappropriate supplement to the quotations already made.†

Before dismissing the present subject, it is proper for me to

* [Book I. chap. i.; Vol. I. pp. 17-19, tenth edition.]

† [Probably *Letters on the Utility and Policy of employing Machines to shorten Labour, occasioned by the late Disturbances in Lancashire*, &c., 1782. But this pamphlet I have never seen, and the Notes do not supply Mr. Stewart's quotation.]

mention, as an additional limitation of Mr. Smith's doctrines, that in certain cases great advantages have been gained by a judicious concentration of all the different employments connected with a particular manufacture under the same general superintendence and management; advantages which Mr. Smith represents as only attainable by pushing the subdivision of labour to a greater extent. In proof of this remark, I shall read a short quotation from an anonymous work which states some facts well worthy of attention in the present argument. The publication to which I allude is entitled, *Observations founded on Facts, on the Propriety or Impropriety of Exporting Cotton Twist*, published in the year 1803.* As an additional illustration of the same thing, reference is made by the author to Mr. Thorpe's manufactory at Leeds, where the same work is said to be now performed by thirty-five persons, to execute which in a far more imperfect manner, required, eighteen years ago, 1634 persons.

In offering the criticisms with which I concluded my lecture yesterday, on the favourite speculation of Mr. Smith with respect to the division of labour, I must again remark, that I do not censure his doctrines as erroneous, but only as partial and incomplete. Of the importance of the division in promoting the progress of the arts, and as a very striking feature in the present state of society in England, I am abundantly aware. I only mean to say, that it is not the sole cause of the progress of the arts, or of the diffusion of wealth among the body of the people;—that there are various other causes with which it is altogether unconnected, and that even where its effects are the greatest, it generally co-operates with other causes much more powerful in their operation.

A farther limitation of Mr. Smith's doctrine with respect to the connexion between the division of labour and national wealth, is suggested by this consideration, that if it is just in all its extent, it would necessarily follow, that in every country where the division of labour is carried to a great extent, the

---

* [Perhaps 1805; see Watt. Like the former the Notes give no quotation from this pamphlet, of which I am equally ignorant.]

condition of the people must be actually easy and prosperous. This conclusion surely would be very wide of the truth. Before men can think of the accommodations of life, it is necessary that they should be provided with the means of subsistence; and the abundance of these must always depend on the state of Agriculture,—an art, to the perfection of which the division of labour contributes less than to that of any other art whatsoever. Indeed, where this art is neglected, or does not receive adequate encouragement, one of the greatest sources of national distress may be found in the encroachment which the poor man is led to make on the funds, which are destined for procuring food, by those artificial wants which the arts of accommodation provoke and multiply.

With respect to the limit to which the division of labour may be carried, it is fixed, according to Mr. Smith, in all cases by the extent of the market. Before a person dedicates himself entirely to one employment, says Mr. Smith, he must have a reasonable ground of assurance, that he will be able to exchange the surplus produce of his labour for the commodities which he may want of a different nature, and accordingly, in a country which is thinly peopled, we find some individuals uniting a variety of different employments; while in those cases where the market is extensive, and where large capitals are employed in trade, the imagination can hardly fix any limits to the progressive simplification of manufacturing art. It must at the same time be remembered, that these circumstances, though indispensable requisites, are not those alone on which this progress depends, as sufficiently appears from the powerful stimulus which has been applied in this country by the pressure of our public burdens, and also by the competition of foreign nations. In the different parts of Great Britain, illustrations may be collected of all the various gradations in the simplification of manual operations, from that state of society where the farmer is butcher, baker, and brewer to his own family, to the prevalent and almost ludicrous extreme of refinement which is exhibited in the manufacture of a pin. In some parts of the Highlands of Scotland, not many years ago, every peasant, according to the *Statistical Accounts,* made his own shoes of leather tanned by himself. Many a shepherd and cottar too, with his wife and children, appeared at church in clothes which had been touched by no hands but their own, since they were shorn from the sheep and sown in the flax field. In the preparation of these, it is added, scarcely a single article had been purchased, except the awl, needle, thimble, and a very few parts of the iron-work employed in the weaving. The dyes, too, were chiefly extracted by the women from trees, shrubs, and herbs.

The remarks quoted from Mr. Smith at our last meeting, naturally lead our attention to the effects of the separation of professions in consolidating the social union, and in organizing the political system, by multiplying the mutual connexions and dependencies of the different members of a community. There is nothing, indeed, in the history of human affairs more striking than this obvious fact, that in proportion as the intellectual and moral faculties of the species are unfolded and cultivated, and in proportion as the joint wealth and power of the community increase, individuals, considered apart, should become more and more connected with one another, and man should be rendered more necessary to man. I need hardly add, that this separation of professions, which, by limiting some men to the labour of the hands, and allowing others to cultivate their intellectual powers, fits the one to govern, and the others to be governed, and establishes in a state, that good order and tranquillity which are incompatible with the habits of uncivilized life. The Son of Sirach has described this state of things with beautiful simplicity:—" The wisdom of a learned man cometh by opportunity of leisure: and he that hath little business shall become wise.—How can he get wisdom that holdeth the plough, and that glorieth in the goad, that driveth oxen, and is occupied in their labours, and whose talk is of bullocks? He giveth his mind to make furrows, and is diligent to give the kine fodder. So every carpenter and work-master, that laboureth night and day: and they that cut and grave seals, and are diligent to make great variety, and give themselves to counterfeit imagery, and watch to finish a work. The smith also sitting by the anvil, and considering the iron work, the vapour of the fire wasteth his flesh, and he fighteth with the heat of the furnace: the noise of the hammer and the anvil is ever in his ears, and his eyes look still upon the pattern of the thing that he maketh; he setteth his mind to finish his work, and watcheth to polish it perfectly. So doth the potter sitting at his work, and turning the wheel about with his feet, who is alway carefully set at his work, and maketh all his work by number; he fashioneth the clay with his arm, and boweth down his strength before his feet; he applieth himself to lead it over; and he is diligent to make clean the furnace.—All these trust to their hands: and every one is wise in his work. Without these cannot a city be inhabited: and they shall not dwell where they will, nor go up and down: they shall not be sought for in public counsel, nor sit high in the congregation: they shall not sit on the judges' seat, nor understand the sentence of judgment: they cannot declare justice and judgment; and they shall not be found where parables are spoken. But they will maintain the state of the world, and all their desire is in the work of their craft.—But he that giveth his mind to the law of the most High, and is occupied in the meditation thereof, . . . he shall serve among great men, and appear before princes."*

There is, it must be confessed, at the same time, one view of this subject which is not altogether so pleasing; I mean the effect which, in the more advanced stages of commercial and manufacturing refinement, is produced by the subdivision of labour on the intellectual and moral qualities of those who are doomed to be the instruments of all those blessings to their fellow-citizens. It is justly remarked by Dr. Ferguson in his *Essay on the History of Civil Society,* "The artist finds that the more he can confine his attention to a particular part of any work, his productions are the more perfect, and grow under his hands in greater quantities. Every undertaker and manufacturer finds, that the more he can subdivide the tasks

* [*Ecclesiasticus,* xxxviii. 24—xxxix. 4.]

of his workmen, and the more hands he can employ on separate articles, the more are his expenses diminished and his profits increased." . . . . " Every craft may engross the whole of a man's attention, and has a mystery which must be studied or learned by a regular apprenticeship. Nations of tradesmen come to consist of members, who, beside their own particular trade, are ignorant of all human affairs, and who may contribute to the preservation and enlargement of their commonwealth, without making its interest an object of their regard or attention." . . . " Many mechanical arts, indeed, require no capacity, they succeed best under a total suppression of sentiment and reason; and ignorance is the mother of industry as well as of superstition. Reflection and fancy are subject to err, but a habit of moving the hand or the foot is independent of either. Manufactures accordingly prosper most where the mind is least consulted, and where the workshop may, without any great effort of imagination, be considered as an engine, the parts of which are men."*

This view of the moral effects of the division of labour, which is at least equally important with the former, is illustrated at length by the author now quoted, with his usual ingenuity and eloquence. To contrive some method of obviating or diminishing this misfortune, which seems at first view to be inseparably connected with the growth of commercial prosperity, is one of the most important problems of legislation. The remedy which at first suggests itself, is the establishment of a system of national instruction, adapted peculiarly to the lower orders of men. But the prosecution of this subject would lead me into too extensive a field of speculation. I cannot, however, quit this article without remarking, that the evil, though a real one while it lasts, naturally leads the way to its own correction, so as to render it probable that it is but a step in the progress of human improvement. In confirmation of this remark, a variety of proofs crowd on me; but I shall confine my attention to one consideration, which follows as an obvious corollary from the foregoing principles. I have already endeavoured to ex-

* [Part IV. sect. i.]

plain, in what manner the division of labour leads to the invention of machines. When the simplification has been carried so far as to convert, according to Dr. Ferguson's metaphor, a workshop into an engine, the parts of which are men, the next step is that which converts it into an engine, literally so called, where the place of men is supplied by mechanical contrivances. The ultimate tendency, therefore, of this process, is to substitute mechanical contrivances for manufacturing work, and to open a field for human genius in the nobler departments of industry and talent. There are some other respects, besides, in which the invention of machines counteracts the effects of that division of labour by which it is facilitated. I have heard it remarked, for example, as an advantage resulting from the subdivision of labour, that it obstructs the transplantation of manufactures from one country to another, tending thereby to preserve to a nation which has once outstripped its neighbours, the superiority which it has gained. The effect of mechanical inventions, unquestionably, is to encourage and accelerate this transplantation, rendering the progress of arts and manufactures over the globe more and more an operation of capital. If the former be advantageous in a national view, the latter acts with a more extensive influence on the fortunes of the human race. Indeed, its partial inconvenience, with respect to the stability of some branches of foreign trade, is much more than counterbalanced by its tendency to support manufactures over the whole face of our own country, so as at once to distribute their beneficial effects, and to prevent the evils with which they are attended when carried to an undue excess in a particular district. But I have already dwelt longer on this general topic than perhaps was requisite; and I hasten to other discussions more circumscribed in their object, though intimately connected with those in which we have been engaged.

The result of the reasonings which I have now stated, with respect to the division of labour is, that however extensively this principle may operate as one cause of the improvement of the arts, and of the general diffusion of the accommodations of life among the members of a commercial society, yet that a variety of other causes co-operate no less powerfully to the same effect ; more particularly the invention of machinery, the application of chemistry to the arts, and the facilities afforded to commercial exchanges by roads, bridges, canals, harbours, and the arts of navigation. In one common tendency, as I remarked in my lecture yesterday, all these different expedients agree with the division of labour, and with each other ; I mean their tendency to save or to supersede labour ; and therefore I should be disposed to substitute, instead of the phrase "*division of labour,*" as employed by Mr. Smith, the more general phrase, "*economy of labour,*" a phrase which points out with precision the common qualities from which the division of labour, the invention of machinery, the facilities afforded to commerce, and the application of chemistry, derive all their value.

CHAPTER II.

[OF MONEY, THE CIRCULATING MEDIUM.]

[SECT. I.—OF THE ORIGIN AND USE OF MONEY.]

THE Division of Labour, wherever it has been carried to any considerable extent, presupposes the establishment of some common medium of exchange. Without this previous arrangement it would be impossible for an individual to devote himself exclusively to a particular species of employment; divesting himself of every care for the supply of his other wants, and trusting to the fruits of his own labour for the power of commanding the produce of that of his neighbours ; and it is thus that the use of money becomes a powerful, and indeed necessary auxiliary to the other circumstances which lay the foundation of the progressive improvement of the species. It would lead me into a detail inconsistent with my present plan, to attempt the slightest historical sketch with respect to the origin of this invention, and to the successive forms which it assumes in proportion as the operations of commerce become more extensive and complicated. These different stages in this history, from the first and simplest operations of barter, to the refinements of paper credit, have been traced by various writers, particularly by Mr. Harris in his *Essay upon Money and Coins*,* and by Mr. Smith in the *Wealth of Nations*.†

---

* [In two parts. The first was published in 1757, the second in 1758. The work is anonymous: but by Mr. M'Culloch it is ascribed to Joseph Harris, Assaymaster of the Mint; whereas by Watt and the Catalogues in general, the author is called William Harris, D.D.,—which last is, I presume, an error.—Mr. Stewart's reference will be found in Part I. chap. ii.]

† [Book I. chap. iv.; Vol. I. p. 83, *seq.*, tenth edition.]

In process of time, among all civilized nations, gold, silver, and copper have supplanted all other commodities as the great instruments of commerce. For this purpose, indeed, these metals are so admirably adapted, that we may justly consider them, particularly the two first, as destined for it by nature, independently of all convention or of all laws.[1]

The circumstances which recommend silver and gold as the fittest materials for money, are chiefly the following.—*First*, When pure, and unmixed with base metals, they have everywhere the same characteristics, and in all respects the same qualities. *Secondly*, They are divisible into minute parts, which are again susceptible of a complete re-union by fusion. *Thirdly*, They are durable, portable, easily kept, and not liable to injury from want of use. *Fourthly*, They are susceptible of any form, and any impression. *Fifthly*, They are not too common, nor to be obtained without a valuable consideration in land and labour. To the provision which nature has thus made for facilitating commerce, in the qualities which so remarkably characterize these metals, it may be worth while to add the advantages which we derive from the variety of metals in which these qualities are to be found. In rich and commercial countries, coins of gold and silver alone would by no means answer all the purposes of exchange. Coins of gold and silver are not well adapted for that retail trade in which, however, the greatest number of subjects are principally concerned. Coins of silver, again, are too bulky for larger payments. It is necessary, therefore, that coins should be made of different metals. Accordingly, in all such countries, this has taken place sooner or later in the progress of commercial refinement. With respect to the history of the coins in England, a great deal of very curious information has been lately brought together, and very perspicuously stated by Lord Liverpool, in his *Treatise on the Coins of the Realm*, [1805.]

The enumeration which has been already given of the qualities which so peculiarly fit the precious metals to perform the

[1] See Turgot, [*Sur la Formation et la Distribution des Richesses*, sect. xlv. Œuvres, Tome V. p. 48.]

function of media of exchange, seems of itself fully sufficient to account for the universal use made of them in commerce, abstracting altogether from the useful purposes to which they are applicable in the various arts. In stating this remark, it is scarcely necessary for me to add, that I would by no means be understood to deny the important uses of which gold and silver are susceptible, or the intrinsic value which they derive from their beauty and subserviency to the arts of decoration. On this subject I am ready to admit all that has been urged by Mr. Smith, in that part of his work where he attempts to shew that, except iron, they are more useful than any other metal. He says—" The demand for those metals arises partly from their utility and partly from their beauty. If you except iron, they are more useful than perhaps any other metal. As they are less liable to rust and impurity, they can more easily be kept clean; and the utensils either of the table or the kitchen are often upon that account more agreeable when made of them. A silver boiler is more cleanly than a lead, copper, or tin one; and the same quality would render a gold boiler still better than a silver one. Their principal merit, however, arises from their beauty, which renders them peculiarly fit for the ornaments of dress and furniture. No paint or dye can give so splendid a colour as gilding. The merit of their beauty is greatly enhanced by their scarcity. . . . These qualities of utility, beauty, and scarcity, are the original foundation of the high price of those metals, or of the great quantity of other goods for which they can everywhere be exchanged. This value was antecedent to, and independent of, their being employed as coin, and was the quality which fitted them for that employment. That employment, however, by occasioning a new demand, and by diminishing the quantity which could be employed in any other way, may have afterwards contributed to keep up or increase their value."*

In the whole of this passage I certainly agree with Mr. Smith, excepting where he says, that the intrinsic value of gold and silver was the quality which fitted them for their employ-

* [Book I. chap. xi.; Vol. I. p. 268, *seq.*, tenth edition.]

ment as coin. It appears to me, that this intrinsic value, which I shall allow to gold and silver in its fullest extent, ought to be regarded in the theory of money as merely accidental circumstances, from which it is proper to abstract with all possible care, as tending only to embarrass our conceptions; for the same reason, that in studying the theory of mechanics, we abstract from the effects of friction, the rigidity of ropes, and the weight of the materials of which machines are composed. The considerations, undoubtedly, mentioned by Mr. Smith, add to the exchangeable value of money, by increasing the demand for the materials of which it is made, in the very same manner as this value would be increased by a deficiency to the same extent, in the ordinary supply coming from the mines. But I cannot help thinking, that the quantity of gold and silver employed in the arts, bears but a very trifling proportion to that which circulates in the shape of money or bullion over the commercial world, so trifling, indeed, as to render it of little moment in the present argument, or at most to place it on the same footing with those circumstances in mechanics, from which, though it is necessary to attend to them in practice, it is nevertheless convenient to abstract in theory, in studying the principle on which any of the simple mechanical powers produces its effect. At any rate, when gold is converted into coin, its possessor never thinks of anything but its exchangeable value, or supposes a coffer of guineas to be more valuable, because they are capable of being transformed into a service of plate for his own use; whatever satisfaction the possessor of a service of plate may derive from the consideration that it may be converted into guineas. Why, then, should we suppose, that if the intrinsic value of gold and silver were annihilated completely, they might not still perform, as well as now, all the functions of money, supposing them to retain all those recommendations formerly stated, which give them so decided a superiority over everything else which could be employed for the same purpose. Supposing the supply of the precious metals, at present afforded by the mines, to fail entirely all over the world, there can be little doubt that all the plate now in existence would be gradually converted into money, and gold and silver would soon cease to be employed in the ornamental arts. In this case, a few years would obliterate entirely all idea of the intrinsic value of these metals; while their value would be understood to arise from those characteristical qualities which recommend them as media of exchange. But so far from sinking in their exchangeable value, they would every day become more valuable in the market than before, in proportion as their quantity was diminished by the slow waste occasioned by commercial circulation. Mr. Smith's doctrine, at the same time, I must own, coincides with the general opinion on this subject; and Mr. Harris carries it so far, as to propose it as a questionable point, whether coins would have preserved their value and been continued as money, if silver and gold had not been applicable to other purposes. I confess I can see no good reason for this observation; as, independently of the intrinsic value of these metals, their peculiar adaptation to their different ends, as signs or measures of value, could not have failed to have given them an exclusive title to this employment. I am therefore disposed to think, that Bishop Berkeley was not wide of the truth, (for I would not go so far as to adopt his idea in its full extent,) when he proposed the following doubts in his pamphlet, entitled *The Querist*, "Whether money is to be considered as having an intrinsic value, or as being a commodity, a standard, a measure, or a pledge, as is variously suggested by writers? And whether the true idea of money, *as such*, be not altogether that of a ticket or counter?"* The ingenious author certainly did not mean, in this query, to deny that gold and silver have an intrinsic value, but only to insinuate, that this is an accidental or secondary consideration from which we ought to abstract entirely in forming a precise idea of their function as money. This is perfectly evident from the qualifying words "*as such*," which he introduces into the Query.

The same functions might be performed by a variety of other metals, but by none which unites so many advantages; and

* [Query xxiii.]

hence the general consent of mankind in applying them to this purpose; in consequence of which they have come to be essentially distinguished from those local media of exchange to which accidental circumstances have given currency in particular nations. It is this general consent alone which distinguishes them, when employed as money, from anything else which circulates in a country; from the paper currency, for instance, which circulates in Scotland and England. Were this island insulated from the rest of the world, the former, as a medium of exchange, would possess no advantage over the latter, excepting in so far as it diminished the opportunities of fraud; nor would it make the smallest difference on the national wealth, whether the circulating medium consisted of gold or paper, or whether the materials were abundant or scanty. This observation, self-evident as it may appear to some, may perhaps to others require a little illustration.

In a country which had no communication with others, it is obvious and indisputable, that the precious metals, when formed into money, would be useful only as a medium of exchange and scale of valuation. On this supposition, the observation of Anacharsis the Scythian, quoted by Mr. Hume in one of his *Political Discourses*, seems to be perfectly just, that gold and silver appeared to be of no use to the Greeks, but to assist them in enumeration and arithmetic.* I shall afterwards, however, endeavour to show, that Mr. Hume carried this principle a great deal too far, when he concluded, that the prices of commodities are regulated entirely by the plenty or scarcity of the coin in circulation.†

In a country which has commercial dealings with others, the case is very different; the precious metals being, by those essential qualities formerly mentioned, so much distinguished from the other media of exchange that have been occasionally employed, that they are objects of universal request among mankind; influencing in a great variety of ways, by their local plenty or scarcity, the relative condition of nations.

Among the other commodities which have been used for the

* [*Essays*, Vol. I. Of Money.] † [Ibid.]

same purpose, the small shells, called *Cowries*, which are employed in Africa and some parts of Asia, are perhaps the most deserving of attention, when we consider, notwithstanding their total inutility in every other respect, the value set upon them as media of exchange over such extensive regions of the earth. "I am informed from good authority," says Major Rennell, " that about a hundred tons of Cowries are annually shipped from England alone to Guinea. These are originally shipped from the Maldive Islands to Bengal, and from Bengal to England. In Bengal, twenty-four hundred more or less are equal to a shilling, and, notwithstanding, some articles in the market may be purchased for a single cowry. But in the inland parts of Africa, they are about ten times as dear, varying from two hundred and twenty to two hundred and eighty. M. Beaufoy was told that in Kassina they were at the rate of about two hundred and fifty; and Mr. Park reports, that they are about the same price at Sego, but *cheaper* at Timbuctoo, which is about the *centre* of the cowry country; *dearer* towards Manding, which is the western extremity of it. Hence they are probably carried in the first instance to Timbuctoo, the gold market, and thence distributed to the east and west."[1]

It would be a curious speculation to examine the combinations of circumstances which thus affect the value of an article that derives its whole worth from its arbitrary application to facilitate commercial operations. The facts which have been stated are sufficient to show, that the minute subdivision of value which these shells are fitted to express, has created a demand for them even where the precious metals are in abundance; and this demand would manifestly be much greater if the precious metals did not exist at all. These last, however, abstracting entirely from their application in the useful arts, are incomparably better adapted for the purposes of exchange than cowries, or any other substitute which has yet been thought of, and therefore I have not the smallest doubt, that their employment as media of exchange would have been as universal as it

[1] [*Proceedings of the Association for promoting the Discovery of the Interior Parts of Africa*, &c., 1798.] Appendix, p. 86.

now is, though they had possessed no intrinsic utility or value whatever. In consequence, indeed, of these qualities, the attention of men was directed to them at an earlier period than it otherwise would have been; and the estimation in which they were held as articles of merchandise, may have suggested their advantageous properties as media of exchange. But the only utility which is essential to gold and silver as media of exchange, is their peculiar adaptation to that purpose; and though I would not take it upon me to say that their uses in the arts detract from their value in this respect, yet these are so far from being essential to their qualities as money, that they are in some respects disadvantageous, by rendering the theory of money more complicated than it otherwise would have been.

Having mentioned the extensive use of Cowries as a medium of exchange, I cannot help taking notice here, though the subject is not immediately connected with our present inquiry, of some particulars concerning the current prices of some commodities estimated in this way, extracted from the last communication which was received in this country from Mr. Mungo Park, and which is dated 16th November 1805. The particulars which I have to state, are copied from a letter received by me some time ago from a friend in London, who had an opportunity of perusing the original document. In this letter Mr. Park states, that in Manding, a town containing eleven thousand inhabitants, he opened a booth for the sale of European commodities, of which he took down some of the prices in cowries. Thus, a piece of gold worth in our currency twelve shillings and sixpence, sold for three thousand cowries. A dollar, sold by Mr. Park as a piece of European manufacture, brought from six to twelve thousand cowries. Currency for currency, a cowrie is stated to be worth the twentieth part of our penny. A prime male slave brought forty thousand cowries; a prime female slave ninety thousand; one young female slave brought forty thousand; a horse, from two to ten prime male slaves; a fat cow, fifteen thousand cowries; an ass, seventeen thousand; a sheep, from three to five thousand.

The doctrine which the foregoing observations tend to establish is, if I mistake not, agreeable to the opinion of Mr. Locke, who observes, "that the general consent of nations has placed an imaginary value on silver, because of the qualities fitting it for the purposes of exchange."* This remark of Locke's has been severely commented on by Mr. Law, in a small treatise entitled *Money and Trade Considered*.† "It is reasonable to think," he says, " silver was bartered, as it was valued, for its uses as a metal, and was given as money according to its value in barter. The additional use of money to which silver was applied, would add to its value, because, as money, it remedied the disadvantages and inconveniences of barter; and consequently the demand for silver increasing, it received an additional value equal to the greater demand its use as money occasioned.

" And this additional value is no more imaginary than the value silver had in barter, as a metal; for such value was because it served such uses, and was greater or less according to the demand for silver as a metal, proportioned to its quantity. The additional value silver received from being used as money, was because of its qualities which fitted it for that use, and that value was according to the additional demand its use as money occasioned.

" If either of these values be imaginary, then all value is so; for no goods have any value, but from the uses they are applied to, and according to the demand for them, in proportion to their quantity."‡

I confess, it does not appear to me that Mr. Law's reasonings are precise or conclusive. In as far as his criticism refers to Mr. Locke's use of the word *imaginary*, I do not think it necessary to enter into any argument concerning its justice, but I own that the idea which Mr. Locke meant to express, appears to me clear and unquestionable. That idea was, that the general consent of men, by adopting silver as the medium of exchange, bestows on it, in addition to the recommendations which it derives from its subserviency to the arts, a value which

---

* [(First) *Considerations on Interest and Money*.]
† [First published in 1705.]
‡ [Chap. i. p. 15, *seq.*, Glasgow edition, 1750.]

it did not intrinsically possess. This ideal value is precisely of the same kind with that which the credit of a bank stamps on paper currency, with this difference, that the latter is local, while the former is universal. Mr. Locke's remark farther intimates, that the general consent of men was not the effect of caprice, but of certain peculiarities in the nature and qualities of silver, which have eminently fitted it for the purposes of exchange; a proportion which coincides exactly with an assertion formerly quoted from Turgot, [p. 334,] that gold and silver seem destined by nature to be the great instruments of commerce, independently of all law and of all convention.

In further prosecution of the same argument, Mr. Law adds, " that he cannot conceive how different nations could agree to put an *imaginary* value on anything, especially upon silver, by which all other goods are valued; or that any one country would receive that as a value, which was not valuable equal to what it was given for; or how that imaginary value could have been kept up."* The extensive use which is made of cowries in Africa, and some parts of Asia, may serve as a sufficient answer to these observations. Nor is the fact less applicable, though we admit, that these shells, being used in countries where gold and silver are also employed, are therefore to be considered merely as tokens or representatives of the precious metals; for if articles possessing no intrinsic value, should possess a value as representing the precious metals, why might not gold and silver derive their value from the useful commodities which they represent and enable us to purchase?

" But," says Mr. Law, " for the same reasons a crown passing in France for seventy-six sols, should pass in Scotland for seventy-six pence, and in Holland for seventy-six stivers. But on the contrary, even in France where the crown is raised, it is worth no more than before when at sixty sols."† I must confess that I do not understand the scope of this argument, nor can I conceive how it applies to the question under discussion. According to the literal interpretation of this passage, Mr. Law is combating a phantom of his own imagination; for, by whom

* [Ibid.] † [Ibid.]

was it ever supposed that one nation adopted the money of another, ascribing to the precious metals an imaginary value for no other reason than that others had done the same ? I have before said, that the general use of the precious metals is the obvious result of those circumstances which so peculiarly adapt these metals for the purposes of money. This general coincidence Mr. Locke expresses by the word *consent*. But it is perfectly evident from the context, that he did not mean consent arising from any stipulation or imitation among nations; but a consent analogous to that which Cicero ascribes to the human race, in the fundamental principles of religion and virtue. If this observation be just, it affords a sufficient explanation of the fact, that a crown may pass in France for seventy-six sous, while in Scotland it may not bring seventy-six pence, nor in Holland seventy-six stivers. The properties which universally belong to the precious metals, account completely for the universality of their use as media of exchange ; but it would be surprising, indeed, if all nations had adjusted their values agreeably to some common standard. The case of the precious metals is similar to measures of longitudinal extension. In taking the standard of these from the human body, there has been a pretty general consent among nations. But it would not follow from this, that the Paris foot, and London foot, &c., should be exactly of the same length. Such a coincidence could have resulted only from an express compact. The truth however is, that in consequence of the commercial connexions of different nations, the relative values of the coined metals have been pretty accurately adjusted in the general market of the world ; and it is owing to this that all arbitrary operations in the mints of particular States are unjust, inexpedient, and in many respects ineffectual ; a consequence which has not escaped the notice of Mr. Law himself.*

* [Mr. Stewart probably refers to the following passage:—" It is unjust to raise or allay money, because, then all contracts are paid with a lesser value than was contracted for; and as it has bad effects on home or foreign trade, so no nation practises it that has regard to justice, or understands the nature of trade and money."—(*Money*, &c. Chap. iv. p. 79, *seq.*, Edit. 1750.) And so on throughout the chapter.]

It must not, therefore, be imagined, when I lay so great stress on the properties of the precious metals, abstracting from their intrinsical value, in studying the theory of money, that I would mean to insinuate any apology for those arbitrary operations on the coinage, which have been so often practised by different princes. If gold and silver possessed no intrinsic value, such operations might be no less iniquitous than they always have been; for their iniquity arises, not from the useful purposes to which the precious metals are subservient in the arts, but from the universality of their employment as media of exchange. And, indeed, one of my chief reasons for dwelling so long on the present subject, was to prevent so very important a truth as that which relates to the good faith that ought to be maintained with regard to the coinage, from being placed on what I conceive to be an unsound foundation. The pains which Mr. Law has bestowed on this argument is the more surprising, that the doctrine which he wishes to refute would have accorded better with the general scope of his book than that which he supports; and indeed, in one passage, he seems to give up completely the very point for which he had been so long contending. "Money is not the value for which goods are exchanged, but the value by which they are exchanged; the use of money is to buy goods, and silver, while money, is of no other use."* An observation which coincides entirely with that above quoted from Mr. Hume, [p. 338.]

From the function of the precious metals as media of exchange, they gradually and naturally came to form the common scale of valuation. For this end, indeed, they are admirably adapted, from the mathematical exactness with which metals, in consequence of their divisibility and fusibility, are fitted to express every conceivable variation of value; a quality, indeed, of so much importance in their use as money, that it probably contributed more than anything else to establish their employment among commercial nations. The existence, too, of such a standard, would necessarily render the ideas of relative value much more precise and definite than they otherwise would have

* [Chap. vii. p. 188. Edit. 1750.]

been; by leading men to an arithmetical statement of relations, which probably, in the infancy of commerce, would have been estimated in a very gross and inaccurate manner.

The *two* great functions, then, of the precious metals, when employed for the purposes of *Money*, are to furnish, *first*, a universal *medium of exchange;* and *secondly*, an accurate *scale of valuation*. The truth is, that the second idea is, in some measure, involved in the first; and it is for this reason that I have not included it in my definition; for although in rude nations articles have been used as media of exchange, which are incapable of expressing all the different gradations of value, such could not possibly have furnished the means of carrying on the business of a great commercial country; it is therefore implied necessarily in the nature of money, that it furnishes an accurate scale of valuation ; and consequently this last function of money is to be considered as inseparably connected with that universality of its use, to which I have directed your attention as its leading and fundamental property.

To the conclusion which the foregoing reasonings tend to establish, I know it has been objected, that it is obviously contradicted by the perpetual variations that take place in the relative values of money and of commodities. When we see that silver, according to its plenty or scarcity, combined with other circumstances, fluctuates in its exchangeable value compared with that of corn, do we not ascribe an intrinsic value to the one as well as the other ? and may not silver be considered as the commodity, and corn the price, with as little impropriety as the converse ?—For my own part, I do not perceive the force of this objection. That gold and silver may be considered as commodities, I allow. But would not the case have been the same although they had possessed no intrinsical qualities whatever ? and would not their adaptation to the purposes of commerce, and their employment as media of exchange, have occasioned a considerable demand for them ? Indeed, may I not venture to add, that these circumstances would have rendered the demand for them as great as it is at present ? Of what intrinsic utility, for instance, are cowries, which perform the functions of money over a great part of Africa and Asia? and does not even this local employment of them render them an article of commerce and a commodity for sale in the hands of those traders who, after bringing them from Bengal, ship them again to Guinea?

The same doctrine concerning the precious metals will be found perfectly consistent with the principles which regulate the Course of Exchange between different countries. Even when they exist in the shape of Bullion, what constitutes their exchangeable value is their convertibility into the current coins of the country; and any increased demand for these in a particular country may be regarded, not as a symptom of any new call for them for the purposes of the arts, but as a symptom of some accident in the course of trade which has drained the country of its circulating specie. The truth of all this indeed is virtually acknowledged in those countries where a *paper currency* forms the chief circulating medium; and accordingly, whatever objections may be made to bank notes, from their supposed tendency to raise the prices of commodities, or from their insecurity in case of a revolution, no one, abstracting from these and similar circumstances, would at any time wish to see silver and gold, when able to supply himself with paper. But of this subject of Paper Currency, I shall afterwards have occasion to treat fully. In the meantime, I shall only observe, that its advantages are necessarily confined to countries which enjoy the blessings of a free and settled government. Were such governments generally established, paper would everywhere supply more and more, except in the smaller operations, the ordinary medium of circulation; and the precious metals would be limited in a great measure to the functions of liquidating the debts of different nations, and regulating the quantity of the circulating medium by restraining the paper currency within its due limits.

The observations which I have hitherto made on the subject of metallic money, apply equally to Silver and Gold; both of which are used, without any discrimination, in common mercantile transactions. It is necessary, however, according to the

CHAP. II.—OF MONEY, THE CIRCULATING MEDIUM. (§ 1.) 347

opinion of all our latest and best writers on Political Economy, that *one* of these metals should be considered as the standard or level, or measure of value ; with respect to which, the other is to be regarded as a mere commodity ; for silver and gold, in their mutual relations, like other commodities, are variable in their value, according as the quantity of either is increased or diminished. Consequently, it is not possible that they should both be the measure of value at the same place and time. This doctrine is maintained by Sir William Petty, Mr. Locke, and Mr. Harris, the last of whom speaks of silver as the measure of value in this country. On the other hand, it is one great object of Lord Liverpool's late publication on the Coinage, [1805,] to demonstrate, that gold coin has now become in this country the measure; and that this is the idea not only of the people of Great Britain, but of all the merchants of foreign countries who have any intercourse with it, and even of those who deal the most extensively in the precious metals.

" After full consideration of this subject," says his Lordship, " I offer as the result of my opinion,—*First*, That the coins of this realm, which are to be the principal measure of property and instrument of commerce, should be made of one metal only. *Secondly*, That in this kingdom the gold coins only have been for many years past, and are now in the practice and opinion of the people, the principal measure of property and instrument of commerce. In a country like Great Britain, so distinguished for its affluence and for the extent of its commercial connexions, the gold coins are best adapted to be the principal measure of property; in this kingdom, therefore, the gold coin is now the principal measure of property and standard coin, or, as it were, the sovereign archetype by which the weight and value of all other coins shall be regulated. It is the measure of almost all contracts and bargains, and by it, as a measure, the price of all commodities, bought and sold, is adjusted and ascertained."

In answer to Mr. Locke, who had said " that gold is not the money of the world and measure of commerce, nor fit to be so," his Lordship observes, " It is difficult to determine what Mr.

Locke means, when he asserts that gold is not fit to be the money of the world. Gold, as a metal, is equally homogeneous, equally divisible into exact portions or parts, and not more consumable, or more subject to decay, than silver; gold has some of those qualities even in a higher degree than silver. Mr. Locke must mean, therefore, that gold is, on account of its value, not fit to be the money of the world, or the measure of property and commerce. It cannot, I think be doubted, that the metal of which this principal measure of property is made, should correspond with the wealth and commerce of the country for which it is intended. Coins should be made of metals more or less valuable in proportion to the wealth and commerce of the country in which they are to be the measure of property. In very poor countries coins have been, and still are, principally made of copper, and sometimes even of less valuable materials. In countries advanced to a certain degree of commerce and opulence, silver is the metal of which coins are principally made. In very rich countries, and especially in those where great and extensive commerce is carried on, gold is the most proper metal, of which this principal measure of property and this instrument of commerce should be made; in such countries gold will in practice become the principal measure of property, and the instrument of commerce, with the general consent of the people, not only without the support of law, but in spite almost of any law that may be enacted to the contrary, for the principal purchases and exchanges cannot then be made, with any convenience in coins of less valuable metal."

I must own I do not fully see the force of his Lordship's reasoning upon this subject; but Lord Liverpool seems to have reflected so much upon it, and enjoyed such opportunities of being well informed in all things relating thereto, that I am doubtful of my own opinion, wherever I am forced to differ from him. Of the advantages, indeed, which he thus enjoyed, his Lordship appears to have been fully sensible; and in one place of his book, appears to express an opinion pretty strongly of the inability of speculative men, that is, men without his practical knowledge, to oppose or criticise his opinions.

Admonished by these hints, I shall not on this occasion prosecute the discussion of this complicated subject any farther.

I cannot, however, dismiss the subject altogether, without taking notice of an idea which has been suggested by many political writers, and which is well entitled to a careful consideration, though I do not mean to offer any decided opinion with regard to it;—that the stamp of the sovereign affixed to the metals which compose the current coin, ought alone to denote the degree of purity, and that their value ought to depend totally on their weight. The only inconvenience which would attend this measure, would be the difficulty of breaking through the present plan, and the trouble which would be occasioned by the necessity of weighing. Of these, the last only is permanent in its operation. The conveniences which would attend a general adoption of this plan, would be great. It would put an end to all clipping, washing, and paring of the coins, and to all that jobbing which proceeds from a minute knowledge of the state of the currency in different countries. In truth, such a regulation, if everywhere adopted, would secure to the world at large those advantages which Holland derived from the Bank at Amsterdam.

[SECT. II.—OF REAL AND NOMINAL PRICES.]

The remarks which I now proceed to offer, relate to a distinction intimately connected with the subject which has just been under our consideration; I mean that between the real and nominal prices of commodities. In the practical conclusion which Mr. Smith ultimately adopts on the question to which this distinction applies, I do not differ from him very widely; though I think that it has been stated by him in too general and unqualified terms. But as I deem the metaphysical process by which he arrives at this conclusion is by no means satisfactory, and as I have been often puzzled with it myself, I shall offer no apology for making a few observations on it, premising only, that I consider the question to which I am first to direct your attention, as chiefly an object of speculative curiosity.

"Every man is rich or poor," says Mr. Smith, "according to the degree in which he can afford to enjoy the necessaries, conveniences, and amusements of life. But after the division of labour has once thoroughly taken place, it is but a very small part of these with which a man's own labour can supply him. The far greater part of them he must derive from the labour of other people, and he must be rich or poor according to the quantity of that labour which he can command, or which he can afford to purchase."*—It appears to me that the latter clause of this sentence is by no means a just inference from the former; and the only conclusion to which it properly leads, is that every man is rich or poor according to the means which he possesses of purchasing those necessaries, conveniences, or amusements, which are supplied by the labour of others. That the riches of an individual do not depend on the quantity of labour which he can command, is obvious from what Mr. Smith himself has so ingeniously shown with regard to the effects of the division of labour in increasing its productive powers. [See p. 312, *seq*.]—In a country, therefore, where a separation of arts and professions has taken place, the national riches depend much less on the quantity of labour, than on the skill of the labourer, a proper division of work, and the advantages which are derived from the use of machinery. Consequently no estimate can be formed of the comparative riches of individuals from merely knowing the quantities of labour which they are able to command.

"The value of any commodity, therefore," continues Mr. Smith, "to the person who possesses it, and who means not to use or consume it himself, but to exchange it for other commodities, is equal to the quantity of labour which it enables him to purchase or command. Labour, therefore, is the real measure of the exchangeable value of all commodities."†—I have sometimes thought that part of the obscurity in which Mr.

---

* [*Wealth of Nations*, Book I. chap. v.; Vol. I. pp. 43, 44, tenth edition.]
† [Ibid.]

Smith has involved this subject, arises from the vague use which he makes of the phrase "measure of value." I need not remark, that this expression is borrowed from the mathematical sciences, in which important advantages are sometimes gained by employing one species of quantity to measure another. Thus angles are measured by the arc of a circle; and velocities and forces are measured by a reference to extended magnitudes. This seems to be the idea which Mr. Smith has annexed to the word throughout the greater part of the chapter in question. But in this sense, the speculation cannot possibly admit of any useful application; as he confesses that it is difficult, or rather impossible, to ascertain the proportion between different quantities of labour. For he proceeds:—

"Though labour be the real measure of the exchangeable value of all commodities, it is not that by which their value is commonly estimated. It is often difficult to ascertain the proportion between two different quantities of labour. The time spent in two different sorts of work, will not always alone determine this proportion. There may be more labour in an hour's hard work, than in two hours' easy business; or in an hour's application to a trade which it cost ten years' labour to learn, than in a month's industry at an ordinary and obvious employment. But it is not easy to find any accurate measure either of hardship or ingenuity. In exchanging, indeed, the different productions of different sorts of labour for one another, some allowance is commonly made for both. It is adjusted, however, not by any accurate measure, but by the higgling and bargaining of the market, according to that sort of rough equality which, though not exact, is sufficient for carrying on the business of common life."

"Every commodity," he adds, however, "is more frequently exchanged for, and thereby compared with other commodities, than with labour. It is more natural, therefore, to estimate its exchangeable value by the quantity of some other commodity, than by that of the labour which it can purchase. The greater part of people, too, understand better what is meant by a quantity of a particular commodity, than by a quantity of labour.

The one is a plain palpable object, the other an abstract notion, which though it can be made sufficiently intelligible, is not altogether so natural and obvious.

"When barter ceases, and money has become the common instrument of commerce, every particular commodity is more frequently exchanged for money than for any other commodity.... It is more natural and obvious, therefore, to estimate the value of commodities by the quantity of money, the commodity for which they are immediately exchanged, than by that of the commodity for which they are exchanged only by the intervention of another commodity. Hence it comes to pass, that the exchangeable value of every commodity is more frequently estimated by the quantity of money, than by the quantity either of labour or of any other commodity which can be had in exchange for it."*

From this quotation, it appears manifestly that there is no analogy between Mr. Smith's conclusion touching the mensuration of value by labour, and the measures employed by mathematicians. These last substitute quantities easily compared for quantities that are compared with greater difficulty ; whereas the measure of value proposed by Mr. Smith is acknowledged to be founded on a mere abstract notion. The truth is, however, that what Mr. Smith was really in quest of in this chapter, was not a measure of value, but a universal standard for the measurement of value ; or, in other words, a unit fixed in the unalterable principles of human nature, by a comparison with which, the comparative values of money at different times might be estimated. It is obvious that it gives us no idea of the wealth of an individual to say, that in the time of Henry VII. his income amounted to £5000, unless we also knew how far a pound sterling would go in these days.

On what principle, then, *shall the value of money at different times be estimated, or how shall the real prices of commodities and labour be computed?* This I conceive to be the simple statement of the question, which Mr. Smith undertakes to resolve; and in this, as in many others, a precise idea of its

* [Ibid. pp. 45, 46.]

nature will be found to contribute much to the success of our inquiries.

That labour is the real measure of the exchangeable value of all commodities, Mr. Smith attempts to show in the second paragraph of his fifth chapter, by a different process of reasoning, but, in my opinion, one not more satisfactory.

"The real price of everything," he observes, "what everything really costs to the man who wants to acquire it, is the toil and trouble of acquiring it. What everything is really worth to the man who has acquired it, and who wants to dispose of it, or change it for something else, is the toil and trouble which it can save to himself, and which it can impose upon other people. What is bought with money or with goods, is purchased by labour, as much as what we acquire by the toil of our own body. That money or those goods, indeed, save us this toil. They contain the value of a certain quantity of labour, which we exchange for what is supposed, at the time, to contain the value of an equal quantity. Labour was the first price; the original purchase-money that was paid for all things. It was not by gold or by silver, but by labour that all the wealth of the world was originally purchased; and its value to those who possess it, and who want to exchange it for some new productions, is precisely equal to the quantity of labour which it can enable them to purchase or command."*

The fallacy of the argument contained in this passage, consists in the application to all the various stages of society, of a description which applies only in fact to that rude period which preceded the accumulation of stock, and, what may be regarded as nearly coeval in point of time, the establishment of positive institutions regulating the acquisition and protecting the enjoyment of property. I have endeavoured to shew, in my other course of lectures, that prior to the establishment of law, the only foundation of an exclusive and permanent property is labour; and hence it seems to follow, as a necessary consequence, that in this rude state of things, the only circumstance which could regulate the exchangeable value of commodities,

* [Ibid. p. 44.]

was the quantity of labour which the preparation of them required; some allowance being probably made for superior hardship incurred, or skill exerted. This incontrovertible principle, accordingly, Mr. Smith turns in various strong lights; after which, he makes an abrupt conclusion, with which it is not easy to trace its connexion, that the value of a commodity to those who possess it, and want to exchange it, is precisely equal to the quantity of labour which it can enable them to command. It is difficult to reconcile this passage, considered at least in its application to the more advanced periods of society, with the analysis which Mr. Smith has given in a different chapter, of the component parts of the price of commodities :—" As soon as stock has accumulated in the hands of particular persons, some of them will naturally employ it in setting to work industrious people, whom they will supply with materials and subsistence, in order to make a profit by the sale of their work, or by what their labour adds to the value of the materials. In exchanging the complete manufacture either for money, for labour, or for other goods, over and above what may be sufficient to pay the price of the materials, and the wages of the workmen, something must be given for the profits of the undertaker of the work, who hazards his stock in this adventure. The value which the workmen add to the materials, therefore, resolves itself in this case into two parts, of which the one pays their wages, the other the profits of their employer upon the whole stock of materials and wages which he advanced."*

With these principles in his view, it is not a little curious that Mr. Smith should have satisfied his mind with the reasoning just quoted from another part of his work.

Another metaphysical argument afterwards offered by Mr. Smith in proof of the same proposition, is, that "as a measure of quantity, such as the natural foot, &c., which is continually varying in its own extent, never can be an accurate measure ; so a commodity, like silver or gold, which is continually varying in its own value, can never be an accurate measure of value. But equal quantities of labour must at all times be of equal

* [Ibid. Book I. chap. vi. ; Vol. I. p. 72, tenth edition.]

CHAP. II.—OF MONEY, THE CIRCULATING MEDIUM. (§ 2.)   355

value to the labourer;"* and so on.—The step of this reasoning to which I would more particularly direct your attention, is that in which it is said, that equal quantities of labour must at all times be of equal value to the labourer. What idea are we here to annex to the term *value?* In the previous chapter, we are told that this word has two different meanings; sometimes expressing the utility of a commodity, and sometimes the power of purchasing other goods. The first of these is called value in use, the other value in exchange. The distinction is illustrated by the examples of water and a diamond. The same distinction, illustrated by the very same examples, occurs in Mr. Harris's work *On Coins*, and in the treatise by Mr. Law, entitled, *Money and Trade Considered.* I have some doubts, however, with respect to its accuracy; for what is value in use, but a circuitous expression for utility; and what possible advantage can arise from substituting the former phrase for the latter? On the other hand, is not the idea of value in exchange sufficiently conveyed by the word value; which in speculations of this sort is seldom or never employed as synonymous with intrinsic utility, and which in itself seems to involve the very nature of the comparison? Both of these, and similar phrases, have been employed in the present discussion. The principal advantage of the common mode of speaking over that employed by Mr. Smith, is, that the latter, after distinguishing the two kinds of value, often makes use of the word without any limiting epithet; and thereby not only puzzles his readers, but imposes on himself. Thus, when it is said that a commodity like silver, which is continually varying in its own value, can never be an accurate measure, the word value plainly means exchangeable value. But this word as plainly alters its meaning in the next sentence, when it is remarked, that equal quantities of labour are of equal value to the labourer. Here the word value cannot mean exchangeable value, as it is expressly supposed that the exchangeable value varies. We must, therefore, conclude, according to Mr. Smith's definition, that it was value in use which he meant; though I need hardly

* [Ibid. chap. v.; Vol. I. p. 48, tenth edition.]

observe, it is rather an awkward mode of expressing the simple proposition, that equal quantities of labour always cost the same exertion to the labourer, to say, that equal quantities of labour will always be of equal value to the labourer. It is in this last sense however alone, that the proposition can be interpreted. There is no difference, therefore, between labour and silver and gold, which entitles the former to be established as a standard of value, in preference to the latter. And where Mr. Smith adds, that in those cases where the same quantities of labour purchase different quantities of goods, it is the value of the latter which varies, not of the former, the assertion amounts merely to this, that the exchangeable value of labour varies, while the labourer continues to make the same sacrifices of his ease and happiness. But might not this proposition be converted in many cases to the necessaries of life, &c., the exchangeable value of which varies, while their value in use remains the same?

Mr. Smith's doctrine on this subject has been plainly suggested by that state of society which preceded the accumulation of stock, when the labour of one man being universally exchanged against that of another, the exchangeable value of commodities was thus rated according to the quantities of labour which they could command. How wide a difference there is between this state of things, and the circumstances of a community like ours, where the labourer has to exchange his labour, not only against the labour of his fellow-citizen, but against value arising from the profits of stock and the rents of land, and where commodities involving all the three constituents of price are continually exchanged against one another. The sacrifices which the labourer makes, must, indeed, remain always the same, and he will naturally be led to bestow the epithets of cheapness or dearness, according to the extent of his own exertions. But how does this afford a standard or fixed value for comparing different values in different ages and nations? Is it not evident, that those who subsist by labour form only one of the classes of society; that the price of labour enters as an element into that of most of the commodities which are purchased by the other classes; and that the same circumstances which are favourable to the one class, are equally so to the other? Why, therefore, should the standard of value be taken from the labour of one class in preference to the limited revenue of the other?

A very important distinction, however, follows in the next paragraph, though it has been introduced with a sort of apology for the deviation from strict philosophical accuracy, for which I must own I see no reason. "In this popular sense, therefore, labour, like commodities, may be said to have a real and a nominal price. Its *real* price may be said to consist in the quantity of the necessaries and conveniences of life which are given for it, its *nominal* price in the quantity of money. The labourer is rich or poor, is well or ill rewarded, in proportion to the real, not to the nominal price of his labour."* It is somewhat surprising that Mr. Smith should not have seen, after stating those very just and accurate views, that they apply not only to labour, but to commodities of every description. Mr. Smith says, that the nominal value of a commodity is the quantity of money, its real value the quantity of the conveniences and necessaries of life which it will purchase. Is not this a more precise, as well as a more obvious and intelligible mode of speaking, than to measure the price of commodities by their price in labour; a thing which Mr. Smith himself tells us is a mere abstract notion, and which must have its own real price measured ultimately by this very standard?

My last lecture was chiefly occupied with an examination of Mr. Smith's doctrine, concerning the *real* and *nominal* price of commodities,—a doctrine which, as I have already hinted, seems to me to be rather of a metaphysical than of a political nature. Indeed, Mr. Smith himself acknowledges that it does not admit of any practical application of which we can avail ourselves in comparing together the prices of commodities at different periods. It is not the wages of labour, it must always be remembered, either nominal or real, by which this ingenious

* [Ibid. Book I. chap. v.; Vol. I. p. 49, tenth edition.]

writer proposes to measure the price of commodities; for he tells us himself, in the same chapter, that the subsistence of the labourer, or the real price of his labour, is very different in different circumstances, "more liberal in a society advancing to opulence, than in one standing still," &c. It is the quantity of labour employed by the labourer, which he holds out again and again, not as affording an approximation to the truth, but as a universal standard by which we may, with the greatest accuracy, estimate the comparative values of different commodities, as well from century to century, as from year to year. He acknowledges, at the same time, that it is a test to which we cannot appeal in fact.*

From this passage, if I do not misunderstand it, it appears to have been admitted by Mr. Smith, that his theory does not afford a rule, of which we can avail ourselves for the purpose of actually calculating the comparative value of prices at different times and places. He seems, at the same time, to have considered the theory as mathematically accurate in itself, but as unsusceptible of a practical application. If the remarks which I made yesterday be just, the theory, even considered abstractly, proceeds on an erroneous principle. In some of the practical rules which Mr. Smith afterwards suggests, I agree with him very nearly, under proper limitations. But I am unable to conceive their connexion with the premises from which he deduces them. I shall, therefore, endeavour to establish the justness of my own opinions on this point; in doing which, I may perhaps be able to point out some of the circumstances which have misled the speculations of this very profound writer.

In general, it will be remembered, that the precise object of the present inquiry is, to find some standard by which we may compare the exchangeable value of commodities at different times and places, or something by which the varying price of the precious metals, when considered as media of exchange, may be estimated. In the observations which I am to make on this subject, I shall retain Mr. Smith's language, in order

* [See the quotation given above, p. 351.]

to point out more clearly in what respects I differ from his opinions; taking care, however, when I make use of the word value, to add the terms *intrinsic* or *exchangeable*, according to the sense in which I wish to be understood. The same distinction, as I have already hinted, may perhaps be expressed by the terms *utility* and *value*; but, on the present occasion, I flatter myself that by adopting Mr. Smith's phraseology, I shall be able, with greater conciseness, to show in what the defects of his reasoning consist.

The following general principles, which I shall state with all brevity, are intended to facilitate some of our subsequent reasonings. They may, perhaps, also be found to throw additional light on some points which I have already noticed.

I. It was before observed, in quoting Mr. Smith's distinction between Value *in use*, and Value *in exchange*, that a commodity may possess the one species of value in the greatest possible degree, while it possesses little or none of the other. As a necessary limitation, however, of this remark, it may be proper to add, that although value in use does not imply any value in exchange, yet value in exchange necessarily implies some degree at least of value in use. The truth of this is manifest; for value in exchange depending, as I shall afterwards have occasion to show, on the proportion between the demand and the supply, some intrinsic recommendation, either real or apprehended, must be supposed to account for the demand which the object occasions. This recommendation may, indeed, be of the most trifling nature; arising, perhaps, merely from beauty, fashion, or curiosity. But whether trifling or important, some degree of it must either belong to the object, or be generally ascribed to it, before it can become the subject of competition to purchasers.

II. The degrees of *utility* are infinite in number, extending from those slight and evanescent recommendations which operate on the fancy or caprice of the opulent, to what is necessary for the support of life. Articles of the last kind possess the highest degree of utility, and are, I think, the only ones to whose value in use it is possible to annex any definite meaning.

III. However slight the intrinsic utility of a commodity may be, a certain degree of scarcity, combined with a certain degree of demand, may bestow on it any conceivable *value in exchange;* that is, the caprice of the opulent may incline them to purchase it, by parting with any given quantity of the superfluous articles of use or necessity which they may possess. In this case, the greatness of its exchangeable value means nothing more than the power which it conveys to the possessor of purchasing a comparatively great quantity of other commodities; the exchangeable value of these things in the market being to each other inversely as their quantities.

IV. As the terms, price and exchangeable value, necessarily imply the relation of one thing to another, the common impressions of high and low price, or great and small exchangeable value, convey no definite ideas whatever, excepting to those who have in view some standard of comparison. A difficulty, therefore, occurs here precisely similar to that which has so long puzzled mathematicians on the subject of a universal standard of longitudinal extension. But fortunately, the speculations of political economists do not require the same mathematical accuracy in their solution, which is so desirable in the other case. Whatever room for regret the astronomical or natural philosopher may find in the looseness of the language employed in different ages and nations with respect to longitudinal measures, very little inconvenience is experienced by those whose speculations come home immediately to the business of common life. For all purposes of this kind, common language, which has adopted the dimensions of the human body as a standard, is sufficiently definite and precise; for though the Roman foot, the Paris foot, &c., deviate considerably from a mathematical equality, yet as we have reason to believe, that in different ages the average stature of man has varied only within very narrow limits, this measure of extension is, in most instances, sufficient for the purposes of the historian, politician, and philologist. In like manner, in Political Economy, the great object of research is, to obtain some standard of price or exchangeable value, not exhibiting to all mankind a mathematical sameness or stability, for that is impossible in the nature of things, but bearing such a relation to the fixed circumstances of the human race as may reduce the vagueness of ordinary language within such limits as to enable one age or nation, to avail itself of the political experience of another. Thus when we look at a drawing, it is impossible to form an estimate of the magnitude of the object which the painter meant to represent. But if a human figure is introduced into the landscape, though the size of men is subject to some variation, it affords us at least such a standard of comparison, as reduces the difference between the painter's conception and ours to a comparative trifle. The application of this illustration to the present subject is sufficiently obvious.

. V. It seems farther evident, in the fifth place, that in order to obtain such a standard as we are now in quest of, it is necessary to fix on some commodity for which the demand shall at all times bear, as nearly as possible, the same proportion. Were the case otherwise, the exchangeable value of this commodity must be subject to occasional variations; insomuch, that, on the one hand, by a conceivable increase of the demand, the supply continuing the same, the exchangeable value of the commodity might rise to a monopoly price; or, on the other hand, by a conceivable increase of the supply, without a change on the demand, its exchangeable value might be extinguished altogether. This last supposition has been actually realized in the case of water.

VI. In the sixth place, the uniformity of the demand for a commodity, can arise only from its being a necessary of life; as, in every other case, fashion and accidental circumstances may be supposed more or less to operate.

VII. In the seventh place, a regular adaptation of the supply to the demand, can exist only in things which depend on human industry, proportioning its exertions to the known extent of the market.

Agreeably to these principles, corn, or whatever constitutes the ordinary food of the people, seems more likely to furnish a standard of valuation than anything else. *First*, The demand is less subject to variation, the commodity itself forming to the great mass of the people a necessary of life; and the consumption of individuals among the labouring classes of mankind, subsisting on the same species of food being found, in different ages and nations, to approach wonderfully near to the same standard. *Secondly*, The quantity of corn raised may be expected to adapt itself within narrow limits to the effectual demand. The value in use, therefore, of this commodity, may be considered as remaining always the same.

We have thus arrived at the very same conclusion which Mr. Locke has deduced from a different view of the same subject; and as the general scope of his reasoning seems to be just in itself, and to afford some additional illustrations of the subject which I have been considering, I shall quote the substance of his argument as stated by himself in his *Considerations on Lowering the Rate of Interest.*

[§ 15.]—" That supposing wheat a standing measure, that is, that there is constantly the same quantity of it, in proportion to its vent, we shall find money to run the same variety of changes in its value, as all other commodities do. Now that wheat in England does not come nearest to a standing measure, is evident by comparing wheat with other commodities, money, and the yearly income of land, in Henry VII.'s time and now; for supposing that in the first of Henry VII., N let 100 acres of land to A for sixpence per annum per acre, rack-rent, and to B another 100 acres of land, of the same soil and yearly worth with the former, for a bushel of wheat per acre, rack-rent, (a bushel of wheat about that time being probably sold for about sixpence,) it was then an equal rent. If, therefore, these leases were for years yet to come, it is certain that he that paid but sixpence per acre, would pay now fifty shillings per annum; and he that paid a bushel of wheat per acre, would now pay about twenty-five pounds per annum, which would be near about the yearly value of the land, were it to be let now. The reason whereof is this: that there being ten times as much silver now in the world (the discovery of the West Indies having made the plenty) as there was then, it is nine-tenths less worth now, than it was at that time; that is, it will exchange for nine-tenths less of any commodity now, which bears the same proportion to its vent, as it did two hundred years since, which of all other commodities wheat is likeliest to do. For in England, and this part of the world, wheat being the constant and most general food, not altering with the fashion, not growing by chance, but as the farmers sow more or less of it, which they endeavour to proportion, as near as can be guessed, to the consumption, abstracting the overplus of the precedent year in their provision for the next, and *vice versa*, it must needs fall out that it keeps the nearest proportion to its consumption (which is more studied and designed in this than other commodities) of any thing, if you take it for seven or twenty years together; though, perhaps, the plenty or scarcity of one year, caused by the accidents of the season, may very much vary it from the immediately precedent, or following. Wheat, therefore, in this part of the world, (and that grain which is the constant general food of any other country,) is the fittest measure to judge of the altered value of things, in any long tract of time; and therefore, wheat here, rice in Turkey, &c., is the fittest thing to reserve a rent in, which is designed to be constantly the same for all future ages. But money is the best measure of the altered value of things in a few years, because its vent is the same, and its quantity alters slowly. But wheat, or any other grain, cannot serve instead of money, because of its bulkiness, and too quick change of its quantity. For had I a bond to pay me one hundred bushels of wheat next year, it might be a fourth part loss, or gain to me; too great an inequality and uncertainty to be ventured in trade, besides the different goodness of several parcels of wheat in the same year."

It appears from these very judicious observations of Mr. Locke, as well as from what I had occasion to state formerly, that the accuracy of wheat, considered as a standard of valuation, proceeds on the supposition, that the quantity constantly bears the same proportion to the demand. But though this may be expected to be the case on the average of a number of years, the proportion must necessarily vary much, as Mr. Locke has suggested, from year to year, in consequence of the accidents of the seasons.

Hence, I apprehend, arises the true principle of the rule for measuring prices by the wages of labour, as these do not vary from year to year with the money price of corn, but in general are regulated by its average price. It is not, therefore, in consequence of any metaphysical theory concerning labour considered abstractly, that I would appeal to the wages of labour as a measure of value; I merely consider them, when accurately ascertained, and when due allowances are made for collateral circumstances, as an evidence of the average price of corn and the necessaries of life, at any particular period. Mr. Smith's reasoning, you will observe, reverses this order, and deduces the rule founded on the money price of corn from a metaphysical speculation concerning the fixed and unalterable value of labour.

The oldest writer by whom I have found the wages of labour suggested as a criterion for ascertaining the real price of commodities, [in 1765,] is Mr. Rice Vaughan, who, after a variety of preliminary observations extremely deserving of attention, expresses himself thus:—

" But there is only one thing from whence we may certainly track out the prices, and which carries with it a constant resultance of the prices of all other things which are necessary for a man's life; and that is the price of labourers' or servants' wages, especially those of the meaner sort. And as there is to be found no other certain and constant cause of the raising of the prices of all things, but two, viz., the one, the raising of the values of monies; the other, the great abundance of gold and silver coming into these parts, in this latter age, out of the Indies; although the hire of labourers did continually rise, yet it did rise so much and no more, as the value was raised. But after the discovery of the Indies, you shall find the price of the labourers' wages raised in proportion, far exceeding the raising of monies; and therefore, for my part, I am certainly persuaded, that as long as the values of monies are raised, and the

Indies do yield that abundance of gold and silver which they do, that both the hire of labourers, and generally the price of all things, especially of those things necessary for life, will rise; however, for a year, two or three, through uncertain accidents, sundry particulars may stand at a stay, or abate, but that the hire of labourers and servants carrieth with it a resultance of the prices of all things generally necessary for a man's life; besides, that reason doth convince that there must be a convenient proportion between their wages and their food and raiment, the wisdom of the statute doth confirm it, which doth always direct the rate of labourers and servants to be made with a regard of prices of victuals, apparel, and other things necessary to their use."*

The same criterion of price or value is repeatedly referred to by Mr. Harris in his *Essay on Coins*, [1757.] But he does not appear to me to have been so successful as Mr. Rice Vaughan, in fixing on the real grounds on which the opinion rests. The following are the principal passages in his book relative to this subject:—

" The values of land and labour do, as it were of themselves, mutually settle or adjust one another; and as all things or commodities are the products of those two, so their several values are naturally adjusted by them. But as in most productions *labour* hath the greatest share; the value of labour is to be reckoned the chief standard that regulates the values of all commodities, and more especially as the value of land is, as it were, already allowed for in the value of labour itself."†

" It may be reasonably allowed, that a labouring man ought to earn, at least, twice as much as will maintain himself in ordinary food and clothing, that he may be enabled to breed up children, pay rent for a small dwelling, find himself in necessary utensils, &c.; so much, at least, the labourer must be allowed, that the community may be perpetuated. And as the world goes, there is no likelihood that the lowest kind of labourers will be allowed more than a bare subsistence; if they

* [*A Treatise of Money*, &c., chap. xi. p. 105, *seq.*]
† [Part I. chap. i. § 7.]

will not be content with that, there will be others ready to step into their places; and less, as above observed, cannot be given them. And hence the quantity of land that goes to maintain a labourer becomes his hire; and this hire again becomes the value of the land, the expenses of manuring and tilling it being also included."*

In another passage he observes,—" Though we reckon by money, yet labour and skill are the main standards by which the values of all or most things are ultimately ascertained, and there will require a greater or less bulk of money, to purchase the very same thing, according as there is a greater or less quantity of money in circulation; that is, according as the material of money is cheaper or dearer, or in greater or lesser plenty."†

In these extracts, notwithstanding the general indistinctness which runs through the passages now quoted, there are some hints not undeserving of attention: for although the author has not touched on what appears to me to be the fundamental principle, yet he has suggested some collateral advantages which we derive from the wages of labour considered as a test of the exchangeable value of gold and silver at different periods.

Of these, the two following seem to be the most important:—
First, As the wages of common or unskilled labour may be presumed to be nearly the minimum at which an individual with a family can be subsisted, the knowledge of this minimum affords the lowest points of the scale on which the comparative riches of individuals are to be graduated. In proportion as their daily income rises above this point, they are removed from the lowest class of independent citizens, and rank higher or lower, among the superior orders of the community. In the *second* place, a tolerable estimate may be formed of the power and influence of an individual, from the number of labourers to whom he can furnish employment; and as far as the value of labour regulates the price of commodities, a knowledge of its

* [Ibid. § 8.] † [Ibid. chap. ii. § 22.]

current price will enable us to form an estimate of the effective power of money, at any particular time, in commanding a supply of the conveniences and accommodations of life.

From the foregoing reasonings, it sufficiently appears that if the current price of labour could be accurately ascertained in different times and places, it would furnish to the political economist important lights for comparing the actual circumstances of mankind in different states of society. It is, however, but very rarely that this accuracy can be obtained. The price of corn, on the other hand, though it has been but in few cases regularly recorded, is yet in general better known, and has been more frequently taken notice of by historians and political writers. To these, accordingly, we are forced to appeal in inquiries of this nature. In doing so, however, it is necessary always to remember, that the standard of comparison must be taken, not from the accidental prices of particular years, but from the average prices of a considerable period.

It appears farther from what has been stated, that neither the current wages of labour, nor the average price of corn, important as they are in the light of political data, can furnish anything like a mathematical standard for judging of the effective power of money, or the exchangeable value of commodities in different countries. A great variety of other circumstances must be taken into account, in order to form a reasonable estimate. After all, we can only hope to obtain such an imperfect help to our conceptions, as the average height of the human figure affords, when it is the only scale introduced into a landscape.

To what degree the wages of labour are liable to be affected by accidental circumstances, particularly by the advancing, stationary, or declining state of the society, has been shown very fully and ably by Mr. Smith himself, in the eighth chapter of his first book. Beside, however, the considerations there suggested, many others must be combined, in order to obtain the necessary corrections of the conclusions to which we are led by the standard of value now recommended. But the statement of these will be less tedious, when introduced in the course of the practical applications of this doctrine which will afterwards occur.

There is one consideration, however, so obvious and important, that I think it proper to mention it in this place; I mean the necessity of paying due attention to the general habits of the people in the article of food, before we build any reasonings on the prices of what are now considered as necessaries of life. This remark I take the earliest opportunity of stating, because it leads to the correction of a very fertile source of error in political speculations; and in no instance, perhaps, is it more likely to mislead us, than in the conclusions which we form with respect to the condition of the labouring classes, and the value of money, at different periods, from the comparative prices of *wheat alone*, forgetting that this was not the common food of the people till very lately, and that even at present it is only one of their various articles of subsistence.

From the household book of Sir Edward Coke, it appears that in the year 1596, rye-bread and oatmeal formed a very considerable proportion of the diet of servants, even in the greatest families.—In 1626, barley-bread is stated in the grant of a monopoly by King Charles to be the usual food of the lower classes.—Of the relative proportion of wheat consumed in England and Wales about the era of the Revolution, some idea may be formed from an estimate of the produce of the arable land by Gregory King, whose schemes, according to Dr. Davenant, are all so accurate as not to be controverted.—In the supplement to the *Corn Tracts*, there is an estimate of the proportional consumption of the different kinds of grain about thirty years ago, which deserves attention on account of the esteem in which the author of that work [Ch. Smith] has always and most deservedly been held by the best judges, for the extent and accuracy of his information. After remarking that bread made of wheat has become much more generally the food of the common people since the year 1689, than before, he adds, that "it is still very far from being the food of the people in general," &c., estimating the bread consumers in 1764 at not more than one-half of the population.—Mr. Benjamin Bell, in

CHAP. II.—OF MONEY, THE CIRCULATING MEDIUM. (§ 2.) 369

a volume of Essays published some years ago, and which contain some important views concerning the agricultural interests of this country, which he has illustrated by a large collection of facts, ascertained with uncommon care, states the proportion of the whole inhabitants of Great Britain, who are fed on oats and barley, at a fourth of the whole population, giving it at the same time, as his opinion, that the estimate probably falls short of the truth. Indeed, I apprehend there can be little doubt that it does so very considerably.

I have entered into these details, in order to show with how great latitude it is necessary to receive all those estimates of the efficiency, or exchangeable value of money, at different times and places, which are founded on a comparison of the prices of wheat. A similar remark may be made with respect to those inferences which have been so often drawn from the same data, in proof of the misery of the lower orders, occasioned by the astonishing fluctuations of the prices of necessaries during the earlier periods of our history. That these inferences are just, when confined within certain limits, I do not mean to deny. But it is certainly pushing them too far, when we assume the wide ranges in the price of this article at particular times, as a scale for measuring the abundance or scarcity of necessaries at these periods. Thus, for example, when Stowe informs us, that in the year 1317, the harvest in England was all got in before the 1st September, and that wheat from £4 a quarter fell to 6s. 8d., this is a fact sufficient of itself to demonstrate by how small a proportion of the people wheat was then regarded as an indispensable necessary. The variation in the price of oats, as stated on the same authority, is no less astonishing, being from £3, 4s., to 5s. 4d. But it is very observable, that no mention is made of the price of barley, which appears then to have formed the ordinary food of by far the greater proportion of the people; an omission which affords a presumption, that its fluctuations were confined within much narrower limits. In the year 1270, the price of wheat fell to 6s. 8d. per quarter, while the rate of wages was 1d. a-day in harvest, and $\frac{1}{2}$d. out of harvest. In such circumstances, it is quite superfluous to remark, that the average price of wheat had no relation whatever to the price of labour.

I shall take this opportunity of remarking, though the observation has not any immediate connexion with the present argument, that in accounting for the different prices of butchers' meat at different periods, some allowance ought to be made for the changes in the national habits with respect to food, which arose naturally from the Protestant Reformation. It is observed by Dr. Campbell, in his *Political Survey of Great Britain*, that before the Reformation the people may be supposed to have lived one-third of the year on fish. I presume he meant to say, that during one-third of the year fish served as a substitute for flesh: and I am inclined to think that this estimate is rather below than above the truth, as a paper, preserved among the Harleian Manuscripts, affords a proof, that even in the time of Queen Elizabeth, the number of fish-days appointed for the royal household was one hundred and forty-five. Dr. Campbell elsewhere remarks, that in consequence of the regard paid to Lent, the rising stock was preserved; and that it was with a view to this circumstance that so many proclamations were issued for keeping Lent long after the reformed religion was established. It appears, too, that while this demand continued, the sea was ransacked for many articles which would now be rejected by the meanest persons, but which were then presented at the best tables. Thus, in the Appendix to the tenth volume of Dr. Henry's *History of Great Britain*, a bill of fare is given, which contains porpoises and seals, as " part of the goodly provisions collected for the installation of an Archbishop of York." (1466.)

The observations already made on the difference in the relative importance of wheat as an article of request in national diet at different periods, will explain sufficiently the circumstances which give to the wages of common labour, wherever they are accurately ascertained, an advantage over the average price of wheat as a standard for estimating the exchangeable value of money. " They carry with them," to use the words of Rice Vaughan, " a constant resultance of the prices of all other things necessary for a man's life." The political regulations, however, it must be confessed, which in almost every country prevent the wages of labour from finding their proper level, together with the varying effects of villanage, from the first decline of that institution till its final abolition, render even facts of this description less accurate tests of the exchangeable value of money, than we should be apt to conclude from a theoretical view of the subject. But notwithstanding this objection, these undoubtedly form the most important data to which we can appeal in comparing together the effective powers of money in different periods of society.

Were it possible to ascertain with accuracy the rates of wages in different times, and to combine them with the prices, not only of the necessaries, but of the conveniences and luxuries of life, it would throw more light on that most interesting branch of history, the condition and manners of the people, than is to be collected from all the narratives which record the political and military transactions of our ancestors. It is much to be regretted that our earlier writers were so little aware of this truth, and that among modern authors a false idea of historical dignity should prevent a due attention to the scattered details which may still be gleaned from a careful and industrious examination of our ancient monuments. To the universality, indeed, of this remark, Mr. Hume's history forms a striking exception; and it is to the sanction of his name that we are probably indebted, in a great measure, for those researches which have rendered the work of Dr. Henry so valuable an accession to the stock of British literature.

[SECT. III.—ON THE EFFECTS OF PLENTY OR SCARCITY OF THE PRECIOUS METALS UPON PRICES.]

I now proceed to offer some remarks on the principles by which the relative values of money and commodities are adjusted in commercial transactions. It is a subject of extreme difficulty, and I am much afraid that what I have to state will tend more to invalidate the reasonings of others, than to establish any satisfactory conclusions of my own.

I begin with examining a speculation of Montesquieu, which has contributed greatly to mislead those of his successors. This I shall state in Montesquieu's own words, after which I shall consider particularly the different steps of his argument.

"Money is the price of merchandise or manufactures. But how will this price be fixed? that is to say, by what price of money will each thing be represented?

"If we compare the mass of gold and silver in the whole world, with the quantity of merchandise therein contained, it is certain that every commodity or merchandise in particular, may be compared to a certain portion of the entire mass of gold and silver. As the total of the one is to the total of the other, so part of the one will be to part of the other. Let us suppose that there is only one commodity or merchandise in the world, or only one to be purchased, and that this is divisible like money, a part of this merchandise will answer to a part of the mass of gold and silver, the half of the total of the one to the half of the total of the other; the tenth, the hundredth, the thousandth part of the one, to the tenth, the hundredth, the thousandth part of the other. But as that which constitutes property amongst mankind is not all at once in trade; and as the metals or money which are the signs of property, are not all in trade at the same time, the price is fixed in the compound ratio of the total of things, with the total of signs, and that of the total of things in trade, with the total of signs in trade also. And as the signs which are not in trade to-day, may be in trade to-morrow; and the signs not now in trade may enter into trade at the same time, the establishment of the price of things always fundamentally depends on the proportion of the total of things to the total of signs." . . .

"If since the discovery of the Indies, gold and silver have increased in Europe in the proportion of one to twenty, the price of provisions and goods must have been increased in the proportion of one to twenty. But if, on the other hand, the number of articles of merchandise has increased as one to two, it necessarily follows that the price of these articles and provisions has risen in the proportion of one to twenty, and fallen in proportion of one to two,—it necessarily follows, I say, that the proportion is only as one to ten."¹

It is observed by Sir James Steuart,* that this theory of Montesquieu is of an older date than his writings, being alluded to in one of the papers of the *Spectator*, and very explicitly stated by Mr. Locke. The ideas of this last writer are strongly expressed in a passage which has been already quoted during this Lecture, from his considerations on lowering the rate of interest.†

It is, however, from Montesquieu and Mr. Hume, that this theory has chiefly derived its authority, and it is surprising to what a degree it has influenced the opinions of commercial politicians since their time, although neither of these eminent writers have attempted any explanation whatever of the principle on which it proceeds. In the passage above quoted from the *Spirit of Laws*, it is said to be certain; and it is represented by Mr. Hume as next to a self-evident proposition,— " That the prices of everything depend on the proportion between commodities and money, and that any considerable alteration on either has the same effect, either of heightening or lowering the price. Increase the commodities, they become cheaper; increase the money, they rise in their value. As, on the other hand, a diminution of the former, and that of the latter, have contrary tendencies.

" It is also evident, that the prices do not so much depend on the absolute quantity of commodities and that of money which are in a nation, as on that of the commodities which come or may come to market, and of the money which circulates."‡

The same doctrine has been repeated by numberless writers of a later date; and among others, by Dr. Wallace, in a small book entitled *Characteristics of the present Political State of Great Britain;* a coincidence the more remarkable that it is the great object of the latter to oppose some consequences that

¹ *Spirit of Laws*, B. XXII. c. vii., viii.   † [Above, p. 362.]
* [*Political Œconomy*, Book II. chap.
xxviii.; *Works*, Vol. II. p. 84.]   ‡ [*Essays*, Vol. I. Of Money.]

have been deduced by Mr. Hume, and I apprehend, very logically, from the theory.

"Let us suppose," says Dr. Wallace, "that there is a certain quantity of money and of commodities in any country. The quantity of money may be said to represent the commodities, and to determine the prices of them. The prices of *particular* commodities may vary in different circumstances; but if the *sums* of the money and of the commodities continue much *the same*, the prices, *on the whole*, cannot much alter. In such a case, if no more money comes into the country, unless the dispositions of the people are remarkably changed by some extraordinary accident or revolution, it will be very difficult to carry on a great deal of more work on a sudden, as speedily to increase the sum of the commodities.

"But, if a great sum of money should be brought into the nation at once, and be distributed in any way whatever, provided the labouring and industrious part of the nation do not get such sums as will keep them idle; though some part of it would undoubtedly be hoarded up, and would thereby be rendered useless, yet the greatest part of it would be employed and become useful. . . . Every one would be enabled to spend a little more, and to carry on his business better. By these means there would be everywhere more labour. Of course, the commodities, or *real* riches, which are quite *different* from *money*, would be greatly increased.

"Again: If the stock of money should be increased by this industry; or, if *another sum* of money should be introduced by other means, and be distributed as before, this would again increase the stock of commodities. And so on continually, or to a certain limit."*

The general conclusion in which these authors agree, has been adopted with great zeal by Mr. Arthur Young, who has produced various arguments in defence of his opinion, which I do not think it necessary to quote.

Among the consequences inferred by Mr. Hume from this doctrine, the two following are the most important:—The *first*

* [Part I. pp. 21-23.]

is the advantage of hoarding large sums in public treasuries, so as to prevent completely their circulation. The *second* consequence deduced from this principle is, that banks, funds, and paper credit of every kind are injurious to the commerce and wealth of a nation. The contrariety of these conclusions of Mr. Hume to the prevailing opinions among our best political writers, together with their alarming aspect when considered in relation to the policy of this country, excited the attention of Dr. Wallace, the learned and ingenious author of the *Dissertation on the Numbers of Mankind;* and gave rise to the publication just quoted, in which he opposes the applications which Mr. Hume makes of Montesquieu's principle, without, however, expressing any doubts concerning the principle itself.

The most elaborate refutation that I know of these speculations of Montesquieu and Mr. Hume, is in Sir James Steuart's *Political Œconomy;* and I shall, accordingly, avail myself freely of his ideas wherever I find them to my purpose; attempting, as far as I am able, to avoid that profusion of vague and indefinite words with which this very ingenious and well-informed writer is so apt to obscure his meaning. Much additional light has been thrown on this subject by several foreign authors, particularly by Mr. Pinto, in his celebrated *Essay on Circulation and Credit.* I need scarcely add, with respect to Mr. Smith, that in treating of this important article of Political Economy, as far as it was connected with his great plan, he has displayed his usual superiority over all other writers; establishing, in the most satisfactory manner, some general principles which conclude decisively against the theory in question. But I shall avoid his view of the subject, as it is more generally known, and as he has passed over some topics more slightly than he probably would have done, if Mr. Hume had not given the sanction of his name to Montesquieu's errors. [?]

In order to avoid circumlocution, I shall distinguish this doctrine by ascribing it to Montesquieu; although, from what has been already said, it appears to have been current in this country at a much earlier period. I shall direct my remarks, too, more particularly against his statement of the doctrine than against Mr. Hume's, as he has been at more pains to explain the sense in which he wishes it to be understood. Indeed, in his attempt to unfold the nature of his doctrine, it is surprising that he did not discover the vagueness of the ideas which he annexes to the words which he employs.

"Let us suppose," says Montesquieu, "that there is but one commodity to be bought and sold," &c. [above, p. 372.] In this passage, he uses the French word *répondre*, by which he would seem to intimate, that the tenth or hundredth part of the commodities is equal in exchangeable value to the tenth or hundredth part of the money. But whether this was Montesquieu's idea or not, it is of little consequence, as it follows necessarily from his fundamental principle, that the whole money in circulation is either equal in value to the whole commodities, or that it is equal to some determinate part, such as a half, &c., and that this proportion never varies. Unless we admit this conclusion, we must reject the general principle, that the price of commodities varies proportionally with the quantity of money. The truth is, that it is not an easy matter to put any precise or intelligible interpretation on the language which has been employed by Montesquieu, and those who have followed him on this subject. They tell us that the money *represents* a commodity; that it is the *sign* of the commodity; that it *answers to* the commodity. These are expressions which, if they have any determinate meaning, seem to imply, that the whole of the money is equal to the whole of the commodity, the half to the half, and so on in proportion. If this be not the meaning of these expressions, when introduced in order to prove or illustrate the principle, that prices must bear relation to the quantity of money, what other interpretation can be put upon them?

"Were a statesman," says Sir James Steuart, "to perform the operation of circulation and commerce, by calling in, from time to time, all the proprietors of specie in one body, and all those of alienable commodities, workmen, &c., in another; and were he, after informing himself of the respective quantities of each, to establish a general tariff of prices, according to our author's [Hume's] rule; this idea of *representation* might easily be admitted, because the particles of manufactures would then seem to be adapted to the pieces of the specie, as the rations of forage for the horses of an army are made larger or smaller, according as the magazines are well or ill provided at the time; but has this any resemblance to the operations of commerce?"*

It is indeed wonderful how much this subject has been perplexed by the use of words that are indefinite or equivocal in their meaning. Coin has been called a representation; and because it is a representation, it must bear an exact proportion to the thing represented. And since in some particular examples this representation has been found to hold, the rule has been made general. If, for instance, a merchant has £1000 worth of grain, the thousandth part of the commodity is said to be equivalent to the thousandth part of the sum, because both are determinate in their quantity. But the parcels of this corn, though exactly proportioned to the quantities of money, do not draw their value from this proportion, but from the total value of the whole mass; a value which is determined, not by the amount of the specie in the country, but by the complicated operations of competition. To call coin a representation of commodities and labour, because the possession of the one commands the enjoyment of the other, is plainly an abuse of language. Coin, indeed, by being the established medium of exchange, may be regarded as a universal equivalent. But it is not the only equivalent for things alienable; for although it were banished altogether, alienations and exchanges would still continue, though in a more inconvenient form. And even at present this takes place in many instances, as where a peasant receives meat and clothes as an equivalent for personal service.

Why, then, should coin be considered as the representation of all the manufactures and industry of a country more than any other equivalent? If it did represent or answer to them, in the only sense in which the proposition seems intelligible, it

* [*Political Œconomy*, Book II. chap. xxviii.; *Works*, Vol. II. p. 100.]

would follow that "every commodity of a country," as Sir James Steuart observes, "should be sold, like the parcel of grain in the foregoing example, by the rule of three."* If the proposition, indeed, be supposed to imply no more than this, that the value of every commodity is reckoned in pounds, shillings, and pence, the word representation is not inaptly employed. But in this sense the proposition is nugatory, and altogether foreign to the present question.

It is not, however, in considering coin as the only equivalent for things vendible, that the principal fault of this theory consists. When stripped of equivocal language, it will be found necessarily to involve the following supposition: that as in every bargain of buying and selling, the price paid is equivalent to the thing bought,—therefore, for everything bought, there must exist a sum of money of equal value; a proposition of which the fallacy is obvious, as it overlooks completely that virtual multiplication of the quantity of money which arises from its circulation. It takes for granted that money has been employed which was never given in payment before, and never will be given again; a supposition which is contrary to one of the most familiar and indisputable facts, that a guinea will pass through many hands in a day, and in the course of a year may pay for a hundred times its value in commodities. It may be proper to illustrate this idea a little more fully, because, familiar as the fact is, it leads to consequences which have not always been attended to, in discussing the question now under consideration.

In Mr. Pinto's *Treatise on Circulation and Credit*, it has been shewn with much ingenuity, how a quick circulation makes money go far in exchanges. And the following anecdote is mentioned by this very well-informed writer as an illustration:—" Pendant le siège de Tournay en 1745, et quelque temps auparavant, la communication étant coupée, on était embarrassé, faute d'argent, de payer le prêt à la Garnison. On s'avisa d'emprunter des Cantines la somme de 7000 florins. C'était tout ce qu'il y avoit. Au bout de la semaine les 7000

* [Ibid. p. 102.]

florins étaient revenus aux Cantines, où la même somme fut empruntée encore une fois. Cela fut répété ensuite jusqu'à la reddition pendant sept semaines, de sorte que les mêmes 7000 florins firent l'effet de 49,000 florins."* It was, therefore, with very good reason, that Bishop Berkeley long ago proposed the following query, " Whether less money swiftly circulating be not in fact equivalent to more money slowly circulating ?"†

From these observations it seems evident, that the quantity of money and notes in circulation, must bear but a small proportion to the value of goods to be bought and sold, and that this proportion must vary according to the quickness with which the money circulates or shifts from one hand to another. According to Mr. Pinto, there is not in the whole world half the silver coin which would pay all the expenses of Paris for a single year, if the same piece were never to change its possessor but once.

In order to illustrate this subject a little farther, I shall suppose that a labouring man gains ten shillings a week, which he receives always on Saturday, and that he spends proportionally through the week these ten shillings on his family, so as to have no money in his pocket next Saturday. This man may be said, on a medium, to be possessed of five shillings; and a hundred men in this situation may be said to be in possession of £25. This is all they have used, though they have each of them spent ten shillings a week.

I make a second supposition, that each of these men lives on credit; that his ten shillings are spent by the time they are earned; and that every man pays his debt when he receives his weekly wages. In this case, the money may never have been a single hour in their hands; and it is a chance of a hundred to one, if they are masters of twenty shillings amongst them; and yet each of them, as before, spends ten shillings a week.

I have only another supposition to make, that each of these hundred labourers will live at the same rate as formerly; that they ask no credit; and that they are paid their wages once a year. They will thus receive at once £26; which, having no

* [Partie I. p. 34, Note, orig. edit.]   † [*Querist*, Q. xxii.]

other use for their money, they will gradually spend on their families in the course of a year, at the rate of ten shillings a week. It is evident, that these men will at *a medium* be possessed of £13 a piece, and that their whole money will be equal to £1300; though their wages and consumption are the same as those of a hundred men who could not produce twenty shillings among them.

The obvious inferences from these suppositions are, *firstly*, that £25 with a quick circulation, will go as far as £1300 with a slow circulation; *secondly*, that even where the circulation is equally quick, £1 with credit will purchase as much as £25 without credit; and, *thirdly*, that as both *the circulation and quantity of money* may vary in consequence of a variety of causes, both natural and moral, it is extremely improbable that the money in circulation should always bear a fixed and invariable proportion to the value of all the commodities used in commerce. Yet it is demonstrable, that if the price of commodities bears a constant proportion *to their total amount*, as Mr. Hume and Montesquieu have both maintained, the whole amount of the commodities must either be equal to the whole money, or bear some fixed and invariable proportion to it.

As a farther proof of the fallaciousness of the reasonings formerly quoted from Montesquieu, it may be worth while to take notice of some remarkable facts which have been preserved with respect to prices among the ancients. These facts will exhibit a striking contrast to the state of modern Europe, and will, I hope, throw some additional light on the subject under discussion, the simple structure of society in the ancient world enabling us to trace whatever relation subsists between the quantity of money and its exchangeable value, more easily than when it is affected by such a complication of circumstances, as operate so powerfully on that order of things which falls under our observation. The same facts will afford an additional illustration of what I have already so often remarked concerning the essential changes which, in modern Europe, trade, and industry, and the freedom of the lower orders, have produced on the circumstances of mankind.

"It is a question with me," says Sir James Steuart, "whether the mines of Potosi and Brazil have produced more riches to Spain and Portugal than the treasures heaped up in Asia, Greece, and Egypt, after the death of Alexander furnished to the Romans, during the two hundred years which followed the defeat of Perseus and the conquest of Macedonia."* Soon after this inundation of wealth, the Roman republic went to destruction; and a succession of the most prodigal princes ever known in history succeeded each other for two hundred years; giving all the circulation to these treasures which was compatible with the actual state of commerce at the time. It is, however, extremely remarkable, that while in consequence of the extravagance of the Romans, the prices of superfluities rose to an excessive height, those of necessaries kept astonishingly low. Of this the most satisfactory evidence is produced by Dr. Wallace, in his *Dissertation on the Numbers of Mankind;* and by Dr. Arbuthnot in his *Tables of Ancient Coins.*

In times somewhat earlier, before this great influx of money, the cheapness of the necessaries of life was much greater. According to Polybius, the Sicilian medimnus of wheat was even in his time sold commonly in some parts of Italy at four oboli, and the same quantity of barley for two: at which rate, if we admit Dr. Wallace's computation, the English quarter of wheat would have sold at a price equivalent to about fifteen pence. Polybius informs us farther, that there was such plenty of provisions in the north of Italy at that time, that a traveller was well entertained at an inn with all necessaries, and seldom paid more than a quarter of an obolus, equal to a third of a penny. Long before this period, however, immense prices had been paid for things merely ornamental; and the plenty of money could not fail to be great.

But afterwards, the contrast between the extravagance of the rich, and the simple manners of the people in general, became far more conspicuous under Augustus. In illustration of this, I shall point out a few facts, taken at random from Dr. Arbuthnot's work on *Ancient Coins, Weights, and Measures.*

* [*Political Œconomy*, Book II. chap. xxx.; *Works*, Vol. II. p. 135, *seq.*]

Before proceeding to these, I shall just mention that the debts of Julius Cæsar, before he had been in any public office at Rome, amounted to 1300 talents, a sum which Dr. Arbuthnot estimates at £221,875 sterling. According to a Latin translation of Appian, the debts of the same person, before he held any foreign command, amounted to £2,000,000 sterling. A Greek manuscript has a different reading, and states them at half this sum. But, on either supposition, the fact is sufficient to convey an idea of the quantity of the precious metals which then existed in Rome; for as great debts are the effect of great credit, so they are an indication of great riches. Æsopus the player, as noticed by Arbuthnot, spent a sum equal to £4000 sterling on a single dish; Vitellius the Emperor consumed upon one supper a sum equal to £87,000 sterling, and in the course of seven months that he continued Emperor, spent upon eating and drinking a sum amounting to upwards of £4,000,000 sterling.

I have mentioned these facts, chiefly to have an opportunity of introducing a most extraordinary circumstance, that nearly about the same time when the debts of Julius Cæsar amounted to the enormous sum stated above, Pomponius Atticus, who lived with great hospitality, and even with some degree of simple elegance, associating with all the first characters in Rome, did not spend more than £9, 13s. 9d. a month, or in the whole year £116, 5s. On this point we have the decisive evidence of Cornelius Nepos, in the following remarkable passage:—" Nec hoc præteribo, (quanquam nonnullis leve visum iri putem,) cum imprimis lautus esset Eques Romanus, et non parum liberaliter domum suam omnium ordinum homines invitaret; scimus non amplius, quam terna millia aeris, peræque in singulos menses, ex Ephemeride cum expensum sumtui ferre solitum. Atque hoc non auditum sed cognitum prædicamus. Sæpe enim propter familiaritatem. domesticis rebus interfuimus."*

These facts appear to me to illustrate strongly the essential difference between the state of society in ancient and modern times. In truth, the circulation of money among the Romans

* [*Excellentium Imperatorum Vitæ*, Atticus.]

had little or no resemblance to what is now called circulation in our systems of Political Economy. Fortunes were then made by corruption, fraud, and plunder, instead of trade and regular industry. The consequence was, that there was no relation whatever between the prices of articles ministering to the desires of the great, and of articles subservient to the necessities of the poor. It is to be observed, too, that in the curious examples collected by Dr. Arbuthnot, of such articles as brought the most extravagant prices, we only find those which could not be multiplied in proportion to the demand. These prices, therefore, arose not from the abundance of money, but from the impossibility of suiting the supply to the market. The cheapness of necessaries did not proceed from their plenty, but from the small number of individuals who were led by their situation to purchase them. As none who were fed by the labour of slaves, or on grain distributed gratuitously, had any occasion to go to market, the competition must have been confined to a comparatively inconsiderable portion of the community. The manner, too, in which the market was then provided, must be taken into account. It was supplied partly by the surplus corn produced on the lands of great men, laboured by slaves, who, being fed on the lands, the surplus cost a mere trifle; and as the number of buyers was very small, this surplus must necessarily have been sold very cheap. Besides, the grain distributed among the people must have kept down the market, as a part of it must have sometimes been superfluous to those who received, and consequently must have come to be sold in competition with that which was raised at private expense.

In judging of the very low prices of grain in our own country some centuries ago, similar considerations must be taken into account. A very large proportion of the inhabitants then drew their subsistence directly from the soil, and consequently, the demand for grain in the markets must have been comparatively inconsiderable. In such a state of society, the demand must have been proportioned, not to the consumers, but to the buyers.

Shall we, therefore, say, that the quantity of money in a State has no effect whatever on price? That it does not vary with it proportionally, and that in estimating its effects on the commercial system, the rate of circulation must always be combined with the amount of the circulating mass, is a proposition abundantly evident. Much, too, must depend on the manner in which the money is distributed, among the different classes of the community, and in various other circumstances connected with the condition and habits of the people, of which it is easy to perceive the general influence, but which it is impossible to subject to calculation in accounting for particular phenomena. It does not, however, follow from this as a consequence, that the relative proportion of money and commodities, though not the only cause which regulates prices, may not, in certain circumstances, operate on them very powerfully, how difficult soever it may be from the extreme complacency of the subject, to trace the extent of its influence.

A distinction of Mr. Smith's relative to this question is extremely worthy of attention, though it may be doubted whether it authorizes all the important consequences which he supposes it to involve.

"The quantity of the precious metals may increase in any country from two different causes: either, first, from the increased abundance of the mines which supply it; or secondly, from the increased wealth of the people from the increased produce of their annual labour. The first of these causes is no doubt necessarily connected with the diminution of the value of the precious metals; but the second is not.

"When more abundant mines are discovered, a greater quantity of the precious metals is brought to market, and the quantity of the necessaries and conveniences of life for which they must be exchanged being the same as before, equal quantities of the metals must be exchanged for smaller quantities of commodities. So far, therefore, as the increase of the quantity of the precious metals in any country arises from an increased abundance of the mines, it is necessarily connected with some diminution of their value.

"When, on the contrary, the wealth of any country increases, when the annual produce of its labour becomes gradually greater and greater, a larger quantity of coin becomes necessary in order to circulate a greater quantity of commodities; and the people, as they can afford it, as they have more commodities to give for it, will naturally purchase a greater and a greater quantity of plate. The quantity of their coin will increase from necessity, the quantity of their plate from vanity and ostentation, or from the same reason that the quantity of fine statues, pictures, and of every other luxury and curiosity, is likely to increase among them. But as statuaries and painters are not likely to be worse rewarded in times of wealth and prosperity, than in times of poverty and depression, so gold and silver are not likely to be worse paid for."* After illustrating at some length this remark, Mr. Smith states, that " From about 1570 to about 1640, during a period of about seventy years, the variation in the proportion between the value of silver and that of corn held a quite opposite course. Silver sunk in its real value, or would exchange for a smaller quantity of labour than before; and corn rose in its nominal price, and instead of being commonly sold for about two ounces of silver the quarter, or about ten shillings of our present money, came to be sold for six and eight ounces of silver the quarter, or about thirty or forty shillings of our present money."†

On this distinction Mr. Smith founds his reply to Mr. Hume's celebrated argument against banks and paper credit. "These," says Mr. Hume, "render paper equivalent to money, circulate it throughout the whole state, make it supply the place of gold and silver, raise proportionably the price of labour and commodities, and by that means either banish a great part of those precious metals, or prevent their farther increase. What can be more short-sighted than our reasonings on this head? We fancy, because an individual would be much richer, were his stock of money doubled, that the same good effect would follow were the money of every one increased; not considering that

* [*Wealth of Nations*, Book I. chap. xi.; Vol. I. p. 294, *seq.*, tenth edition.]
† [Ibid. p. 299, *seq.*]

this would raise as much the price of every commodity, and reduce every man in time to the same condition as before. It is only in our public negotiations and transactions with foreigners, that a greater stock of money is advantageous; and as our paper is there absolutely insignificant, we feel, by its means, all the ill effects arising from a great abundance of money, without reaping any of the advantages.

"Suppose that there are twelve millions of paper which circulate in the kingdom as money, (for we are not to imagine that all our enormous funds are employed in that shape,) and suppose the real cash of the kingdom to be eighteen millions: Here is a State which is found by experience to be able to hold a stock of thirty millions. I say, if it be able to hold it, it must of necessity have acquired it in gold and silver, had we not obstructed the entrance of these metals by this new invention of paper. *Whence would it have acquired that sum?* From all the kingdoms of the world. *But why?* Because, if you remove these twelve millions, money in this State is below its level, compared with our neighbours; and we must immediately draw from all of them, till we be full and saturate, so to speak, and can hold no more. By our present politics we are as careful to stuff the nation with this fine commodity of bank-bills and chequer-notes, as if we were afraid of being over-burthened with the precious metals.

"It is not to be doubted, but the great plenty of bullion in France, is in a great measure owing to the want of paper-credit. The French have no banks: merchants' bills do not there circulate as with us: usury or lending on interest is not directly permitted; so that many have large sums in their coffers: great quantities of plate are used in private houses; and all the churches are full of it. By this means, provisions and labour still remain cheaper among them, than in nations that are not half so rich in gold and silver. The advantages of this situation, in point of trade, as well as in great public emergencies, are too evident to be disputed."*

In opposition to this doctrine, Mr. Smith labours to prove,

* [*Essays*, Vol. I. On the Balance of Trade.]

that "the whole paper money of every kind which can easily circulate in any country, never can exceed the value of the gold and silver of which it supplies the place, or which, the commerce being supposed the same, would circulate there if there had been no paper money."* A few pages after Mr. Smith proceeds to an examination of Mr. Hume's doctrine in the following words:—

"The increase of paper money, it has been said, by augmenting the quantity, and consequently diminishing the value of the whole currency, necessarily augments the money price of commodities. But as the quantity of gold and silver, which is taken from the currency, is always equal to the quantity of paper which is added to it, paper money does not necessarily increase the quantity of the whole currency. From the beginning of the last century to the present time, provisions never were cheaper in Scotland than in 1759, though, from the circulation of ten and five shilling bank-notes, there was then more paper money in the country than at present. The proportion between the price of provisions in Scotland and that in England, is the same now as before the great multiplication of banking companies in Scotland. Corn is, upon most occasions, fully as cheap in England as in France; though there is a great deal of paper money in England, and scarce any in France. In 1751 and in 1752, when Mr. Hume published his *Political Discourses*, and soon after the great multiplication of paper money in Scotland, there was a very sensible rise in the price of provisions, owing, probably, to the badness of the seasons, and not to the multiplication of paper money.

"It would be otherwise, indeed, with a paper money consisting in promissory notes, of which the immediate payment depended, in any respect, either upon the good-will of those who issued them, or upon a condition which the holder of the notes might not always have it in his power to fulfil, or of which the payment was not exigible till after a certain number of years, and which in the meantime bore no interest. Such a paper money would, no doubt, fall more or less below the value of gold

* [*Wealth of Nations*, Book II. chap. ii.; Vol. I. p. 448, tenth edition.]

and silver, according as the difficulty or uncertainty of obtaining immediate payment was supposed to be greater or less; or according to the greater or less distance of time at which payment was exigible."*

That this reasoning of Mr. Smith involves some very sound and important principles, cannot be disputed. At the same time, I believe, it is now very generally admitted, that it also involves some material mistakes and oversights. The assertion, in particular, that the whole paper money of every kind that can easily circulate in any country, never can exceed the value of the gold and silver of which it supplies the place, is an assumption completely refuted by our actual experience since Mr. Smith's time. Indeed, if we had had no such experience, it would have been easily susceptible of refutation from a theoretical view of the subject. On this point, however, I shall not now enlarge, as it will again come under our consideration before the completion of these lectures.

Another oversight of still greater consequence, is almost equally manifest, I mean the inattention manifested by Mr. Smith to that remarkable depreciation in the value of money which has taken place during the last century, and more especially during the present reign. To what causes this depreciation is to be ascribed, whether to the substitution of factitious instead of real money, or to the weight of our public burdens, or to both of these circumstances combined, is a different question, on which I shall afterwards hazard some remarks. But the fact is too obvious to the most careless observer to admit of a moment's controversy. The truth seems to be, that Mr. Smith has been led to his general conclusion, by too partial attention to the price of corn as a standard of the value of money. He did not sufficiently reflect on the effects of an extended and improved agriculture in preventing an increase of the price of grain, in comparison with that of other commodities. He was farther confirmed in his opinion by the partial view which he took of the nature of paper-credit, already noticed. Proceeding on the supposition that factitious money

* [Ibid., pp. 490-492.]

could only supply the place of that quantity of gold and silver which would otherwise have circulated in its stead, he could perceive no possible way in which it could have any tendency to depreciate the value of money ; and as the best information which he could obtain, satisfied him, that the annual supply of bullion from America did not materially exceed the annual consumption, it appeared to him, as a necessary consequence, that the common complaints of a depreciation in the value of money were altogether founded in ignorance and prejudice.

During the eventful interval which has elapsed since the publication of the *Wealth of Nations*, the question concerning the effects of paper currency on prices has assumed completely a new aspect, inasmuch, that granting all Mr. Smith's principles in their fullest extent, no fair inference whatever could be drawn from them at all applicable to the present condition of the commercial world ; as his whole reasoning on this subject proceeds on the supposition, that the issues of bank-notes are limited by the obligation of paying them in specie on demand. But the problem still remains concerning the effects on prices of a paper currency that is not convertible at pleasure into gold and silver. On this point, however, I shall not at present enlarge.

Having been led to allude to the depreciation of money, I shall avail myself of the opportunity which the subject affords, to mention a circumstance which escaped me yesterday, in treating of the real and nominal prices of commodities.

In the passage which I then quoted, [above, p. 362,] from Mr. Locke, that profound writer observes, that " wheat in this part of the world, (and that grain which constitutes the general food of any other country,) is the fittest measure to judge of the altered value of things in any long tract of time. Therefore, wheat here, rice in Turkey, &c., is the fittest thing to reserve a rent in," &c.

That this principle of Mr. Locke, although stated by him in terms much too strong and unqualified, contains a great deal of truth and good sense, I formerly remarked ; and the utility of the practical rule which it recommends, has been sufficiently confirmed by the experience of those who have had the prudence to adopt it. It is remarked by Mr. Smith, in his *Wealth of Nations*, that "the rents in England which have been reserved in corn, have preserved their value much better than those which have been reserved in money." I have introduced this passage from Mr. Smith, merely to do justice to the uncommon foresight of the great man, by whose advice the memorable statute, mentioned by Mr. Smith, was passed, which first introduced a provision of this sort into college leases. This person was Sir Thomas Smith, principal Secretary of State to Edward VI. and Queen Elizabeth; whose merits in this respect cannot fail to rise in our estimation, when we consider how very near he lived to the period when the depreciation of the precious metals first furnished a subject of political discussion. One of his biographers gives an articulate account of this provision.

SECT. IV.—OF MONEY AS THE STANDARD OF VALUE.

From the reasonings which I have been for some time past engaged in stating, in opposition to Montesquieu and Hume, we were led to conclude, that the prices of goods, more particularly of articles of the first necessity, have much less connexion with the quantity of the precious metals at the time, than these two writers seem to have supposed. For a complete discussion of the subject, I shall refer to the second book of Sir James Steuart's *Political Œconomy*, and to the digression concerning the variations in the value of silver and gold, in the eleventh Chapter of the first Book of Mr. Smith's *Inquiry*.

The remaining observations which I think it necessary to state, on the money price of commodities, I shall despatch in a very few words; referring to Mr. Smith's *Inquiry* for his doctrine concerning the component parts of price in what he calls the natural price of commodities, as distinguished from that which they actually bring in the market. It is sufficient for my purpose to mention one or two of his most important principles.

From an analysis of the price of different articles, Mr. Smith was led to infer, that in every society the price of any commodity resolves itself into one or other, or all of these three following parts: *the price of labour,—the rent of land,*—and *the profits of stock and wages;* and in proportion as a commodity is more manufactured, that part of the price which resolves itself into profit and wages, becomes greater in proportion to the other two, &c.

He further observes, that "There is in every society or neighbourhood an ordinary or average rate both of wages and profit in every different employment of labour and stock. This rate is naturally regulated, as I shall show hereafter, partly by the general circumstances of the society, their riches or poverty, their advancing, stationary, or declining condition ; and partly by the particular nature of each employment.

"There is likewise in every society or neighbourhood an ordinary or average rate of rent, which is regulated too, as I shall show hereafter, partly by the general circumstances of the society or neighbourhood in which the land is situated, and partly by the natural or improved fertility of the land.

"These ordinary or average rates may be called the natural rates of wages, profit, and rent, at the time and place in which they commonly prevail."*

Mr. Smith afterwards states, that "The natural price, therefore, is, as it were, the central price, to which the prices of all commodities are continually gravitating. Different accidents may sometimes keep them suspended a good deal above it, and sometimes force them down even somewhat below it. But whatever may be the obstacles which hinder them from settling in this centre of repose or continuance, they are constantly tending towards it." . . . .

"But though the market price of every particular commodity is in this manner continually gravitating, if one may say so, towards the natural price, yet sometimes particular accidents, sometimes natural causes, and sometimes particular regulations of police, may, in many commodities, keep up the market price, for a long time together, a good deal above the natural price."†

Abstracting even from these circumstances, there are other

* [Ibid. Book I. chap. vii.; Vol. I. p. 82, tenth edition.]   † [Ibid. pp. 87, 90.]

causes which may produce the same effect. These Mr. Smith refers to three heads: First, Particular accidents giving one society of men an advantage over others; secondly, Local peculiarities of soil and climate; and thirdly, Particular regulations of police. An illustration of these circumstances would lead me into details inconsistent with my general plan.

With respect to the relative market prices of different commodities, the general principle, I may add, is subject to various important limitations, but they rise or fall according to the scarcity, compared with the demand. In applying this rule, proper allowances must be made for various accidental circumstances. Thus, if there is more grain in a country than supplies the demand, the price will fall because grain is a perishable commodity. In broad cloth, again, if there be more than sufficient for the demand, the price will be less liable to be affected, because it can be longer kept than grain, and at a smaller expense. The truth of the maxim, too, it must be remembered, depends on the supposition that the demand and the quantity destined for the supply are both limited.

Another general principle, which I have already in some measure hinted at, it may not be improper again to notice, as I shall probably refer to it more than once in the course of our future inquiries. Abstracting from legislative interference, and all aids to the indigent, whether legal or voluntary, it seems evident that in a free country, where the lower orders have nothing to depend upon but the fruits of their own industry, a limit is necessarily fixed on the price of articles of the first necessity, by the wages of labour. Mr. Smith has shown, with much ingenuity, that the money-price of labour has a tendency to adjust itself not to the temporary or occasional, but to the average or ordinary price of the necessaries of life, and that the average price of corn is regulated by the value of silver, that is, by the richness or barrenness of the mines which supply the market with that metal. On the other hand, it appears to be, at least, equally clear, that however much the price of corn may vary from year to year, the wages of labour fix a limit beyond which it cannot rise, abstracting from the circumstances already mentioned. On this point, Sir James Steuart reasons thus :—

"The *number* of the buyers of subsistence, nearly determines the *quantity* to be sold; because it is a necessary article, and must be provided in a determinate proportion for every one, and the more the sale is frequent, the more the price is determinate. Next, as to the standard; this, I apprehend, must depend upon the faculties of the buyers, and these again must be determined by the extent of those of the greatest number of them; that is to say, by the extent of the faculties of the lower classes of the people. This is the reason why bread, in the greatest famine, never can rise above a certain price; for did it exceed the faculties of the great classes of a people, their demand would be withdrawn, which would leave the market overstocked for the consumption of the rich; consequently, those persons who in times of scarcity are forced to starve, can be such only whose faculties fall, unfortunately, below the standard of those of the great class; consequently, in countries of industry, the price of subsistence never can rise beyond the powers to purchase of that numerous class, who enjoy nothing beyond their physical-necessary; consequently, never to such an immoderate height as to starve considerable numbers of the people, a thing which very commonly happens in countries where industry is little known, where multitudes depend merely upon the charity of others, and who have no resource left so soon as this comes to fail them.

"The faculties, therefore, of those who labour for a physical-necessary, must, in industrious nations, determine the standard value of subsistence, and the value in money which they receive for their work, will determine the standard of their faculties, which must rise or fall according to the proportion of the demand for their labour."*

I have quoted this passage in Sir James Steuart's words, because, though somewhat obscurely expressed, it suggests a principle, sound and important; and because it seems, on a superficial view, to be contradicted by facts, which a few years

* [*Political Œconomy*, Book II. chap. xxviii.; *Works*, vol. II. pp. 82, 83.]

ago fell under our observation. In reality, however, the fact and theory are perfectly consistent, inasmuch as the latter, proceeding on the supposition that the poor have no resources but their own industry, is plainly inapplicable to a state of things where the poor are secured in a legal provision, and where a general spirit of humanity prompts to such exertions as this country never fails to exhibit during the pressure of a scarcity. It must be remembered, too, that the ordinary principles which regulate the prices of necessaries, were, during the late years of dearth, deranged completely by the sudden emission of an immense quantity of paper occasioned by the stoppage of issues of specie at the Bank of England, a circumstance of which I shall have occasion to take particular notice afterwards, and which, therefore, I shall content myself at present with merely mentioning.

On this question, I know, very opposite opinions have been entertained by some writers of high reputation for commercial knowledge. One writer, Mr. Boyd,* overlooking almost entirely the effects of the scarcity occasioned by the bad harvest in 1799, a scarcity demonstrated beyond the possibility of a doubt, and relieved very imperfectly by importations, amounting in twelve months to seven or eight millions sterling;—has ascribed in a pamphlet, which for some time gained a large share of the public attention, the high price of necessaries during the following winter, chiefly to the rapid addition which had been made to the circulating medium. That the augmentation of the quantity of money, or of paper performing the functions of money, has a tendency to depreciate that money or paper, he states, as a principle universally recognised, and as no less invariable in its operation than the law of gravitation.

In opposition to this reasoning, an author of the highest personal respectability, Sir Francis Baring,† and of unquestionable eminence as a commercial politician, has stated it confidently as a first principle, though without offering the slightest proof

---

* [*A Letter, &c., on the Stoppage of Issues in Specie at the Bank of England*, &c. 1800.]

† [*Observations on the Publication of Walter Boyd, Esq., M.P.*, &c. 1801.]

CHAP. II.—OF MONEY, THE CIRCULATING MEDIUM. (§ 4.) 395

of it, that bank-notes circulating at par cannot contribute to raise prices by any possible means. Into the discussion of these questions I cannot enter at present; although I must own that the subject does not appear to me to have been exhausted in either of these publications.

One consideration only which I shall endeavour to illustrate very fully in another part of the course, I shall suggest very briefly; that abstracting altogether from the point in dispute between these two writers, the sudden addition made to the circulating medium of this country, about the very period when the scarcity took place, may have operated very powerfully on prices, by a process of which neither of them has taken any notice. In consequence of this addition an increased facility was given to all who possessed credit, to add to the fund of their expenditure, and such as felt their limited incomes inadequate to meet the increasing exigencies of the times, were enabled, by encroaching silently on their capitals, or by anticipating their future resources, to relieve themselves from the pressure of the present moment, and to maintain their former rank in society. Their consumption accordingly, was not diminished to the same extent as it must otherwise have been from absolute necessity, and that economy, which is the natural and most effectual palliative for the evils of scarcity, was thus counteracted in its operation.

This inconvenience, however great as it is, was certainly accompanied with a consequence, on which it is impossible to reflect without satisfaction, although it probably contributed more than any other single cause to enhance the price of necessaries. The circumstance to which I allude is the increased facility which the higher and middling classes thus acquired of enlarging the funds of their charity. That the amount of voluntary contributions was in this manner greatly augmented, cannot, I think, be reasonably denied; and that these, added to the legal provisions for poor, rendered the price of provisions much higher than it otherwise would have been, seems equally indisputable. The competition was thus kept up much beyond what the unassisted means of the poor could have produced; and the operation of those circumstances was prevented which would have limited prices long before they approached that height which they actually reached. Numbers must have been left to perish from want of food; and a melancholy remedy would have been provided against the evils of dearth, by a diminution of the numbers of competitors. But on this subject I shall again have an opportunity of treating before the conclusion of these Lectures.—(*End of Interpolation from Notes.*)

[SECT. V.—OF INTEREST.]

Having finished the very slight view which our time permitted me to take of *money* considered as *a medium of exchange*, and of the principles which regulate its value in relation to that of commodities, I proceeded (at our last meeting) to consider the tendency which this important invention has, to facilitate the accumulation of stock or capital, which Turgot and Mr. Smith have shown to be so intimately connected with the increase of *National Wealth;* in this respect its effects in promoting the progress of society are no less striking than those which it produces, (as I had occasion formerly to remark,) by facilitating the separation of professions, and the distribution of labour among the different orders of the community.

Before the introduction of gold and silver in trade, undertakings of every kind, but especially those of manufactures and of commerce, must evidently have been extremely confined, on account of the perishable nature of every other species of property which could be employed as a medium of exchange, and the trouble attending the preservation of them. " A great number of those arts," as M. Turgot observes, " which are indispensable for the use of the most indigent members of society, require that the same materials should pass through many different hands, and undergo, during a considerable space of time, difficult and various operations. Such, for example, is the art of preparing leather for the purposes of the shoemaker. Whoever has seen the work-house of a tanner, must immediately perceive the impossibility of *one*, or even *several* indigent persons providing themselves with leather, tan, utensils, &c., causing the requisite buildings to be erected, and procuring the means of their subsistence till such time as their leather can be sold. In this art, and many others, must not those that work have learned the craft in some degree before they begin to exercise it on materials which are not to be obtained without expense? In what manner are the materials to be collected for the manufactory; the ingredients and the necessary tools for their preparation? How shall this multitude of workmen subsist till the commodity comes to market; a multitude of whom none individually could earn his subsistence by the preparation and sale of a single hide? Who shall defray the expenses for the instruction of the apprentices, and maintain them till their labour can be useful? All this, it is manifest, requires the aid of a proprietor of capital, who shall supply the advances necessary for the purchase and preparation of materials, and for the wages of the workmen employed in preparing them. This capitalist, on the other hand, will naturally expect that the sale of the commodity will not only return to him his advances, but will afford an emolument sufficient to indemnify him for what his money would have procured him, if he had turned it towards the acquisition of land; and, moreover, a salary due to his trouble, and attention, and risk. In proportion as the capital returns to him by the sale of his works, he employs it in new purchases for supporting his family, or maintaining his manufactory. By this continual circulation he lives on his profits; accumulating what he can save to increase his stock, and thereby to enlarge his enterprises still farther."*

Similar observations might be made to illustrate the necessity of advances for lucrative enterprises in commerce, and also in agriculture, wherever the cultivation of land is carried on to a considerable extent.

All such enterprises, therefore, must necessarily have been confined within very narrow limits, till the accumulation of stock was facilitated by the introduction of *money ;* an inven-

* [*Réflexions sur la Formation et la Distribution des Richesses,* § lxi.; *Œuvres,* Tome V. pp. 65-67.]

tion which thus appears to be not only subservient to the prompt *circulation of wealth*, but to be essentially connected with its production.

Since capitals then are indispensably necessary to all lucrative enterprises, a certain command of stock may be said, in the ordinary course of things, to be implied in every reasonable project for the augmentation of personal property. And it is thus, that according to the common proverb, " Money has the power of begetting money," [" Money breeds money."] Hence those industrious individuals who have not adequate funds of their own, will be willing to share the profits of their enterprises with such owners of capital as may agree to trust them with the employment of their *stock*. On this principle is founded in reason and equity the practice of lending upon *interest ;* or, in other words, the *commerce of money*. The lender *selling* the use of his stock, and the borrower *buying* it, in a manner perfectly analogous to that in which the proprietor of an estate *sells*, and the farmer who rents it *buys* or *hires* the temporary use of the land.

Of this subject I propose to treat at greater length than of some other articles that may appear at first view, of still more fundamental and general importance. My principal reason for doing so is, that it leads to some interesting discussions which continue to divide the opinions of very eminent writers; and which have been less exhausted than most of the questions connected with this part of the course, by the profound and comprehensive speculations of Mr. Smith.

One of the first authors who in this country investigated with success the principles that regulate the rate of interest, was Mr. Hume, in his *Political Discourses*, published in 1752. Long indeed before his time, political writers had admitted the general maxim, that a low rate of interest was the most certain of all signs of national prosperity; but they seem very generally to have misapprehended the manner in which these two effects are connected. The lowness of interest was ascribed by Locke, Law, and Montesquieu, to the abundance of money, in proof of which they appealed to the fall of interest, through the greater part of Europe, since the discovery of the Spanish West

Indies. But this doctrine, as Mr. Hume observes, is contradicted by the most obvious facts. " Interest in Batavia and Jamaica is at ten per *cent.*, in Portugal at six, though these places, *as we may learn from the prices of everything*, abound much more in gold and silver than either London or Amsterdam."* The fact is unquestionably as Mr. Hume states it, although the test to which he appeals, in the difference of prices, is not perhaps so conclusive as he appears to have imagined.

As a further presumption against the same doctrine, Mr. Hume remarks, that " Prices have risen about four times since the discovery of the Indies, and gold and silver have probably multiplied much more ; but interest has not fallen much above half. The rate of interest, therefore, is not derived from the quantity of the precious metals."†

The same conclusion to which Mr. Hume is thus led by an induction from facts, is very clearly and concisely deduced by Mr. Smith from a theoretical view of the subject.

" Before the discovery of the Spanish West Indies, ten per cent. seems to have been the common rate of interest through the greater part of Europe. It has since that time in different countries sunk to six, five, four, and three per cent. Let us suppose that in every particular country, the value of silver has sunk precisely in the same proportion as the rate of interest, and that in those countries, for example, where interest has been reduced from ten to five per cent., the same quantity can now purchase just half the quantity of goods which it could have purchased before. This supposition," continues Mr. Smith, " will not probably be found anywhere agreeable to the truth ; but it is the most favourable to the opinion we are going to examine ; and even upon this supposition it is utterly impossible that the lowering of the value of silver could have the smallest tendency to lower the rate of interest. If a hundred pounds are in those countries now of no more value than fifty pounds were then, ten pounds must now be of no more value than five pounds were then ; whatever were the causes that lowered the value of the capital, the same must necessarily have lowered

* [*Essays*, Vol. I. Of Interest.]   † [Ibid.]

that of the interest, and exactly in the same proportion. The proportion between the value of the capital and that of the interest must have remained the same, though the rate had never been altered. By altering the rate, on the contrary, the proportion between these two values is necessarily altered. If a hundred pounds now are worth no more than fifty were then, five pounds now can be worth no more than two pounds ten shillings were then. By reducing the rate of interest, therefore, from ten to five per cent., we give for the use of a capital which is supposed to be equal to one half of its former value, an interest which is equal to one-fourth only of the value of the former interest."*

" High interest," according to Mr. Hume, " arises from *three* circumstances ;—a great demand for borrowing,—little riches to supply that demand,—and great profits arising from commerce ; and these circumstances are a clear proof of the small advance of commerce and industry, not of the scarcity of gold and silver. Low interest, on the other hand, proceeds from the three opposite circumstances : a small demand for borrowing, great riches to supply that demand, and small profits arising from commerce,—circumstances which are all connected together, and proceed from the increase of industry and commerce, not of gold and silver."† This analysis of Mr. Hume's seems to be accurate and satisfactory ; and I shall accordingly, in the further prosecution of the subject, follow the arrangement which he has adopted, beginning, in the *first* place, with the causes and effects of a *great or small demand for borrowing*.

"When a people," says Mr. Hume, " have emerged ever so little from a savage state, and their numbers have increased beyond the original multitude, there must immediately arise an inequality of property ; and while some possess large tracts of land, others are confined within narrow limits, and some are entirely without any landed property. Those who possess more land than they can labour, employ those who possess none, and agree to receive

* [*Wealth of Nations*, Book II. chap. iv.; Vol. II. p. 39, *seq.*, tenth edition.]
† [*Essays*, Vol. I. Of Interest.]

a determined part of the produce. In this manner the society comes to consist of two orders of men, *proprietors and cultivators ;* and a *landed interest* arises with privileges, and views, and habits, strikingly discriminated from those which belong to the other members of the community. As the spending of a settled revenue is a way of life entirely without occupation, men have so much need of somewhat to fix and engage them, that pleasures, such as they are, will be the pursuit of the greater part of the landholders, and the prodigals among them will always be more numerous than the misers. In a state, therefore, where there is nothing but a landed interest, as there is little frugality, the borrowers must be very numerous, and the rate of interest must bear a proportion to it. The difference depends not on the quantity of money, but on the habits and manners which prevail."*

This reasoning of Mr. Hume is perfectly just in the main; but the conclusion is perhaps expressed in too unqualified a manner. In a state where there is *nothing* but a landed interest, it is manifest that whatever the waste and profusion of the proprietors may be, it is scarcely possible that their expense should in general exceed their income, because there are, *by the supposition,* no articles of luxury in commerce to form an object for their expenditure. Mr. Hume's reasoning, therefore, seems rather to apply to a country where commerce has made a certain progress, although not a considerable one ; such a progress as to excite in the landed interest a taste for the luxuries and vanities of life, without having established a monied interest of sufficient opulence to supply the increased demand for borrowing. And, if I am not mistaken, this view of the subject receives confirmation from a fact mentioned by Mr. Hume himself, in the *first* edition of his *Political Discourses,* that about four centuries ago, money in Scotland, and probably in other parts of Europe, was only at five per cent., and afterwards rose to ten before the discovery of the West Indies.

This fact Mr. Hume states, on the authority of an eminent lawyer, who had verified it by an examination of ancient papers

* [Ibid.]

and records; and it certainly forms an exception to Mr. Hume's general proposition, inasmuch as the monied interest in Scotland was still more inconsiderable four centuries ago than towards the end of the fifteenth century. Of its state at the former period, an idea may be formed from the account of Froissart, (who was at Dalkeith in the year 1360,) and who tells us, that "even in the *Doulce Escoche*, or lowlands, a complete ignorance prevailed of the commonest arts of life. The meanest articles of manufacture, horse-shoes, harness, saddles, bridles, were all imported, ready made from Flanders." The same author estimates the houses in Edinburgh, then the capital, at four thousand, and tells us that they were small wooden cottages covered with straw. In the reign of Robert II., (about the year 1380,) the inhabitants of the capital are supposed to have hardly exceeded sixteen thousand.[1]

Before the end of the following century, commerce and luxury had made considerable progress. In a poem, written during the reign of James III., and entitled *Tales of the Priests of Peebles*, "taverns and dice are reprobated; and a merchant's cupboard of plate is estimated at three thousand Scottish pounds, or about seven thousand five hundred of modern sterling currency."[2] The same poem complains of the degeneracy of the Peers from the wisdom, virtue, and valour of their ancestors, and that in consequence of their frequent poverty, they endeavoured to replenish their coffers by unworthy marriages with the opulent bastard daughters of priests, or heiresses of merchants, or by selling the right of marriage of their sons to rich commoners.[3]

In such a state of society it is certainly not surprising that the rate of interest should have risen greatly beyond what it was in times of comparative simplicity; and yet, if Mr. Hume's conclusion were admitted without any limitation, the case should have been reversed. He seems indeed to have been sensible of this himself; for he remarks, (after stating the fact now under consideration,) that the lowness of the rate of

---

[1] See Pinkerton, [*History of Scotland*. 1797, Vol. I. p. 148, and p. 25.]
[2] Ibid. p. 433.
[3] Ibid. pp. 435, 436.

interest in Scotland four centuries ago, was owing to this, that though the lenders were then few, the borrowers were still fewer. This concession, however, is plainly in direct opposition to his general principle; and confirms the necessity of that limitation with which I already said it ought to be adopted.

From what has been now observed, it appears, both *a priori*, and from the fact, that the rise of interest in Scotland before the discovery of the West Indies, resulted from the *first* operation of an infant commerce on the manners of a people among whom the national wealth was accumulated *chiefly*, but not *exclusively* in the hands of the landed proprietors; whatever opinion, however, we may form on this point, it is equally clear that the demand for borrowing depends on the general state of manners and habits, and not on the quantity of the precious metals.

The case is precisely similar with regard to the *second* circumstance mentioned in Mr. Hume's enumeration,—*the quantity of stock which exists to supply the demand of the borrowers.* This effect also depends on the habits and way of living of the people, not on the quantity of gold and silver. In order to have, in any state, a greater number of lenders, it is not sufficient, nor requisite, that there be great abundance of the precious metals. It is only requisite that the property, or command of that quantity which is in the state, whether great or small, should be collected in particular hands, so as to form considerable sums, or compose a great monied interest. This begets a number of lenders, and sinks the rate at which money may be borrowed; and it evidently depends, not on the quantity of specie, but on particular manners and customs which accumulate a superfluity of specie in the hands of a certain description of individuals.

This description of individuals, too, naturally arises, in the farther progress of society, from the physical circumstances of our condition, combined with our moral constitution. The rude materials of all those objects which minister to our wants, are derived ultimately from the ground; but they are seldom furnished by nature in that form in which they can be applied to immediate use. There must, therefore, beside the cultivators and proprietors of land, be another order of men, who, receiving from the former the rude materials, work them into their proper form, and retain part for their own use and subsistence. In the infancy of society, these contracts betwixt the artisans and the peasants, and betwixt one species of artisan and another, are commonly entered into immediately by the persons themselves, who, being neighbours, are readily acquainted with each other's necessities, and can lend their mutual assistance to supply them. But when men's industry increases, and their views enlarge, it is found that the most remote parts of the state can assist each other as well as the more contiguous; and that this intercourse of good offices may connect together in a thousand ways the most different orders of individuals in the most extensive and populous community. Hence the origin of *merchants*, who serve as agents betwixt those parts of the state that are wholly unacquainted, and are ignorant of each other's necessities. It is manifest, too, that as the people increase in numbers and industry, the difficulties of their mutual intercourse must increase; and of consequence the business of the agency or merchandise will become so complicated as naturally to divide and subdivide itself into various branches, from the same causes which give rise to the division of labour in the mechanical arts, and to the separation of trades and professions. In all these commercial transactions, it is necessary and reasonable, that a certain part of the commodities should remain with the merchant, to whose industry and skill in facilitating their exchanges, the existence of a great proportion of them is entirely owing; and thus gradually arises and multiplies that order of men, called the *Commercial Interest*, who have exerted so powerful an influence over the policy and manners of Modern Europe.

I have already illustrated the effects of Manufactures and Commerce in exciting a spirit of Agricultural industry, by leading the husbandman to increase his surplus produce, in order to have something to give in exchange for the articles that minister to his comfort or vanity. Commerce, at the same time, turns to account every particle of the produce of this industry, and instead of allowing it to perish on the spot where it is obtained, circulates it through the state, so as to render it at once an addition to the national stock, and a stimulus to the industry of others. Of this circulation merchants are the great agents and instruments; and as they take a more enlarged and comprehensive survey of the different interests of the community than any other description of men, they acquire a far greater command of the circulating stock. The habits of frugality, too, naturally connected with their education and profession, and that love of money, which is the never-failing consequence of commercial pursuits, render their expenditure less in proportion to their revenue than that of landed proprietors, or even than those of men who follow the more liberal walks of lucrative industry. In this manner, while they open channels for the free circulation of wealth, and thereby increase its quantity, they become themselves *basins* or *reservoirs* in which this wealth is locally accumulated. It is on this accumulation of wealth in particular hands, more than on the general wealth of the community, that the supply of stock to satisfy the demand for borrowing depends; and it appears from what has been said, how much both the existence of the stock and its partial accumulations are the consequences of commerce.

It may be said, indeed, that the increase of commerce, if it adds to the number of lenders, adds also to the number of borrowers, or rather that it creates a *new order* of borrowers, who contract debts, not from necessity, but to increase their capital and enlarge their trade. The observation is just, undoubtedly; but the two circumstances do by no means compensate each other: for, in a great commercial country, there will be always a large proportion of individuals, who, after having acquired a competency by their industry, will be desirous to indulge in ease and indolence; and a still larger proportion of their descendants who, inheriting affluence from their forefathers, will be unwilling to burden themselves with the cares of a laborious profession. Such individuals constitute what is properly called the *Monied Interest*, in contradistinction not only to the landed interest, but to the trading and manufacturing interests in which the owners themselves employ their own capitals. The growth of this monied interest, or, in other words, the quantity of stock to supply the demand of borrowers, will evidently keep pace with the general increase of capital, that is, with the increase of national stock.[1]

The stock belonging to the monied interest, it is farther manifest, is not at all regulated by the value of the *money*, whether paper or coin, which serves as the instrument of the loans. The capitals are, indeed, commonly lent out and paid back in money; and hence the lenders are distinguished by the name of the *Monied Interest;* but the truth is, (as Mr. Smith remarks,*) that the money is merely *the deed of assignment*, (as it were,) which conveys from one hand to another those capitals which the owners do not care to employ themselves. Those capitals may be greater in any proportion than the amount of the money which serves as the instrument of their conveyance; the same pieces of money successively serving for many different loans, as well as for many different purchases. The truth of this observation is sufficiently obvious from what was formerly stated on the subject of *Circulation.*— [P. 378, *seq.*]

While the progress of commerce thus creates a monied interest, it undoubtedly adds to the number of borrowers; but, by doing so, it does not necessarily raise the rate of interest. To understand the reason of this, it is of importance to attend to the different effects produced by a demand for money to be spent in consumption, and a demand for money to be employed in trade. The former has, undoubtedly, a tendency to raise the rate of interest; and there is no fixed limit which it may not be conceived to pass, as there is no fixed limit to the extravagance and improvidence of the prodigal. But the case is very different with respect to the latter; for the rate of interest paid by merchants will be always limited by the profits of trade; and the same circumstances which produce an increase in their

---

[1] Smith, Vol. II. p. 120, Irish Edition. [*Wealth of Nations*, Book II. chap.   iv.; Vol. II. p. 35, *seq.*, tenth edition.] * [Ibid.]

demand for borrowed money, must necessarily sink these profits, by bringing a greater number of mercantile stocks into competition with each other. It is evident that when the stocks of many rich merchants are turned into the same trade, their mutual competition must tend to lower its profits; and, in like manner, when there is an increase of stock in all the different trades carried on in the same society, the same competition must produce the same effect in them all. It is farther evident, that the *præmium* given by a merchant for the use of money, will be proportioned to the profit he expects to make by his commercial speculations. And, accordingly, this is the *third* circumstance mentioned by Hume as a cause of low interest;—*low profits arising from commerce.*[1]

As low profits arising from commerce necessarily produce a low rate of interest, so a low rate of interest has a tendency, in its turn, to reduce still more the profits of trade, by inducing many to continue their stock in commerce, in order to derive from it all the advantages which the capitalist has a right to expect when he superintends the employment of his own money. It is owing to this circumstance, that in Holland almost every man is a man of business; for the interest of money is so low, that none but the very wealthiest people are able to live on the revenue which their capital affords. The Dutch carry on trade upon lower profits than any people in Europe; but low as these profits are, they are sufficient to render trade the general and fashionable pursuit in a country, where people of good credit are accustomed to borrow at three per cent., and where Government was able to borrow at two. These two causes, therefore, low profits and low interest, mutually act and react on each other; and they are both of them necessary consequences of an extensive and flourishing

---

[1] If the foregoing observations be well founded, they lead to a limitation or correction of the terms in which Hume states the *First* cause he assigns for the low interest of money,—*a small demand for borrowing;* for this cause operates in the way he mentions, only in a country where the mercantile interest bears but a small proportion to the rest of the community. I would propose, therefore, to add to his words ; *a small demand for borrowing among those classes who live by their revenue.*

commerce. We may add, that, as low profits arise from the increase of commerce and industry, they serve in their turn to the farther increase of commerce, by rendering the commodities cheaper, increasing their consumption, and heightening the industry.

"In this manner," says Mr. Hume, "if we consider the whole connexion of causes and effects, interest is the true barometer of the state, and its lowness is a sign almost infallible of the flourishing condition of a people. It proves the increase of industry, and its prompt circulation through the whole state, little inferior to a demonstration. And though, perhaps, it may not be impossible but a sudden and a great check to commerce may have a momentary effect of the same kind by throwing so many stocks out of trade, it must be attended with such misery and want of employment to the poor, that, besides its short duration, it will not be possible to mistake the one case for the other."*

From the reasonings which have been already stated, and which, I must not at present attempt to recapitulate, we were led to conclude with Mr. Hume, (in opposition to the opinions of Locke, Law, and Montesquieu,) that the rate of interest has no necessary connexion with the plenty or scarcity of the precious metals, depending entirely on the habits and manners of a people, more particularly on the state of their commerce and industry. The result of the whole was, that the lowness of interest may be regarded as an almost infallible sign of a flourishing commerce, evincing at once an active spirit of national industry, and a prompt circulation of wealth through all those channels in which it can be employed with advantage.

I shall only take notice farther before leaving this part of the subject, (and the remark may probably appear superfluous, after what has been already stated,) of the two different senses in which the *value of money* is to be understood in commercial disquisitions. On some occasions this phrase expresses the quantity of the precious metals we give in exchange for com-

* [*Essays*, Vol. I. Of Interest.]

modities: on other occasions, it expresses the proportion between a sum of money, and the interest it bears in the market.

These *two* different modes of valuing *money* have, in truth, very little connexion with each other, inasmuch as its exchangeable value in relation to the different articles of trade may be *low*, while the rate of interest is *high*, and *vice versa*. *One* obvious reason of this (although not the only one) is, that the money brought into the market for the purchase of commodities, is that which is circulated to procure the necessaries and accommodations of life: that which is lent on interest, is what is actually drawn out of circulation to be accumulated into a capital.

I should hardly have thought it necessary to mention this ambiguity in the word *value*, when applied to money, if it had not escaped the attention of some respectable writers.

In a late publication (for example) on the *Corn Trade*,[1] there are some tables for converting the ancient money of England and of Scotland, into the present sterling money, which tables, we are told, proceed on the two following principles:—

1. In England and in Scotland, at the time of the Conquest, there were *twenty* shillings in the coinage pound of silver, which continued with very little variation in England, till the year 1347, and in Scotland till 1306; but now, there are *sixty-two* shillings in the coinage pound of silver in both kingdoms, so that £100 at that time, were equal to £310 of the present money, in point of sale or denomination.

2. Prior to the sixteenth century, the interest or yearly value of money, in both England and Scotland, was about sixteen per cent.; whereas it is now reduced to five per cent.

"Money therefore," says this author, "being raised or reduced in value according to its yearly legal produce, £100 bearing interest at ten per cent., is equal in value to £200, bearing only five per cent.; and so of other sums in proportion. So that £100 of ancient money, being equal in value to £310 in point of denomination, and money being now

[1] Dirom's *Inquiry*, &c. [Lond. 1796.]

worth only five per cent. yearly, therefore the £310, with the interest at sixteen per cent., were equal to £992 of the present money."

On these principles, accordingly, a laborious table has been constructed, exhibiting the prices of wheat in England from 1223 to 1784; *first,* in the money of the times; and *secondly,* in what is supposed to be an equivalent *money price* at present.

It is sufficiently obvious, that in the observations now quoted, the two meanings of the phrase *value of money,* which have just been distinguished, are confounded together.

It would be easy to confirm and illustrate the foregoing reasonings by an appeal to facts, as well as to reconcile to them some apparent exceptions which occur in the history of commercial nations. I must, however, at present, confine myself to a few particulars, which seem to me more peculiarly interesting from their connexion with the history of this country, and to one or two anomalous cases which may be supposed, at first view, to contradict our general conclusions.

The first English Act of Parliament in which we find any rate of interest mentioned, is the 37th of Henry VIII., enacted in 1546. This Act prohibits, under severe penalties, all interest above ten per cent., and consequently proves, that before that period, a higher rate of interest had sometimes been taken. In the earlier ages of the English history, all loans of money for interest were regarded as usurious;—a prejudice which prevailed also all over the rest of Europe, and which (as will afterwards appear) is not altogether of modern origin. In the very preamble to this law of Henry VIII., the practice of taking interest is stigmatized as immoral and criminal; and although it authorized it, from political considerations, yet the prejudice continued so strong, that in the following reign (of Edward VI.) the Statute of Henry was repealed, and all interest prohibited. By the 13th of Elizabeth, the Statute of Henry VIII. was revived with additional clauses, still prohibiting the taking of interest above ten per cent. It appears from D'Ewes's *Journal of Queen Elizabeth's Parliaments,* that while this Act was depending in the House of Commons, it occasioned warm debates, and drew from many of the members violent invectives against usury or interest of every kind, as unchristian, detestable, and damnable. It was said to be,—" præter naturam,"—" idem ac hominem occidere,"—" proxima homicidio," &c. &c.[1]

Mr. Hume (in the Third Appendix to his *History of England*) remarks, that "by a lucky accident in language, which has a great effect on men's ideas, the invidious word *usury*, which formerly meant the taking of any interest for money, came at this period to express only the taking of exorbitant and illegal interest." The Act of Queen Elizabeth violently condemns all *usury*, but permits ten per cent. *interest* to be paid.

I shall have occasion afterwards to consider the origin of these prejudices against usury, and also to examine the policy of those restrictions which our legislators have thought proper to continue on money loans to the present day. In this inquiry I have referred to the English laws, only as affording a document of the different rates at which money appears to have been actually lent at different periods; for although the legal rate of interest does not with precision determine the market rate, (as it merely fixes the limit which it cannot exceed,) yet as the object of our lawgivers has plainly been to adapt the changes in the legal rate, to that market-rate which would naturally have arisen from the varying circumstances of society, and as the market-rate has been, on the whole, *below* the legal rate, the progress of our laws affords us sufficient *data* for comparing the actual rates of interest in England, with the general principles formerly stated.

The Law of Elizabeth authorizing interest under ten per cent., continued in force till the 21st of James I. (1623,) when it was made penal to take above eight per cent. Soon after the Restoration, it was reduced to six per cent., at which rate, by the way, it had been fixed nine years before under the usurpation of Cromwell; and by the 12th of Queen Anne it was farther reduced to five per cent., at which rate it still continues.

[1] Postlethwayt, [*Dictionary*, &c., Art. *Interest.*]

It appears, therefore, that since the reign of Henry VIII., a gradual abatement in the rate of interest has accompanied the growing commercial prosperity of the country. The demand for money at that epoch must have been great in consequence of the general spirit of improvement which was rising over the kingdom, and at the same time the ready money accumulated in the coffers of individuals comparatively inconsiderable. The kings of England, both before and after this period, borrowed large sums in Genoa and the Netherlands, and so low was their credit, that beside the exorbitant interest of ten or twelve per cent., they were obliged to make the city of London join in the security.[1] It is somewhat curious, that the Act which, in 1623, reduced the interest of money to eight per cent., states in its preamble the declining circumstances of the nation, although it affords itself the most unequivocal of all documents of its advancing wealth; for (as Mr. Chalmers justly remarks) " such laws can never be safely enacted till all parties, the lenders as well as the borrowers, are properly prepared to receive them." Accordingly, Stowe tells us (speaking of the reign of James VI.) " that it would in time be incredible, were there not due mention made of it, what great increase there is, within these few years, of commerce and wealth throughout the kingdom; of the great building of royal and mercantile ships; of the repeopling of cities, towns, and villages; beside the sudden augmentation of fair and costly buildings." Nor will this account be suspected of any exaggeration, when we reflect, that during the reign of James the nation enjoyed a longer interval of peace than it has ever done since, no less than twenty-two years of almost uninterrupted tranquillity; a fact which has been alluded to by some historians, as involving a reproach on his glory as a sovereign, although, in truth, it is more than sufficient to expiate all the follies and absurdities which debased his character.

The picture given by Lord Clarendon of the state of England during the first part of the reign of Charles I., is no less flattering. Nor was the progress of the country, although

[1] Guthrie, [*History*, &c.]; Chalmers's *Estimate*, p. 29.

interrupted for a time by the civil wars, retarded on the whole by that event. On the contrary, Mr. Chalmers has remarked, that " these wars, unhappy as they were while they continued, both to king and people, produced in the end the most salutary influences, by bringing the higher and lower ranks closer together, and by continuing in all a vigour of design and activity of practice, that in prior ages had no example."[1]

One of the first consequences of real hostilities, was the establishment of taxes, to which the people had seldom contributed, and which produced before their final conclusion, the sum of £95,512,025. In this estimate, indeed, are included the sales of confiscated lands, compositions for estates, and such other more oppressive modes of raising money; but the wealth of the country may be judged of from this, that there were collected by *excises* only £10,200,000, and by *tonnage and poundage* £5,700,000. The opulence which industry had been collecting for ages, was thus brought into circulation by means of the tax-gatherer; and the evils resulting from the dormant hoards of country gentlemen, and other descriptions of individuals, remedied, in a great measure, by the liberality with which they contributed to the wants of the sovereign.

In consequence of these and other causes, the legal rate of interest was reduced in 1651 to six per cent. And the same rate was continued by a law of Charles II., passed soon after the Restoration.

The activity and ardour which the civil commotions of the country had excited, began now to be turned to the arts of peace. The several manufactures and new productions of husbandry that were introduced from abroad, before the Revolution, not only formed a new epoch, but evince a vigorous application to the useful arts, in the intermediate period. The common highways were repaired and enlarged, and rivers were deepened for the purposes of water conveyance, while foreign trade was increased by opening new markets, and by withdraw-

[1] Eden, [*State of the Poor*,] Vol. I. p. 146; Chalmers's *Estimate*, p. 37, second edition.

ing the alien duties, which had always obstructed the vent of native manufactures.

But above all, says Mr. Chalmers, the change of manners, and the intermixture of the higher and middle ranks by marriages, induced the gentry, and even the younger branches of the nobility, to bind their sons apprentices to merchants, and thereby to ennoble a profession that was before only gainful, to invigorate traffic by their greater capitals, and to extend its operation by their superior knowledge. And accordingly, Child, Petty, and Davenant, agree in asserting that the commerce and riches of England did never, in any former age, increase so fast as in the busy period from the Restoration to the Revolution. From an authentic account of *the customs*, (referred to by Mr. Chalmers,) it appears that they were more than doubled during this short interval; and we are told by Dr. Davenant, that the tonnage of the merchant ships was, in the year 1688, double of what it had been in 1666; and the tonnage of the Royal Navy, which in 1660 was only 62,594 tons, was in 1688 increased to 101,032 tons.[1]

Towards the end of King William's reign, the interest of money began to fall; and it continued so low, even amid the pressures of the subsequent war, that Parliament enacted in 1713, that the legal interest should not rise higher than five per cent. after September 1714. This law continues in force in the present times; and since the period it was enacted, the market rate seems to have been, *on the whole*, below the legal rate, notwithstanding the effects of the funding system, and of some other accidental circumstances in keeping up the rate of interest. About seven years ago, the Bank of England was in the practice of discounting bills at four per cent. And in the reign of George I., the natural rate of interest fell to three per cent., while the Government seldom borrowed at more than four.[2]

The effects produced on the market rate of interest by *public loans*, and more particularly by those high gratuities which, in times of difficulty, Government is under the necessity of giving,

[1] Guthrie, [*History*, &c.] p. 311.   [2] Chalmers's *Estimate*, &c., p. 98.

are sufficiently evident. But on this subject I shall not enlarge at present; although it is of great importance, not only in consequence of its connexion with the variations of *interest* in this country, but with those general principles which influence the progress of national improvement.

During the whole period which has been now under our review, from the reign of Henry VIII. till the present century, while the interest of money has been gradually diminishing, the wages of labour (which may be expected always to increase with the increase of national stock) have been continually rising.

Agreeably to the same general principles, we find a small difference in the market rate of interest in the two United Kingdoms, corresponding to their unequal measures of national prosperity. The market rate of interest in Scotland is rather higher than in England, although the legal rate of interest be the same in both. In the latter country, the competition of great and numerous stocks in every branch of trade, must necessarily diminish the profits of the trader; and the diminution is still farther aggravated by that increase in the wages of labour which a superabundance of stock produces. In Scotland, the comparative poverty of the country is accompanied with consequences precisely opposite.

In Ireland the legal rate of interest is six per cent. An attempt was made a few years ago to lower it to five, but without success. I am not acquainted with the arguments which were employed on the opposite sides of the question; but the consideration which appears to have had the chief weight was, that a considerable portion of the stock and capital of the kingdom was English; that the only temptation the proprietors had to lay it out in Ireland was the additional interest paid there, and that if this were reduced the greater part of it would be withdrawn.[1]

In France, the legal rate of interest has not been always regulated by the market rate, during the course of the present

[1] Crumpe's *Essay*, &c., [1796,] p. 340. (In pencil.—Mem.—To inquire about the Register of Mortgages in Ireland and in England.—Lord Mansfield.)

century, but has been, in several instances, violently altered by Government for political purposes. In 1720, it was reduced from five to two per cent. In 1724, it was raised to three and one-third per cent. In 1725, it was again raised to five per cent. In 1766, during the administration of M. Laverdi, it was reduced to four per cent. The Abbé Terray raised it afterwards to the old rate of five per cent. Although, however, the legal rate of interest in France has frequently been lower than in England, the market rate has generally been higher, the ingenuity of borrowers and lenders being employed there as in other countries, to evade the law, where it did not happen to be accommodated to the commercial circumstances of the nation. From this statement of the comparative market rates of interest in France and in England, it would appear that the profits of trade were higher in the former country than in the latter; a conclusion which is strongly corroborated by another well-known fact, that many British subjects have chosen to employ their capitals rather there than at home, notwithstanding the low degree of importance which was attached in France to mercantile opulence. If the foregoing principles concerning interest be just, we must also conclude from these facts, that the accumulation of stock in France was less than in England, or at least, that the national prosperity was not so rapidly advancing; and, accordingly, we find, that the wages of labour were lower, and the condition of the common people greatly inferior, in respect of the comforts and accommodations of life.

In earlier times the case was different. About the period when Elizabeth fixed the rate of interest at ten per cent., Henry IV. of France reduced it from eight and one-third per per cent. (at which it was fixed by Francis I., anno 1522 [1]) to six and one-half per cent; a fact which Mr. Hume refers to in his *History*, as evincing the great advance of France above England in commerce about the middle of the sixteenth century. In the Appendix to the twenty-fifth volume of the *Monthly*

[1] Sir James Steuart's *Political Œconomy*, [Book IV. chap. iv.; *Works*, Vol. III. p. 156.]

Review, a writer who professes to speak from good information concerning the present state of that kingdom, (1798,) assures us, that the interest of money is from six to seven per cent., all restraints upon usury being now taken away. The same writer tells us, that the wages of labour have in general risen greatly of late, and that in some places the wages of rustic labour have been nearly doubled. These facts, supposing them to be accurately stated, afford no exception to our general principles; for the interest of money appears to have risen in a very inconsiderable proportion when compared with the wages of labour, more particularly when it is considered that, even under the old Government, the market rate of interest was higher than in England. Indeed, there can be little doubt that in our own country, the market rate of interest would be at present six or seven per cent. if the legal restraints were abolished.

If we extend our view to our West Indian colonies, we find the same general principles apply, although the results are somewhat different, in consequence of particular combinations of circumstances. As a new colony must always for some time be more understocked in proportion to the extent of its territory, than the greater part of other countries, the stock which exists, as Mr. Smith has remarked,* is applied to the cultivation only of what is most fertile and most favourably situated, the lands near the sea-shore, and along the banks of navigable rivers—lands, too, which are frequently purchased at a price below the value even of their natural produce. Stock employed in the purchase and improvement of such lands must yield a very large profit, and consequently afford to pay a very large interest. As the colony increases, the profits of stock gradually diminish. When the most fertile and best situated lands have been all occupied, less profit can be made by the cultivation of what is inferior both in soil and situation, and less interest can be afforded for the stock which is employed. In the greater part of our colonies, accordingly, both the legal

---

* [*Wealth of Nations*, Book I. chap. ix.; Vol. I. p. 140, *seq.*, tenth edition.]

and the market rate of interest have been considerably reduced during the course of the present century. As riches, improvement, and cultivation have increased, interest has sunk; so that, although still higher than in this part of the world, it is low when compared with what it was at a more early period. It runs in general from six to eight per cent.

But although the rate of interest in these colonies is plainly regulated by the general principles formerly explained, it must be confessed, that it does not appear, on a superficial view, to bear the same relation to the wages of labour which it does in Europe. The truth is, (as Mr. Smith has further observed,*) that new colonies are not only understocked, in proportion to the extent of their territory, but underpeopled in proportion to the extent of their stock. The rapid accumulation of their stock, at the same time, enables the planters to increase the number of their hands faster than they can find them in a new settlement, and, of consequence, those whom they do find are very liberally rewarded. This combination of high wages of labour and of high profits of stock, is seldom to be found but in the peculiar circumstances of new colonies. And even in these, as improvement goes on, their mutual relation comes to approach more and more to the general theory. Thus, in the West Indies, while the profits of stock have gradually diminished during the last hundred years, the wages of labour continue unabated. The reason, according to Mr. Smith, is obvious, for "the demand for labour increases with the increase of stock, whatever be its profits; and after these are diminished, stock may not only continue to increase, but to increase much faster than before."† The connexion between the increase of stock, and that for the demand for useful labour, is fully explained by Mr. Smith in that part of his work where he treats of the accumulation of stock.‡ The further illustration of it has no connexion with our present subject.

Another case is mentioned by the same ingenious and pro-

* [Ibid.] (In pencil.—Memorandum. † [Ibid.]
—Consult Bryan Edwards.) ‡ [Ibid. Book II., *passim*.]

found writer, as affording an apparent exception to the foregoing doctrine; I mean the case of a country whose state has been suddenly altered by the acquisition of new territory, or of new branches of trade. Here "the profits of stock, and with them the interest of money, may rise, even although the country is fast advancing in the acquisition of riches. The stock of the country not being sufficient for the whole accession of business, which such acquisitions present to the different people among whom it is divided, is applied to those particular branches only which afford the greatest profit. Part of what before had been employed in other trades, is of course withdrawn from them, and turned into some of the new and more profitable ones. In all those old trades, therefore, the competition comes to be less than before; and as the market is less fully supplied with the different sorts of goods, their price rises more or less, and yields a greater profit to those who deal in them, and who can therefore afford to borrow at a higher interest. . . . This accession of business, to be carried on by the old stock, must diminish the quantity employed in a great number of particular branches in which the competition being less, the profits must be greater."* So that, through all the different branches of trade, both old and new, the demand for borrowed money must necessarily yield a higher interest to the lenders.

In Bengal, and the other British settlements in the East Indies, the wages of labour are very low, while the profits of stock and the interest of money are very high. The truth is, that the same cause which lowers the wages of labour, viz., the diminution of the capital stock of the society, or of the funds destined for the maintenance of industry, raises the profits of stock. By the wages of labour being lowered, the owners of what stock remains in the society can bring their goods cheaper to market than before, and at the same time they can sell them dearer, as the market is not so well supplied. These unnatural profits, arising from the ruined state of these countries, afford of consequence a proportionally exorbitant interest. "In Bengal,"

---

* [Ibid. Book I. chap. ix.; Vol. I. p. 142, tenth edition.]

according to Mr. Smith, "money is frequently lent to the farmers at forty, fifty, and sixty per cent., and the succeeding crop is mortgaged for the payment. As the profits which can afford such an interest must consume almost the whole rent of the landlord, so such enormous usury must in its turn eat up the greater part of these profits."* And hence, on the one hand, the rapid accumulation of wealth by our countrymen in that part of the world; and on the other, the oppressed and impoverished condition of the natives.

In a country which had obtained that complete measure of opulence and of population of which its physical advantages admitted, and which at the same time was not on the decline, both the wages of labour and the profits of stock would probably be very low. The country being, by the supposition, fully peopled, the competition for employment would reduce the wages of labour to that *minimum* which was just sufficient to prevent the race of labourers from diminishing; and the stock being fully adequate to all the business that could be transacted, the competition would be as great, and consequently the rate of profit as low as possible.

It may be doubted, however, whether this hypothetical case was ever realized in its full extent in the history of mankind. At first view, perhaps, China may appear to approach to the description; and undoubtedly it seems to have continued longer in a stationary condition, than any other country with which we are acquainted. It is, however, very well remarked by Mr. Smith, that although China may have acquired that full complement of riches which is consistent with the nature of its laws and institutions, there is the greatest reason to believe that this complement is far short of what its physical advantages might admit under a different system of policy. Of this a judgment may be formed from the contempt in which foreign commerce is held; from the exclusion of foreign vessels from all the ports, one or two excepted; and above all, from the oppressive extortions to which men of small capital are liable from the inferior mandarins. This last circumstance of itself, added to

* [Ibid. p. 143.]

the comparative security of the rich, must establish a monopoly in favour of the latter, and increase greatly the profits of trade. Accordingly twelve per cent. is said to be the common interest of money in China.[1] The wages of labour are no higher than what is sufficient for the most scanty subsistence of the labourer, the population being incomparably beyond what the stock engaged in business is able to employ.

In what has now been said, we have considered the riches or poverty of a country as the *only* causes which influence the rate of interest. It is possible, however, that other adventitious circumstances may operate to the same effect. When the law, for example, does not enforce the performance of contracts, the precariousness of repayment places all debtors in the same situation with persons of doubtful credit, and subjects them to the same usurious conditions. In accounting for the high rate of interest during the earlier periods of the modern history of Europe, this cause ought not to be overlooked.

The same effect takes place in a still greater degree where the law absolutely prohibits interest. Necessity must frequently produce evasions of the law; and in such cases a premium will be expected, not only in proportion to the profits to be made by the use of the money, but to the danger to which the lender is exposed in the event of a discovery.

From the general principles which we have now been endeavouring to illustrate, it is easy to conceive in what manner the prices of commodities may sometimes continue stationary while the wages of labour are progressive; for the same cause which raises the wages of labour, (viz., the increase of national stock,) has a tendency to lower the profits of the merchant, and, consequently, the variations in these two elements of price may so balance each other, as to bring the commodity to the market at the same rate as before.

Before leaving this part of our subject, it may be worth while to add, that the ordinary market price of land is regulated, in every commercial country, by the ordinary market

---

[1] (In pencil)—Postlethwayt states the rate of interest in China at thirty per cent. See *Dictionary*, Article, *Interest.*—Consult Sir G. Staunton.

rate of interest. If the return to be expected from vesting a capital in land, were equal to what could be obtained by lending the same sum upon interest, the superior security, together with the other advantages connected with landed property, would induce every person who wished to derive an income from his money without superintending the employment of it himself, to prefer the former species of income to the latter. The truth is, that these advantages are such, as to compensate a certain difference in the pecuniary return, and accordingly the market rent of land may be always expected to fall short of the market interest of money. What the difference between them is, in particular cases, will no doubt depend somewhat on the judgment or fancy of the individual; but it is evident that there are certain limits within which it must be confined. If the pecuniary difference was very great, the market would be glutted with land, its ordinary price would fall, and the balance would be restored. On the other hand, if the advantages of landed property were more than sufficient to compensate the pecuniary difference, everybody would buy land, and the rise in its price would restore the natural proportion between the rent of a capital so employed and the market rate of interest. When interest was at ten per cent., land was commonly sold for ten and twelve years' purchase. As interest sunk to six, five, and four per cent., the price of land rose to twenty, five-and-twenty, and thirty years' purchase; so that, in general, the price of land may be expected to vary inversely with the value of money.

In farther illustration of this subject, I may observe, that land, when let on lease, may be considered as so much capital let out by landlords to the farmers; and consequently, a very close analogy must exist between the condition of the capitalist, or landed interest, and that of the properties of disengaged capital, or monied interest. A pecuniary augmentation of rent, however, is not an augmentation of the rent of the capital alone, but of the capital itself, being immediately convertible into property, by a rate determined by the number of years' purchase which land may be worth in the market. In this respect, too, the same general principles apply to the rent of land, and to the interest of money, any additional annual dividend declared by our chartered companies instantly resolving itself into capital.

This doctrine, at the same time, it is necessary to remark, although just and unquestionable in the main, must be understood with certain limitations. Landed property has many circumstances peculiar to itself, which, by stamping upon it a value independent of the pecuniary returns it affords, prevents its price from being regulated by the same general principles which apply to other articles of commercial speculation. Local causes, for example, may, in particular districts, alter the general proportion of buyers to sellers, and may thus occasion a local rise or fall in the price of land, while the market rate of interest is nearly the same over the whole kingdom.[1] In places where thriving manufactures have been established, land has been observed to sell more briskly, and for more years' purchase than in other districts, for there the number of buyers may be expected to exceed the number of sellers. In such manufacturing districts, the riches of one set of men not arising from the extravagance and waste of another, as it does in other places where men live idly on the produce of their land, the industrious part of the community brings an increase of wealth from a distance, without injuring the interests of their neighbours. And when the thriving tradesman has got more than he can well employ in trade, his next thoughts are to look out for a purchase in the vicinity, where the estate may be under his eye, and may remove neither himself nor his children from the business to which they have been accustomed. The extraordinary demand for land, therefore, in such situations, must occasion an extraordinary enhancement of its price.

In regulating the proportion, too, between the price of land and the value of money, a good deal, it is evident, will depend on the habits of the landed gentry in point of frugality or of dissipation. Where it is fashionable for them to live beyond

---

[1] See Locke, Vol. II p. 20. [(First) *Considerations on Interest and Money.*]

their income, debts will increase and multiply, and lay them under a necessity, first of encumbering and then of selling their estates. This is generally the cause why men part with their land, for it happens rarely that a clear and unencumbered estate is exposed to sale merely for a pecuniary profit. Mr. Locke remarks, that " there is scarce one in a hundred that thinks of selling his patrimony, till mortgages have pretty well eat into the freehold, and the weight of growing debts force the proprietor, whether he will or no, out of his possessions. . . . . It is seldom," he adds, " that a thriving man turns his land into money, to make the greater advantage ; the examples of it are so rare, that they are scarce of any consideration in the number of sellers."

"This I think may be the reason," continues the same writer, " why, in Queen Elizabeth's days, (sobriety, frugality, and industry, bringing in daily increase to the growing wealth of the kingdom,) land kept up its price, and sold for more years' purchase than corresponded to the *interest* of money, then busily employed in a thriving trade, which made the natural interest much higher than it is now, as well as the legal rate fixed by Parliament."[1]

In these observations of Mr. Locke there is much truth and good sense, but I apprehend that they are by no means so strictly applicable to the present state of our country as they were at the time when he wrote. The attachment to landed property is now greatly diminished. The personal consideration arising from it has sunk in the public estimation, in consequence of the progress of commerce and of luxury, and the rank of an individual is measured chiefly by the extent of his expenditure. The extravagance and dissipation of the metropolis, are preferred to the simple and frugal enjoyments of the country ; and land, like any other article of property, is valued chiefly in proportion to the revenue it affords. Although, therefore, it still possesses, and must necessarily possess, certain advantages over every other species of property, these advantages are not so great now as they formerly were, and conse-

[1] Vol. II. p. 26. [Ibid.]

quently the price of land may be expected to be more accurately regulated by the interest of money, than when the feudal ideas were more prevalent, and the commerce of England comparatively in its infancy

The question concerning the expediency of subjecting the commerce of money to the regulation of law is to be considered in another part of the course.

In the observations which I have hitherto made on National Wealth, my principal object has been, to illustrate some of the most important elementary principles connected with that article of Political Economy, with a view chiefly to facilitate and assist your studies in the perusal and examination of Mr. Smith's *Inquiry*. The greater part of these disquisitions have been entirely of a speculative nature, aiming merely to analyze and explain the actual mechanism of society, without pointing out any of the conclusions, susceptible of a practical application, to which they may lead. A few disquisitions of this last description may, indeed, have insensibly blended themselves with our analytical inquiries; but in these instances I have departed from my general plan, and my only apology is, that the limits of my course left me little prospect of being able to resume, in a systematical order, the consideration of the questions which gave occasion to these digressions.*

* [Book II. is concluded in the ensuing Volume.]

APPENDICES

TO BOOKS FIRST AND SECOND.

APPENDICES.

APPENDIX I.—To B. I. Ch. ii. § 3.

Quotation on Population from Pinto.

[It has been thought proper to adduce fully the following passage, alluded to by Mr. Stewart in p. 203; and a reference to this Appendix ought to have been there subjoined.—*Ed.*

" Pour faire sentir qu'il y a un *maximum* et dans la population et dans l'agriculture, je prie le lecteur de promener son imagination sur les observations suivantes. Supposons d'abord toute l'Europe aussi peuplée qu'elle est susceptible de l'être ; elle contiendra par estimation quatre ou cinq fois autant d'habitans qu'il y en a actuellement d'établis. Dans ce cas là, il faudroit de toute nécessité que tout son sol fût exactement cultivé pour nourrir tant de monde. Nous voulons encore accorder, que par une législation et par une administration supérieures, tous les gradins des classes fussent bien distribués, en un mot qu'il y eût une proportion, et une harmonie exacte dans toutes les parties des divers Etats et Gouvernemens.

" L'Europe parvenue à ce point de population et de culture, qu'en arriveroit-il ? Arrêteroit-on le progrès ultérieur de la population ? Comment l'arrêteroit-on ? On seroit forcé d'envoyer des Colonies en Amérique et ailleurs. Mais cette ressource ne suffiroit pas ; il est à craindre qu'on ne fût contraint de susciter de cruelles et funestes guerres en attendant la peste et la famine. Ce dernier fléau ne tarderoit pas à faire des ravages ; il seroit amené naturellement par cette grande et universelle population qu'on suppose établie. Les fruits annuels de la terre seroient sans contredit annuellement consumés par les habitans respectifs de chaque Pays. Or il est certain que, selon le cours de la Nature, les récoltes manquent dans tous les pays après un certain nombre d'années. Toutes les contrées seroient donc forcément réduites tour à tour à mourir de faim ; chaque pays, ayant besoin de ses propres productions pour nourrir ses propres habitans, ne pourroit pas pourvoir ses voisins. Poussons plus loin nos observations.

" Il y a des Naturalistes qui prétendent que notre globe terrestre n'a qu'une croûte végétale, qui s'épuise par la culture, et devient en fin aride et stérile. On prétend que les déserts de l'Arabie ont autrefois été des contrées fertiles, et les premières habitations du genre humain.

" Sans approfondir cette question, tout le monde sait que la terre rajeunit par le repos; il lui est souvent nécessaire pour conserver sa fécondité. Personne n'ignore l'impatiente végétation dont une terre neuve se presse de récompenser les premiers soins du laboureur. Il faut donc des alternatives de repos et de culture; il faut des vivres de réserve, des terres incultes, des pays inhabités, pour l'ordre, l'harmonie et la conservation du tout. Il paroît probable qu'il n'entre point dans le dessein de la Providence, que le globe que nous habitons soit partout également cultivé et peuplé. Cet état momentaire de perfection d'opulence, s'il pouvoit exister, ameneroit donc les plus grands malheurs. Nous ne connoissons pas le souverain bien; les imperfections apparentes conspirent souvent à la conservation du tout. Nous ne voyons qu'une partie du tableau; de faux jours nous éblouïssent; la perfection n'est pas l'apanage d'une seule partie, mais le résultat du tout.

"La population excessive a toujours enfanté la guerre, qui, en se tournant contre sa cause, la diminue et la détruit.

"Multiplier les hommes, dit M. de Mirabeau, [the elder,] sans multiplier les subsistances, c'est les vouer au supplice de la faim. Ce phénomène est rare, et ne peut arriver que par un vice d'administration et de police; mais, d'un autre côté, multiplier les subsistances sans multiplier les consommateurs, c'est une chimère destructive, et qui ne peut jamais exister au delà d'une année. Les bornes physiques de la population d'un pays ne sont pas invinciblement assujetties aux productions de son territoire, quand le commerce et la navigation, secondés du crédit, de la circulation, et des biens fictifs, sont en bon état: témoin la Hollande. C'est plutôt la culture qui est invinciblement assujettie à la consommation intérieure, ou à l'exportation précaire Nationale. Quand la population excède les richesses, le vice est inhérent au corps de l'Etat. C'est que toute la machine politique est détraquée. Il faut pour-lors porter ses regards partout, et remédier à tout à la fois. Il faut pour-lors, comme Mylord Bolingbroke dit à un autre sujet, imiter les grandes opérations de la nature, et non celles de l'art, toujours lentes, foibles et imparfaites. Nous ne devons pas procéder comme fait un statuaire en formant une statue, dont il travaille tantôt la tête, tantôt une autre partie; mais nous devons nous conduire comme la nature agit en formant un animal, ou toute autre de ses productions; *Rudimenta partium omnium simul parit et producit;* elle jette à la fois le plan de chaque être et les principes de toutes ses parties. Tous les végétaux et les animaux croissent en volume, et augmentent en forces; mais ils sont les mêmes dès le commencement. Il faut une puissance coërcive, qui contienne les ordres de l'Etat, comme la clef d'une voute contient le corps du bâtiment. Dans un grand Royaume, l'agriculture, le commerce, les manufactures, la circulation, le crédit public, la police intérieure, la finance, l'état de guerre, les colonies, la navigation, la marine, le luxe modéré, tout doit marcher dans une proportion réciproque, pour conserver l'harmonie de l'Etat, le bon ordre et la prospérité d'une Nation.

"L'étendue des frontières ne fait pas seule la puissance d'un Etat; mais c'est un grand avantage, qui comporte un plus grand nombre de sujets qui peuvent trouver leur subsistance. Le grand nombre seul avec une subsistance physique, n'est pas encore le tout; il faut que l'aisance s'y trouve; et cette aisance, dans le grand nombre, exige plusieurs classes, et ne sauroit être confinée aux seuls travaux de l'agriculture. Si la population en France étoit à son comble, le débouché extérieur, ou l'exportation des grains, seroit presque inutile. Elle doit être regardée comme un supplément ou comme un remède au manque de population pour l'article de la culture, et comme un véhicule de commerce pour soutenir l'agriculture, et favoriser la population. Mais ce n'est pas l'accroissement de la population, qui est le vrai secret de l'Administration ; c'est l'harmonie de toutes les parties, et l'équilibre de toutes les classes."*]

APPENDIX II.—To B. II. Ch. ii.

Notes on the [Parliamentary] Bullion Report.

(*Sent by Mr. Stewart to Lord Lauderdale, in February, March, and April,* 1811.)

NOTE I.

(*Feb.* 26,) *Bullion Report*, p. 7.—" The same rise of the market price of gold above its mint price will take place, if the local currency of this particular country, being no longer convertible into gold, should at any time be issued to excess. That excess cannot be exported to other countries, and not being convertible into specie, it is not necessarily returned upon those who issued it ; *it remains in the channel of circulation, and is gradually absorbed by increasing the prices of all commodities.* An increase in the quantity of the local currency of a particular country, will raise prices in that country, exactly in the same manner as an increase in the general supply of precious metals raises prices all over the world."

This reasoning is qualified and restricted in another part of the Report, by some just observations upon the effects of a quick or slow circulation, in augmenting or diminishing the powers of money as a medium of exchange, (see page 26 ;) but very little use is made, in the general argument, of these important and indeed essential limitations ; and they seem to have been still less attended to in some of the best pamphlets which have lately appeared on the same subject. " If the currency of a country," says Mr. Blake, " is increased, while the commodities to be circulated by it remain the same, the currency will be diminished in value with respect to the commodities, and it will require a larger proportion of the former to purchase a given quantity of the latter ; or, in other words, prices will rise. If we were in the habit of considering money as purchased by commodities, instead of commodities being purchased by money, the diminution in the value of money from its abundance would be immediately apparent."—" Mr. Thornton admits, in the most explicit manner, that if the quantity of circulating medium is permanently augmented, without a corresponding augmentation of internal trade, a rise will invariably take place in the price of exchangeable articles. Indeed, this is a principle upon which all the writers on Commerce, both practical and speculative, are agreed ; they have thought it so undeniable as to require no particular illustration, and have rather assumed it as an obvious truth than as a proposition that depended on inference. Upon this idea is founded Mr. Hume's well-known argument against Banks, and it is equally implied in Dr. Smith's confutation of that objection ; it forms the foundation of those presumptions from which Mr. Boyd has

* [PINTO, *Traité de la Circulation et du Crédit*, Amst. 1771. Partie iv. p. 221, *seq.*]

lately inferred an improper increase of Bank of England paper; and it is implicitly admitted likewise by Mr. Thornton, one great object of whose book is to persuade the public that there has been no such increase."[1]—" Without entering, therefore," continues Mr. Blake, "into an unnecessary argument, I shall, for the present, assume as admitted, that the increase of currency, while the commodities to be circulated remain the same, will be attended with an increase of nominal prices, and a correspondent depreciation in the value of money."[2]

That there is a great deal of truth in this doctrine, when properly explained and modified, I do not deny; but it is surely not entitled to be assumed as a political axiom; nor is it even correctly true in the form in which it is here stated. It is, in fact, the very same doctrine with respect to prices, which was advanced by Locke, Montesquieu, and Hume; and which Sir James Steuart has, I think, refuted by very satisfactory (though very ill expressed) arguments, in his *Political Œconomy*. (Book II. chap. xxviii.) The only difference is, that whereas Locke and Montesquieu assert that the prices of commodities are always *proportioned* to the plenty of money in a country, the authors referred to in the foregoing extract, (with the exception of Mr. Hume,) content themselves with saying, that "the *increase* of currency, while the commodities to be circulated remain the same, will be attended with an *increase* of nominal prices."

That the principle, even when thus corrected, does not appear altogether self-evident, is shewn sufficiently from what was already hinted concerning the effects which may be produced by a change in the *rate* of circulation. Bishop Berkeley long ago proposed it as a Query,—" Whether *less* money swiftly circulating be not, in effect, equivalent to *more* money slowly circulating; and whether, if the circulation be reciprocally as the quantity of coin, the nation can be a loser?"[*] It is, at least, a *possible* case then, in theory, that, on the one hand, an increase in the quantity of money may be so counterbalanced by a decrease in the rate of circulation, as to leave the relation between money and commodities the same as before; and that, on the other hand, the quantity of money may remain unaltered, (nay, may suffer a great diminution,) while in consequence of an accelerated circulation, its influence upon prices, and upon everything else, may be increased in any given ratio. In general, before we draw any inferences from the mere increase of currency, it is as necessary to ascertain the fact, whether its circulation be likely to be, on the whole, accelerated or retarded, as it is, in computing the *momentum* of a moving body, to combine the velocity of its motion with the quantity of its matter.

---

[1] *Edinburgh Review*, Vol. I. p. 178.

[2] Blake's *Observations*, &c., p. 44.—To the same purpose it is observed by Mr. Huskisson, that "although a general increase of prices in all the ordinary commodities of any country is not, in itself, an indication of the depreciation of its currency, (it being always possible that such an effect may arise from other causes;) yet this general increase of prices *could not fail* to be produced by an increase of the precious metals."
—[*Question on the Currency*, &c.,] pp. 24, 25.

" If the circulation of any country were performed exclusively by gold, and the supply of that metal were, from any imaginable cause doubled, whilst the quantity of gold and the demand for it should continue the same in all ordinary parts of the world, the price of gold in such a country would be diminished. This diminution of the price of gold would appear in the *proportionate* rise of all commodities."—[*Ibid.*] pp. 26, 27.

[*] [*Querist*, No. 22.—*Vide supra*, pp. 378, 379.]

An examination of the circumstances by which the circulation of money is liable to be affected, appears to me to be still a *desideratum* in the theory of commerce. Mr. Thornton has touched slightly on the subject in his book on *Paper Credit;* but his reasoning is not at all convincing to my mind. "The causes," he observes, "which lead to a variation in the rapidity of the circulation of bank-notes may be several. *In general, it may be observed, that a high state of confidence serves to quicken their circulation; and this happens upon a principle which shall be fully explained.* It must be premised that, by the phrase, a more or less quick circulation of notes, will be meant a more or less quick circulation of the whole of them on an average. Whatever increases that reserve, for instance, of Bank of England notes which remains in the drawer of the London banker, as his provision against contingencies, contributes to what will here be termed the less quick circulation of the whole. Now a high state of confidence contributes to make men provide less amply against contingencies. At such a time, they trust, that if a demand upon them for a payment, which is now doubtful and contingent, should actually be made, they will be able to provide for it at the moment; and they are loath to be at the expense of selling an article, or of getting a bill discounted, in order to make the provision much before the period at which it shall be wanted. When, on the contrary, a season of distrust arises, prudence suggests that the loss of interest arising from a detention of notes for a few additional days should not be regarded."[1]

Agreeably to the same view of the subject, it is observed in the *Bullion Report,* as a proof, that "the effective currency of the country depends upon the quickness of circulation, as well as upon its numerical amount," that "a much smaller amount is required in a high state of public credit, than when alarms make individuals call in their advances, and provide against accidents by hoarding; and in a period of commercial security and private confidence, than when mutual distrust discourages pecuniary arrrangements for any distant time."—(P. 26.)

In both of these passages, there appears to me to be an indistinctness of thought as well as of expression. In the *first* place, I have great doubts of the correctness of the assertion, "that a high state of confidence seems to quicken the circulation of bank notes." A rapid circulation of money, it must be observed, is by no means implied in that briskness and activity of commerce which is measured by the number of commercial exchanges, and which is sometimes, but very inaccurately, called *the circulation of commodities.* The manufacturer may supply the merchant, the merchant the shopkeeper, and the shopkeeper his customers, without the intervention of any money, till it come out of the pockets of the consumers; the place of money being supplied, during the previous process, by the mutual credit of the parties: and it is evident, that in proportion to the quickness of the process, and to the high state of confidence at the time, the employment of money will be the less necessary. If the rapidity of circulation be, at such a period, increased *on the whole,* it is not because the money passes more rapidly than before through the same number of hands, but because the multiplication of hands which have now acquired by their industry the means of partaking in the national opulence, has enlarged the circle in which its movements are performed.

But, *secondly,* admitting Mr. Thornton's general assertion to be true, I do not

[1] *Inquiry into the Nature and Effects of the Paper Credit of Great Britain,* Chap. III. p. 47, seq.

see that the reasoning either in his Book or the Report, affords any explanation of the fact. The notes which, during a period of alarm, are kept in the drawers of bankers and others, as a provision against contingencies, cannot surely be said with propriety to have *their circulation retarded*. They are abstracted from circulation altogether; and if the same demand for a circulating medium continues as formerly, the notes which remain to supply this demand cannot fail, in proportion to the reduction in their amount, to pass with an accelerated rapidity from one hand to another. The truth is, if I do not deceive myself, that in both the passages last quoted, two very different things are confounded together:—1. The effect of credit and confidence in superseding the necessity of ready money payments, by a settlement of accounts at distant periods of time; and, 2. The effect of a quick circulation in rendering a given quantity of currency equivalent to a larger one with a slow circulation. Both of them have a tendency to economize the numerical amount of currency; but they depend on very different causes, and are by no means necessarily combined in their operation.

It is justly remarked in a passage which you have quoted from Quesnai in your pamphlet on the Irish Bank, that "the money of a poor nation must be proportionally more considerable than that of a rich one; for no more can remain with either, than the sum of which they have need for their sales and for their purchases. Now, among poor nations the intervention of money becomes indispensably necessary in the operations of commerce. Everything must there be paid for in ready cash; because no one can there rely on the good faith of another." The same observation is applicable to a rich commercial country, in times of distrust and alarm; and explains sufficiently the increased demand which arises for a circulating medium at such a crisis. A circulation of money or paper *then* takes place, in numberless cases, where its intervention was before superseded by general confidence and credit. As to the *rapidity* of circulation, I cannot help thinking, that a general want of confidence must tend powerfully to *increase* it, by adding to the number of ready money payments; and, in so far as this takes place, it must necessarily (by the virtual multiplication of the currency) counteract the pressure of the existing evil. From the Statement of the Committee, they seem to consider the increased demand for notes in a time of distrust, as a consequence of the circulation being slower than usual.

The aim of the reasoning quoted above from Mr. Thornton's book, was probably to suggest, as an indirect apology for the increased issue of notes from the Bank, that the effect of this increased issue is partly to correct the inconveniences of that retarded circulation which he supposed to exist. If the foregoing remarks have any foundation, the effect of this increased issue upon prices, must, in fact, exceed that of its numerical amount, in the same proportion in which the rate of circulation has been quickened by the peculiar circumstances of the times.

It is to be observed, besides, that the most considerable part of the increase of Bank of England notes since 1798, has been in the article of small notes, (*Report*, p. 25;) and there cannot be a doubt that the case has been the same in a far greater degree with the issues of country banks, although no estimate is given by the Committee of the increased circulation of *their* notes, not exceeding two pounds two shillings. (P. 29; see also p. 149.) Now, it is chiefly in the case of *small notes* that circulation operates in producing a virtual multiplication of paper currency·

for the same reason that "a shilling," according to an observation of Mr. Smith, "changes masters more frequently than a guinea, and a halfpenny more frequently than a shilling."* In reply to a question addressed by the Committee to Mr. Francis Baring—("Do you not believe that the amount of small notes should be left out of the account in comparing the present amount of notes in circulation with that existing before the restriction?") I find the following answer stated in the *Report:*—"Instead of being left out in a comparative view, I fear the small notes *rather tend to increase the difficulty beyond their due proportion;* because they cannot be withdrawn, without an issue of specie to an equal amount, and stand therefore in the front of the battle." I am inclined to think he might also have added, that they tend to increase the difficulty *beyond their due proportion,* inasmuch as their *commercial momentum* (if I may be allowed the expression) is increased in an incomparably greater degree than that of the larger notes, by the rapidity of circulation.

In farther illustration of the proposition, "that the mere numerical return of the amount of bank-notes out in circulation, cannot be considered as at all deciding the question, whether such paper is or is not excessive,"—it is stated in the *Report,* as a circumstance which *above all* deserves attention, that "the same amount of currency will be more or less adequate, in proportion to the skill which the great money-dealers possess in managing and economizing the use of the circulating medium. Your Committee (it is added) are of opinion, that *the improvements* which have taken place of late years in this country, and particularly in the district of London, with regard to the use and economy of money among bankers, and in the mode of adjusting commercial payments, must have had a much greater effect than is commonly ascribed to them, in rendering the same sum adequate to a much greater amount of trade and payments than formerly."—(P. 26; see also p. 147.)

Upon the supposition that the issues of the bank had been *diminished* precisely to the extent of this economy, it seems evident, that the circulation of the country, so far as it can be supposed to have any influence upon *prices,* could not have been at all affected by these *late improvements.* The bank-notes formerly employed in conducting this business, were found, it would appear, to be a clumsy and expensive instrument for accomplishing an end that could be attained as effectually without its assistance ; and this being the case, the new arrangements were unquestionably *improvements in point of economy* to the London bankers. With respect to the general circulation of the country, the effect in both cases must have been exactly the same.

On the other hand, as, in point of fact, the issues of the bank have increased immensely since these economical arrangements have taken place, the amount of the notes thus economized must either be added to the mass of circulating medium which is employed in carrying on the exchanges of the London district, or must serve to enlarge the basis on which the circulation of the country banks is to be reared. The effect must be similar to those other improvements which (according to the *Report*) "have taken place in this country, with regard to the use and economy of money among bankers, and in the mode of adjusting commercial payments."

* [*Wealth of Nations,* Book II. chap. ii.; Vol. I. p. 486, tenth edition.]

It is also worthy of observation, that this economy is confined to the *larger* notes, and that, in the same proportion, the means are acquired of increasing the issues of the *small* ones.

In what I have hitherto said, I have proceeded on the general principle assumed in the *Report*, "That every change in the *effective currency* of the country, (including under this phrase the *quickness of its circulation*, as well as *its numerical amount*,) must occasion a corresponding change in the price of commodities;" and the result of the whole is, that the operation of the cause must, upon this supposition, have been incomparably greater than the mere numerical amount would lead us to apprehend. I must, however, confess, that I can see no evidence whatever for the truth of this doctrine; and if you think it worth your while to read my observations on the subject, I shall state in another letter the grounds of my doubts. In the meantime, I shall only add, that I am perfectly satisfied with the *conclusion* of the Committee, that the increased issues of bank-notes *have* occasioned a depreciation of our currency, or, in other words, a general rise of prices. I differ from them only in the *manner* in which I conceive this depreciation to have been brought about. According to their view of the subject, the effect is represented as resulting from the cause, no less immediately and obviously than a fall in the exchangeable value of wheat after an abundant harvest; or, if any explanation is hinted at, it is by means of some metaphorical phrase, which only serves to throw the difficulty a little more into the shade. "The issues of the bank," we are told, "cannot be exported to other countries, and not being convertible into specie, it is not necessarily returned upon those who issued it; it remains in *the channel of circulation*, and is gradually *absorbed* by increasing the prices of all commodities."[1] To me it appears, that without attending particularly to the various modes in which the additional currency enters into circulation, (whether issued by the Bank of England in advances to Government, and in discounts to merchants, or by country banks in discounts to traders, to farmers, and to other classes of the community,) and following it out through the various steps of its progress, till it finds its way into the pockets of those who are to employ it in consumption, it is neither possible to form a precise idea of the nature of the disorder, nor to speculate safely concerning the means by which it may be alleviated.

The omission of this preliminary discussion strikes me as the most important defect in the *Report*. Something approaching to it is attempted by Mr. Blake in his pamphlet, and the outline which he has sketched is very distinct and satisfactory, as far as it goes.[2] It is only surprising that a writer, to whom this view of the subject had presented itself, did not assume, *as the foundation of his general argument*, this explanation of *the process* by which the over-issues of the bank tend to augment the prices of commodities, instead of having recourse to the very vague and incorrect principle, "that it is impossible such an increase should have taken place in the quantity of *any commodity* that is given in exchange for *others*, whose quantity is not augmented in the same proportion without affecting their comparative value."[3] This misapplication of the word *commodity* to bank-notes, is not peculiar to Mr. Blake,[4] and it is extremely apt to mislead a careless reader.

[1] *Report*, p. 7.

[3] [*Observations*, &c.] pp. 78-83.

[2] Ibid. p. 44.

[4] " It is generally admitted, that the value of a *commodity* depends greatly on i s scarcity or

It is not even, in my opinion, accurately applied to gold and silver *while in the shape of coins*, were it for no other reason than this, (and I apprehend there are several others no less conclusive,) that *commodities* cannot, like *coins*, be virtually multiplied by circulation. The essential difference between such coins and paper currency is, that the former are at all times *convertible into a commodity*, by being put into a crucible, serving, in their new form of bullion, to liquidate the accounts of different nations, and to furnish a link for connecting together the commercial transactions of mankind in every quarter of the globe.

Note II.

[*March.*]—In my former paper, I took notice of the general principle which seems to me to be assumed in the *Bullion Report*, "That every change, &c.—(*Supra*, p. 436.) I intended to have stated, at some length, my doubts about the correctness of this proposition, but shall confine myself at present to one or two of the most obvious objections to which it is liable.

1. It may, I think, be now assumed as a first principle, that the mere increase of gold and silver in a country does not necessarily raise prices. The reasonings of Sir James Steuart on this head appear quite decisive, and could not have failed to have made a greater impression on the public mind, if they had been expressed with the clearness and precision of Mr. Hume or Mr. Smith. Now, if this principle be once granted, it necessarily follows, that prices are not regulated solely by the amount of currency, *even when combined with the rate of its circulation.* In proof of this, it is sufficient to observe, that an accelerated circulation operates entirely by the *virtual* multiplication of the currency; and therefore, whatever effect may result from this acceleration, might have been produced by a *real* multiplication of the currency, the rate of circulation remaining the same as before.

In speculating concerning prices, the *quickness of circulation* deserves our attention, only in so far as it may be supposed to afford a proof of the general diffusion of the currency through the great mass of consumers. But of this last fact, a quick circulation, considered singly, by no means furnishes unequivocal evidence, as the money may, in consequence of various causes, pass more rapidly from hand to hand, while it still moves in the same circle as before; and even where the two circumstances, of an accelerated and of an extended circulation, happen to coincide, the effects on price are evidently to be ascribed, *not* to the quick circulation, but to the multiplication and competition of purchasers. The quick circulation is itself, in this case, only a collateral *effect* of that general diffusion of wealth upon which, much more than on the quantity of currency in the country, the prices of commodities will be found to depend. Indeed, neither the one nor the other (nor any other cause whatsoever,) can possibly raise the price of any article, but by first increasing the competition of purchasers in a greater proportion than the quantity of goods which the market supplies.

2. Another proof that "the *momentum* of the circulating medium does not of

plenty. Now, there has been, within these twelve years, a remarkable increase in our amount of bank-notes," &c.—Mushet, *Inquiry into the Effects on Currency, &c.*] p. 20.

itself regulate prices," may be collected from the effects of CREDIT in supplying to those individuals who possess it, for all essential purposes, the place of ready money. A man whose credit is good, or, in other words, who is known to possess valuable property at his own disposal, may command, at all times, what commodities he pleases, though he should happen, at the moment, to have neither a guinea nor a bank-note in his pocket. The only inconvenience he will suffer from his want of ready money is, that he will be obliged to pay a proportionally higher price for what he purchases ; and, consequently, where there is a competition of such purchasers, a scarcity of circulating medium, instead of *lowering* prices, will infallibly tend to *increase* them.

From these principles it follows, that no fixed proportion can exist between the quantity of currency in a country and the amount of commercial exchanges to which it is subservient, inasmuch as this proportion must vary, not only with the rate of circulation, but with the degree of credit and confidence generally prevalent, and with the skill of bankers and merchants in economizing the use of money in their mutual dealings. Nor would the problem be of much use if it could be solved; for none of these circumstances has any direct connexion with the high or low prices of commodities. Indeed, *credit*, under whatever form it may appear, must always tend to raise prices, *at least as high*, as the money would have done, whose place it supplies.[1]

In illustration of this, I shall avail myself of a passage in Pinto's *Traité de la Circulation et du Crédit*, which I shall transcribe at length, as you are not likely to have the book at hand :—" La circulation réelle de la monnoie est prodigieuse dans la dépense ournalière et domestique qu'on appelle négoce ; le même écu peut *cascader* en 24 heures, par cinquante mains différentes, et aura représenté cinquante choses par la circulation qu'il a essuyée ; si donc ces cinquante personnes s'assembloient la nuit, elles trouveroient avoir dépensé et payé 50 ecus, et il n'y en a eu cependant qu'un d'effectif, qui par la circulation en représente cinquante. On n'a qu'à observer, qu'il n'y a pas dans tout l'univers la moitié de l'argent à quoi se monte la dépense qu'on fait en un an dans la seule ville de Paris, si l'on comptoit tout l'état de dépense qu'on fait, et qui se paie en argent, depuis le 1 Janvier jusqu'au dernier Décembre, dans tous les ordres de l'état, depuis la maison du roi, jusqu'aux mendians qui consomment un sol de pain par jour.

" Cette circulation est immense par la multiplicité des operations simultanées et répétées partout et à chaque moment ; mais il y a une autre circulation en gros, qu'on fait à la faveur du crédit, et du papier, qui représente l'argent, comme l'argent représente les choses. L'exemple de l'écu fait voir qu'un négociant particulier, qui a du crédit, peut, indépendamment des termes qu'on lui accorde pour les paiemens de ses achats, faire circuler son papier et se prévaloir de celui des autres, et multiplier par-là les ressorts de son commerce, en facilitant la circulation. Une lettre de change a souvent dix endossemens, et représente souvent la même

---

[1] The effect of credit in supplying the place of a circulating medium, and that of mercantile skill in economizing the use of it, (which last is, at bottom, nothing more than a more ingenious and refined extension of the same substitute,) have been remarked by Thornton, and various other late writers; but none of them appear to me to have been aware, that whatever effects are produced by a circulating medium on prices, must be equally produced by every possible expedient which can be devised to keep accounts between debtor and creditor, without its intervention.

valeur à dix personnes différentes. Voilà des choses importantes; quoiqu'assez connues, elles ne méritent pas le nom de triviales." *

In a note to this passage, the following anecdote is mentioned by the author:— "Pendant le Siège de Tournay en 1745," &c.†

This fact, which is adduced by Pinto merely to shew that a small sum with a quick circulation may be virtually equivalent to a large sum with a slow circulation, leads to some other consequences no less important, by placing in a strong light the effects of credit in facilitating the operations of commerce, where there is an apparent deficiency in the circulating medium. The paymaster, by borrowing 7000 florins seven times over from the sutlers, borrowed, during the course of the siege, to the amount of 49,000 florins. Supposing that there had been no specie to be had in the garrison, it is evident that the same transactions might have been carried on by means of paper money issued by the paymaster, and accepted in payment by the sutlers; and therefore the only use of these weekly loans was to keep the garrison in good humour, by the regular handling of their pay in that currency to which they were accustomed. Or, supposing the sutlers to have given credit to every soldier to the extent of his pay, and that accurate accounts had been kept of all their mutual dealings, might not the whole business have been managed (without any inconvenience whatever but the trouble arising from the petty details of book-keeping) without any circulating medium at all? In such a peculiar combination of circumstances as this, the only essential advantage derived from a circulating medium (whether we suppose it to consist of specie or of paper) would seem to resolve into its effect in superseding the task of recording the mutual bargains of individuals; or (as Anacharsis concluded somewhat too precipitately with respect to the use of gold and silver among the Greeks) a circulating medium would seem to answer no purpose whatever, but that " of assisting the memory in numeration and arithmetic." Mr. Hume, when he wrote his *Essay on Money*, seems to have thought that the case would be the same with a nation cut off from all commercial connexion with foreigners; overlooking a variety of important considerations, which I shall pass over here, as they have no immediate connexion with the present argument. Whatever opinion we may form on this point, one thing seems indisputable, that in the example of the garrison as described by Pinto, the amount of circulating medium could have no effect whatever *on prices;* that there would have been exactly the same with a circulation of 7000 florins as with one of 49,000—and that (supposing credit to be completely established among all parties) they would not have fallen, although no circulating medium had been employed as an instrument of commerce.

I have thus arrived at the same conclusion which you state in your last letter, when you express your doubts whether " a mere excess of *circulating medium, if it confined itself to those duties which a circulating medium properly performs*, could produce a rise of prices." For my own part, I am disposed to go a step farther, and to entertain some doubts, whether a general rise of prices would be necessarily produced by this superabundant currency, even on the supposition that it consisted wholly of gold and silver, so as to form (according to Mr. Smith) a real addition to the national capital. Mr. Hume, in his *Essay upon Interest*, states an imaginary case, that " by miracle, every man in Great Britain should have five pounds

* [Partie I. p. 33, *seq.*, orig. edit.]   † [Quoted above, p. 375.]

slipt into his pocket in one night, in which case," he adds, " the whole money that is at present in the kingdom would be much more than doubled :" and he observes very justly, that in these circumstances "there would not next day, nor for some time, be any more lenders, nor any variation in *the interest*." The next sentence is not so unexceptionable. " Were there nothing but landlords and peasants in the state, this money, however abundant, could never gather into sums ; and *would only serve to increase the prices of everything*, without any farther consequence." In what proportion it would serve to increase prices, Mr. Hume has not said explicitly ; but it is evident, that upon the principle which he has assumed in his *Essay on Money*, (and which is unfolded still more fully by Locke and Montesquieu,) it ought to do much more than *double* the prices of all the commodities in the kingdom. The palpable absurdity of the conclusion, in this instance, affords a sufficient refutation of the premises from which it is deduced. The real fact would manifestly amount to this, and to nothing more, that every man would be enabled to add five pounds to his capital or to his expenditure. What possible effect could this have on the prices of any commodities, but those which are in request among the lowest order of the people ? Nor is it easy to conceive, that even on these prices, the permanent effect would be very considerable. How different would be the influence of the same addition to the capital (either real or fictitious) of the country, if it were all to issue from the shops of bankers in the form of advances to Government, or of discounts to merchants, manufacturers, farmers, and landed proprietors!

It would appear, therefore, that it is not the quantity of money added, at any time, to the capital of a country, which can, of itself, produce a general rise of prices ; unless this accession of capital is determined by political or commercial arrangements, to flow in those channels which may alter the former relation between the demand and supply of the market. According to Montesquieu's doctrine, the prices of all commodities should not only rise, but *all of them* should rise in the very same proportion ; in contradiction to the evidence of our daily experience, that while the prices of certain articles are rising, those of others are falling, in consequence of causes which have no connexion whatever either with the quantity of money, or with the quantity of commodities.

What you afterwards remark on the indirect connexion between high prices and an increased circulating medium, is precisely the proposition I had in my mind when I said formerly, that the extraordinary issues of paper currency since the stoppage of cash payments, had affected prices chiefly *by the manner* in which these notes have entered into circulation. Nothing, in my opinion, can be more satisfactory on this head than the simple statement you have given of *the fact*. "*By the same act* with which a bank increases the circulating medium of a country, it issues into the community a mass of fictitious capital, which serves not only as circulating medium, but creates an additional quantity of capital to be employed in every mode in which capital can be employed." The explanation you have given of the process by which this affects the prices of commodities, coincides so exactly with all my own ideas, that it would be quite superfluous for me to follow out the speculation any farther.

The radical evil, in short, seems to be, not the mere over issue of notes, considered as an addition to our currency, but the anomalous and unchecked extension of *credit*, and its inevitable effect in producing a sudden augmentation of prices by a sudden augmentation of demand. The enlarged issues deserve attention, chiefly as affording a scale for measuring how far this extension has been carried. The same degree of credit, if it could have been given without the intervention of paper currency, would have operated exactly in the same way upon prices, and upon everything else.

Mr. Thornton's opinion is plainly in direct opposition to this conclusion, and can, I think, be accounted for only by the credit which he has unconsciously lent, on various occasions, to the specious but fallacious theory of Montesquieu and Hume. "It is by the amount," he observes, "*not* of the loans of the Bank of England, but of its paper; or, if of its loans, of these merely as indicating the quantity of its paper, that we are to estimate the influence on the cost of commodities. The same remark," he adds, "may be applied to the subject of the loans and paper of country banks."[1] The converse of these propositions would, in my apprehension, be much nearer to the truth.

An idea similar to that which Mr. Thornton has here expressed, seems plainly to be implied in the explanation given by the Bullion Committee, of the difference between "the effects of an advance of capital to merchants, and an additional supply of currency to the general mass of circulating medium. "If the advance of capital only be considered, as made to those who are ready to employ it in judicious and productive undertakings, it is evident there need be no other limit to the total amount of advances than what the means of the lender, and his prudence in the selection of borrowers, may impose. But, in the present situation of the bank, intrusted as it is with the function of supplying the public with that paper currency which forms the basis of our circulation, and at the same time not subjected to the liability of converting the paper into specie, every advance which it makes of capital to the merchants in the shape of discount, becomes an addition also to the mass of circulating medium. In the first instance, when the advance is made by notes paid in discount by a bill, it is undoubtedly so much capital, so much power of making purchases, placed in the hands of the merchant who receives the notes; and if those hands are safe, the operation is so far, and in this its first step, useful and productive to the public. But as soon as the portion of circulating medium in which the advance was thus made, performs in the hands of him to whom it was advanced this its first operation as capital, as soon as the notes are exchanged by him for some other article which is capital, they fall into the channel of circulation as so much circulating medium, and form an addition to the mass of currency. The necessary effect of every such addition to the mass is to diminish the relative value of any given portion of that mass in exchange for commodities."*

The very same doctrine occurs in a different form in the following passage of Mr. Huskisson's pamphlet :—"The state of our currency, in regard to its diminished value, is no other than it would be if our present circulation, being retained to the same amount, were, by some sudden spell, all changed to gold, and, by

---

[1] The illustration which Mr. Thornton has given of this remark, affords a most satisfactory refutation of the opinion which it is employed to establish. (Pp. 313, 314.)

It is difficult to reconcile the above passage with the very judicious observations which Mr. T. has made in pp. 258-260 of the same book.

* [*Report*, p. 23.]

another spell, not less surprising, such part of that gold, as by its excess created a proportionate diminution in its value here, with reference to its value in other countries, would not by exportation, or otherwise, find its way out of our separate circulation."[1] The *simile* is quite correct, so far as it goes; but in order to render the parallel complete, Mr. Huskisson should have added, as *a third spell*, not less indispensably necessary than the two others: That all the issues of gold should be confined to the shops of our bankers, to be put in circulation by them in the shape of advances to Government, or of mercantile discounts; and that our bankers should have the same profits in issuing gold, as they have at present in the issues of their own paper. If the gold were all to emanate from the same sources as the paper, and to flow afterwards in the same channels, the results in both cases could not fail to be precisely the same.

NOTE III.

The general result of the reasonings which I have hitherto stated is, that the increased issues of paper currency since the year 1797, have operated on the prices of commodities chiefly by means of that sudden extension of *credit* which they necessarily suppose; and of the communication of this credit to those classes of individuals whose capitals have the greatest influence on the state of the market. Had the increased issues been divided into equal shares, according to the population of Great Britain, and had every inhabitant of the island received his trifling *quota* at one and the same instant, how comparatively insignificant would the effects have been!

This conclusion agrees, I think, perfectly in substance with that which you have formed, when you observe, in your last letter, that "by the same act with which a bank increases the circulating medium of a country, it issues into the community a mass of fictitious capital, which serves not only as circulating medium, but creates an additional quantity of capital to be employed in every mode in which capital can be employed." My own statement, however, appears to me to have this advantage, that it comprehends not only those mercantile discounts which have a *remote* effect on the market by being employed as capital, but those discounts which affect the market *immediately*, by furnishing the means of an enlarged expenditure. It is worthy of attention too, that even mercantile discounts operate on the market in the latter way as well as in the former; it being presumable, that every merchant (and more particularly, every speculative merchant) will raise his style of living in proportion to the magnitude of his commercial transactions. The same luxury and vanity extend themselves downwards through all the inferior orders of traders and men of business; the peculiar circumstances of the times having been so long unfavourable to habits of sober economy, and having so strong a tendency to encourage a general spirit of extravagance and improvidence, by facilitating the means of its indulgence. Hence, to those persons who live on fixed incomes, an additional sort of depreciation in the value of money, (a depreciation quite distinct from the effects either of taxation or of high prices;) I

[1] *The Question Concerning the Depreciation of our Currency Stated and Examined*, p. 107 note.

mean *that* which arises from new ideas of competency, and of the scale of expenditure necessary to support the condition of a gentleman.

I have dwelt the longer on this particular view of the subject, considered in contrast with that adopted by Mr. Thornton, (and apparently sanctioned in the last passage quoted from the *Bullion Report*,) because the two opinions lead obviously to two very different conclusions concerning the nature of the remedy suited to the disorder. The one opinion suggests the propriety of limiting credit through the medium of a restricted currency; the other of limiting the currency through the medium of a well-regulated and discriminating credit. If the radical evil were merely an excess of circulating medium, operating as such without the combination of any other cause, it would follow, that a reduction of this quantity, by whatsoever means it were to be brought about, and however violent the effects which it might threaten, would be the only measure competent to the attainment of the end. But if, on the other hand, this excess be only symptomatic of another malady, with which, from particular circumstances, it happens to be co-existent, (of an extension of credit, to wit, calculated to derange the pre-existing relations of demand and supply;) in that case, the restriction and *regulation* of this credit ought to be regarded as the primary object, and the reduction of our circulating medium attended to solely as an indication that the cure is progressive.

Of the most expedient means to be employed for this purpose, I am not qualified to form a judgment. But I cannot help observing, that if a repeal or a relaxation of the anti-usurious laws were a thing not quite impracticable, it would go to the root of the mischief by a process more effectual, and at the same time more gentle and manageable in its operation, than any other that I can imagine. It is observed in the *Bullion Report*, that "the law which in this country limits the rate of interest, and of course the rate at which the bank can legally discount, exposes the bank to still more extensive demands for commercial discounts. While the rate of commercial profit is very considerably higher than five per cent., as it has lately been in many branches of our foreign trade, there is in fact no limit to the demands which merchants of perfectly good capital, and of the most prudent spirit of enterprise, may be tempted to make upon the bank for accommodation and facilities by discount."*

To the same purpose, Mr. Thornton long ago remarked, that " in order to ascertain how far the desire of obtaining loans at the bank may be expected at any time to be carried, we must inquire into the subject of the quantum of profit likely to be derived from borrowing there under the existing circumstances. This is to be judged of by considering two points: the amount, first, of interest to be paid on the sum borrowed; and, secondly, of the mercantile or other gain to be obtained by the employment of the borrowed capital. The gain which can be acquired by the means of commerce, is commonly the highest which can be had; and it also regulates in a great measure, the rate in all other cases. We may, therefore, consider this question as turning principally on a comparison of the rate of interest taken at the bank with the current rate of mercantile profit.

" The bank is prohibited, by the state of the law, from demanding, even in time of war, an interest of more than five per cent., which is the same rate at which it discounts in a period of profound peace. It might, undoubtedly, at all seasons,

* P. 23.

sufficiently limit its paper by means of the price at which it lends, if the legislature did not interpose an obstacle to the constant adoption of this principle of restriction.

"Any supposition that it would be safe to permit the bank paper to limit itself, because this would be to take the more *natural* course, is, therefore, altogether erroneous. It implies that there is no occasion to advert to the rate of interest in consideration of which the bank paper is furnished, or to change that rate according to the varying circumstances of the country.

"At some seasons an interest, perhaps, of six per cent. per annum, at others of five, or even of four per cent., may afford that degree of advantage to borrowers which shall be about sufficient to limit, in the due measure, the demand upon the bank for discounts. Experience in some measure proves the justice of this observation; for, in time of peace, the bank has found it easy to confine its paper, by demanding five per cent. for interest; whereas, in war, the directors have been subject, as I apprehend, to very earnest solicitations for discount, their notes, nevertheless, not being particularly diminished. It is, therefore, unreasonable to presume that there will always be a disposition in the borrowers at the bank to prescribe to themselves exactly those bounds which a regard to the safety of the bank would suggest. The interest of the two parties is not the same in this respect. The borrowers, in consequence of that artificial state of things which is produced by the law against usury, obtain their loans too cheap. That which they obtain too cheap, they demand in too great quantity."[1]

I had written thus far, when the *Edinburgh Review* for February was put into my hands. It contains a pretty long article on the Depreciation of Paper Currency, including remarks on the chief pamphlets which have lately appeared on the subject. I have only had time, as yet, to read four or five of the first paragraphs, in one of which there is a passage which surprised me a good deal by the looseness of the statement, both in point of thought and of expression. "Mr. Ricardo is in our opinion particularly entitled to praise for the manner in which he has laid down two most important doctrines,—long known, indeed, and acknowledged by those who have maturely considered these subjects, but not unfrequently overlooked by others.

"The first is the grand doctrine, which may be said to be the main hinge on which the principles of circulation, whether consisting of a paper currency, or of the precious metals, must necessarily turn;—the doctrine, that every kind of circulating medium, as well as every other kind of commodity, is necessarily depreciated by excess, and raised in value by deficiency, compared with the demand, without reference either to confidence or intrinsic use. This doctrine follows immediately from the general principles of supply and demand, which are unquestionably the foundation on which the whole superstructure of political economy is built."[2]

In justice to some propositions which I have already hazarded, I cannot pass over these magisterial remarks without examining the legitimacy of the inference mentioned in the last sentence. This will give me an opportunity of adding a few

[1] *Inquiry into the Nature and Effects of the Paper Credit of Great Britain*, Chap. I. pp. 267, 268.
[2] No. XXXIV. p. 341.

illustrations which escaped me formerly in the hurry of writing. But I find I must delay proceeding farther till another post.

Note IV.

I was afraid, that in the foregoing papers, I had dwelt much longer than was necessary on the refutation of acknowledged prejudices; but some remarks in the last *Edinburgh Review* convince me, that either my own ideas are completely unfounded, or that something is still wanting to place the question at issue in the proper point of view. The following is the passage which appears to me to be more particularly exceptionable. " Mr. Ricardo . . . . . is built." (Same as quoted in last page.)

I before objected to the application of the word *commodity* to paper currency, or even to the precious metals *while in the shape of coin;* for this obvious reason, that there is nothing in the commercial transferences of commodities which bears the most distant analogy to the virtual multiplication of a bank-note, or of a guinea, by means of a quick process of circulation. If there were any such analogy, the sutlers mentioned in the anecdote quoted above from Pinto, might, without the aid of a miracle, have multiplied at pleasure the number of loaves and fishes in their canteens, according to the wants of the garrison.

It is not unusual, indeed, among writers on Political Economy, to speak of the circulation of *commodities* or of *goods*, as well as of the circulation of *money;* but the expression is extremely vague and inaccurate, inasmuch as the word *circulation* must, in these two cases, be used in very different acceptations. In the following instance, Mr. Thornton appears to have departed very widely from his customary precision of language. "Montesquieu alludes, in a manner so imperfect, as to be scarcely intelligible, to those effects of the different degrees of rapidity, in the circulation both of money and of goods, which it has been one object of this work to explain. It is on the degree of rapidity of the circulation of each, combined with the consideration of quantity, and not on the quantity alone, that the value of the circulating medium of any country depends."[1] To this last sentence, I must own, I cannot annex any clear idea. Mr. Thornton has, indeed, explained more distinctly than any other English author I know, the effects of a quick circulation of *money;* but as to a quick circulation of *goods*, (if the word circulation be, in both instances, used in the same sense,) I am unable to form any conjecture concerning the meaning which he annexes to the phrase.

Nothing, I think, but this common misapplication of the word *commodity* to a *circulating medium* could have suggested the observation which occurs in the next sentence of the *Edinburgh Review*. "This doctrine follows immediately from the general principles of supply and demand, which are unquestionably the foundation on which the whole superstructure of Political Economy is built." Upon this sentence, accordingly, I must take the liberty of offering a few remarks; for, surely, if these principles have so weighty a fabric to support, we cannot be at too much pains to ascertain correctly, in what sense we ought to understand them.

And here I must observe, in the *first* place, that there are few, if any, political maxims, which admit, like the axioms in mathematics, of a literal and unqualified

[1] *Inquiry into the Nature and Effects of the Paper Credit of Great Britain*, Chap. xi. p. 307.

application in all imaginable combinations of circumstances. They are, in general, abbreviated, and consequently loose statements of important conclusions, adopted by their conciseness to serve as aids to the memory; but requiring, when they are assumed as principles of reasoning, the exercise of our own common sense, in supplying those indispensable conditions and exceptions, which are to be collected from their spirit rather than from their letter. That this observation applies forcibly to the maxim now before us, a few very slight hints will be sufficient to show.

Prior to the present discussions about paper currency, the *Corn Trade* had been, for a good many years, the favourite subject of speculation to Political Economists; and in *this* particular speculation, the *general principles of supply and demand* may, with great truth, be said to be the foundation on which all our reasonings must be built. The demand is here constant, universal, and imperious; and the supply, at the same time, such as must necessarily be brought to the market, within a period of no great extent, from the perishable nature of the commodity and the expense which it involves in the keeping. It is not, therefore, surprising, that the habitual use of the words *demand* and *supply*, in speaking of the *Corn Trade*, should have facilitated to hasty reasoners the extension of a similar conclusion to other branches of trade of a very different nature; and to which that conclusion cannot be fairly applied, without many modifications and restrictions. An obvious example of this occurs in the article of *wine*, which being kept at no expense, while it increases in value with its age, may, notwithstanding a moderate demand and an abundant supply, keep up its price for years, in defiance of the general maxim. Upon the whole, however, due allowance being made for obvious exceptions of this sort, the truth of the maxim may be safely admitted; provided always the demand, and the quantity destined for supplying it, be of such a nature as to be confined in their variations within that range which experience teaches us to allow for the possible fluctuations of the market. If the *supply* be inexhaustible, (as in the instance of water in this country,) the principle becomes altogether unmeaning; the commodity possessing, on that supposition, no exchangeable value whatever. Nor does it become less nugatory, if we suppose, on the other hand, the demand to be unlimited, as I apprehend, happens very remarkably with respect to *money, considered as a subject of property.* The demand for it (or, at least, for something *convertible* into it) is unbounded, and frequently increases in proportion to the abundance in which it is possessed. Political arithmeticians have employed themselves in attempting to ascertain the quantity of bread and of butcher's meat that individuals may be supposed to consume at an average; but who has ever thought of fixing a limit to the *auri sacra fames?* *In this respect, at least,* if we choose still to call money *a commodity,* we must allow it to be a commodity *sui generis;* and, therefore, not to be rashly subjected to those sweeping maxims which regulate the prices of wheat or of broad cloth.

"Crescit amor nummi, quantum ipsa pecunia crescit;
Et minus hanc optat, qui non habet."—[*Juvenalis*, V. xiv. 140.]

Another circumstance, which has given rise to this mistaken view of the subject, is a want of attention to the distinction between the *use* of money and the *property* of money. No man certainly would choose to *borrow* money beyond what he really wants, or what he can turn to profit; and, in proportion to the urgency of the demand, or the prospect of greater profit by the employment of it, he will be willing to give a higher interest. The natural and equitable rate of interest will be determined by the demand there is for borrowing, and the plenty there is to supply that demand; and hence it is, that in a country situated as Great Britain now is, (a country where a *maximum* for the rate of interest is fixed by law, and where the prospect of commercial profit is tempting to adventurers,) it is altogether absurd to suppose, as some respectable persons have done, that "the bank ought to regulate their issues by the public demand;"—"a principle," says Sir F. Baring, "which I consider as dangerous in the extreme, because I know by experience that the demand for speculation can only be limited by the want of means."—(*Report*, p. 133.) The inevitable consequence of this is, a general rise of prices, (or what amounts to the same thing,) a depreciation in the value of our circulating medium;—a *depreciation*, however, I must again repeat, which is not (like the fall in the price of wheat after a plentiful crop) the immediate or necessary consequence of mere superabundance, otherwise the same effect might have been produced (which it manifestly could not) by slipping a twenty shilling note into the pocket of every inhabitant of the kingdom. The *primary* cause of the depreciation is the artificial cheapness in the rate at which, in consequence of the laws against usury, the use of money may be obtained, combined with the security which the Bank enjoys, in yielding to the public demand, in consequence of the stoppage of cash payments. But these considerations do not belong to this part of my argument.

The authority of Mr. Smith's name (although he has expressed himself on this topic in very general terms) has probably contributed not a little to induce many persons to adopt, without a due examination, the doctrine which I have been endeavouring to refute. "The quantity," he observes, "of the precious metals may increase in any country from two different causes; either, first, from the increased abundance of the mines which supply it; or, secondly, from the increased wealth of the people, from the increased produce of their annual labour. The first of these causes is, no doubt, necessarily connected with the diminution of the value of the precious metals; but the second is not."[*]

On both these points, I must acknowledge, I am disposed to differ very considerably from Mr. Smith, (at least in the unqualified form in which he has here expressed his opinion,) but I shall confine myself at present to the *first clause* of his proposition. I shall send you afterwards, if you desire me to do so, the grounds of my doubts with respect to the second.

"It is a question with me," says Sir James Steuart, "whether the mines of Potosi and Brazil have produced more riches to Spain and Portugal within these two hundred years, than the treasures heaped up in Asia, Greece, and Egypt, after the death of Alexander, furnished to the Romans during the two hundred years which followed the defeat of Perseus and the conquest of Macedonia? From the treasures mentioned by all the historians who have written of the conquest of these kingdoms by the Romans, I do not think I am far from truth when I compare the treasures of the frugal Greeks to the mines of the New World."[†]

[*] [*Wealth of Nations*, Book I. chap. xi.; Vol. I. p. 294, tenth edition.]
[†] [*Political Œconomy*, Book II. chap xxx.; *Works*, Vol. II. p. 135, *seq.*]

Mr. Hume himself has said, that "money, after the conquest of Egypt, seems to have been nearly in as great plenty at Rome, as it is at present in the richest European kingdoms."*

It is, however, a fact, equally striking and indisputable, that while, in consequence of the later Romans, the prices of superfluities rose to an excessive height, those of necessaries kept astonishingly low. Of this, the most satisfactory evidence may be found in Arbuthnot's *Tables of Ancient Coins*, and in Wallace's *Dissertation on the Numbers of Mankind*.†

It will be said, that no inference whatever can be justly founded on any parallel between the statistical details of ancient and of modern times; and that the low prices of the necessaries of life in Rome, notwithstanding the plenty of money, may be explained in the most satisfactory manner from the cultivation of the land by slaves, and from a variety of other causes which have no existence among us. Now, this is the very point for which I am contending; that the plenty of the precious metals does not *necessarily* raise prices, and that *these* are influenced by many other circumstances of a perfectly different nature. The effects of wealth obtained by war and rapine, I consider as perfectly analogous to those of gold and silver obtained by the discovery of a new mine; and, therefore, I take for granted, that had the money in Rome been drawn immediately from the bowels of the earth, the prices of necessaries would not have been affected in a greater degree,—the political condition of the people and the state of manners remaining the same.

The trifling wages of labour in India afford another illustration of the same thing.

Mr. Smith afterwards remarks, that the discovery of the abundant mines of America seems to have been the sole cause of this diminution in the value of silver in proportion to that of corn. It is accounted for accordingly in the same manner by everybody; and there never has been any dispute either about the fact, or about the cause of it."‡ But surely, during this period, a variety of other causes of the most powerful efficacy were operating on the condition of mankind in this part of the world; and without the co-operation of some of these, the discovery of the American mines would no more have raised the price of corn in modern Europe, than the sudden influx of wealth from the conquered provinces did in ancient Rome. On the other hand, I have no doubt that those causes would have raised prices, (I do not say to the same degree,) although the mines had not been discovered. Nay, it is far from being improbable, that this discovery retarded, instead of accelerating the progress of mercantile ingenuity in introducing the later improvements of banks and of paper currency, by means of which (while they continued to be regulated by principles founded on good sense and good faith) such a source of real wealth and prosperity was opened to this country.

NOTE V.

If I had looked over the whole of the article in the *Edinburgh Review* which I referred to in my last, I would not have troubled you with so large a packet. After reading more than twenty pages farther, I was agreeably surprised with the following passage :—

* [*Essays*, Vol. I. Note P.]
† [See above, p. 381, *seq.*]
‡ [*Wealth of Nations*, Book I. chap. xi.; Vol. I. p 300, tenth edition.]

APPENDIX II.—TO B. II. CH. II.—BULLION REPORT. 449

"Whenever, in the actual state of things, a fresh issue of notes comes into the hands of those who mean to employ them in the prosecution and extension of a profitable business, a difference in the distribution of the circulating medium takes place, similar in kind to that which has been last supposed; and produces similar, though of course comparatively inconsiderable effects, in altering the proportion between capital and revenue, in favour of the former. The new notes go into the market as so much additional capital, to purchase what is necessary for the conduct of the concern. But before the produce of the country has been increased, it is impossible for one person to have more of it, without diminishing the shares of some others. This diminution is effected by the rise of prices, occasioned by the competition of the new notes, which puts it out of the power of those who are only buyers, and not sellers, to purchase as much of the annual produce as before. While all the industrious classes,—all those that sell as well as buy, are, during the progressive rise of prices, making unusual profits, and, even when this progression stops, are left with the command of a greater portion of the annual produce than they possessed previous to the new issues.

"It must always be recollected, that it is not the *quantity* of the circulating medium which produces the effect here described, but the *different distribution* of it. If a thousand millions of notes were added to the circulation, and distributed to the various classes of society exactly in the same proportions as before, neither the capital of the country, nor the facility of borrowing, would be in the slightest degree increased. But, on every fresh issue of notes, not only is the quantity of the circulating medium increased, but the distribution of the whole mass is altered. A larger proportion falls into the hands of those who consume and produce, and a smaller proportion into the hands of those who only consume."[1]

Now, the *substance* of all this seems to me to be perfectly sound and satisfactory, (although I think it might have been more unexceptionably expressed;) but I confess I am at a loss how to reconcile it with the "GRAND DOCTRINE, that every kind of circulating medium, as well as *every other kind of commodity*, is necessarily depreciated by excess, and raised in value by deficiency, compared with the demand." Or, supposing for a moment that the two passages may be so explained as to be not inconsistent with each other, it must still be acknowledged that the conclusion in which the foregoing reasoning terminates, does not "follow *immediately* from the general principles of supply and demand," as applied to the circulating medium.

NOTE VI.

[*April* 12.]—Your solution of the difficulty with respect to the rapid rise of silver since the increased issues of the Bank, by means of purchases of Exchequer Bills, appears to me to be sound and satisfactory. Whether the additional notes be, in the first instance, issued to Government or to the merchants, the ultimate effect will, I conceive, be exactly the same. In both cases, they must pass very soon into the hands of the bankers, who will employ them again in discounts; and who, in proportion to the increased amount of the notes, will have the means of their accommodation enlarged. Indeed, I cannot imagine how it is possible, by any creation of

[1] No. XXXIV. p. 364.

circulating medium on the part of the bank, to raise the prices of commodities, unless it either adds to the capital of merchants so as to increase the demand, while the supply in the market continues the same; or augments, by an increased facility of borrowing, the funds of those classes who fall under the description of consumers.

The more I reflect on the figurative language commonly employed on this subject, I am the more at a loss how to comprehend its meaning. When it is said, for example, in the *Bullion Report*, " that the excess of the present currency of this country not being exportable to other countries, nor convertible into specie, remains in the channel of circulation, and is gradually absorbed by increasing the prices of all commodities," I find it utterly impossible for me to annex any precise idea to the proposition. By what sort of *gradual process* are the superabundant issues *absorbed* in the prices of commodities; and to what sort of elective attraction is it owing that this *gradual absorption* is so much greater in the case of some commodities than of others? This metaphorical view of the subject is the more to be regretted, that, by placing on a wrong foundation the very important conclusion with respect to the depreciation of our present currency which it is employed to support, it has furnished to different writers the means of involving the conclusion itself in some degree of obscurity. Mr. Coutts Trotter, for instance, in a pamphlet which has just reached me, (and which, however erroneous and superficial in its views, may be regarded as a fair specimen of the prevailing misconceptions among men of business,) proceeds all along on the supposition, that, in order to shew there has been no excess in the bank issues, it is sufficient to remark, that no man carries about with him in his pocket, or locks up in his drawer, a greater number of bank-notes than he finds necessary for his immediate expenditure. Hence he seems disposed to infer, that as the additional issues do not stagnate in the channel of circulation so as to overflow its banks, any more than the limited issues did prior to the restriction, there exists no superfluity of currency to be absorbed in the prices of commodities. The truth is, that it is not a superfluity of currency in the hands of consumers that is the *cause* of the advanced prices; but, on the contrary, it is the advanced prices which render an amount of currency, that would otherwise have been superfluous, absolutely necessary for the daily expenditure of the consumer.[1] In other words, it is the rise of prices produced by the extension of credit and the creation of fictitious capital implied in the enlarged issues, that gives full employment to the same issues considered in their capacity of circulating medium. Indeed, it might be easily shewn, that the rise of prices must occasion a *scarcity* rather than a superfluity of circulating medium: for a great deal of what Davenant and others have stated with respect to the disproportion between the cause and the effect, in the rise of price produced by a *deficient supply* of corn or of other necessary commodities, will be found to hold equally with respect to the rise of price produced by an *increased demand* operating on a limited supply. The amount of increased issues, therefore, considered in their capacity of circulating medium, cannot possibly keep exact pace with the advanced prices which they have previously

---

[1] I speak here of the economical consumer, or as to those who enlarge their scale of living in proportion to the facility of obtaining credit, their increased consumption operates on the market in the same way as the increased demand occasioned by mercantile discounts.

occasioned by increasing demand, in their double capacity of mercantile capital and of funds for expenditure.

Having mentioned Mr. Trotter's pamphlet, I cannot help taking notice here of some remarks which he has made in reply to that account of the rise of prices which seems to me the only satisfactory one, and on which I think *the whole argument* on that point ought to be rested. "It is maintained," he says, "that the facility with which bank-notes are procured from the bank, by the mode of discount peculiar to commercial men, calls into existence an increase of purchasers in our markets, whose competition heightens the price of every article." On this sentence, (which Mr. Trotter seems to consider as a first-rate absurdity from the two points of admiration which he has placed at the end of it,) he proceeds to remark as follows:—" This will not be urged by any person acquainted with the subject of *production;* an increase of capital (which this is to the small degree in which it exists) never raises the price of commodities, but has exactly the opposite effect; an increase of *consumers*, in any given state of supply, will raise the price of every article which is the object of their wants, and the enhanced price will continue until the stimulus of the increased demand has created a proportionably increased production;—but a competition of consumers is regulated by principles quite distinct from a competition of merchants, who buy to sell again: these must always have in view the price which the article they are in treaty for will obtain at its ultimate market; and, whether there be ten such competitors or a hundred, whether each has carried to the place of competition one hundred pounds of bank-notes, or one thousand, he must still be limited, in the offer he can afford to make, by the price which he expects to obtain in selling again. So far, indeed, from this increased capital being the occasion of high prices, it is one of the principal means of keeping them down;—a competition of capitalists, like a competition of manufacturers, restricts their respective profits."[1] In answer to this reasoning it may be observed:—1. That merchants and consumers are here stated in contrast to each other, as if they were two classes of persons completely distinct, whereas, in fact, every merchant is also to be considered as a consumer; and, (in a commercial country like Great Britain,) a very great proportion of the consumers may, without any improper latitude in the use of the word, be considered as merchants. The enlarged accommodation, therefore, that a merchant receives, in the form of commercial discounts, while it enables him to increase his speculations as a trader, enables him also to defray the enlarged expenditure which he incurs as a consumer, and even encourages him to add to the scale of his consumption. 2. The *immediate* or *proximate effect* of a competition of capitals, is here confounded with its *ultimate tendency*. That prices are always reduced in the long run by an increase of demand, where it is possible by human industry to increase the supply in proportion, is a maxim admitted by all writers on Political Economy; but that *the first effect* of the increased demand is to raise prices, is another maxim no less indisputable than the former. It is under this first or proximate effect that we are now suffering, and under this effect we must (while things continue on their present footing) every day suffer more and more, unless by some miracle the supply of commodities should be rendered as easy and as instantaneous as the extension of credit and the creation of capital. That "a competition of capitalists, like a

[1] *Principles of Currency and Exchanges applied to the Report of the Bullion Committee*, p. 37.

competition of manufacturers, restricts their respective profits," is indeed true; and it is reasonable and fortunate that it should be so, where all their capitals are equally the fruits of regular and useful industry. The melancholy fact in this country at present is, that the profits of men of real capital are restricted by the competition of those who have none, and that the prudent and steady trader feels himself jostled out of his way by the bolder adventurer. It is no less hard, that the expenditure of the former, in his capacity of consumer, should, at the same time, be augmented by the competition of the latter.

I forgot to take notice, in my last letter, of your remarks on the inconveniences that might be expected to result, *under the present state of our paper currency*, from the repeal of the Anti-Usurious Laws. With these remarks I perfectly agree, but I always proceeded on the supposition, that the Bank was to be obliged, within a limited time, to resume its cash payments; a supposition, which, I think may be assumed as an indisputable postulatum, whatever other subsidiary measures may be thought useful for accomplishing the proposed end. It still appears to me, that, while the Bank is previously preparing for this resumption by narrowing its discounts, a relaxation of these laws would contribute more than anything else to smooth the way towards this great object, by furnishing the means of such a prudent solution in the distribution of credit, as might moderate the violence of the shock, which both the commercial and agricultural interests of the country must inevitably sustain before things are brought round again to their ancient and natural course.

I must now relieve you, for the present, from this voluminous correspondence, but I have still floating in my head a variety of crude ideas about some other parts of the *Report*, which I shall put in writing during the summer, and submit to your consideration, when I shall have the pleasure of seeing you at Dunbar. I have little doubt that my objections to some of these arise from my want of sufficient information.

If I have stumbled upon anything that you think worth shewing to Horner, I can have no objection to your communicating my papers, either in whole or in part, to one in whom I have so entire a confidence, provided only you mention to him my anxiety that nobody whatever shall hear of such a communication. I meant to have written to himself on the subject, but as the *Report* was already before the public, and as the most popular objections to it have been confined to those points which seemed to me the least vulnerable, I thought it better to delay proposing my doubts till both of us should have a little more leisure. I have sometimes wished that I had seen the *Report* before it was printed, as nothing would have given me greater pleasure than to have contributed anything, however trifling, towards its improvement. But this I regret the less, as I take for granted, that nothing of any consequence is to be expected at the present moment, and that there will still be ample time for discussion before the business can be brought forward with any prospect of success.

www.ingramcontent.com/pod-product-compliance
Lightning Source LLC
Chambersburg PA
CBHW051854300426
44117CB00006B/384